The Handbook of Canadian Film

The Handbook of Canadian Film

Second Edition

Eleanor Beattie

**Peter Martin Associates Limited
in association with Take One Magazine**

Canadian Cataloguing in Publication Data

The handbook of Canadian film

(PMA/Take one film book series; 4)

Includes bibliographies and indexes.
ISBN 0-88778-130-6 bd.   ISBN 0-88778-131-4 pa.

1. Moving-pictures — Canada. I. Title. II. Series.

PN1993.4.C3B4 1977   791.43'0971   C77-001157-8

Design: Diana McElroy and Tim Wynne-Jones

The PMA/Take One Film Book Series is published by Peter Martin Associates Limited, 280 Bloor Street West, Toronto, Ontario M5S 1W1, in association with *Take One* magazine, Post Office Box 1778, Station B, Montreal, Quebec H3B 3L3; distributed in the U.K. by Tantivy Press, 108 New Bond Street, London W1Y 00X.

General Editors: Peter Lebensold, Joe Medjuck

Acknowledgements

A Handbook of Canadian Film is the result of the cheerful collaboration of many filmmakers and the people who help produce and distribute their films. I take all responsibility for the errors and omissions and acknowledge the generous help provided by the following people and organizations: the Canada Council for allowing me to travel across the country to meet filmmakers and the Ontario Arts Council for enabling me to hire assistants; Ron Blumer and Sandra Gathercole who always came through, and Vivian Geeza who was instrumental in reorganizing the book; Pierre Allard and the Bibliothèque nationale, Jean-Pierre Bastien and the Cinémathèque québécoise, and Michelle Bischoff and the National Film Board whose files form the basis of this book; Connie Tadros of *Cinema Canada* and *Cinéma-Québec*, Kirwan Cox, Gilles Marsolais, Evelyn McCartney (of the Directors' Guild), Linda Beath and Peter Morris who were generous with their information; the indexer France Arioli, the transcriber Anna Arioli, my editors Kathy Vanderlinden and Joe Medjuck, and my publishers Carol and Peter Martin—I thank them all.

Contents

How to Use This Book

The core of this book consists of 131 short entries on individual filmmakers, arranged in alphabetical order, with filmographies and suggestions for further reading. In the filmographies, the production company is noted after the title of each film and provides a good lead to the distributor. (The NFB, for example, distributes most of its own films.) When a film is not distributed by its producer, the distributor has been included. The majority of the filmmakers included are directors; the other important and essential members of the film community—producers, cameramen, sound engineers, critics, script-writers and musicians—are discussed in various articles throughout the book.

For film students, An Introduction to Canadian Film provides a historical framework, offers a perspective, and identifies some general works on the Canadian film industry. The Film Study section includes suggestions for setting up a film society and for locating film study centres, film courses and film archives.

For filmmakers, the section Making Films lists sources to contact when trying to finance a film and when looking for technical help and advice. This section also includes professional associations involved in the film industry, cooperative productions and film festivals.

For teachers and librarians, the section Using Films offers suggestions for film study, including where to find films and film-related material for various levels. The Film Publications section and the Bibliography list useful books, catalogues, periodicals and directories.

In this revised second edition of the *Handbook*, the following sections have been added: Community Film and Video, Native People and Film, Political and Third World Films, and Women in Film. The book has been reorganized in, we hope, a more useful format. It was not our plan to repeat the work of others but to refer to it and indicate what is available. In fact, this whole book is a kind of directory, an open-ended listing which continues to invite additions and point out areas where further investigation and research are needed. While it does not pretend to be a work of criticism, this book does carry a critical point of view which is reflected in the subjects chosen and discussed.

NOTES

Financing of Films: CFDC

10. (1) The objects of the Corporation are to foster and promote the development of a feature film industry in Canada, and without limiting the generality of the foregoing, the Corporation may, in furtherance of its objects,

(a) invest in individual Canadian feature film productions in return for a share in the proceeds from any such production;

(b) make loans to producers of individual Canadian feature film productions and charge interest thereon;

(c) make awards for outstanding accomplishments in the production of Canadian feature films;

(d) make grants to filmmakers and film technicians resident in Canada to assist them in improving their craft; and

(e) advise and assist the producers of Canadian feature films in the distribution of such films and in the administrative functions of feature film production.

Canadian Film Development Corporation Annual Report, available from: 800 Place Victoria, Suite 2220, Montreal, Quebec H4Z 1A8. (Tel: (514) 283-6363) or 111 Avenue Road, Suite 602, Toronto, Ontario M5A 3J8 (Tel: (416) 966-6436).

Cinema Canada, no. 15. Special issue celebrating the 35th anniversary of the NFB.

An Introduction to Canadian Film

Since 1968, when the Canadian Film Development Corporation (CFDC) went into operation, Canada has produced over 250 feature films; unfortunately, very few Canadians and almost no one outside our borders have seen more than a handful of these titles. On the other hand, since 1939, when the National Film Board (NFB) was established, Canadian-produced shorts have become well-known, and have established Canada as the world's leader in documentary films. What accounts for the success of the NFB and the failure of the CFDC in reaching audiences with their respective films? Why have Canadian feature films failed to crack the domestic market, not to mention the international market?

Despite the success or failure of the NFB and the CFDC, Canada now has a complete film industry producing shorts, documentaries and feature films. We have a wealth of talent and a growing reputation, garnered largely at international film festivals, and confirmed at the 1975 Cannes Film Festival when Michel Brault, an alumnus of the NFB, won the Best Director Award for his feature on the October Crisis, **Les ordres.**

John Grierson founded the NFB on a political and cultural ideal which still serves as a solid base for our growing film industry.

NOTES

Variety, November 17, 1971, PR. 28-60, a special issue on "Canada's 'Nervous' Film Boom".

The Feature Film Industry in Canada, a thesis submitted by R. Jock to the School of Business Administration, University of Western Ontario, London, Ontario, in April 1967. Available from the Centre de documentation cinématographique (Bibliothèque nationale), 360 McGill Street, Montreal, Quebec H2Y 2E9.

Rodney James has written a thesis, *The National Film Board of Canada and its Task of Communication*. Published in 1968 by the US Department of Health, Education and Welfare, Washington, it is available from them and also available for reference at the National Film Board library in Montreal.

Statistics Canada, *Annual Catalogue (#63-206) on Motion Picture Production*. Available from Publishing Centre, Supply and Services Canada, Ottawa.

"Sex Is Out", an article by Marc Gervais in the *Montreal Star,* July 24, 1971, discusses the record of the CFDC and interviews the CFDC chairman, Gratien Gélinas, and executive director, Michael Spencer.

Le cinéma: autre visage du Québec colonisé, a manifesto of l'Association professionnelle des cinéastes du Québec. Available from Association des réalisateurs de films du Québec, 3466 St-Denis, Montreal, Quebec H2X 3L3.

"Donner un cadre à une industrie", by Luc Perreault in *La Presse*, June 19, 1971. An interview with François Cloutier, Quebec Minister of Cultural Affairs, on the problems of developing a national cinema of Quebec.

L'Etat et l'industrie du cinéma, by André Poirier, January 1963, Ecole des hautes études commerciales, University of Montreal. Available from the Centre de documentation cinématographique (Bibliothèque nationale), 360 McGill Street, Montreal, Quebec.

L'Industrie du cinéma dans la province du Québec, by Jacques St. Laurent, March 25, 1962. Available from the Centre de documentation cinématographique (Bibliothèque nationale), 360 McGill Street, Montreal, Quebec.

How to Make or Not to Make a Canadian Film (Comment faire ou ne pas faire un film canadien). André Paquêt, editor (La Cinémathèque canadienne, 1967). The most complete historical description of cinematic events in Canada, listed chronologically from 1898 to 1967.

The annual reports of the Department of Trade and Commerce in the Dominion of Canada and later Canada (1917-1941) have sections on film in the country. Any large library should have these books, and they are available at the Centre de documentation cinématographique (Bibliothèque nationale), 360 McGill Street, Montreal, Quebec.

This organization has gone a long way towards developing an attitude and feeling for Canada, allowing millions of people to see NFB productions in schools and halls across the country. There is an increasing awareness that an appreciative milieu is of the utmost importance for the development of our indigenous cinema. Students are now using Canadian productions in film study courses, and they are assisted by critical film magazines and film study centres. Out of this milieu have grown co-operatives in major Canadian centres—Vancouver, Edmonton, Regina, Halifax, Winnipeg, St. John's, Toronto and Montreal—to assist independent filmmakers in the production and distribution of their films. But Canadian filmmakers are no longer content to work only in the major centres; there is now a desire among filmmakers to remain and to work in the communities that fostered them. (And despite the expressed intention of the Secretary of State to decentralize the CFDC and the NFB, little has been accomplished.) Finally, and most importantly, there is a growing Canadian public taking an increased interest in seeing the films it has supported (to the tune of over 20 million dollars) through taxes; and,when given the opportunity, the public has responded to the product it helped finance. In 1975, for example, **The Apprenticeship of Duddy Kravitz** was one of the top 25 money-earners in box-office receipts in Canada. But despite **Duddy's** box-office success and the critical success of such films as **Mon Oncle Antoine, Rejeanne Padovanni, Les ordres, Paperback Hero, Bar salon, Eliza's Horoscope, The Rowdyman, Between Friends**—the list is long —and despite our talent, our resources, we are still not seeing our own films because our industry continues to be controlled by foreign exhibition and distribution networks.

Canadian film production is completely divorced from the Canadian box-office. In the last four years, box-office revenues in Canada increased by 100%, reaching an all-time record of $200 million in 1975; revenues earned in Canada by foreign distributors increased by 98.9% to a 1974 total of $54.4 million. And within the same period, Canada became the largest foreign market for American films. All this is not doing Canadian film production any good; profits are flowing out of Canada to finance American feature film production. During the four years the box-office in Canada was booming, local production fell drastically. What little support there is for film production here is being undermined by increasing pressure to make Canada's resources part of a branch plant industry employing technicians to produce essentially foreign material. While branch plant production may be acceptable in the auto industry, it is not acceptable in our cultural life. Although it does have historical precedents, it is not a basis for a Canadian film industry.

Certainly little of early cinema in Canada was indigenous. Exotic snowy plains and Eskimos brought Robert Flaherty to the Hudson

NOTES

The Canadian Film Industry: Past, Present and Future, by Joseph Fox. Thesis submitted to the School of Journalism, Carleton University. Available for reference at the Canadian Film Institute, Ottawa.

Maclean's, June 1, 1943, pp. 40-42. "Propaganda Maestro", by Thelma Lecocq.

Take One, vol. 4, no. 5, pp. 31-33, "Life at the early NFB", by Sol Dworkin.

Cinema Canada no. 16, pp. 52-53. "Roy Tash, C.S.C.", by Harris Kirshenbaum.

Pierre Savignac, *Historique du cinéma canadien.* Mimeographed. Written for *Semaine du cinéma canadien,* January 1965. Available for reference at the NFB library, Montreal, and the Canadian Film Institute, Ottawa.

The National Film Board's publicity department has published in mimeographed form *A Brief History: The National Film Board of Canada* by James Lysyshyn, and assembled a special edition of *New Clips,* dated April 1968, on the history of the Board. Both are available by writing: Information Division, National Film Board, P.O. Box 6100, Montreal, Quebec H3C 3H5.

Dreamland: A History of Canadian Movies 1895-1939 (1974). Directed by Donald Brittain, produced by Kirwan Cox, The Great Canadian Moving Picture Company. 86 min. col. Available from the NFB.

Cinema Canada, no. 16, pp. 54-57. "Dreamland". A. Ibranyi-Kiss interviews Brittain and Cox.

The *Canadian Moving Picture Digest* is a good source of historical information. The following issues tell something of the "Carry On Sergeant" disaster: January 12, February 2 and 23, 1929.

Sparling's extraordinary experiences in early Canadian cinema are documented in his article, "The *Short* Way to Canadian Entertainment", in *How To Make or Not to Make a Canadian Film (La Cinémathèque canadienne, 1967).*

Parts I & II of *Canadian Feature Films, 1913-69* lists chronologically all known films shot in Canada by indigenous and foreign companies between these years. Edited by Peter Morris. Canadian Filmography Series nos. 106 and 107, Canadian Film Institute, 1970, 1972.

History of the National Film Board of Canada, by Marjorie McKay (undated). Available from NFB offices.

Pot pourri, Summer, 1975. "The Grierson Years: 'They wouldn't have been worth a damn without the women'", edited by Pat Thorvaldson. Interviews with women who worked at the NFB during Grierson's reign.

Untitled Report, September 1943; *The Shift of Power in Education,* August 1943; *Searchlight on Democracy,* Spring 1939. Three pieces by Grierson: all available for reference at the Centre de documentation cinématographique, Bibliothèque nationale.

Bay area in 1922 to film **Nanook of the North;** so, too, the western plains and the legendary RCMP attracted all the large Hollywood companies. Great Britain's quota system on film made the Canadian setting particularly attractive. Implemented in 1930, this system considered all production filmed and produced in a commonwealth country as British-made. Out of this situation developed one of the first so-called Canadian talking feature films, **North of '49,** directed by Neal Hart and produced by the short-lived British Canadian Pictures Ltd., and 14 other features produced by Central Films of Victoria.

Although Canadian production companies and distribution outlets were set up, most collapsed. **Carry on Sergeant** (1928), directed by Bruce Bairnsfather, and purported to have cost $500,000, fell by the wayside, a victim of indifferent distribution; for in the field of entertainment films, Canada was simply an extension of the American distribution-exhibition system.

One of the assistant directors working on **Carry on Sergeant** was Gordon Sparling, who later joined the Montreal branch of New York's *Associated Screen News*; his "Canadian Cameos" series lasted from 1931 to 1954, producing over 80 films, among them, **Grey Owl's Little Brother** (1932) and **Rhapsody in Two Languages** (1934). Some indigenous films did grow out of the need to build and populate the country; the Canadian Bioscope Company, a branch of Urban (G.B.), was founded in 1900 to make films for the Canadian Pacific Railways to stimulate British immigration to the west.

The period from 1914 to 1922 was important to Canadian commercial cinema. Numerous shorts and features were made including **Evangeline** (1913), produced by the Halifax Canadian Bioscope and directed by E.P. Sullivan and W.H. Cavanaugh; but few of these succeeded in crashing the big American market. The exceptions were those produced by Ernest Shipman whose films were international; but his success lasted only until 1922 when the vertical integration of the Hollywood film industry squeezed out Shipman and other Canadian producers.

In the meantime, the Canadian Government Motion Picture Bureau (founded in 1921 out of the Exhibits and Publicity Bureau) was introducing one part of the country to another through the medium of film. Among their productions were **Lest We Forget** (1935) which focused on Canada's role in World War I, and **Heritage** (1939), directed by J. Booth Scott, which dealt with the ten-year drought in western Canada.

The National Film Board, which later incorporated the Canadian Government Motion Picture Bureau, was the result of John Grierson's coming to Canada in 1938 to help formulate the government's film policy and to act as film commissioner. The National Film Board Act states that the duties of the commissioner are "to advise upon the making and distribution of national films designed

NOTES

Homage to John Grierson, La Cinémathèque canadienne on the occasion of the National Film Board's 25th Birthday, 1964. Out of print, it is available in film study libraries and contains testimonials and a filmography.

McGill Daily Supplement, February 28, 1972, edited by Ronald Blumer. "John Grierson: 1898-1972".

A valuable collection of Grierson's writings have been edited by Forsyth Hardy in *Grierson on Documentry* (London: Collins, 1946).

Don't Look at the Camera, by Harry Watt. (Elek Books Limited, 1974). Memories of Grierson and the G.P.O.

For recent interviews with Grierson see "John Grierson: 'I derive my authority from Moses'", an interview with Ronald Blumer in *Take One,* vol. 2, no. 9. Also see "John Grierson: The 35mm Mind", interview with Darlene Kruesel in *McGill News,* March 1971.

"Political Film". A talk by John Grierson followed by a panel discussion recorded from *Ideas,* CBC, Nov. 25, 1970. Cat. no. 546L. One hour. Available from *CBC Learning Systems,* Box 500, Terminal A, Toronto, Ontario.

Le Devoir, February 26, 1972. "Le coeur et l'esprit", by Roger Blais and Françoise Jaubert.

Cinéma-Québec, vol. 1, no. 9, pp. 32-35. "Le rêve de Grierson", by Rodney James.

Motion, vol. 4, no. 5, pp. 6-8. "The Canadian Indian Summer of John Grierson", by Elspeth Chisholm.

The National Film Board of Canada: The War Years, edited by Peter Morris. Canadian Filmography Series no. 103 (Canadian Film Institute, Ottawa, 1965, second edition, 1972), p. 32.

Hye Bossin, editor of the *Canadian Film Weekly,* which started in 1942 and continued into the 60s, recalls the participation of Canadian Jews in those early days in his *Stars of David* (The Canadian Jewish Congress, 1965).

See Tom Daly's article of personal reminiscences, "From 'World in Action' to 'Man in His World'", in *How to Make or Not to Make a Canadian Film* (La Cinémathèque canadienne, 1967).

"The Private Film Industry in Canada and its Relation to Government", by F. R. Crawley. A speech given to the Conference on CInformation, November 12, 1971. Available from Crawley Films, Ottawa, Toronto, or Montreal. Judith Crawley, *The Quality of a Nation* (Crawley Films, 1962).

For a complete description of this period in Quebec, see the following publication: *Vingt ans de cinéma au Canada français* by Robert Daudelin. (Québec: Ministère des affaires culturelles, 1967). The section on the history of Quebec cinema was reprinted in *Objectif,* May 1967, pp. 18-20.

to help Canadians in all parts of Canada to understand the ways of living and the problems of Canadians in other parts". Grierson's formulation of the documentary film as a powerful tool for the discovery and illumination of the ordinary world shaped and continues to influence Canadian cinema.

The war years brought an accelerated need for propaganda and information films; Britain needed support and the U.S. was being encouraged to enter the war. Grierson, as first film commissioner, invited a number of foreign directors to the Board: Stuart Legg directed the Board's first film, **The Case of Charlie Gordon** (actually produced under the old Motion Picture Bureau in 1939); he then created the "Canada Carries On" and "World In Action" series. Such films as **The War for Men's Minds** (the Allies' answer to Leni Riefenstahl's **Triumph of the Will**), **Churchill's Island** and **The Gates of Italy** attempted to supply mass educaton for a democratic world. Joris Ivens, the great Dutch filmmaker, came to make **Action Stations!** (1942); Evelyn Spice-Cherry (who continues to work in Regina) and Norman McLaren (who likewise still delights us) came and stayed. Other directors included Raymond Spottiswoode (**Quebec—Path of Conquest**), George L. George (**Handle with Care**) and Ernest Bornemann (**Target Berlin**). It is estimated that the "World in Action" films were seen by an international audience of 30 million people.

Canadians, too, were drafted into the film front of the war effort: Sydney Newman came from Toronto to make **Trainbusters** (1943), a film about the fighter plane pilots; Tom Daly, a brilliant editor, worked with Stuart Legg in piecing together stock-shots, newsreel and captured footage; Julian Roffman, Michael Spencer, James Beveridge, Gudrun Parker, and Guy Glover began making their contributions during this vital period.

Budge and Judith Crawley, who had won an award in New York in 1938 for their short, **Ile d'Orléans,** received contracts from the National Film Board during the war years. Later the Crawleys became heavily involved in sponsored films (their all-time hit was **The Loon's Necklace,** made in 1948 for Imperial Oil) which gave rise to a whole new generation of professional personnel).

After the war, production companies began to mushroom across the country — among them, Parry Films and Trans-Canada Film Company in Vancouver, and Chetwynd Films in Toronto. But the biggest boom took place in Quebec. There, in addition to the founding of Peterson Productions and Les films Lavoie, Quebec Productions and Renaissance Films—two large studios—were built, producing such films as **Un homme et son péché** (Paul Gury, 1948), **Le gros Bill** (René Delacroix, 1949) and **Tit-coq** (Gratien Gélinas and René Delacroix, 1952).

This period of feature film production ended with the introduction of television in 1952, but television did stimulate the growth of the film society movement (the Canadian Film Institute was found-

NOTES

Filmographie d'Albert Tessier, by René Bouchard, Collection documents filmiques du Québec. (Les Editions du Boreal Express Ltée, distributed by Fides). A study of the prehistory of Quebec cinema and the precursor of cinema direct.

The complete story of the work produced by the filmmakers in Unit B at the NFB, their search for, and indeed, the building of more manageable equipment, the development of their new approach and its cross-fertilization in France and the United States has yet to be thoroughly investigated by film historians. The following articles, however, are available:

"A Note on Candid Eye", by Wolf Koenig, in *How To Make or Not To Make a Canadian Film* (La Cinémathèque canadienne, 1967).

Terence Macartney-Filgate: The Candid Eye, edited by Charlotte Gobeil, in Canadian Filmography Series no. 104 (Canadian Film Institute, Ottawa 1966). Available at film study libraries.

"En courant derrière Rouch" Parts 1, 2 & 3, by Claude Jutra in *Cahiers du cinéma* (Paris), no. 113, (November 1960), pp. 32-43, no. 115 (January 1961), p.23-33, no. 116 (February 1961), pp. 39-44.

"Le cinéma direct nord-Americain", by Louis Marcorelles, in *Image et son,* no. 183, (April 1965), pp. 47-54.

"The Innocent Eye: An Aspect of the Work of the National Film Board of Canada", by Peter Harcourt (on Tom Daly's Unit B) in *Sight and Sound,* no. 65 (Winter 1964).

"Comment se porte le micro-cravate à Montréal", Andre Martin in *Artsept,* no. 2, (April/June, 1963), pp. 26-39. The issue called "Le cinéma et la vérité" deals in part with the Candid Eye Unit.

"Michel Brault et Claude Jutra, racontent Jean Rouch" (interview with R. Daudelin and M. Patenaude), in *Objectif,* no. 3 (December 1960), pp. 3-16. "Entretien de deux cinéastes" (Brault and Jutra talk about Jean Rouch and Norman McLaren), in *L'Ecran* (Montreal), no. 2, pp. 7-15.

Movie (Britain) no. 8 (April 1963) discusses *cinéma-vérité* and the role which the National Film Board group, in particular, Brault, has played.

Liberté, vol. 8, no. 2-3 (March-June 1966). The whole issue is dedicated to Canadian cinema, with an article by Georges Dufaux and Jean-Claude Labrecque, "Le fameux cinéma candide", pp. 84-90.

Eléments pour un nouveau cinéma by Louis Marcorelles (Paris: UNESCO, 1970). Includes a section on the National Film Board's Candid Eye Unit.

See *Homage to the Vancouver CBC Film Unit.* (La Cinémathèque canadienne, 1964).

ed out of the old National Film Society), the concept of Canadian film awards, amateur film production (Claude Jutra won first prize in the 1949 Canadian Film Awards for **Mouvement perpetuel**) and film criticism (*Découpages,* a Montreal-based film magazine, had Pierre Juneau, Michel Brault and Marc Lalonde on its editorial board). With television came the demand for speedier production. The National Film Board began turning out series of half-hour films; film adapted to television brought new techniques for a fresh look at the everyday world: "Petites Médisances" was directed by Jacques Giraldeau, with camera by Michel Brault, and Bernard Devlin produced "On the Spot" (Sur le vif). Perhaps best-known is the "Candid Eye" series produced by Tom Daly's Unit B; Wolf Koenig, Michel Brault, Roman Kroitor and Terence Mac-artney-Filgate directed such gems of craftsmanship and teamwork as **The Days Before Christmas**, **The Back-breaking Leaf**, **Glenn Gould** and **Lonely Boy**. Other members of the "Candid Eye" team were John Spotton, Georges Dufaux and Stanley Jackson. This unit was a training ground and inspiration for many young people, including Gilles Gascon and Jean-Claude Labrecque, who later formed the French Unit.

The National Film Board's animation department also became involved in television work. During the war years, Norman McLaren had gathered talent around him — George Dunning, René Jodoin, Jim McKay, Evelyn Lambart, Grant Munro, Robert Verrall and Maurice Blackburn — and most had stayed on. Television created another animation centre in the CBC's Toronto Graphics Department founded by David McKay; it employed such artists as Dennis Burton, Warren Collins and Carlos Marchiori.

With the formation of the French Unit at the National Film Board in 1959 (following the Board's move from Ottawa to Montreal), French-Canadian cinema was revived. Those assertive efforts of Michel Brault, Gilles Groulx, Claude Jutra, Claude Fournier, Arthur Lamothe and Marcel Carrière resulted in such seminal films as **Les raquetteurs**, **La lutte**, **Golden Gloves**, **Les bûcherons de la Manouane** and **Québec—USA**.

The demand for televised drama found the National Film Board producing a series for the French network entitled "Panoramique", produced by Guy Glover. The Vancouver CBC film unit, founded in 1953 by Stan Fox, Jack Long and Arla Saare, had been producing short documentaries by Allan King, Daryl Duke and Gene Lawrence. With Ron Kelly's **A Bit of Bark** in 1959, they began to produce dramatic shows, including "Caribou Country", the series written by Paul St-Pierre and directed by Philip Keatley. Harvey Hart returned to Canada in 1962 to head up "Festival", a dramatic series at CBC Toronto, and the dramatic productions of Eric Till, Arthur Hiller, Harvey Hart and Paul Almond became familiar to the Canadian public.

An outgrowth of the intense television production was the

NOTES

See "Conversations on film with Arthur Hiller and Sidney Furie", in *Canadian Cinematography*, January-February 1966, pp. 13-16.

Liberté, "Cinéma si", vol. 8, no. 2-3 (March-June 1966). A special issue on Canadian cinema with reprints of reports by the L'Association professionnelle des cinéastes du Québec to the Quebec government, recommendations by that body to the federal government, and many other articles by filmmakers reflecting on the industry.

Cinéma-Québec, vol. 1, no. 7 (Summer 1971). Special issue on production, distribution and exhibition of Canadian films, particularly Quebec films.

Le Devoir, Sept. 12, 1970. "La Société de développement de l'industrie cinématographique à l'heure du choix", by Jean-Pierre Tadros.

The Private Film Industry in Canada and its Relation to Government, a speech by F. R. Crawley to the Conference on Canadian Information at the Chateau Montebello, November 12, 1971. Available from Crawley Films Limited in Ottawa.

Minutes of Proceedings and Evidence of the Standing Committee on Broadcasting, Film and Assistance to the Arts, House of Commons, Issue no. 7, May 6, 1971. These minutes from the annual accounting of the CFDC to the Committee contain some fascinating exchanges and arguments on the direction of the industry, and particularly on the "crucial problem" of distribution. Available from Publishing Centre, Supply and Services Canada, Ottawa.

Minutes of Proceedings and Evidence of the Standing Committee on Broadcasting, Film and Assistance to the Arts, House of Commons, February 26, 1970. Representatives of Le Syndicat général du cinéma present and discuss their brief to the Committee on problems in the industry. Available from Publishing Centre, Supply and Services Canada, Ottawa.

renewed activity in feature-length films: Julian Roffman directed
The Bloody Brood (1958) and Canada's first and only 3-D
feature, **The Mask** (1961); Norman Klenman and William Davidson co- directed four of Morley Callaghan's stories in **Now That
April's Here** (1958) and Sidney Furie made two films in 1959, **A
Dangerous Age** and **A Cool Sound from Hell**. These attempts to
establish a viable commercial film industry met with little success.
The years following found many of our filmmakers departing for
either Hollywood or England.

But while Canada was losing many of its veteran filmmakers,
young people in the universities organized film crews and found
professional help. **Seul ou avec d'autres** (1962) was made at the
University of Montreal with the cooperation of Michel Brault;
directed by Denis Héroux, Denys Arcand and Stephane Venne, it
received limited commercial distribution. At the University of
British Columbia in 1963, Larry Kent directed his first feature, **Bitter Ash**, which was banned in British Columbia and became a
cause célèbre as it moved from university to university on the
underground circuit. In 1965, David Sector's **Winter Kept Us
Warm**, made with a cast and crew from Ryerson and the University of Toronto, met with commercial and critical success. But
perhaps the independently-made film which had the strongest effect was Claude Jutra's **A tout prendre** (1963), an intensely personal film using Jutra's skills as an actor, and combining the
qualities of fiction and the documentary.

The first feature films made by the National Film Board came in
the midst of this independent activity: **Pour la suite du monde**
grew out of the 13 half-hour shows, produced for the CBC by
Crawley Films, about the isolated French Canadians living on the
north shore of the St. Lawrence River. One of the writers of the
series, Pierre Perrault, went on to make two other films, **Le règne
du jour** and **Les voitures d'eau**, completing a now classic trilogy
of great poetic strength. Another feature film produced in this
same year, **The Drylanders** (1963), was also a thematic investigation of a man's relationship to his land and country; directed by
Don Haldane and produced by Peter Jones, it told a story of the
pains and joys of western pioneer life. Starring Frances Hyland
and Don Francks, the film had moderate success.

But, while **Pour la suite du monde** and **The Drylanders** expressed rural and traditional values, two young men — one from
Toronto, the other from Montreal—found an intense challenge in
urban life. In **Nobody Waved Goodbye**, Don Owen told a story of
embattled youth. Taking a critical yet sympathetic stance towards
his characters who were coping with a society which operated on
confused values, Owen summed up the spirit of a generation. His
successful efforts encouraged another young filmmaker in Montreal, Gilles Groulx; his hero Claude, a young Québécois, and
Barbara, a Jewish Montrealer, embody the personal, social and

NOTES

Motion Picture Theatres and Film Distributors, annual catalogue (63-207), available from the Dominion Bureau of Statistics, gives statistics on film revenues, number of films exhibited in Canada and the percentage of Canadian films exhibited in Canada.

Rapport sur la distribution du film, Institut canadien d'éducation des adultes, September 1967. Available from that organization at 506 St. Catherine St. East, Suite 800, Montreal, Quebec.

"I am going to take you back to 1949 when Mr. C.D. Howe became quite alarmed about the dollar drain out of this country, and about where all that money was going. When he looked around he found that a large proportion of it was going out through Famous Players. Mr. Howe asked Mr. Fitzgibbons, who was then the President of Famous Players, to come up here to Ottawa and have a little chat about that. He thought that perhaps some of that money should stay in the country and they should perhaps use it to build up a Canadian film industry or make some of those films inside the country.

"To cut a long story short . . . Mr. Fitzgibbons came out laughing with an agreement referred to as the Canadian Co-operation Project which said that they were not to get involved in the Canadian film industry because it was too young and it could not do the job anyway. However, because of the money they were taking out of the country, they agreed to do a big job of propaganda for us . . . 'to make sure that every time we have a feature film that makes reference to your country, we will spread it around the world'. What this meant in effect was that in a particular script, instead of the man coming from Canton, Ohio, they wrote in that he came from Moose Jaw, Saskatchewan. That was their Canadian contribution."

—From *Minutes of Standing Committee on Broadcasting.*
Films and Assistance to the Arts, 1969-70

Backlot Canadiana. Film by Peter Rowe on the Canadian Cooperation Project deal offered by Hollywood. To see it, contact CBC, Box 500, Station A, Toronto, Ontario M5W 1E6.

political complexities of the early sixties. Robert Daudelin describes the appearance of **Le chat dans le sac** as "a moment of intense joy. . . . At last we were confronted by a film which really belonged to us, one in which we were happy to recognise ourselves and see ourselves close to. **Le Chat dans le sac** was (and remains) the image of our most recent awakenings, as much through its stripped-down form as through its voluntarily confused subject."

The year 1964 also brought the first efforts of Jean-Pierre Lefebvre, poet and critic on the now defunct film review, *Objectif;* and the following year, Gilles Carle delighted popular audiences with the Christmas story of a snowplow driver in his **La vie heureuse de Léopold Z**.

During the mid-sixties, television news programs, such as "Document" and "This Hour Has Seven Days", encouraged the production of film documentaries; Patrick Watson, Douglas Leiterman and Beryl Fox produced such memorable films as **The Mills of the Gods**, **The Chief** and **Seven Hundred Million**. Ron Kelly's document on the Depression, **The Thirties: A Glimpse of a Decade**, won him his first Wilderness Award. The kind of public, non-personal documentary evolved by the Candid Eye Unit gave way to much more intense and intimate portraits; CBC refused to telecast Dick Ballentine's **Mr. Pearson**, as well as Allan King's **Warrendale**, which went on to gather popular success in independent houses.

With the founding of the Canadian Film Development Corporation in 1967, Canada made a seemingly serious commitment to feature film production; the Corporation was allotted 20 million dollars of public money "to foster and promote the development of a feature film industry". As a result, Canada has seen a breakthrough in the area of production; many of the features produced with the assistance of the CFDC have received international recognition. However, there has been no corresponding breakthrough in the distribution-exhibition of these films.

In setting out the guidelines for the establishment of the CFDC, on June 20, 1966, then Secretary of State Judy Lamarsh stated in the House of Commons:

Many countries, in order to encourage the distribution of their own films, have applied quotas. We have chosen, however, not to introduce this kind of restriction in the Bill at this time. Canadian films must therefore make it on their own merits. But in rejecting quotas, we are counting on film distributors and cinema chains to give more than ordinary support to the aims of this program.

Every film-producing country in the world has some form of protection for its indigenous production. Bergman did not spring forth a cinematic genius with his first film. He was extended, numerous times, with assistance through quotas and levies by a

NOTES

"Les Cinéastes québécois: un aperçu", by Robert Boissonnault. Master's thesis presented to the Departement de Sociologie, Université de Montréal, 1971. An analysis of the structure of filmmaking in Quebec, related to Radio-Canada, the CBC, the NFB, large theatre chains and cinemas. Available for reference at the Bibliothèque nationale, Montreal.

Cinéma (Paris) no. 176. pp. 47-79. "Paradoxes québécois", by Albert Cervoni; "Table ronde de jeunes réalisateurs", by Gérard Langlois; "Lettre de Québec", by Pierre Veronneau.

Rapport sur la situation du cinéma au Québec, Robert Daudelin, Montreal, 1970. Available for reference at the Centre de documentation cinématographique, Bibliothèque nationale, Montreal.

Cinema Canada, no. 18, pp. 36-43. "Beyond Words! The Quebec filmmakers' occupation of the censorship office", by Robin Spry.

Cinema Canada, no. 6 (February-March 1973), pp. 34-35, 43, "The Film Industry in Ontario", a brief submitted to the Ontario Ministry of Industry and Tourism by John F. Bassett in behalf of the Exploration Team on Film Industry, January 1973.

The membership of the CMPDA consists of Columbia Pictures of Canada, International Film Distributors Ltd., Paramount Pictures Corp. (Canada) Ltd., Twentieth Century-Fox Corporation, United Artists Corporation (MGM Canada Ltd), Universal Films (Canada) Ltd., Warner Brothers Distributing (Canada) Ltd., Astral-Bellevue-Pathe representing Columbia, and Bellevue Film Distributors Ltd. representing Avco Embassy. "... these companies earned $56 million in theatrical film rentals, or approximately 93% of the total film rental earned in Canada in 1974. The balance of approximately $2.8 million remained to be shared among the 74 other distribution firms operating in Canada during 1974". p.261 of the "Distribution Exhibition Section" of the Tompkin's Report. Formally the Bureau of Management Consulting Film Study, commissioned by the Department of the Secretary of State and presented to the Secretary of State on June 15, 1976.

Some fascinating background on the large theatre chains and distributors in Canada can be gleaned from an old government report, Investigation into an Alleged Combine in the Motion Picture Industry in Canada. 234 pp. Department of Labour, April 30, 1931. Available at the Centre de documentation cinématographique (Bibliothèque nationale), 360 McGill Street, Montreal, Quebec. It must be noted that the case was heard in the Ontario Supreme Court, without jury, and on March 18, 1932 the accused were discharged.

Cinema Canada, no. 22, pp. 18-22. "Hollywood's Empire in Canada: The Majors and the Mandarins through the Years", by Kirwan Cox.

Cinema Canada no. 25, pp. 22-26. "Rocca's Big Fight: The Rocca brothers built some theatres in the Maritimes only to find their access to first-run features blocked by certain 'understandings' between the big theatre chains and major film distributors", by Kirwan Cox.

country which made a commitment to nurture its home product. Bergman's early films were given theatre time and the benefit of a levy whereby a percentage of the revenues on all films exhibited in his country were turned back to local production to assist film-makers in achieving competence or, in the case of Bergman, far more. If Bergman had been a Canadian he would have been de-nounced as a failure without being given an opportunity to make more than one or two films; he would have become another Hiller, Jewison, Kotcheff, Furie or Duke, extremely competent Canadian filmmakers working in another country and cut off from their cultural roots. The decision of the Canadian government to continue ignoring the experience of other countries in the matters of quota and levy, coupled with Canada's cultural vulnerability because of the accessibility of the American product, has meant that Canadian films have been denied an audience.

Famous Players Limited and Odeon Theatres (Canada) Limited, two multinational, basically foreign-owned corporations, own or control more than 66% of the commercial cinemas in Canada. In distribution, the foreign control is even greater; seven American and two Canadian distributors acting as agents for American distribution companies, form the Canadian Motion Picture Distributors Association (CMPDA), and the members of this group control more than 90% of all commercial theatrical film rentals in Canada.

On February 4, 1976, a group of filmmakers initiated an applica-tion under the Combines Investigation Act charging that illegal agreements exist among these major exhibitors and distributors which augment their control of the market. George Destounis, president of Famous Players Limited, in an interview for the CBC in 1975, explains how the system works:

> It's been an historical fact that . . . major distributors aligned themselves with either one circuit or the other. People like Paramount, Warner's and United Artists will play 100% Famous and people like Columbia, and two-thirds Universal and one-third Fox would play Odeon. . . . It was agreed, I understand, [in the] early forties how the breakdown [worked] when Odeon was first formed.

In other words, there is a quota—guaranteed screen time—for Hollywood films in the majority of theatres in Canada; in fact, many of the poorer films of these distributors often receive better exhibition treatment in Canada than they do in the United States. Our country has become a "dumping ground" for the films of American distribution companies, which shipped earnings of $54.4 million in 1974 from the Canadian market. The result is that only a small percentage of the films produced in this country ever reach a Canadian audience. When they do, they are generally exhibited, without proper promotion, in a small number of theatres in major

NOTES

Proposals for Canada's Film Policy. Brief presented to the Secretary of State, May 1972, by the Toronto Filmmakers' Co-op. Available from the Co-op, and for reference in film libraries.

Cinema Canada, no. 6 (February-March 1973) pp. 28-31. "How to make a profit doing what we really should be doing anyway". Brief presented to the Ontario Film Study Group by K. Cox and S. Gathercole representing the opinion of the Toronto Filmmakers' Co-op and the Canadian Film-makers' Distribution Centre.

"Because of foreign domination, box-office revenues in Canada leave the country at an alarming rate—most particularly to the parent companies in the United States—where they are re-invested in the production of more American films. Canada is the largest single foreign source of income for the American film industry. Thus, while the government puts money into the production end of the industrial cycle, it is literally pouring out of the country at the other, severely impeding economic growth." From a speech by the Hon. J. Hugh Faulkner, Secretary of State to the Standing Committee on Broadcasting, Film and Assistance to the Arts, April 29, 1976.

Cinema Canada, no. 12, pp. 48-53. "Council of Canadian Filmmakers: Policy Statement on Feature Films".

Cinema Canada, no. 6 (February-March 1973), pp. 38-42. "Canadian film industry panel", held in 1973 with George Destounis, President of Famous Players, Canada; Bill Fruet and Allan King, filmmakers; John Hofsess and Gerald Pratley, critics; Michael Spencer, director of CFDC; and Sandra Gathercole, Canadian Council of Filmmakers.

New Canadian Film, vol. 6, nos. 4-5 (February-March 1975), pp. 29-30. The issue is dedicated to an evaluation of the Canadian film industry in 1974.

Criteria, vol. 2, no. 1 (February 1976). "The Politics of Film in Canada", edited by Ardele Lister. Eleven interviews with people involved in the politics of film. Available for 75c from *Criteria*, 1145 West Georgia Street, Vancouver, B.C. V6E 3H2.

Take One, vol. 4, no. 4, pp. 22ff. "The Wit and Wisdom of the Canadian Film Industry", by Joseph Bechstein. A report on the second Canadian Film Symposium in 1974.

The Canadian Film Digest, January 1973. "Production in Canada Today: A Mari Usque ad Mare".

Variety, May 25, 1976. Reviews of **Breaking Point** and **Shoot.**

Weekend Magazine, July 17, 1976, pp. 16-19. "The Shadow of the Eagle", by Martin Knelman.

Canadian Forum, November-December 1973, pp. 37-40. "Is There a Canadian Cinema?", by Peter Harcourt.

Take One, vol. 4, no. 3, pp. 24-30. "Being Canadian means always having to say you're sorry", by Robert Fothergill.

centres only. Without access to the exhibition network, films produced by the Canadian industry are costing us millions of dollars with very little cultural or economic return. This is a fraud.

It is perhaps too obvious to say that to continue production one must sell what has already been produced. The Canadian Film Development Corporation began operation in 1968 as a government bank, loaning money for the production of feature films. It was stipulated that the CFDC would finance half the cost, and that the other half was to come from private investment. And private investors did materialize, not because there was money to be earned from the films themselves—in many cases the films had no potential exhibition outlets—but because of a tax loophole which allowed investors sizable tax write-offs for a non-return investment. When that loophole was closed in 1972, investment dried up, production was strangled and low-budget features not dependent on private investment were invented by the CFDC as a mechanism to justify their existence, while production of major feature films fell to an all-time low. For a period of time in 1975, the Treasury Board cut off all funds to the CFDC, the bank was dry, and the CFDC was powerless.

But the growing interest in our film industry brought even more strident demands from many quarters for a legislated levy and quota. Seeing the writing on the wall, Famous Players and Odeon in 1975 volunteered a quota of four weeks a year of Canadian films in major cinemas and a voluntary levy amounting to $1.7 million per year. A statistical quarterly analysis shows that neither Famous Players nor Odeon has honoured its voluntary quotas for the first year of the agreement. At the time of writing, Odeon is slow on its commitment to invest in Canadian film, while Famous Players has exceeded its commitment. The problem is that in many instances Famous Players has invested in essentially American films made in Canada rather than in Canadian films. (See articles in *Variety* and *Weekend Magazine*.) It is clear that we face a growing problem of branch plant production. If we had a legislated levy or tax rather than a voluntary levy, the CFDC would be the decision-making body of Canadian feature film production. As it is, decisions about who and what films to support are now and will increasingly be made in New York. The foreign distribution-exhibition network has wound up benefiting and controlling the few measures designed to counteract their control of the Canadian film industry.

The existence of a Canadian film industry is no longer in question; the question now is whether this industry is in danger of betraying its heritage. If it develops as a supermarket cinema, if it trades on commercialism, if it is essentially derivative, then it will be merely a branch plant industry, flaccid and faceless. But if it is rooted in this country's historical and immediate experience, if it gives a face to our unique aspirations, if it draws on the resources of the congregation which is Canada, then its appeal will be distinct, dynamic—and international. The films of Sweden, Italy, France, of Bergman, Fellini, Godard, and the success of the NFB at home and abroad bear this out. The fate of the feature film industry depends now on whether the governments of Canada, both federal and provincial, act swiftly and decisively to permit the development of an indigenous rather than a branch plant film industry in Canada.

Filmmakers

Film People

ACOMBA, DAVID

Born in Montreal in 1944, David Acomba studied film at Northwestern University and the University of Southern California. After working in the United States he joined the CBC in 1967 to produce and direct a 26-week series, "Sunday Morning", a 45-minute variety program with live music, satire and information. Acomba has combined his interest in film and music to produce some exceptional music specials for television, including **Mariposa: A Folk Special**, **Outerplaces**, with Robert Charlebois, and the first Anne Murray special, **Straight, Clean and Simple**, which introduced network stereo in 1971. Acomba's first feature film, **Slipstream**, won the best film, best director and best sound awards at the 1973 Canadian Film Awards. Screenplay was by Bill Fruet (from an original story by Acomba), with camerawork by Marc Champion, music by Brian Ahern and sound by Alan Lloyd.

Filmography
The Time is Now (1966). Prod: Independent. 15 min. b&w.
Summer's Gone After Today (1967). Prod: Independent. 24 min. col.
Mariposa: A Folk Special (1969). Prod: CBC. 60 min. col.

Rock I (1970). Prod: D. Acomba, CBC. 60 min. col.
Rock II (1971). Prod: D. Acomba, CBC. 60 min. col.
Somewhere (1971). Prod: D. Acomba, CBC "Program X". 30 min. col.
King Paddy (1971). Prod: D. Acomba, CBC "Telescope". 30 min. col.
Straight, Clean and Simple (1971). Prod: D. Acomba, CBC. 60 min. col.
Slipstream (1973). Prod: James Margellos, Pacific Rim Films Ltd. 92 min. col. Dist: Cinepix.
Outerplaces (1974). Prod: D. Acomba, CBC. 60 min. col.
Three Women (1975). Prod: D. Acomba, Sharon Keogh CBC. 90 min. col.
Valdy Sings About Newfoundland. Prod: D. Acomba, OECA, BBC "The Camera and the Song". 26 min. col.
Work in progress: **The George Harrison Tour**. Prod: D. Acomba. 90 min. col.

Bibliography

Cinema Canada, nos. 10/11, pp. 28-31, "Alberta Todd-ao: David Acomba Whips Up a Storm with **Slipstream**", Harris Kirshenbaum (interview); *Globe and Mail,* August 25, 1969, "Mariposa on Film: Cutting 41,000 Feet to 2,000 Takes a Lot of Time", Leslie Millin; *Montreal Star,* April 11, 1970, "Acomba, Rock and That Festival Feeling", Cynthia Gunn; *Canadian Film Digest,* January 1973, p. 11, "David Acomba and Another Musical Ride", Lloyd Chesley; *Cinema Canada,* no. 8 (June/July 1973), p. 64, review of **Slipstream**, Montague Smith; *La Presse,* November 17, 1973, "La Liberté du joueur de cornemuse", Luc Perreault; *Saturday Night,* January 1974, Marshall Delaney on **Slipstream**; *Séquences,* no. 75 (January 1974), p. 27, review of **Slipstream** by Robert-Claude Bérubé; *The Canadian Forum,* February 1974, pp. 33-36, "Three Canadian Films", Robert Fothergill; *Télérama,* Paris, no. 1260 (March 9, 1974), p. 71, review of **Slipstream** by Laredj Karsallah; *Film Culture,* New York, nos. 58-60 (1974), pp. 268-92, "Filmexpo and the New English Canadian Cinema", Seymour Stern, on **Slipstream**, p. 277ff; *Variety,* October 2, 1974, p. 152, critique of **Outerplaces**.

ALMOND, PAUL

Paul Almond was born in Montreal in 1931. After studying at McGill University he worked on his BA and Master's at Oxford, where he was actively involved as president of its poetry society and editor of a literary magazine. After graduation, he travelled with a repertory company in England, joining the CBC in Toronto in 1954 as a director. He directed many dramas, in particular with the "Festival" series — among them, **Point of Departure**,

Shadow of a Pale Horse, **Under Milkwood**, **Julius Caesar** and **Romeo and Jeannette**; **The Hill**, which he wrote and produced, won the 1957 Ohio Award. He later directed a number of episodes in the series "Wojeck", "RCMP" and "Forest Rangers", and the American series "Alfred Hitchcock Presents". **The Puppet Caravan**. (La roulotte aux poupées), with a scenario by Marie-Claire Blais, was the first bilingual drama produced by CBC's English and French networks having the same cast and production personnel. With **Journey** Almond completed a trilogy of features he both wrote and produced; all three starred Geneviève Bujold.

Filmography (incomplete)

A Phoenix Too Frequent (1958). Prod: CBC "Television Theatre". 60 min. b&w.

Backfire (1961). Prod: Merton Park Production Co.,England. 59 min. b&w.

The Dark Did Not Conquer (1963). Prod: CBC. 60 min. b&w.

Journey to the Centre (1963). Prod: CBC. 60 min. b&w.

October Beach (1964). Prod: CBC, "Telescope". 30 min. b&w.

7 Up (1964). Prod: Granada, England, "World in Action". 45 min. b&w.

Mother and Daughter (1964). Prod: CBC "Telescope". 11 min. b&w.

Let Me Count the Ways (1965). Prod: CBC "Festival". 90 min. b&w.

The Puppet Caravan (La roulotte aux poupées). Prod: CBC "Festival"/"Les beaux dimanches". 60 min.

Isabel (Isabel) (1968). Prod: P. Almond, Quest Film Productions Ltd. 108 min. col. Dist: Paramount.

Act of the Heart (Acte du coeur) (1970). Prod: P. Almond, Quest Film Productions Ltd. 103 min. col.

Journey (Détour) (1972). Prod: P. Almond, Quest Film Productions Ltd. 97 min. col. Dist: Astral Communications Ltd.

Fellowship (1976). Prod: CBC. 90 min. col.

Work in progress: **Solstice**.

Bibliography

Paul Almond: The Flame Within, Janet Edsworth, Canadian Filmography Series no. 11, available from the Canadian Film Institute. It contains a complete filmography, an interview and criticism; *La Presse*, June 3, 1967, p. 33, "Geneviève Bujold et Paul Almond: la lutte avec l'ange", Luc Perreault (interview); *Inner Views: Ten Canadian Film-makers*, J. Hofsess (McGraw-Hill Ryerson, 1975), pp. 129-142; *Montreal Star*, September 26, 1970, pp. 21-22, "Life is Knowing How to Live It", Martin Malina (interview); *Séquences*, October 1970, pp. 4-8, "Entretien avec Paul Almond", Léo Bonneville (interview); *Cinema Canada*, no. 4 (October/November 1972), pp. 30-38, "Paul Almond's **Journey**: Dream and Reality", George Csaba Köller (interview); *La Presse*,

September 26, 1970, p. D9, "L'iceberg québécois", Luc Per-
reault; *Time,* September 28, 1970, pp. 9-13, "Geneviève Bujold:
The Flame Within"; *Rélations,* no. 354 (November 1970), pp.
313-314, review of **Acte du coeur** by Yves Lever; *Globe and
Mail,* October 7, 1972, "Almond's **Journey** is a Murky Allegory",
Martin Knelman; *Le Devoir,* November 21, 1972, p. 12, "Paul
Almond: un réalisateur à découvrir", Jean-Pierre Tadros; *Take
One,* vol. 3, no. 7, p. 35, review of **Journey** by Bob Fothergill; *La
Presse,* November 10, 1972, "La fille à la dérive", Luc Perreault;
Séquences, no. 71, (January 1973), pp. 26-27, review by Jean-
René Ethier; *The Province,* Vancouver, April 17, 1973, "The Vivid
Moment Before Death's Final Darkness", Michael Walsh; *
Cinéma-Québec,* vol. 2, no. 4, pp. 9-13, "Eurydice deux fois
perdue", Michel Euvrard.

ARCAND, DENYS

Called a filmmaker of "demystification", Denys Arcand brings a
strong political and social argument to his work. He was born in
Deschambault, Quebec in 1941, and worked on the review *Parti
pris* before studying history at the University of Montreal. There he
made his first film, **Seul ou avec d'autres**, in a student group
with the help of Michel Brault on camera. Arcand joined the NFB
in 1963 where his **On est au coton**, a social-political document
on the Quebec textile workers, precipitated an internal crisis in
1970; the film was never released. His experiences in making that
film were incorporated in his script for **Gina**, a fictional feature
about textile workers and a documentary film crew. **Réjeanne
Padovani** was chosen to run in one of the non-competitive events
of the festival at Cannes, "La quinzaine des réalisateurs", and
was judged the best in the series by *Le Monde.*

Filmography

Seul ou avec d'autres (1962). With Denis Héroux and Stephane
Venne. Prod: Denis Héroux, Association générale des etudiants
de l'Université de Montréal. 65 min. b&w.
Champlain (1963). Prod: André Belleau, Fernand Dansereau,
NFB. 28 min. col.
La route de l'ouest (1964). Prod: André Belleau, NFB. 28 min.
col.
Les Montréalistes (Ville-Marie) (1964). Prod: André Belleau,
NFB. 28 min. col.
Montréal un jour d' été (Montreal on a Summer Day) (1965).
Prod: Raymond-Marie Léger, OFQ and Les Cinéastes associés.
12 min. col.
Volley Ball (Volleyball) (1966). Prod: Jacques Bobet, NFB. 13
min. b&w.
Parcs atlantiques (Atlantic Parks) (1967). Prod: André Belleau,

Jacques Bobet, NFB. 17 min. col.

On est au coton (1970). Prod: Marc Beaudet, Guy L. Côté, Pierre Maheu, NFB. 120 min. b&w.

Québec: Duplessis et après... (1972). Prod: Paul Larose, NFB. 115 min. b&w.

La maudite galette (1972). Prod: Cinak, Les Films Carle- Lamy. 105 min. col.

Réjeanne Padovani (Réjeanne Padovani) (1973). Prod: Marguerite Duparc-Levebvre, Cinak. 90 min. col. and b&w. Dist: Cinepix.

Gina (1974). Prod: Luc Lamy, Carle-Lamy Productions. 90 min. col. Dist: Cinepix.

Bibliography

Cinéastes du Québec no. 8: Denys Arcand, 1971, CQDC, contains a long interview with Arcand and others involved in the filming of **On est au coton** with passages from the sound track plus criticism by Réal La Rochelle, a filmography and bibliography; *Le Devoir*, January 25, 1975, p. 13, "Je me refuse à réfléchir", Denys Arcand; *How to Make or Not to Make a Canadian Film* (La cinémathèque canadienne, 1967), "Speaking of Canadian Film", Denys Arcand; *Cinéma-Québec*, September 1973, pp. 17-23, "**Réjeanne Padovani**: un film dramatique pour provoquer une série de sentiments", Jean-Pierre Tadros (interview); *Cinema Canada*, no. 13 (April/May 1974), pp. 56-58, "How to Have Your Cake and Eat It Too . . . à la Denys Arcand", Á. Ibrányi-Kiss (interview); *Montreal Star*, January 25, 1975, p. D-12, "Reality As Fiction", Martin Malina (interview); *La Presse*, May 29, 1971, p. D-9, "La violence d'un jeune cinéma (jusqu'ici) doux", Luc Perreault; *Champ libre II*, November 1971, re: the censoring of **On est au coton**; *L'Action*, Quebec, November 9, 1971, a letter from Sydney Newman to M. André l'Heureux, directeur du secrétariat d'action politique, also concerning the censoring of **On est au coton**; *La Presse*, November 25, 1972, "La série noire se porte bien", Luc Perreault; *Montreal Gazette*, October 6, 1973, "A Hard Look at Quebec Politics", Dane Lanken; *Montreal Star*, October 6, 1973, "Corruption Quebec-Style", Martin Malina; *Rélations*, no. 387 (November 1973), p. 318, "**Réjeanne Padovani** ou la conscience dans le béton", Yves Lever; *Le nouvel observateur*, Paris, December 10, 1973, "Messieurs, tueurs et putes: un Canadien féroce nous parle du charme discret de la bourgeoisie québécoise", Jean-Louis Bory; *Globe and Mail*, February 2, 1974, p. 27, "Reflecting Quebec Events through **Padovani**", Betty Lee; *Le Devoir*, February 23, 1974, "Et voilà pourquoi madame est aveugle", Paul Warren; *Cinema Canada*, no. 13 (April/May 1974), pp. 75-76, reviews of **Réjeanne Padovani** by Mark Miller and Natalie Edwards; *Le Devoir*, January 25, 1975, p. 13, "Un film politique qui communique", Robert-Guy Scully; *Le magazine Maclean*, April 1975, p. 12,

"Arcand, cinéaste engagé", Marc Blandford; *Réjeanne Padovani*, Robert Lévesque, ed. (L'Aurore, 1975), dist. by L'Agence de distribution populaire, script and critiques; references in *Le cinéma québécois: tendances et prolongements, L'aventure du cinéma direct,* and *Inner Views: Ten Canadian Film-makers (McGraw-Hill Ryerson, 1975), pp. 145-157.*

ARIOLI, DON

Don Arioli was born in Rochester, N.Y., in 1937 and began his storytelling career as an actor before joining Jim MacKay's animation company in Toronto, Film Design. His first work included animated segments for the CBC children's program "Butternut Square" and government sponsored films; he was invited to join the National Film Board in 1966 where he has written and designed a number of storyboards, among them **Tax is Not a Four Letter Word** (directed by Mike Mills for the Department of National Revenue), **The House that Jack Built** (La maison de Jean-Jacques) directed by Ron Tunis, **Best Friends** (Nos meilleurs amis) directed by Bob Browning for the Department of National Health and Welfare, **In a Nutshell** directed by Les Drew and **Tilt** (Tilt) directed by Arioli for the World Bank. Arioli also directed **The Specialists** which was co-produced with Zagreb Films; co-operation with the Yugoslavian studio has led to Zlatko Grgic directing a number of Arioli storyboards — **Hot Stuff** (Le feu? Pas pour les hommes) for the Dominion Fire Commissioner, **The Sea** and **Who Are We**. In 1973 Arioli directed a 53-minute co-production with Zagreb, **Man: The Polluter**; Hugh Foulds and Kaj Pindal were segment directors. Also in 1973 Barry Nelson directed Arioli's storyboard **Ten — the Magic Number**, and in 1974, **Propaganda Message**. As well as designing anti-smoking, inflation and highway safety clips (the latter directed by Blake James), Arioli did the drawings for **Tickets s.v.p.**; outside the Board he has worked on the storyline of **The Yellow Submarine**, animated and designed segments for "Sesame Street" and **Thinking**, for ABC's "Curiosity Show". As an actor he played in Dusan Makavejev's **Sweet Movie** and in George Kaczender's **U-turn**; he was also involved in an NFB feature as co-writer with director John Howe of **A Star Is Lost**. Arioli is presently working on a storyboard, **What Do You Do, What Are You Doing**, for the Language Commission.

Bibliography
Pot pourri, April, 1972, critical reviews and an interview; *Montreal Gazette,* July 4, 1970, "The Truth about Mickey Mouse", Marilyn Beker; *Montreal Star,* November 17, 1973, "Gloria (That's the Blonde) Teaches English", Martin Malina on **A Star Is Lost**; *Canadian Photography,* February 1974, "Don Arioli: Clown Prince of Animators", Dean Walker.

BAIRSTOW, DAVID

Born in Toronto in 1921, David Bairstow joined the National Film
Board in 1944. As a producer Bairstow has been involved in a
number of projects—*Eye Witness* (1952-1954), a monthly theatrical screen magazine produced by the Board; "Perspective"
(1955- 1958), a television series which dramatized social
problems; "Frontiers" (1958-1960), half-hour documentary essays
for television; and the "Netsilik" series in 1968-1969 which
became the basis of a television series on Eskimo life, "The
Stories of Tuktu". Bairstow spent the year 1969-1970 as exchange
producer with the Australian Commonwealth Film Unit where he
produced, among many others, the theatrical short, **Paddington
Lace**. Some individual films which Bairstow has produced at the
NFB include **Eternal Children**, **Autobiographical A.M. Klein**,
Judoka, **Grierson**, **Script to Screen**, **Tomorrow is Too Late**,
Oceans of Science and **Who Were the Ones**, a short by Michael
Mitchell produced within the Native Indian Training Program of
which Bairstow was executive producer. Bairstow was also producer of the Multi-Culture Film Programme which produced **Our
Street Was Paved with Gold** and **The People of the Book**. In
1973 Bairstow did English adaptations of four French television
shows produced by the National Geographic and in 1974 he re-
signed from the NFB. He is presently preparing filmstrip material
and writing a report on possible NFB-Australia co-production.

Filmography (incomplete)

Royal Journey (1952). Prod: Tom Daly, NFB. 54 min. col.

Men Against the Ice (Aux prises avec les glaces) (1960). Prod:
D. Bairstow, NFB "Frontiers". 24 min. b&w.

Morning on the Lièvre (Matin sur la Lièvre; Amanhecer Sobre O
Lievre) (1961). Prod: D. Bairstow, NFB. 13 min. col.

Music from Montreal (Musiciens parmi nous) (1962). Prod: Peter
Jones, NFB. 29 min. b&w.

Christmas Oratorio (1963). Prod: Peter Jones, NFB. 14 min.
b&w.

The First Mile Up (1963). Prod: D. Bairstow, NFB. 28 min. b&w.

"Arctic Circle" series (1963): **The Early Journeys of Vilhjalmur
Stefansson, The Later Journeys of Vilhjalmur Stefansson,
Henry Larsen's Northwest Passages, Memories and Predic-
tions**. Prod: D. Bairstow. Each 28 min. b&w.

Alexander Mackenzie — the Lord of the North (Alexander
Mackenzie — le maître du nord) (1964). Prod: Richard Gilbert,
NFB. 28 min. col.

Max in the Morning (1965). Prod: D. Bairstow, NFB. 28 min.
b&w.

Instant French (1965). Prod: D. Bairstow, NFB. 21 min. b&w.

Twenty-Four Hours in Czechoslovakia (Dvacet Ctyri Hodiny)
(1968). Prod: Walford Hewitson, NFB. 57 min. col.

Bibliography

Vancouver Sun, December 27, 1951, "**Royal Journey**: Big, Fine Job from NFB", Clyde Gilmour; *Montreal Star*, May 2, 1970, "The Film Scene Down Under: Parallel Patterns", David Bairstow.

BEAUDIN, JEAN

Born in Montreal in 1939, Jean Beaudin studied science and later received his diploma from Ecole des Beaux-Arts in Montreal and studied at the School of Design in Zurich. He joined the National Film Board in 1964 and made a number of mathematical series and then a psychological study, **Vertige**, before his first feature, **Stop**. Serge Gerand won a special award and the 1969 CFA for his music in **Vertige**: camera was by Jean-Claude Labrecque. Beaudin left the National Film Board for a short time to direct a feature on satanism, **Le diable est parmi nous**, with camera by René Verzier.

Filmography

"Géométrie" series, "Mathématiques" series (1966-67). Prod: NFB.

Vertige (1969). Prod: Gilles Boivin, Clément Perron, NFB. 44 min. col.

Le diable est parmi nous (The Possession of Virginia) (1971). Prod: John Dunning, André Link, Cinepix. 92 min. col.

Stop (1972). Prod: Pierre Gauvreau, NFB. 85 min. col.

Les indrogables (1972). Prod: François Séguillon, NFB. 26 min. col.

Trois fois passera... (1973). Prod: Jacques Bobet, NFB. 35 min. col.

Par une belle nuit d'hiver (1974). Prod: Paul Larose, NFB, "Toulemonde parle français". 33 min. col.

Cher Théo (1975). Prod: Paul Larose, Jacques Bobet, NFB. 50 min. col.

Feature work in progress: **J.A. Martin: photographe**. Prod: Jean-Marc Garand, NFB.

Bibliography

Télécinéma, no. 1 (1971), p. 13, "Communication et vérité avec Jean Beaudin", Annie Bergeron; *Séquences*, no. 66 (October 1971), p. 32, "Le cinéma canadien à la dérive", review of **Stop** by Bonneville; *Le Devoir*, March 11, 1972, "Le cinéma québécois s'en prend au diable", Jean-Pierre Tadros; *Séquences*, no. 69 (April 1972), p. 40, review of **Le diable est parmi nous** by Bonneville; *Cinéma-Québec*, vol. 3, no. 4 (December 1973), p. 46-47, Pierre Demers reviews **Les indrogables**; references in *Cinéma et société québécoise*.

BLAIS, ROGER

Blais was born in 1917 in Giffard, Quebec and graduated from the School of Fine Arts in Quebec in 1940 where he later taught. In 1945 he joined the National Film Board as a producer-director and from 1953 to 1956 was director of French Production. Blais has produced numerous films, among them **Trouble-fête** directed by Pierre Patry and Coopératio; and in 1973, **Grierson**. In 1953 Blais directed and produced a series of film "Horizons" for the NFB: **Each Man's Son** (Les mains brisées) was based on a chapter of Hugh McLennan's novel; **Au-delà du visage** was based on the novel by André Giroux; **Shadow on the Prairie** (Ombre sur la prairie) starred the Royal Winnipeg Ballet; **Pantomime** (Le voleur de rêves) starred Guy Hoffman, and **Rehearsal** (Répétition) had a musical score by Harry Somers. In recent years Blais has taught courses in communications and is presently producing a series of short films on concepts developed by John Grierson; the film **Working Class on Film** was directed by Susan Schouten.

Bibliography

Actualité, vol. 2, no. 10 (October 1961), article by Blais on his anthropological and cinematographical expedition to west New Guinea; *La Presse,* Montreal, February 3, 1965, "La co-production, clef de notre industrie du cinéma", Roger Blais; *Actualité,* February 1967, article by Blais on audio-visual techniques at Expo '67; *Perspectives,* March 11, 1973, p. 30, "Voyage: Roger Blais réalisateur à l'ONF chez les Papous en Nouvelle-Guinée", Henriette Major; *Pot pourri,* December 1973, p. 13, review of **Grierson**.

BLOOMFIELD, GEORGE

Born in Montreal in 1930, Bloomfield began his cinematic career at the National Film Board in 1957 after postgraduate work in psychology and philosophy at McGill University. His work in professional theatre led in 1961 to his appointment as professor of acting and directing at the National Theatre School. From 1963 to 1968 he wrote, directed and produced for the CBC drama department in company with Paul Almond, Norman Jewison and Ted Kotcheff. Within the well-known dramatic series "Festival", Bloomfield was responsible for George Ryga's **Man Alive**, M. Charles Cohen's **The True Bleeding Heart of Martin B.**, Pinter's **The Lover** and **The Basement**, and **Heloise and Abelard**. On leaving the CBC in 1968 he directed Ryga's **The Ecstasy of Rita Joe** for the Vancouver Theatre Centre. His first feature film, **Jenny**, written with Martin Lavut, was produced in the United States where he wrote two other scripts, **The Love Song of G. Norman Stoner** and **To Kill a Clown** (produced by Palomar Pictures). Bloomfield returned to Canada in 1973 to direct his third feature, **Child Under a Leaf** (L'enfant de la solitude), produced by Potterton Productions in Montreal. He is currently working on **The Marriage Circle**, **Portrait of A. Mask** and **Paradise Lost** for the CBC.

Bibliography

Cinema Canada, no. 17, pp. 44-47, interview by Stephen Chesley and Á. Ibrányi-Kiss. In same issue, reviews by N. Edwards and M. Miller, pp. 78-80; *Globe and Mail*, October 11, 1974, "Cannon Wasted in This New Tearjerker", M. Malina; *La Presse*, October 19, 1974, "Une façade abattue", Luc Perreault; *Montreal Gazette*, October 19, 1974, "Film in Montreal, **Child**, a Solid Work", Jack Kapica; *Le Devoir*, October 26, 1974, "**Child**: ou le Canada anglais, aussi, a ses navets", André Leroux; *Séquences*, no. 79, p. 34, review of **Child** by Huguette Poitras.

BLUMER, RONALD

Born in Montreal in 1942, Ronald Blumer received his B.Sc. from McGill University and his Master's at Boston University's School of Public Communications in Film Production. In 1968 he returned to McGill's School of Communication where he was John Grierson's graduate assistant. As a sound man, Blumer worked on **Ruby**, a feature film directed by Richard Bartlett in Boston; he had gained this expertise as an NFB summer student in the sound department. In 1973-74 he was director of television production at Allan Memorial Institute working in video feedback. As a teacher, Blumer co-directed with Kirwan Cox in 1970 a coast-to-coast project for young filmmakers financed by Opportunities for Youth, and has lectured at Marianopolis and Vanier Colleges in Montreal. He was the film critic on the Montreal radio show "Daybreak" in 1973-74, has written extensively for film magazines and, in 1975, was interim director of the Frobisher Bay Film Workshop run for the Inuit by the NFB. His films reflect his particular interest in the subject of aging.

Filmography

Solomon's Children (1967). With David Grubin. Prod: Rabbi Kantor, Solomon Schechter Day School. 20 min. b&w.

McGill in Crisis (1967). With John N.W. Smith and Adam Symansky. Prod: CBC "Hourglass". 15 min. b&w.

The Treatment is the Crisis (1971). Prod: Gilbert Rosenberg, Maimondes Hospital and Home for the Aged. 31 min. col.

"Learning to Nurse" (1972). Prod: Moira Allen, McGill School of Nursing. A series of 10 videotapes. Each 10 to 30 min.

Students as Engineers (1973). With Pedro Novak. Prod: School of Engineering, McGill. 20 min. col.

Rescue from Isolation (1973). Prod: Gilbert Rosenberg, Maimondes Hospital and Home for the Aged. 20 min. col.
Beyond Shelter (1976). Prod: Gilbert Rosenberg, Maimondes Hospital and Home for the Aged. 25 min. col.

Bibliography

Take One, vol. 2, no. 9, "John Grierson: I derive my authority from Moses", an interview with Ronald Blumer first printed in the *McGill Reporter; McGill Medical Journal,* vol. 38, no. 3, October 1969, pp. 130-132, "Medical Teaching Films or 'Do You Sleep When You Turn Out the Lights?'", R. Blumer; *McGill Medical Journal,* vol. 39, (Spring 1970), pp.26-29, "Films: Is Science Dead?", R. Blumer; *Cinema Journal,* vol. 9, no. 2 (Spring 1970), pp. 31-39, "The Camera as Snowball: France 1918-1927, R. Blumer; *Cinema Canada,* no. 26 (March 1976), pp.48-49, a review of **Beyond Shelter** by Connie Tadros; *Pot pourri,* Summer 1976, p. 17, a review of **Beyond Shelter** by C.A. Bibby.

BONNIERE, RENE

Born in Lyon, France in 1928, René Bonnière worked in his native land in many aspects of film and television production. He studied editing with Henri Colpi who worked for Alan Renais. Bonnière joined Crawley Films in Ottawa in 1955 and worked closely with Pierre Perrault in directing a series of 13 half- hour films about the north shore of the St. Lawrence River called "Au pays de Neuve-France". Bonnière has worked extensively in both English and French television as well as in the feature film field. His **Amanita Pestilens** introduced Geneviève Bujold in 1964. **Hamlet** is a youthful production photographed with a hand- held camera by Richard Leiterman. Louis Applebaum scored **The Discoverers**; camerawork was by Edmund Long. In 1972-73 Bonnière made several films in Europe for Hobel-Leiterman, including **Chili con Cardin**. **Vicky**, made in 1973 from a script by Grahame Woods, won a Canadian Film Award for best actress for Jackie Burroughs; Woods also scripted **The Disposable Man. A Trip to the Coast** was based on the story by Alice Munro. In recent years Bonnière has produced a number of films for television, including ten in the 1974 season of CBC's "The Collaborators". He also worked with producer Roman Bittman, NFB, on a film for the United Nations Habitat conference in 1976.

Filmography (incomplete)

Craftsmen of Canada (Maîtres artisans du Canada) (1957). Prod: Crawley Films. 30 min.
"Au pays de Neuve-France" ("St. Lawrence North") (1960): **La traversée d'hiver à l'Ile aux Coudres** (Winter Crossing at Ile

aux Coudres); **Attiuk** (Attiuk); **Le Jean Richard** (Jean
Richard); **Tête-à-baleine** (Whalehead); **L'anse Tabatière**
(Winter Sealing at La Tabatière); **Ka-ke-ki-ku** (Ka-Ke-Ki-Ku);
Anse-aux-Basques (Whalehunter at L'Anse-aux-Basques); **En
revenant de St- Hilarion** (Soirée at St. Hilarion); **Diamants du
Canada** (Canadian Diamonds); **Les goélettes** (On the Sea);
Rivière du gouffre (Turlutte); **La pitoune** (Three Seasons);
Toutes Isles (Land of Jacques Cartier). Prod. & Script: Pierre
Perrault, Crawley Films for Radio-Canada. Each 30 min. col.
Abitibi (1961). Prod. René Bonnière, Crawley Films. 30 min. col.
Les Annanacks (The Annanacks) (1963). Prod: R. Bonnière,
Crawley Films, NFB. col.
Les faux visages (False Faces) (1963). Prod: R. Bonnière,
Crawley Films. 60 min. col.
Amanita Pestilens (Amanita Pestilens), (1964). Prod: F.R.
Crawley, Crawley Films. 90 min. col.
Over twenty "Telescopes" for CBC. (1966-71). Among them,
Gratien Gélinas (1967); **Alex Colville** (1967); **Robert
Charlebois** (1970); **Veronica Tennant** (1970); **Farley Mowat**
(1970) and **Jean Gascon** (1971). Each 30 min. col.
Directed a number of dramas in series "Wojeck", produced by
Ron Weyman; "McQueen", also Ron Weyman; and "An-
thology", produced by Ron Weyman and Dick Gilbert, 1968-71.
Other dramas were produced for the series "Canadian Short
Stories" (David Peddie) and "Five Years in the Life" (Michael
Rothery).
Alexis de Tocqueville (1969). Prod: Lister Sinclair, CBC for In-
tertel. 60 min. col.
The Firebrand (1970). Prod: Alice Sinclair, CBC for Intertel. 60
min. col.
Four Day Wonder (1971). Prod: Ron Weyman, CBC "Anthology".
60 min. col.
Hamlet (1972). Prod: R. Bonnière, Crawley Films. 168 min. col.
The Disposable Man (1972). Prod: Ron Weyman, CBC. 60 min. col.
The Debain Family of Quebec (1972). Prod: CBC "Five Years in
the Life". 30 min. col.
The Levesque Family (1972). Prod: CBC "Five Years in the
Life". 30 min. col.
The Discoverers (1972). Prod: Ron Weyman, CBC "Anthology".
60 min. col.
Vicky (1973). Prod: Ron Weyman, CBC "Anthology". 60 min. col.
Limestoned (1973). Prod: R. Bonnière, CBC "Art Magazine". 30
min. col.
McIver (1973). Prod: David Peddie, CBC "To See Ourselves". 30
min. col.
Trip to the Coast (1974). Prod: David Peddie, CBC "To See
Ourselves". 30 min. col.
All the King's Men (1974). Prod: Richard Gilbert, CBC "The Col-
laborators". 60 min. col.

A Touch of Madness (1974). Prod: Richard Gilbert, CBC "The Collaborators". 60 min. col.
May and Frank (1975). Prod: Julian Roffman, CBC. 60 min. col.

Bibliography

Montreal Star, October 20, 1962, p. 43, "$200,000 Movie Being Produced Here", Dusty Vineberg; *Objectif*, October-November 1964, pp. 47-49, "Bandes à part"; *Objectif* 9-10, pp. 22-23 (bio-filmography); *Objectif* 61, pp. 21-22, "Dix-sept artisans du cinéma canadien" (with a descriptive filmography); references in: *Vingt ans de cinéma au Canada français, Jeune cinéma canadien,* and *Le cinéma canadien.*

BORREMANS, GUY

Guy Borremans was born in Belgium in 1934. He began his career as a still photographer and has continued to exhibit photographs; as a cameraman he has worked on numerous films and has won himself an unofficial title as father of an independent québécois cinema. After his arrival in Canada he worked as a cameraman and director of photography on a CBC television series and as a still photographer for *Paris-Match* and *Le Canada.* Borremans worked in the United States for the U.S. Information Agency and in Senegal and the Gaza Strip for the United Nations. While at N.E.T. station WGBH in Boston he shot **What Harvest for the Reaper**, a documentary on migrant labour, that resulted in his being barred from the United States. In 1961 Borremans joined the NFB camera department. He received several awards for the cinematography of **Jour aprés jour** (Perron) and worked on many films including **Dimanche d'Amérique** and **Percé on the Rocks** (Carle); **Golden Gloves** and **24 heures ou plus** (Groulx); **Bûcherons de la Manouane**, **Le mépris n'aura qu'un temps**, **Le perfectionnement**, **Un homme et son boss** and **Mistashipu** (Lamothe); **France revisitée** (Aquin); **Jazz** and **Runner** (Owen); **Ballerina** (Kaczender); **Fabienne sans son Jules** (Godbout); **La beauté même** (Fortier); **Un jeu si simple** (Labrecque); **Les Rolling Stones** (Bensimon); and **Job's Garden** (Richardson). Borremans presently lives in New Brunswick where he teaches photography at the University of Moncton.

Filmography

La femme, l'oiseleur et la maison (1956). Prod: Independent. Now lost.
La femme image (1960). Prod: Independent. 37 min. b&w.
L'homme vite (1964). Prod: Hubert Aquin, NFB. 9 min. col.

Bibliography

Canadian Cinematography, May-June 1963, pp. 3-7, "Guy Borremans Talks About Filmmaking", interview by François Sé-
quillon; *Objectif*, vol. 1, no. 1 (October 1960), pp. 20-22, **La
femme image** reviewed by Jean-Claude Pilon; *L'Ecran*, Montreal,
May 2, 1961, pp. 44-48, critique of **La femme image** by Patrick
Straram; *Objectif 62*, no. 15-16 (August 1962), "L'homme
observe"; *Séquences*, no. 33 (May 1963), "Les cameramen de
l'ONF", Jacques Leduc; *Montreal Star*, November 9, 1965, "Borremans at Galerie Caius", Michael Ballantyne; *Le petit journal*,
Montreal, February 18, 1968, "Guy Borremans, la père du jeune
cinéma québécois: 'Parlez-moi de New York, mais ne me parlez
plus de travailler ici' ", Jean- Claude Germain; *Montreal Star*,
September 14, 1968, "**What Harvest for the Reaper**: A Moving
Social Document"; *Foto*, Amsterdam, no. 4 (April 1971), pp.
32-37, "Fotografen en hun wek: Guy Borremans"; references in:
Dossiers de cinéma: 1 (Montreal: Edition Fides, 1968), on **Jour
après jour**; *Cinéma d'ici*, and *L'aventure du cinéma direct*.

BRASSARD, ANDRE

Stage and film director André Brassard has had a fruitful collaboration with playwright Michel Tremblay who wrote dialogue for
Françoise Durocher, waitress; at the 1972 Canadian Film
Awards, it won three Ftrogs for best non-feature film, best director
and best television drama. Brassard and Tremblay also co-
authored the fantastic tale of east end Montreal, **Il était une fois
dans l'est**, Canada's official entry at the 1974 Cannes Film
Festival. Born in 1947, Brassard began his career directing
amateur theatre before his first professional production with
Tremblay's **Les belles soeurs**. Brassard staged an improvised
piece for the NFB's "Adieu alouette" series in **Backyard Theatre**.

Filmography

Françoise Durocher, waitress (1972). Prod: Pierre Duceppe,
   Jean-Marc Garand, NFB. 29 min. col.
Il était une fois dans l'est (1974). Prod: Pierre Lamy, Les Pro-
   ductions Carle-Lamy. 101 min. col.
In progress: **Le soleil se lève encore sur la rue Bélanger**
   (feature).

Bibliography

Le nouvelliste-perspective, Three Rivers, November 20, 1971, "Le
premier film d'André Brassard", Renault Gariépy; *Québec-
presse*, October 8, 1972, "Toutes les waitress fines du Québec
reçoivent l'hommage d'André Brassard", Robert Lévesque; *Le*

Jour, February 28, 1974, p. 13, "André Brassard: un film pyramide entre Tremblay et Bergman ...", Jean-Pierre Tadros; *Le Soleil*, Quebec, March 2, 1974, "La faune de Tremblay et Brassard en 35mm", Claude Daigneault; *Montreal Star*, March 1, 1974, "Film Overdoes Broken Hearts", Martin Malina; *Montreal Gazette*, March 2, 1974, "Tremblay's Demi- monde Staggers on Film", Jack Kapica; *Le Droit*, Ottawa, March 2, 1974, "Brassard et Tremblay fidèles à eux-mêmes", Murray Maltais; *Le nouvel observateur*, Paris, May 13, 1974, review of **Il était** ..., Jean-Louis Bory; *Cinéma-Québec*, vol. 3, no. 5 (1974), pp. 28-32, "Comment passer du théâtre au cinéma ...", Jean- Pierre Tadros; *Relations*, no. 392 (April 1974), p. 125, review of **Il était**..., L. Lever; *Séquences*, no. 76 (April 1974), pp. 28-29, review by Léo Bonneville; *Cinéma-Québec*, vol. 3, no. 8 (1974), pp. 21-23, "Brassard-Tremblay s'expliquent", Louis Marcorelles (interview at Cannes); *Cinema Canada*, no. 19, pp. 38-39, "An Interview with Michel Tremblay", Brian Clancy; *Cinema Canada*, no. 20, p. 65, "Dreams and Despairs on the Main", review of **Il était**..., Marc Miller; *Il était une fois dans l'est*, Michel Tremblay and André Brassard (Montreal: Editions de l'aurore, 1974), filmscript and stills.

BRAULT, MICHEL

Born in Montreal in 1928, Michel Brault began his film career while in university, collaborating (as cameraman) with Claude Jutra on a number of shorts, and between 1950 and 1951 working on a film magazine, *Découpage*. His work as a cameraman both within and outside of the National Film Board has been impressive and influential; he had been cameraman for two television series, "Petites médisances" and "Images en boîte" before joining the NFB's Candid Eye Unit with Koenig, Kroitor and Macartney-Filgate; he is credited as camerman on **The Days Before Christmas** and **Festival in Puerto Rico** in that series. He later worked with Jean Rouch, the French anthropologist-filmmaker, on **La punition** and **Chronique d'un été** and with Mario Ruspoli on **Regards sur la folie**, **La fête prisonnière** and **Les inconnus de la terre**. In 1962, Brault collaborated with Montreal students Denys Arcand and Denis Héroux to photograph **Seul ou avec d'autres**, and with Claude Jutra on **A tout prendre.** In recent years Brault has photographed key Quebec films: **Faut aller parmi l'monde pour le savoir** by Dansereau, **Mon Oncle Antoine** and **Kamouraska** by Jutra, Groulx's **Entre tu et vous**, and **Le temps d'une chasse**, by Francis Mankiewicz. **Les ordres**, a fictionalized documentary on the October Crisis, won the 1974 "Prix de la critique québécoise" given by the Association québécoise des critiques de cinéma, best direction, best screenplay and best film at the 1975 Canadian Film Awards, and the best director award (shared with Costa-Gavras) at Cannes in 1975. Brault is currently working on a TV series about French folk music and is researching a feature film script.

Filmography

Les raquetteurs (1958). With Gilles Groulx. Prod: Louis Portuagais, NFB. 28 min. b&w.

La lutte (Wrestling) (1961). With C. Jutra, M. Carrière, C. Fournier. Prod: Jacques Bobet, NFB. 28 min. b&w.

Quebec-USA or **L'invasion pacifique** (Visit to a Foreign Country) (1962). With Claude Jutra. Prod: Fernand Dansereau, NFB. 28 min. b&w.

Les enfants du silence (1963). With C. Jutra. Prod: Fernand Dansereau and Victor Jobin, NFB. 24 min. b&w.

Pour la suite du monde (Moontrap) (1963). With Pierre Perrault and Marcel Carrière. Prod: Jacques Bobet and Fernand Dansereau, NFB. 105 min. b&w.

Le temps perdu (The End of Summer) (1964). Prod: Fernand Dansereau, NFB, for "Temps présent". 27 min. b&w.

La fleur de l'âge: section **Geneviève** (1964). Prod: André Belleau and Victor Jobin, NFB. 28 min. b&w.

Québec...? (1966). With Gilles Groulx. Prod: Les Cinéastes Associés Inc. for Office du Film du Québec. 30 min. b&w.

Entre la mer et l'eau douce (1967). Prod: Pierre Patry, Coopératio. 87 min. b&w.

Conflicts (1967). Prod: Crawley Films for the Canadian Pavilion, Expo 67. 4-1/2 min. Two screens. col.

Les enfants du néant (1968). Prod: Pyranha Films, France. 60 min. b&w.

Eloge du chiac (1968). Prod: Guy L. Côté, NFB. 28 min. b&w.

L'Acadie, l'Acadie (Acadia, Acadia) (1971). With Pierre Perrault. Prod: Guy l'Côté and Paul Larose, NFB. 117 min. b&w.

Le bras de levier et la rivière (1973). Prod: In-Media for Radio-Canada. 30 min. col.

Les ordres (Orders) (1974). Prod: Les productions Les ordres. 107 min. col. Dist: Mutuel (French version); New Cinema (English version).

Bibliography

Objectif, no. 3 (December 1960), pp. 3-16, "Michel Brault et Claude Jutra racontent Jean Rouch", interview with Robert Daudelin and Michel Patenaude; *Le Devoir*, December 12, 1961, "Opinion de Jean Rouch: le Canadien Michel Brault est le meilleur opérateur du monde"; *L'Ecran*, (Montreal), no. 2, pp. 7-15, "Entretien de deux cinéastes" *Cahiers du cinéma in English*, no. 4, p. 42, "Ten Questions to Five Canadian Filmmakers" (interview); *La Presse*, June 22, 1968, p. 37, "Michel Brault: pourquoi veut-on parler français?", interview with Luc Perreault; *Séquences*, no. 68 (February 1972), pp. 4-14, "Entretien avec Michel Brault" (inter-

view); *Cinema Canada*, no. 7, pp. 45-46, interview on
Kamouraska; *Le Devoir*, August 10, 1974, interview by Louis Marcorelles; *Pariscop*, Paris, no. 366 (May 28-June 3, 1975), "Ils ont
dit" (interview); *La Presse*, February 8, 1969, "**Les enfants du
néant** de Michel Brault en *Quinzaine*", Louis Marcorelles; *Qu°bec-
presse*, February 13, 1972,"**L'Acadie, l'Acadie** *s'adresse plus aux
québécois qu'aux acadiens . . .*"; *Saturday Night*, December,
1973, p. 43, "The High Cinematic Art of Michel Brault", Marshall
Delaney; *Le Jour*, September 21, 1974, "Un film sur l'humiliation",
Jean-Pierre Tadros; *Globe and Mail*, October 5, 1974, "**Les ordres**
an Eloquent Response to Shame of October, 1970", Martin
Knelman; *Le Devoir*, October 5, 1974, "Ordre et desordre", Jean
Ethier-Blais; *Time*, October 17, 1974, "Night of the Garbage
Bags", Geoffrey James; *This Magazine*, vol. 8, no. 5, p. 10-11,
"Political Cinema in Quebec", Mark Raboy; *Cinéma-Québec*, vol.
4, no. 5, p. 10-15, "Une histoire à suivre Octobre 70 dans le
cinéma québécois", by Yves Lever; *Vie des arts*, vol. 20, no. 78,
pp. 44-45, "Michel Brault, cinéaste exemplaire à propos de son
film **Les ordres**"; **Les ordres**: *un film de Michel Brault*, Gilles
Marsolais, "Le Cinématographe" collection (Montreal: Editions de
l'Aurore, 1975). Dossier of the annotated script, stills, criticism,
bio- filmography with an introduction by Marsolais;
Cinéma-Québec, vol. 4, no. 1, pp. 13-20, discussions of **Les ordres** by Michel Brûle and Pierre Vallières; *Cinema Canada*, no. 17,
p. 77, review of **Les ordres** by Ronald Blumer; *Cinema Canada*,
no. 20, pp. 64-65, "The Quebec Crisis: Once More with Feeling",
Mark Miller; *Cinéastes du Québec no. 11: Michel Brault*. CQDC.
Introduction by Gilles Marsolais. Interview by André La France,
Yves Leduc and Gilles Marsolais. Filmography and bibliography;
Extensive criticism in *Vingt ans de cinéma au Canada français, Le
cinéma canadien* and *Jeune cinéma canadien;* numerous
references in *Essais sur le cinéma québécois* and *L'aventure du
cinéma direct*.

BRITTAIN, DONALD

Master editor and story-teller Donald Brittain was born in Ottawa
in 1928 and attended Queen's University in Kingston. Before joining the National Film Board in 1954, he worked as a reporter and
feature writer for the *Ottawa Journal*. Brittain has been responsible for many important film portraits such as those of Dr. Norman
Bethune, Roy Thomson (in **Never a Backward Step**) and, more
recently, of the early Canadian film industry. As well as scripting
most of his own films, Brittain wrote **The One Man Band that
Went to Wall Street** for the New York Stock Exchange, scripted
and co-produced thirteen documentaries in the series "Canada At
War" and, in NFB's Unit B, the commentary for **Stravinsky**.
Among Brittain's other filmscripts are the animated spoof **What**

on Earth, **The Railrodder**, **Labyrinth** and **Helicopter Canada**. In 1970 he worked with Georges Dufaux and Roman Kroitor on **Tiger Child**, a multi-screen production for the Fuji Group Pavilion at Osaka. While continuing to direct, Brittain has produced Larry Kent's **The Apprentice** for Potterton Productions and acted as special editorial consultant on the NFB portrait, **Grierson**.

Filmography

Setting Fires for Science (Les incendiares) (1958). Prod: Peter Jones, NFB. 20 min. col.

A Day in the Night of Jonathan Mole (1959). Prod: Peter Jones, NFB for the Department of Labour. 29 min. b&w.

Fields of Sacrifice (Champs d'honneur) (1963). Prod: D. Brittain, NFB. 38 min. col.

The Campaigners (1964). Prod: D. Brittain, CBC "This Hour Has Seven Days". 35 min. b&w.

Bethune (Bethune, héros de notre temps) (1964). With John Kemeny. Prod: J. Kemeny & D. Brittain, NFB. 59 min. b&w.

Mosca (1965). Prod: D. Brittain, CBC "This Hour Has Seven Days". 10 min. b&w.

Ladies and Gentlemen, Mr. Leonard Cohen (1966). With Don Owen. Prod: John Kemeny, NFB. 41 min. b&w.

Memorandum (Pour mémoire) (1966). With John Spotton. Prod: John Kemeny, NFB. 58 min. b&w.

Never a Backward Step (La presse et son empire) (1967). With Arthur Hammond and John Spotton. Prod: Guy Glover, NFB. 57 min. b&w.

Saul Alinsky Went to War (1968). With Peter Pearson. Prod: John Kemeny, NFB. 57 min. b&w.

Tiger Child (1970). Prod: Roman Kroitor, Kiichi Ichikawa, Multi-Screen Corp. for Expo '70. 20 min. col.

The Noblest of Callings, the Vilest of Trades (1971). With Cameron Graham. Prod: CBC "CBC White Paper". 90 min. col.

The People's Railroad (1972). With John Spotton. Prod: Potterton Productions for CNR. 60 min. col.

Starblanket, **Catskinner Keen**, and **Cavendish Country** (1973-74). Prod: D. Brittain for NFB "West" series. Each 27 min. col.

Van's Camp (1974). With Les Rose. Prod: D. Brittain, L. Rose for NFB "West" series. 27 min. col.

Dreamland: A History of Early Canadian Movies 1895-1939 (1974). Prod: Kirwan Cox, The Great Canadian Moving Picture Company with NFB. 86 min. b&w.

King of the Hill (1974). With William Canning. Prod: W. Canning, NFB. 56 min. col.

The Summer Before (1975). Prod: Peter Llewellyn, Crawley Films for Royal Bank and COJO. 30 min. col.

Stress: The World of Hans Selye (1975). Prod: Andrew Duffus, Informedia Productions. 27 min. col.

The Players (1975). Prod: Tom Daly, Gil Brealey, NFB and South Australian Film Corporation. 58 min. col.

Volcano: An Inquest into the Life of Malcolm Lowry (1976). Prod: James B. Domville, NFB. 90 min. col.

Mr. Montreal: The Life of Camillien Houde (1976). Prod: James B. Domville, NFB. 60 min. col.

Bibliography

Cinema Canada, no. 15, pp. 36-40, "Green Stripe and Common Sense", interview with Brittain by Ronald Blumer and Susan Schouten; *Cinema Canada*, no. 16, pp. 54-57, "**Dreamland**", interview with Brittain and Kirwan Cox by Á. Ibrányi-Kiss; *Montreal Star*, September 3, 1966, p. 27, "The Face on the Documentary Floor", Stephen Franklin; *Film Quarterly*, England, Winter 1966-67, review of **Memorandum**, Henry Breitrose; *Maclean's*, November 1968, p. 111, "Q: Where's the Best Place to See Canada in '70? A: Osaka", review of **Tiger Child**; *The Canadian Magazine*, April 25, 1970, p. 16, "The Fuji Film — Good, Almost Great", on **Tiger Child**; *Montreal Star*, July 11, 1970, "**Tiger Child** Packs 'em In at the Very Fat Caterpillar Called a Pavilion at Osaka", Harry Reade; *American Cinematographer*, July 1970. Most of this issue dedicated to "Film at Expo '70", with a discussion of **Tiger Child** by Brittain, Dufaux and Kroitor; *Ici Radio-Canada*, vol. 5, no. 26 (June 19, 1971), p. 3, "**Bethune, héros de notre temps**"; *Globe and Mail*, Toronto, October 9, 1974, "Film on Canada's Film History", Blaik Kirby; *Le Devoir*, Montreal, October 11, 1974, "Le Cinéma canadien de 1895 à 1939", Jean Basile; *La Presse*, Montreal, October 19, 1974, "Une histoire partiale du cinéma canadien"; *Box Office*, Calgary, November 4, 1974, "Network Special Traces History of Canadian Movies from 1896", Maxine McBean; *Albertan*, Calgary, February 15, 1975, "Calgary Songwriter in Network Special", Shirlee Gordon; references in *Le cinéma canadien* and *L'aventure du cinéma direct*.

BRUCK, JERRY, JR.

Born in Montreal in 1947, Jerry Bruck graduated in history from Yale in 1968. He learned filmmaking while making **Celebration**, a documentary of President Nixon's inauguration. **I.F. Stone's Weekly** was made with a one-man film crew over a three-year period. It documents the work of the famous journalist who, blacklisted during the McCarthy era, founded his own newspaper and for nineteen years published an independent view of U.S. government. The film won the New York American Film Festival's Emily and John Grierson Awards in 1974. Bruck lives in Montreal.

Filmography

Celebration: The Counter-Inaugural, 1969 (1970). Prod: Jerry
Bruck, Jr. 59 min. b&w.
The Old Corner Store Will Be Knocked Down (1973). Prod:
Jerry Bruck, Jr. 22 min. b&w.
I.F. Stone's Weekly (1973). Prod: Jerry Bruck, Jr. 62 min. b&w.

Bruck distributes his films: P.O. Box 5, Station G, Montreal.

Bibliography

Sight Lines, vol. 7, no. 5 (1974), pp. 9-10 and 23-24, interview
with Bruck by Judith Trojan; *Polemics and Prophecies 1967-1970*,
I.F. Stone, edited by Jerry Bruck (New York: Random House,
1970); *Montreal Star*, October 13, 1973, "62 minutes of I.F.
Stone", David MacDonald; *Village Voice*, New York, November
29, 1973, "The Good Muckraking Life", Nat Hentoff; *Time*,
December 3, 1973, p. 94, review of **I.F. Stone's Weekly**; *Globe
and Mail*, Toronto, July 13, 1974, "Raves for Stone Film But
Canada Can't See It", Betty Lee; *La Presse*, Montreal, September
28, 1974, "Une 'vedette' qui a fait trembler les presidents", Serge
Dussault; *Globe and Mail*, Toronto, October 4, 1974, "The Once
Radical Stone Becomes Institution", Martin Knelman; *Montreal
Gazette*, October 12, 1974, "Bruck Takes His Hero Everywhere",
Jack Kapica; *Cinema Canada*, no. 17, pp. 34-36, "Contrasts &
Similarities", L. Hartt.

BULBULIAN, MAURICE

Born in Montreal in 1938, Maurice Bulbulian worked in the
laboratories of the National Research Council and taught for a
number of years before his work with educational films brought
him to the National Film Board, where he made a number of
teaching loops and a series of films on physics. Together with
Robert Forget he was one of the animators of Vidéographe in
Montreal. Bulbulian's work with the NFB Société nouvelle has produced several films on the problems of workers in the Quebec
forest industry. **La richesse des autres**, shot in northwest
Quebec and in Chile, deals with miners and their problems.

Selected Filmography

La p'tite Bourgogne, (1968). Prod: Robert Forget, NFB Société
nouvelle. 44 min. b&w.
Un lendemain comme hier, (1970). Prod: Pierre Maheu, Paul
Larose, NFB Société nouvelle. 42 min. b&w.
Région 80 (1970). Prod: Normand Cloutier, NFB Société nouvelle.
16 min. b&w.
En ce jour mémorable (1971). Prod: Normand Cloutier, NFB
Société nouvelle. 14 min. b&w.

Dans nos forêts (1971). Prod: Normand Cloutier, NFB Société nouvelle. 89 min. col.

La richesse des autres (1973). With Michel Gauthier. Prod: NFB, Société nouvelle. 94 min. col.

Salvador Allende Gossens: Un témoignage (Salvador Allende Gossens: A Testimony) (1974). Prod: NFB. 19 min. col.

La revanche (1974). Prod: Jean-Marc Garand, NFB. 23 min. col.

Y'a rien là (1976). Prod: Jean-Marc Garand, NFB. 90 min. col.

Bibliography

Politique hebdo, Paris, no. 90, vol. 2, no. 8, "Les merveilles de la vidéo libre au Québec" (interview); *Le Soleil*, January 29, 1972, "**Dans nos forêts** ... juste à l'orée", Ghislaine Rheault; *Le Devoir*, February 9, 1972, p. 13, "Le drame de ceux qui vivent de la forêt", Jean-Pierre Tadros; *La Presse*, February 26, 1972, "On est sorti du bois", Luc Perreault; *Le soleil du Saguenay*, June 21, 1972, "Le film **Dans nos forêts** suscite déception, inquiétude et volonté", Claude Vaillancourt; *Cinéma-Québec*, vol. 2, no. 1 (September 1972), pp. 24-25, "Nos forêts?", Michel Euvrard; *La Presse*, June 9, 1973, "Le pouls des mineurs québécois", Luc Perreault; *La Tribune*, Sherbrooke, June 23, 1973, "Un objectif de la CSN: que tous les travailleurs voient un film précis"; *Cinéma-Québec*, July-August 1973, pp. 33-36, "Continuons le combat", reviews by Richard Gay and Pierre Demers on **Richesse des autres**; *Rélations*, no. 384 (July-August 1973), p. 221, review of **Richesse des autres** by Yves Lever; references in *L'aventure du cinéma direct*.

CARDINAL, ROGER

Director and editor Roger Cardinal was born in Montreal in 1940. After serving the navy as an official interpreter, he studied literature and history at Collège Ste.-Marie, and joined Radio-Canada in 1961 first as assistant editor, then as editor. He worked on several series there, including "Dossier" and "Le sel de la semaine". Cardinal produced and edited a number of commercials for the McLaren advertising agency in Toronto before joining Onyx Films in Montreal, where he is vice-president in charge of the film department. **Barrières architecturales**, an exploration of the world of the handicapped, won a silver medal at the international film festival at Varna, Bulgaria in 1974.

Filmography

Boscoville (1969). Prod: Radio-Canada. 26 min. b&w.

Safari canadien: du côté du Yukon (Yukon 70: The Call of the North) (1969). Prod: Mondo-Vision Inc. for CBC and Paramount. 60 min. col.

Les jeunes kidnappés (1969). Prod: Mondo-Vision Inc. 28 min. b&w.

La collège militaire (1969). Prod: Mondo-Vision for CBC and NFB. 30 min. b&w.

Pourquoi pas (1970). Prod: NFB for Department of National Defence. 20 min. col.

The Storm (Al assifa) (1970). Prod: Roger Cardinal, Mondo-Vision Inc. 60 min. col.

Après-ski (1971). Prod: Harry Cohen, Compagnie Après-ski Inc. with Famous Players. 104 min. col.

Mistassini (1971). Prod: OFQ for Ministry of Communication. 7 min. col.

L'apparition (1972). Prod: Roger Vallée, Les films mutuels/Les films Roger Vallée. 118 min. col.

Français, langue de travail (1973). Prod: OFQ for Office de la langue française. 4 min. col.

Montréal-mode (1973). Prod: Jacques Parent, Briston Films for OFQ. 16 min. col.

Barrières architecturales (1973). Prod: Jean Savard, Briston Films for OFQ, for the Ministry of Education. 39 min. col.

Français, Sorry I Don't (1974). Prod: Yvon Blouin, Onyx Films for OFQ, for Office de la langue française. 25 min. col.

Québec c'est bon (1974). Prod: Onyx Films for OFQ. 15 min. col.

Destination, hospitalité (1974). Prod: Onyx Films for OFQ, for Ministry of Tourism. 16 min. col.

Plus ça change, plus c'est pareil (1974). Prod: Onyx Films for NFB. 30 min. col.

The Game Is the Game (1974). Prod: Onyx Films for NFB. 30 min. col.

The Greatest Snow on Earth (Les plus grandes neige du monde) (1975). Prod: Onyx Films for NFB. 15 min. col.

"Charade" series, including: **Oui ... mais, Banc public, Annie**, and **Casse-tête** (1975). Prod: Onyx Films for Ministry of Education. Total 12 min. col.

Québec congrès (1976). Prod: Onyx Films for OFQ. 12 min. col.

Les jeux de Québec: cinq ans après (The Quebec Games: Five Years After) (1976). Prod: Onyx Films for OFQ, for Ministry of Sports, Recreation and Leisure. 30 min. col.

Bienvenue à Montréal (Bienvenue à Montréal) (1976). Prod: Onyx Films for COJO. 15 min. col.

SMMIS (1976). Prod: John Turner, Onyx Films for NFB, for Department of National Defence. 25 min. col.

Bibliography

Sept jours, no. 198 (March-April 1971), pp. 25-29, "Pour comprendre **Après-ski** et les autres pornographes", Claude Jasmin; *La Presse*, April 3, 1971, "Raté, ce slalom"; *Québec-presse*, March 12, 1972, "Monseigneur Lavoie et la p'tite Manon vedettes de cinéma", Robert Levesque; *Le Devoir*, March 20, 1972, "Une apparition bien navrante", Jean-Pierre Tadros; *Séquences*, no. 69

(April 1972), pp. 40-41, review of **L'apparition** by Léo Bonneville; *Photo journal*, July 1, 1973, "Le premier film du genre sur les handicapés", Claire Harting on **Barrières architecturales**.

CARLE, GILLES

Born in Maniwaki, Quebec in 1929, Gilles Carle studied at the Ecole des Beaux-Arts de Montréal with Henry Eveleigh and Alfred Pellan. He worked as a graphic artist for *Le Soleil*, at La Photogravure de Québec and Radio-Canada, and illustrated *How to Make or Not to Make a Canadian Film*; in 1967 he collaborated on the design of the Quebec Pavilion at Expo. Carle has written novels, plays, short stories and film criticism; he co-founded the film magazine *L'Ecran* and later, *Les éditions de l'hexagone* with Gaston Miron, Oliver Marchand and Louis Portuguais. **La vie heureuse de Léopold Z**, Carle's first feature film, was also the first NFB feature to gain popularity in Quebec movie houses. Carle's work has received critical acclaim outside of Quebec: **La mort d'un bûcheron** and **La vrai nature de Bernadette** represented Canada at Cannes in 1972 and 1973. **La tête de Normande St.-Onge** was shown out of competition at Cannes in 1976.

Filmography

Manger (1961). With Louis Portugais. Prod: Fernand Dansereau, Victor Jobin, NFB. 30 min. b&w.

Dimanche d'Amérique (One Sunday in Canada) (1961). Prod: Jacques Bobet, NFB. 28 min. b&w.

Patinoire (The Rink) (1962). Prod: Jacques Bobet, NFB. 10 min. col.

Natation (Olympic Swimmers) (1963). Prod: Jacques Bobet, NFB. 27 min. b&w.

Pattes mouillées (The Big Swim) (1963). Prod: Jacques Bobet, NFB. 10 min. b&w.

Solange dans nos campagnes (1964). Prod: Fernand Dansereau, Victor Jobin, NFB. 28 min. b&w.

Un air de famille (1964). Prod: Fernand Dansereau, Victor Jobin, NFB. 28 min. b&w.

Les mâles (1970). Prod: Fernand Rigard, Onyx Films/France Films. 113 min. col.

Stéréo (1970). Prod: OFQ for Ministère de l'immigration. 19 min. col.

Percé on the Rocks (Percé on the Rocks) (1964). Prod: Jacques Bobet, NFB. 10 min. col.

La vie heureuse de Léopold Z (The Merry World of Leopold Z) (1965). Prod: Jacques Bobet, NFB. 69 min. b&w.

Place à Olivier Guimond (1966). Prod: André Lamy, Onyx Films Inc. 60 min. col.

Place aux Jerolas (1967). Prod: André Lamy, Onyx Films Inc. 60 min. col.

Le Québec à l'heure de l'Expo (Expo '67: Made in Quebec) (1967). Prod: Raymond-Marie Léger, OFQ for l'Office d'information et de publicité et le ministère de l'industrie et du commerce. 20 min. col.

Le viol d'une jeune fille douce (The Rape of a Sweet Young Girl) (1968). Prod: Onyx-Fournier Ltée. 85 min. col.

Red (1970). Prod: Lamy, Onyx Films/SMA. 101 min. col.

La vraie nature de Bernadette (1972). Prod: Pierre Lamy, Les Productions Carle-Lamy. 97 min. col.

Les chevaliers (1972). Prod: COFCI for ORTF. 55 min. col.

La mort d'un bûcheron (Death of a Lumberjack) (1973). Prod: Pierre Lamy, Carle-Lamy Productions. 115 min. col.

Les corps célestes (The Heavenly Bodies) (1973). Prod: Pierre Lamy, Les Productions Carle-Lamy, Mojack Films and Parc Films, NEF Diffusion, Paris. 105 min. col.

La tête de Normande St.-Onge (1975). Prod: Pierre Lamy, Les Productions Pierre Lamy. 116 min. col.

A Thousand Moons (1976). Prod: Steven Patrick, CBC. 53 min. col.

Feature film script in progress: **Exit**.

Bibliography

Cinéastes du Québec 2: Gilles Carle, CQDC, 1970, Criticism, an interview by Robert Daudelin and Roger Frappier, filmography and bibliography; *Le petit journal*, January 16, 1966, pp. 4, 5, 38, "Gilles Carle: 'Nos films sont encore des échecs' ", interview by Michelle Gélinas; *Québec-presse*, Montreal, November 2, 1969, an interview on **Red**; *Cinéma 69*, Paris, no. 140 (November 2, 1969), interview on **Red**; *Montreal Gazette*, November 22, 1969, "Gilles Carle: from Percé Rocks to Indians", Dane Lanken (interview); *Séquences*, no. 65 (April 1971), pp. 4-15 (interview); *Montreal Star*, November 27, 1971, p. C-1, "Joys of Moviemaking", Martin Malina (interview); *Cinéma*, Paris, no. 169 (September-October 1972), pp. 82-86, "Il faut réinventer la notion d'auteur", interview by M. Amiel; and pp. 118-119, review of **La vraie nature**; *Cinéma-Québec*, vol. 1, no. 9 (1972), pp. 18-21, "Un western religieux?", interview with Carle on **La vraie nature**; *La Presse*, Montreal, January 27, 1973, p. D-11, "Pour un 'cinéma d'auteur' collectif", interview by Georges-Hébert Germain; *Image et son*, no. 267 (January 1973), pp. 24-39, interview; *Cinéma-Québec*, vol. 2, no. 5 (January-February 1973), pp. 19-28, "**La mort d'un bûcheron** . . . en quête d'un film", interview, review; *Téléciné*, Paris, no. 181 (September 1973), pp. 16-17, interview by G. Langlois; *Cinéma-Québec*, vol. 3, no. 1 (September 1973), pp. 28-32, "Créer une certaine imagerie", interview with Jean-Pierre Tadros (on **Les corps**); *Motion*,

November-December 1973, pp. 14-17, interview with James McLarty; *Cinema Canada*, no. 13, pp. 48-52, "Carle's Heavenly Bodies", interview with George Köller; *Montreal Star*, August 24, 1968, "Gilles Carle's Bouillabaisse of Visual Exuberance", Stephen Franklin; *Le Devoir*, Montreal, December 28, 1968 (on **The Rape of a Sweet Young Girl**); *Dossiers de cinéma: 1* (Fides, 1968), on **Percé on the Rocks**; *Le Soleil*, Quebec, June 6, 1970, p. 42, "Gilles Carle, un réalisateur solitaire", Paul Roux; *Le magazine Maclean*, March 1972, pp. 38, 41, 45-49, "Gilles Carle, la québécoise en tête", Jacques Guay; *Le Devoir*, Montreal, February 10, 1973, "Le paradoxe de Gilles Carle", Robert Guy Scully; *La Presse*, Montreal, September 22, 1973, "Gilles Carle: *Les corps célestes* dans l'euphorie de 1938", Serge Dussault; *Le Devoir*, Montreal, September 22, 1973, "Les 'corps' de Carle", Jean-Pierre Tadros; *Séquences*, no. 74 (October 1973), pp. 27-28, review of **Les corps** by Robert-Claude Bérubé; *Toronto Star*, November 26, 1973, "**Death of a Lumberjack** is Junk Entertainment", Clyde Gilmour; *Cinéma-Québec*, vol. 3, no. 3 (November-December 1973), pp. 10-13, "L'univers des **Corps célestes**", Pierre Demers; *Montreal Gazette*, November 1, 1975, "Carle Concerned about Normande's Local Legs", Dane Lanken; *Cinéma-Québec*, vol. 4, no. 8, pp. 6-8, "**La tête de Normande St.-Onge**: Le jeu de la seduction", Jean-Pierre Tadros; references in *Vingt ans de cinéma au Canada français*, *Essais sur le cinéma québécois*, *Jeune cinéma canadien*, *Le cinéma québécois: tendances et prolongements*, *Le cinéma canadien*, *Cinéma d'ici* and *L'aventure du cinéma direct*.

CARNEY, JIM

Born in Shanghai, China in 1935, Jim Carney studied in Ontario and British Columbia and graduated from UBC in 1957 with a B.A. in history and political science. He subsequently attended the Radio Television Institute at Stanford University. Carney began his career as a newspaper and radio journalist. He joined the staff of CBC Vancouver in 1959 as a news editor and moved to CBC Toronto in 1962 as a writer/director/producer for Public Affairs, working on such shows as "Close-Up", "Horizon", "Inquiry" and "This Hour Has Seven Days". Carney's writing credits include Patrick Watson's 1964 documentary on China, **The Seven Hundred Million**, commentary for Bané Jovanovic and Ken Page's **28 Above-Below** and Michael Scott's **Station Ten**; he also wrote English commentary for a Japanese television series, "Women and Society", produced for UNICEF, and researched and wrote a series of scripts, "Science—In Search of Man", for the NFB and the University of California. Carney has also written most of his directed films. He has been freelancing since 1966 and formed

Gemini Productions in 1970. In 1975-76 he was producer for the UN Habitat project responsible for a task force, put together by the NFB, to assist developing countries to produce films for the UN Conference on Human Settlements, 1976.

Filmography

City Song (1961). Prod: J. Carney, CBUT. 20 min. b&w.

House of Cards (1962). Prod: Jim Guthro, CBC "Close-Up". 60 min. b&w.

Three Coffins for Moonbeam (1963). Prod: Patrick Watson, CBC "Inquiry". 60 min. b&w.

Fort Chimo (1964). Prod: Patrick Watson, CBC "Inquiry". 30 min. b&w.

The Isseis (1965). Prod: Patrick Watson, CBC "Inquiry". 25 min. b&w.

At the Moment of Impact—Flight 831 (1965). Prod: Patrick Watson, CBC "Document". 60 min. b&w.

"Children of the World", a series of six 30-min. films (1967-68). Prod: CBC, NET (U.S.) and UNICEF. Directed three segments.

The Day Before Tomorrow (1968). Prod: Denis Hargarve, CBC. 55 min. col. Based on series "Children of the World".

In One Day (Au jour le jour) (1968). Prod: George Pearson, NFB, for the Ministry of Transport. 18 min. col.

The World of One in Five (1969). Prod: Gordon Burwash, NFB. 28 min. b&w.

The Challenge of Change (Le défi du devenir) (1969). Prod: George Pearson, NFB for the Department of Labour. 17 min. col.

Search into White Space (Sous les blancs espaces) (1970). Prod: Barrie Howells, George Pearson, NFB for the Department of Indian Affairs and Northern Development. 16 min. col.

Classroom Television: An Instrument for Educational Change (1971). Prod: Joe Koenig, International Cinemedia for the International Development Through Academy, Washington. 45 min. col.

The Effluent Society (1972). Prod: Douglas Leiterman, Hobel-Leiterman, "Here Come The Seventies". 30 min. col.

A City Is (Ainsi va la ville) (1972). Prod: Barrie Howells, NFB for Central Mortgage and Housing Corp. 18 min. col.

Where Do We Go from Here? (1973). Prod: Rex Tasker, Len Chatwin, NFB, Challenge for Change "Urban Transportation". 22 min. col.

The Century that Broke the Silence (1973). Prod: Brant Ducey, Canadian National Railways. 50 min. col.

Sisters of the Space Age (1974). Prod: Desmond Dew, Colin Low, NFB for Department of National Defence. 29 min. col.

The Great Lakes (1976), Prod: NFB for Environment Canada and U.S. Environmental Protection Agency. 55 min. col.

Bibliography

Pot pourri, November 1972. Issue devoted to films on the environment with a review of **Search into White Space**.

CARRIERE, MARCEL

Born in Bouchette, Quebec in 1935, Marcel Carrière studied electronic engineering, joining the National Film Board first as a summer student and in 1956 full-time as a sound engineer. In this capacity he has been involved with some of the most impressive films produced by the Board: **Lonely Boy**, **Stravinsky**, **Le chat dans le sac**, **Un jeu si simple**, **The Days of Whisky Gap**, **Les raquetteurs** and **Pour le suite du monde**; he was also sound engineer on Godbout and Rouch's **Rose et Landry** and Jutra's first feature, **A tout prendre**. Carrière's developed skills as a humorist were made evident in his feature starring Luce Guilbeault, **OK ... Laliberté**. Carrière travelled to the People's Republic of China in 1973 to make three documentaries and has recently completed his third fiction feature, **Ti-Mine, Bernie pis la gans**.

Filmography

La lutte (Wrestling) (1961). With Claude Jutra, Claude Fournier and Michel Brault. Prod: Jacques Bobet, NFB. 28 min. b&w.

Rencontres à Mitzic (1963). With Georges Dufaux. Prod: Fernand Dansereau, NFB. 27 min. b&w.

Pour la suite du monde (Moontrap) (1963). With Michel Brault and Pierre Perrault. Prod: Fernand Dansereau and Jacques Bobet, NFB. 105 min. b&w.

Villeneuve, peintre-barbier (1965). Prod: Fernand Dansereau, NFB. 16 min. col.

Bois-francs (1966). Prod: Michel Moreau, NFB. 26 min. col.

The Indian Speaks (L'indien parle) (1967). Prod: André Belleau, NFB. 40 min. col.

Les Zouaves or **Avec tambours et trompettes** (1968). Prod: Robert Forget, NFB. 28 min. col.

Better Housing in B.C. (Colombie britannique et l'habitation) (1968). Prod: André Belleau, NFB for Central Mortgage and Housing Corp. 16 min. col.

Episode (1968). Prod: Robert Forget, NFB. 59 min. col.

Saint-Denis dans le temps ... (1969). Prod: Robert Forget, NFB. 84 min. col.

Hotel-château (1970). Prod: Marc Beaudet, NFB. 59 min. b&w.

10 milles/heures (1970). Prod: Marc Beaudet, Pierre Maheu, NFB for Osaka '70. 17 min. col.

Chez nous, c'est chez nous (1972). Prod: François Séguillon, NFB Société nouvelle. 81 min. col.

OK ... Laliberté (1973). Prod: Marc Beaudet, NFB. 112 min. col.

Le grand voyage (1974). Prod: Jacques Bobet, Lawrence Paré, NFB. 44 min. col.

Images de Chine (Glimpses of China) (1974). Prod: François Séguillon, NFB. 69 min. col.

Ping Pong (Ping Pong) (1974). Prod: François Séguillon, NFB. 13 min. col.

Ti-Mine, Bernie pis la gans (1976). Prod: Marc Beaudet, NFB. 130 min. col.

Bibliography

Le Devoir, April 25, 1970 (interview); *La Presse*, November 3, 1973, "Un bricoleur qui a fait carrière", Luc Perreault (interview); *Cinéma-Québec*, vol. 3, no. 3 (1973), pp. 14-18, "Une liberté envahie", on **OK ... Laliberté**, critique by Richard Gay and interview by Jean-Pierre Tadros; *Séquences*, no. 75 (January 1974), pp. 4-13, interview with Léo Bonneville, and pp. 24-25, review of **OK**; *Motion*, January-February 1974, pp. 12-14, interviews with Luce Guilbeault and Marcel Carrière on **OK**, by P.M. Evanchuk; *Canadian Film—Past and Present*, La Cinémathèque canadienne, 1967, article by Carrière on the filming of **Stravinsky**. Available for reference only at film study libraries and reprinted in *Eléments pour un nouveau cinéma*, by Louis Marcorelles, UNESCO, Paris, 1970; *La Presse*, April 25, 1970, on **Saint-Denis dans le temps ...**; *La Presse*, April 28, 1970, "Comment passer un Québec", Luc Perreault; *Image et son*, no. 252 (1971), pp. 243-244; *La Presse*, February 24, 1973, "Deux portraits de trappeurs", on **Chez nous**; *Montréal Matin*, March 4, 1973, "Déportation à la moderne: les délogés de Saint-Octave en exode", on **Chez nous**; *Cinéma-Québec*, vol. 2, no. 6/7 (March-April 1973), p. 57, review of **Chez nous** by Pierre Demers; *Montreal Gazette*, September 21, 1973, "Surprises Greet NFB Crew in China", Dane Lanken; *Montreal Gazette*, November 3, 1973, "**OK ... Laliberté**: warm, winning", by Jay Newquist; *Le Devoir*, November 3, 1973, "Une comédie convenable", Robert Guy Scully; *La Presse*, November 4, 1973, "La vie quotidienne du Québécois moyen", Robert Lévesque; *Montreal Star*, November 6, 1973, "Curious Melocomedy Lacks Drama", Martin Malina; *Rélations*, no. 388 (December 1973), pp. 347-348, review of **OK**; *Le Soleil*, January 5, 1974, "Enfin, un veritable film comique québécois", Claude Daigneault; *Le Soleil*, January 12, 1974, "Marcel Carrière, du documentaire à la fiction"; *La Tribune*, Sherbrooke, April 24, 1974, "Trois Québécois ont contemplé la Chine et ont rapporté un film que Kiné-art présent en grande primeur lundi soir"; *Le Soleil*, July 26, 1974, "Première québécoise du film tourné en Chine par

Marcel Carrière"; *How to Make or Not to Make a Canadian Film*, "Where's the Sound?", Marcel Carrière on his work in sound; references in: *Vingt ans de cinéma au Canada français, Le cinéma canadien, Le cinéma québécois: tendances et prolongements, Cinéma d'ici* and *L'aventure du cinéma direct*.

CARTER, PETER

Born in England in 1933, Peter Carter had his early training in film with the J. Arthur Rank Organization. He joined Crawley Films in 1954 as an assistant editor and later as an assistant director. In the latter capacity, Carter worked closely with Paul Almond, Don Haldane, George Gorman and Fergus MacDonald—all of whom directed segments for the series "R.C.M.P.". After four years in England, Carter returned to Canada as assistant director on Maxine Samuel's "Seaway" and "Forest Rangers", and CBC's "Hatch's Mill". As an associate producer he has been involved with Paul Almond's **Act of the Heart** and **Isabel**, and Eric Till's **A Fan's Notes**, His first feature, **The Rowdyman**, was written by and starred actor Gordon Pinsent; music was by Ben McPeek, and photography by Ed Long. The film was chosen in 1972 for screening at the Karlovyzary Film Festival in Czechoslovakia. Carter has directed over fifty dramatic shows for CBC television series, among them, "Anthology", "Theatre Canada", "Swiss Family Robinson", "Police Surgeon", "Camera 76", "Collaborators" and "Wojeck".

Filmography

Does Anybody Here Know Denny? (1969). Prod: CBC "Corwin". 90 min. col.

The Salient (1970). Prod: CBC "Theatre Canada". 30 min. col.

The Day They Killed the Snowman (1970). Prod: CBC "Theatre Canada". 60 min. col.

God's Sparrows (1970). Prod: CBC "Theatre Canada". 30 min. col.

In Exile (1970). Prod: CBC "Theatre Canada". 30 min. col.

A Token Gesture (1970). Prod: CBC "Theatre Canada". 30 min. col.

Rigmarole (1970). Prod: CBC "Theatre Canada". 30 min. col.

The Mercenaries (1970). Prod: CBC "Anthology". 90 min. col.

The Rowdyman (1972). Prod: Lawrence Dane, Canart Films. 96 min. col. Dist: New Cinema.

Strike (1972). Prod: Ronald Weyman, CBC "Sunday at Nine". 60 min. col.

Sam Adams (1974). Prod: David Peddie, CBC. 120 min. col.

Nest of Shadows (1976). Prod: Stephen Patrick and Ralph Thomas, CBC "Camera 76". 60 min. col.

Bibliography

The Rowdyman, Gordon Pinsent (Toronto: McGraw-Hill Ryerson), 1973; *Ottawa Citizen*, August 27, 1971, "Canadian Actor Turns to Playwriting"; *Maclean's Magazine*, June 1972, p. 85, review of **Rowdyman** by John Hofsess; *The Canadian Forum*, July-August 1972, pp. 30-31, review of **Rowdyman** by David Beard; *Cinéma-Québec*, vol. 2, no. 6/7 (1972), p. 54, review of **Rowdyman** by Francine Laurendeau; *Take One*, vol. 3, no. 4 (1972), p. 36, review of **Rowdyman** by Peter Brigg; *Montreal Gazette*, February 3, 1973, "*The Rowdyman* is Far From a 'Newfie' Joke'", Dave Billington; *Le Devoir*, February 10, 1973, "Un amusant excentrique", Luc Perreault; *Séquences*, no. 72 (April 1973), pp. 28-29, review of **Rowdyman** by Robert-Claude Bérubé.

CHABOT, JEAN

Born in Saint-Jean-Baptiste in 1945, Jean Chabot received his BA and studied economics at the University of Montreal. He then made a number of short films and worked in Montreal at Cinéfilms as an assistant cameraman and editor. As a critic, Chabot has written for *Le Devoir*, *Sept-jours*, and *Cinéma-Québec* and his interviews feature prominently in the dossier *Cinéastes du Québec* published by Le Conseil québécois pour la diffusion du Cinéma. Chabot's first feature film, **Mon enfance à Montréal**, a surreal and poignant image of a family locked in poverty, was produced within the program "Premières oeuvres" at the National Film Board. His second feature, **Une nuit en Amérique**, is a detective story written by Chabot with music by Walter Boudreau and l'Infonie.

Filmography

Le chapeau (1965). Prod: Independent. 30 min. col.
Dormez-vous (1965). Prod: Independent. 30 min. b&w.
Porte silence (1966). Prod: Independent. 15 min. b&w.
Des pas dans l'univers (1967). Prod: Independent. 10 min. b&w.
Un bicycle pour Pit (1968). With Clovis Durand. Prod: Independent. 20 min. col.
Mon enfance à Montréal (1970). Prod: Jean-Pierre Lefebvre, NFB. 65 min. b&w. Dist: Faroun.
Des images travaillent (1971). Prod: Ateliers audio-visuels du Québec for OFQ. 3 min. col.
Travelling Blues or **Le cinéma en question** (1971). Prod: Ateliers audio-visuels du Québec for OFQ. 11 min. col.
Une nuit en Amérique (1973). Prod: Guy Bergeron, ACPAC. 93 min. col. Dist: Cinepix.
Chants corporels (1973). Prod: OFQ for SGME "Enfance inadaptée". 28 min. col.

Histoire de pêche (1975). Prod: Marc Beaudet, NFB. 50 min.
col. Feature script in progress: **Atchigan**.

Bibliography

Québec-presse, February 14, 1972, *"Mon enfance à Montréal,*
l'histoire d'une enfance déracinée et brisée" (interview);
Séquences, no. 79 (January 1975), pp. 4-14, interview by Léo
Bonneville; *L'Action Québec*, July 24, 1969, review of **Un bicycle
pour Pit** by Jean-Pierre Guay; *Québec-presse*, February 15,
1970, "Les points sur les 'i' ", Jean Chabot; *La Presse*, March 7,
1970, "Cinéma québécois: la relève", Luc Perreault; *Le Devoir*,
January 20, 1971, "Un témoignage de Jean Chabot et une précision de Jacques Parent", Jean-Pierre Tadros; *La Presse*,
February 13, 1971, "Jean Chabot"; *Le Devoir*, February 13,
1971, "Deux jeunes cinéastes face à la réalité", Jean-Pierre
Tadros; *La Presse*, November 25, 1972, "La série noire se porte
bien", Luc Perreault; *Cinéma-Québec*, vol. 3, no. 8 (1974), pp.
33-38, articles on **Une nuit en Amérique** by Jean-Pierre Tadros
and Pierre Demers; *Séquences*, no. 79 (January 1975), pp. 31-32,
review by Janick Beaulieu.

CHAPMAN, CHRISTOPHER

Born in Toronto in 1927, Chrostopher Chapman is well-known as a
director of poetic films on nature. Working first as a designer,
Chapman began his film career by working alone with a Bolex
camera, joining Crawley Films for eight months after making his
first independent film, **The Seasons.** The multiple-dynamic image
technique ('split screen') was pioneered by Chapman for **A Place
to Stand** (Ontario Pavilion, Expo '67) and later used in Ontario's
contribution to Osaka '70. As many as 15 images work together
on a 70mm image with a 12-track sound system. In 1968, Chapman worked with Gower Champion on his mixed-media Broadway
show, *The Happy Time,* creating a 70mm film sequence. **Toronto
the Good** was also a multi-media production, and **Volcano** used
70mm/Imax techniques. Chapman is currently working on an NFB
film on alternative agriculture.

Filmography

The Seasons (1953). Prod: C. Chapman. 18 min. col.
Quetico (1958). Prod: C. Chapman for Quetico Foundation. 20
min. col.
Essay in Film (1960). Prod: C. Chapman, CBC. 10 min. b&w.
Village in the Dust (1961). Prod: C. Chapman for Imperial Oil. 20
min. col.
Saguenay (1962). Prod: Crawley Films for Aluminum Co of
Canada. 20 min. col.

The Persistent Seed (Le vert vivace) (1963). Prod. Hugh O'Connor, NFB. 14 min. col.

Enduring Wilderness (Jardins sauvages) (1964). Prod: Ernest Reid, NFB. 28 min. col.

Loring and Wylie (1964). Prod: C. Chapman, CBC "Telescope". 30 min. b&w.

Magic Molecule (La molécule magique) (1964). With Hugh O'Conner, Prod: Nicholas Balla, NFB. 9 min. col.

Expedition Bluenose (1964). Prod: Maurice Taylor, John Trent, Taylor Television Production for CBC. 60 min. col.

A Place to Stand (1967). Exec. Prod: C. Chapman, Prod: David Mackay, TDF Artists Limited for the Ontario Government. 17½ min. col.

Impressions 1670-1970 (1970). Prod: Christopher Chapman Ltd. for the Hudson's Bay Co. 34 min. col.

Ontario (1970). Prod: Christopher Chapman Ltd. for the Ontario Government and Osaka '70. 24 min. col.

Festival (1970). Prod. Christopher Chapman Ltd. 20 min. col. (a shortened, six-track version of **Ontario** for Ontario Place, Toronto).

Canada (1972). Prod: Christopher Chapman Ltd. for British Petroleum. 28 min. col.

Toronto the Good (1973). Prod: Christopher Chapman Ltd. for Ontario Place Corporation. 13 min. col.

Volcano (1974). Prod: Christopher Chapman Ltd. for Ontario Place Corporation. 7 min. col.

Bibliography

Food for Thought, Canadian Association for Adult Education, April 1958, pp. 319-325, "An interview with Christopher Chapman"; *The Globe Magazine,* May 9, 1959, pp. 16-17, "He Believes He Can Make His Kind of Film and Make a Living", Dean Walker (interview); *Canadian Cinematography,* January-February 1965, pp. 3, 6, 7, "Shooting **Expedition Bluenose**", C. Chapman; *Weekend Magazine,* no. 45 (1968), "Christopher Chapman is Collecting the Magic", James Quig; *Globe and Mail,* July 12, 1969, "Chris Chapman Has Two Places to Stand", Melinda McCracken; *Globe and Mail,* June 3, 1970, "Ontario at Expo '70: More of the Same"; *Toronto Star,* October 30, 1970, p. 7, a letter by Chapman headed "Is Call of the Wilderness Getting Too Dim to Hear?"; *Toronto Star,* March 6, 1973, "Chapman's New Film Makes Canada a Place to Sleep", Wayne Edmonstone (on **Canada**); *Toronto Star,* March 15, 1973, "Movieman Chris Chapman Captures Volcano's Fury"; *Globe and Mail,* May 11, 1973, "Icelandic Volcano on Cinesphere Screen"; *Globe and Mail,* May 21, 1973, "More thrills from Imax", by Margaret Hogan. *Globe and Mail,* November 3, 1973, "Chapman Turns Imax Lenses on

Erupting Volcano'', Betty Lee; *How to Make or Not to Make a Canadian Film* (La cinémathèque canadienne, 1967), ''The British of **A Place to Stand''**, by Chapman; references in *Le cinéma canadien.*

COTE, GUY L.

Born in Ottawa in 1925, Guy Côté (assisted by his wife Nancy) has made an important contribution in all areas of Canadian cinema; his work at the National Film Board involved both the production and distribution of film; his own directing career began in amateur film circles at Oxford with the abstract film-ballet, **Between Two Worlds.** As a critic, Côté has contributed to leading world film magazines and his private collection of critical documentation, one of the largest and most impressive in Canada, is now housed in (indeed, forms the basis of) Le Centre de documentation cinématographique of the Bibliothèque nationale in Montreal. In the area of film education, Côté founded the bulletin, *Canadian Newsreel,* in 1952 as a liaison between film societies, and later organized (with Dorothy Burritt) the Canadian Federation of Film Societies. This organization, in collaboration with the Canadian Film Institute, still encourages thousands of people in societies across the country to become literate in film. One of the first film archivists in Canada, Côté's personal collection is now owned by La Cinémathèque québécoise; this organization grew out of Connaissance du cinéma which Côté founded in 1962. Another large film archive which exists at the Public Archives and National Library was also co-founded by Côté. Director of the former Montreal Film Festival, founder and first director of L'Association professionnel des cinéastes, he is a pioneer without equal. Côté has produced numerous films including Jacques Leduc's **Chantal en vrac, Nominingue. . .depuis qu'il existe** and **Là ou ailleurs**, Anne-Claire Poirier's **De mère en fille**, Garceau's **Le grand rock**, Groulx's **Où êtes-vous donc?**, and Perrault's **Les voitures d'eau**, **Règne du jour**, and **Un pays sans bons sens**. Côté's own **Les deux côtés de la médaille** documents the life of Bolivian workers.

Filmography (incomplete)

Industrial Canada (Le Canada industriel) (1957). Prod: Nicholas Balla, NFB. 18 min. b&w.

Railroaders (Les cheminots) (1958). Prod: Tom Daly, NFB. 21 min. b&w.

Fishermen (Les pêcheurs) (1959). Prod: Tom Daly, NFB. 22 min. b&w.

Roughnecks (Les maîtres-sondeurs) (1960). Prod: Tom Daly, NFB. 21 min. b&w.

Cattle Ranch (Têtes blanches) (1961). Prod: Tom Daly, NFB. 20 min. col.

Kindergarten (1962). Prod: Tom Daly, NFB. 22 min. b&w.

An Essay on Science (Cité savante) (1962) Prod: Tom Daly, NFB. 20 min. col.

Regards sur l'occultisme, parts 1 & 2 (1965). Prod: André Belleau, NFB. 58 min. each b&w.

Tranquillement, pas vite, parts 1 & 2 (1972). Prod: Normand Cloutier, NFB. 88 min. and 66 min. b&w.

Les deux côtés de la médaille. Race de bronze (part 1); **Risquer sa peau** (part 2) (1974). Prod: François Séguillon, NFB. 87 min. and 79 min. col.

Work in progress: a series of films, "Les vieux amis", produced by the NFB, the first of which is **L'attente**.

Bibliography

Séquences, no. 77 (July 1974), pp. 26-27 (review); also pp. 4-15, interview with Côté by Léo Bonneville; *Cahiers du cinéma*, no. 53 (December 1955), "Canada: un cinéma pratique", Guy Côté; *Dossiers de cinéma: 1*, nos. 11 and 15 (Edition Fides, 1968), on **Roughnecks** and **Cattle Ranch**; *Artscanada*, April 1970, pp. 35-38, "Anybody Making Shorts These Days?", also by Côté; *Le Devoir*, February 3, 1972, "Masse et petits groupes dans l'église", Edmond Robillard on **Tranquillement, pas vite**; *Le Devoir*, February 12, 1972, "Une partialité qui devient vite heurtante", on **Tranquillement, pas vite**; *Cinéma-Québec*, vol. 1, no. 8 (March-April 1972), pp. 21-26, a section by Richard Gay; *Le Devoir*, Montreal, May 8, 1974, review of **Deux côtés** by Pierre Vallières, and May 11, 1974, "Cinéma: **Les deux côtés de la médaille** un très grand documentaire, lumineux et inspiré", André Leroux; *Dimanche-Matin*, Montreal, May 12, 1974, p. 23, "**Risquer sa peau** pour ses vérités" and "Découvrir le Québec en Bolivie", Richard Wallot; *Relations*, July-August 1974, pp. 22-23, "**Les deux côtés de la médaille**: un film sympathique, mais anachronique", Yves Lever; *The Quarterly of Film, Radio and Television*, vol. 7, no. 4, pp. 335-340, "Cinéma sans sense", by Côté; reviews in *Le cinéma québécois: tendances et prolongements, Vingt ans de cinéma au Canada français* (an article by Pierre Pagneau), *Jeune cinéma canadien, Cinéma d'ici* and *L'aventure du cinéma direct*.

Articles on Côté's work as an archivist:

Objectif 62, August 1962, pp. 3-7, "Tous les mémoires du monde", Côté; *Canadian Cinematography*, May-June 1964, pp. 10-11, "Selling Job Must Be Done on Feature Films Says Guy Côté", *Le magazine de la presse*, February 13, 1965, pp. 6, 8-9, "Les mordus du cinéma ont enfin leur musée", Lysiane Gagnon; *Objectif*, April-May 1965, pp. 3-16, "Procès d'une collection",

Pierre Hébert; *The Montrealer,* August 1966, p. 19, "Film
Keeper, Guy L. Côté", Martin Bronstein; *Séquences,* no. 26, pp.
4-5, "Cinéma, art et industrie".

CRONENBERG, DAVID

Born in Toronto in 1943, David Cronenberg studied literature at
the University of Toronto. Severely structured, his two features,
Stereo and **Crimes of the Future,** are philosophically witty comments on the relationship of the technological to the human world.
Virtually a one-man unit, Cronenberg has acted as director, producer, writer and cameraman on all his independently-produced
films. He spent 1971-72 in Europe, scripting his third feature,
Shivers, and working on short spots for CBC.

Filmography

Transfer (1966). Prod: Independent. 7 min. col.
From the Drain (1966). Prod: Independent. 14 min. col.
Stereo (1969). Prod: D. Cronenberg, Emergent Films. 65 min.
   b&w. Dist: New Cinema.
Crimes of the Future (1970). Prod: D. Cronenberg, Emergent
   Films. 63 min. col. Dist: New Cinema.
Secret Weapons (1972). Prod: CBC "Program X". 22 min. col.
Shivers (1975). Prod: Ivan Reitman, DAL/Reitman Productions. 88
   min. col. (Formerly titled **The Parasite Murders**) Dist: Cinepix.
The Victim (1976). Prod: Deborah Peaker, CBC "Peep Show". 29
   min. col.
Work in progress: **Mosquito** (a feature).

Bibliography

Globe and Mail, October 18, 1969, "Happy Film Images and
Money to Boot", K.D. (interview), and August 9, 1969, "New York
Firm Buys Toronto Man's Film" (also an interview); *Film,*
England, no. 58 (Spring 1970), pp. 27-28, "Filmmaking in
Canada" (interview); *Cinema Canada,* no. 22, pp. 23-25, "It'll Bug
You", interview by Stephen Chesley, and p. 44, review of **The
Parasite Murders** by Natalie Edwards; *Montreal Gazette,* June
23, 1969, "**Stereo** — An Interesting First", Jacob Siskind; *Mon-
treal Star,* June 23, 1969, "New Movies: Canadian Film Fresh,
Unconventional", Martin Malina; *Le Droit,* Ottawa, June 24,
1969, "**Stereo** de David Cronenberg", Murray Maltais; *Arts
Canada,* no. 142-143, (April 1970), p. 54, on **Crimes of the
Future**; *Monthly Film Bulletin,* British Film Institute, vol. 38, no.
453 (October 1971), and vol. 38, no. 454 (November 1971), both
articles written by Tony Rayns; *Saturday Night,* July 1974, pp.
17-22, "Just Two Innocent Canadian Boys in Wicked Hollywood",

Norman Snider; *Saturday Night,* September 1975, pp. 83-85,
"You Should Know How Bad This Film Is. After All, You Paid For
It.", Marshall Delaney (on **The Parasite Murders**); *Take One,*
vol. 2, nos. 3 and 6.

DALY, THOMAS

Born in Toronto in 1918, Tom Daly came directly from university
to the National Film Board in 1940, to work with Stuart Legg on
the war propaganda film series, "The World in Action". **Churchill's Island**, **The Gates of Italy** and **The War for Men's Minds**
used stockshots and newsreel footage in hard-hitting war
documents. (**The War for Men's Minds** used footage from Leni
Riefenstahl's **Triumph of the Will**, a film commissioned by
Hitler.) From 1950 to 1964 Daly was executive producer of Unit B
at the National Film Board; consisting of about forty persons, Unit
B made all manner of films — animated, live action, educational
and experimental — and included the Candid Eye Unit which was
making films for television. A producer and editor of wide ex-
perience, Daly was the editor-in-chief on **Labyrinth**, a multi-
screen film produced by the National Film Board for Expo '67.
Among his directed films are those in "The World in Action"
series: **Our Northern Neighbour** (1943), **Inside France** (1944),
Atlantic Crossroads, **Gateway to Asia**, **Ordeal by Ice**, **Road to
Reich** (1945) and **Guilty Men** (1946). Films he produced include:
Universe (Low and Kroitor); **Circle of the Sun**, **The Days of the
Whisky Gap**, and **The Winds of Fogo** (Low); **Paul Tomkowicz,
Street-Railway Switchman** (Kroitor); **Runner** and **Cowboy and
Indian** (Owen); **Satan's Choice** (Shebib), **Prologue**, **Downhill**,
Action and **Reaction** (Spry), **Accident** (Duckworth and Pat
Crawley); **Sad Song of Yellow Skin** and **Waiting for Fidel** (Rub-
bo); **Pandora** and **Sananguagat: Inuit Masterworks** (May); **The
Sloan Affair** (D. Jackson); **Wake up, mes bons amis** (Perrault);
and **Mr. Symbol Man** on Charles Bliss's universal language
system. Tom Daly is an executive producer at the National Film
Board in Montreal.

Bibliography

Pot pourri, September 1973, pp. 2-7, interview; *Objectif,* no. 9-10
(October 1961), pp. 21-22, "Dix-sept artisans du cinéma cana-
dien", a critical article with filmography; *Sight and Sound,* no. 65
(Winter 1964), "The Innocent Eye: An Aspect of the Work of the
National Film Board of Canada", Peter Harcourt on Unit B; *How
to Make or Not to Make a Canadian Film* (Cinémathèque cana-
dienne, 1967), "From 'World in Action' to 'Man in His World'", by
Daly, and "A Note on Candid Eye", Wolf Koenig; *Pot pourri,*
February 1975, issue dedicated to **Mr. Symbol Man**; *Cinema*

Canada, no. 15, pp. 22-23, "Tom Daly, Pioneer Producer", Laurinda Hartt; references in: *Elements pour un nouveau cinéma, Cinéma d'ici* and *L'aventure du cinéma direct.*

DAMUDE, D. BRIAN

Born in 1945 in St. John, New Brunswick, D. Brian Damude studied English and history at McGill and film production at N.Y.U. receiving a Master's degree in fine arts; he later taught film production at Ryerson. Damude has worked in Toronto for Drege Audio Productions and for Nacom Ltd.; starting on a freelance basis at Nacom in 1972, he became director of motion picture productions making television commercials and 18 films — industrial, tourist and educational; **Come Paint and Photograph Us**, which Damude edited, won a third place in the Canadian Travel Film Awards. His multi-media show, **Where It's At**, toured Newfoundland during its 25th anniversary. Damude is presently preparing a comedy to be set in that province and a feature thriller with the working title, **Distortion**.

Filmography

Caged Out (1971). Prod: D.B. Damude, CBC "Programme X". 15 min. col.

Nightmare (1972). Prod: Paddy Sampson, CBC "Programme X". 28 min. col.

Ocean Heritage (1974). Prod: D. B. Damude, Nacom for the Government of Newfoundland. 29 min. col.

Ghost of a Choice (1974). Prod: D. B. Damude, Nacom for the Government of Newfoundland. A two projector film, totalling 45 min. col.

Where It's At (1974). Prod: D. B. Damude, Nacom for the Government of Newfoundland. Multi-media presentation.

Sudden Fury (1975). Prod: Ben Caza, Films Can. Productions. 97 min. col. Dist: Ambassador.

Bibliography

Variety, June 4, 1975 "Reviews from Cannes", G. Pratley on **Sudden Fury**; *Cinema Canada,* no. 22, pp. 31-33, "Visits to the Canadian Countryside", Piers Handling, and same issue, review of **Sudden Fury**, also by Handling.

DANIS, AIMEE

Aimée Danis was born in Maniwaki in 1929 and studied at the University of Ottawa, where she earned a teaching diploma. She worked for Radio-Canada as a script person from 1959 to 1969, as an editor for Films Claude Fournier, and in 1968 became a director at Onyx Films, making some 150 publicity shorts in four years. In 1973 she formed Les productions verseau. **Souris, tu m'inquiètes**, made for the Société nouvelle series "En tant que femmes", uses dramatized sections and interviews to reveal the feelings of a young wife and mother whose quiet life has become unsatisfying, and traces her steps towards a redefinition of self.

Filmography

Six films for Radio-Canada "Cent million de jeunes" series (1968). Each, 30 min. col.

Maryse, pile ou face (1969). Prod: Onyx Films. 30 min. b&w. Six films for Le syndicat de fonctionnaires du Québec in "Les fonctionnaires" series. Prod: Onyx Films. Each 30 min. col.

Québec an 2000. Prod: Onyx Films for the Quebec Pavilion, Terre des Hommes. 10 min. col.

KW + (1970). Prod: Onyx Films for Quebec Pavillion at Osaka. 14 min. col.

La croix sur la colline, L'évadé and **L'adieu au Lys** (1971). Prod: Onyx Films for ORTF/RTB/Radio-Canada series "La feuille d'érable". Each, 60 min. col.

Gaspésie, oui, j'écoute (All Ears to Gaspé) (1972). Onyx Films for Quebec Ministry of Tourism. 13 min. col.

Joie de vivre au Québec (Joie de vivre au Québec) (1972), with Daniel Fournier. Prod: OFQ for Ministry of Tourism. 13 min. col.

Sidbec (Steel Life) (1973). Prod: Onyx Films for Sidbec. 16 min. col.

Souris, tu m'inquiètes (1973). Prod: Anne-Claire Poirier, NFB Société nouvelle "En tant que femmes". 57 min. col.

La bataille de Québec (1974). Prod: Les productions du verseau for Pathé-cinéma "Les grandes batailles de passé". 60 min. col.

Patrick, Julie, Félix et tous les autres (1974). Prod: OFQ for the Minister of Social Affairs. 29 min. col.

Un petit coin bien tranquille (1975). Prod: Screen Gems for Europe I "Jo Gaillard". 60 min. col.

Le règne de quatre (1975). Prod: Les productions du verseau for OFQ. 20 min. col.

La bataille de Yorktown (1976). Prod: Les productions du verseau for Pathé-cinéma "Les grandes batailles de passé". 60 min. col.

Bibliography

Maintenant, November 1974, pp. 28-30, "En tant que femmes", Richard Gay; *La Presse*, September 22, 1975, "Une série dont on parlera longtemps...", Lysiane Gagnon.

DANSEREAU, FERNAND

Born in Montreal in 1928, Fernand Dansereau worked as a journalist before joining the NFB in 1956. One of the founding members of the NFB's French Unit, he helped to produce the French television series, "Temps présent", and later was involved in films dealing with social change for the Société nouvelle unit. While Dansereau has made a number of fiction films — **La canne à pêche** (from a story by Anne Hébert) and **Ca n'est pas le temps de romans** — his interest is in film as a tool of social change. To this end he co-founded In-Media in 1970 as a video animating service. While the company is no longer in existence, Dansereau combined his skills with a group of residents in New Brunswick to create a dramatic story on video; the result is **Simple histoire d'amour**. As a former producer with the NFB, Dansereau has **Golden Gloves**, **Jour après jour** and **Pour la suite du monde** as producing credits.

Filmography

La communauté juive de Montréal (1957). Prod: Guy Glover, NFB. 29 min. b&w.

Le maître du Pérou (1958). Prod: Léonard Forest, NFB "Panoramique". 49 min. b&w.

Pays neuf. (1958). Prod: Guy Glover, Léonard Forest, NFB. 45 min. b&w.

John Lyman, peintre (1959). Prod: Léonard Forest, NFB. 28 min. b&w.

La canne à pêche (1959). Prod. Léonard Forest, NFB "Temps présent". 30 min. b&w.

Pierre Beaulieu (1959). Prod: Léonard Forest, NFB. Two parts, 30 min. each. b&w.

Les administrateurs (1960). With Jacques Godbout. Prod: Léonard Forest, NFB. 60 min. b&w.

Congrès (1960). With Jean Dansereau and Georges Dufaux. Prod: NFB. 28 min. b&w.

Le festin des morts (Mission of Fear) (1965). Prod: André Belleau, NFB. 79 min. b&w.

Ca n'est pas le temps des romans (This is no Time for Romance) (1967). Prod: NFB. 28 min. col.

Saint-Jérome (1968). Prod: Robert Forget, NFB. 114 min. b&w. (plus a series, "Education populaire", 27 films from the original footage, varying in length from 10-62 min).

Tout l'temps, tout l'temps, tout l'temps...? (1969). Prod: Robert Forget, NFB. 115 min. b&w.

Jonquière (1969). Prod: F. Dansereau, S.M.A. Inc. 28 min. b&w.

Québec ski (Quebec Ski) (1970). Prod: Jean Dansereau, Les Cinéastes associés for OFQ. 5 min. col.

Rencontre (1970). Prod: Paul Larose, NFB. 180 min. Unreleased.

Faut aller parmi l'monde pour le savoir. . . (It Is Necessary to
be Among the People of the World to Know Them) (1971). Prod:
In-Media for SSJB and SNQ. 84 min. col.
Vivre entre les mots (1972). Prod: Paul Larose, NFB. 100 min.
Unreleased.
Contrat d'amour (1973). Prod: Claude Godbout, Les Productions
prisma for Radio-Canada "Les joueurs". 26 min. col.
"L'amour quotidien". (1974) With Iolande Rossignol. Prod: Marcia
Couëlle, Radio-Canada. Series of 13 30-min. films.
Simple histoire d'amour (1976). Prod: Rex Tasker, Raymond
Savoie, NFB, Télé-publik. 107 min. b&w video.

Bibliography

Cinéma-Québec, vol. 1, no. 4, pp. 12-21, criticism, interview and
biofilmography; *Le Devoir,* March 21, 1970 (interview); *La
Presse,* April 10, 1971, p. D-9, "J'ai opté pour la libération", and
March 6, 1970 (interviews); *Dossier du cinéastes no. 10: Fernand
Dansereau* (CQDC, 1972), includes a complete filmography,
bibliography, reviews and an interview; *Objectif 65,* no. 32
(August 1965), Jean-Pierre Lefebvre, on **Le festin des morts**;
Liberté, vol. 8, no. 2/3, (March-June 1966), pp. 73-77, an article
by Dansereau; *Séquences,* no. 51 (December 1967), pp. 23-24,
"Dialogue avec des cinéastes canadiens, le travail", Maryse
Grandbois; *Challenge for Change Newsletter,* vol. 1, no. 2, (Fall
1968), "Channelling Change in Quebec: Fernand Dansereau's
Saint-Jérome", and vol. 1, no. 3, (Winter 1968-69), "**Saint-
Jérome**: The Experience of a Filmmaker as Social Animator",
Fernand Dansereau; *La Presse,* February 28, 1970, p. 41, "Le
triomphe du vécu sur la fiction", Luc Perreault; *La Presse,* March
14, 1970, p. 23, "Un secteur de pointe"; *La Presse,* April 10,
1971, p. D-9, "La clé du spectateur", Luc Perreault; *Le Soleil,*
Quebec, April 10, 1971, "A propos de libération"; *Relations,* no.
360 (May 1971), pp. 154-155, critique of **Faut aller**; *Le Jour,*
August 24, 1974, "Perspectives et limites de l'action dramatique
enregistrée sur vidéo", James Dormeyer; *Cinéma-Québec,* vol. 1,
no. 4, pp. 12-21, critique of **Faut aller**; references in *Le cinéma
québécois: tendances et prolongements, Le cinéma canadien,
Jeune cinéma canadien, Cinéma et société québécoise, Eléments
pour un nouveau cinéma, Cinéma d'ici* and *L'aventure du cinéma
direct.*

DANSEREAU, MIREILLE

Born in Montreal in 1943, Mireille Dansereau studied film at the
Université de Montréal and the Royal College of Art in London. It
was in London that she won first prize in the 1969 National Student Film Festival for her film, **Compromise**. Dansereau has

worked in various capacities — as editor, script-assistant, sound-woman, producer, researcher and interviewer — for the CBC, National Film Board and ORTF in Paris. Aside from her film work, Dansereau has videotaped a number of programs for the Board's Challenge for Change Unit on women exploring themselves in work, and for a community group on immigrant women, entitled **Les immigrants**. Her film **Forum** was originally shot on video and she has since directed a video session with students at Sir George Williams University in Montreal. Dansereau was part of the cooperative NFB unit that produced a series of films on women, "En tant que femmes". In 1974 she produced **The Basement**, directed by Vartkes Cholakian.

Filmography

Moi, un jour (1967). Prod: Independent. 10 min. b&w.

Compromise (1968). Prod: Independent. 28 min. b&w.

Forum (1969). Prod: Independent. 60 min. b&w.

Coccinelle (1970). Prod: Independent. 3 min. col.

La vie rêvée (The Dream Life) (1972). Prod: Guy Bergeron, L'Association coopérative des production audiovisuelles. 90 min. col. Dist: Faroun.

J'me marie, j'me marie pas (1974). Prod: Anne-Claire Poirier, NFB, Société nouvelle "En tant que femmes" series, 81 min. col.

Rappelle-toi (1975). With Vartkes Cholakian. Prod: V. Cholakian. 54 min. col.

Work in progress: script on the family for the Challenge for Change program.

Ms. Dansereau's independent films are distributed by Cooperative cinéastes indépendants, Montreal.

Bibliography

Montréal-matin, August 29, 1971, "**La vie rêvée:** dont rêvait Mireille Dansereau", François Piazza (interview); *La Presse*, July 29, 1972, "A quoi rêvent les jeunes filles?", interview and review of **La vie rêvée**, Luc Perreault; *Motion*, January/February 1974, pp. 16-17, "Life as Dreams — Film as Reality", Alexander Hausvater (interview); *Cinema Canada*, no. 5, pp. 26-31, "Women in Canadian Films", interview by A. Ibrányi-Kiss; *La Patrie*, October 13, 1968, "Une cinéaste québécoise à Londres"; *Québec-Presse*, January 18, 1970, "**Forum** ou comment se parler d'amour en se crachant à la figure"; *Montreal Star*, November 14, 1970, "**Forum**: a Nifty Melodrama", Juan Rodriguez; *Montreal Star*, July 27, 1972, "The Struggle to be a Filmland Rarity", Martin Malina; *Le Devoir*, July 29, 1972, p. 15, "Faire des films pour survivre" and "**La vie rêvée:** un collage féministe", Jean-

Pierre Tadros; *Médium-média*, January 1973: the complete issue is dedicated to the series "En tant que femmes"; *Le soleil*, January 11, 1974, "Le film **J'me marie, j'me marie pas** a-t-il changé votre vie?", Claude Daigneault; *Le nouvelliste*, January 14, 1974, "Le film de Mireille Dansereau suscite déjà diverses réactions", Michelle Guerin; *Cinéma-Québec*, vol. 2, no. 3, pp. 30-31, "Jeunes femmes en proie aux images", A. Martin-Thériault; *Take One*, vol. 3, no. 7, pp. 34-35, review of **La vie rêvée** by Kay Armatage; references in *Cinéma d'ici*.

DARCUS, JACK

Darcus was born in 1941 in Vancouver. Before he began making films he was involved in theatre, stage design and painting, working with the Gallimaufry Theatre Company and exhibiting his paintings in West Coast galleries. **Wolfpen Principle,** starring Vladimir Valenta, is Darcus' third feature; cinematography was by Terry Hudson and Hans Klardie, music by Don Druick, editing by Ray Hall. Darcus's interest in wild animals has provided him with a powerful metaphor for the brutality and vulnerability he explores in his films.

Filmography

The Great Coups of History (1969). Prod: J. Darcus. 84 min. b&w. Dist: New Cinema.
Proxy Hawks (1971). Prod: J. Darcus. 77 min. b&w. Dist: New Cinema.
Wolfpen Principle (1974). Prod: Werner Aellen, Image Flow Centre Ltd. 87 min. col. Dist: Faroun.

Bibliography

Motion, November-December 1973, pp. 48-52, interview with Darcus on **Wolfpen** by P.M. Evanchuk; interview with Darcus by Pierre Veronneau, La Cinémathèque québécoise, January 1974, available at film study centres; *Cinema Canada*, no. 13, pp. 42-45, "Filmmaking West Coast Style", interview with Darcus by Á. Ibrányi-Kiss; interview in *Inner Views: Ten Canadian Film-makers*, J. Hofsess (McGraw-Hill Ryerson, 1975), pp. 81-88; *Vancouver Province*, February 6, 1970, "Darcus: The Artist as Film-maker", Neil Arthur; *Vancouver Sun, August 15, 1973*, "A Film-maker Looking Beyond His Own Mudpuddle", Les Wedman; *Maclean's*, February, 1974, "The Better They Are, the Harder They Fall", John Hofsess.

DAVIDSON, WILLIAM

Davidson's career touches on many important events in Canada's film growth. Born in Toronto in 1928, Davidson graduated from the University of Western Ontario and studied at the Lorne Greene Academy of Radio Arts before starting his career as a journalist. In the National Film Board's search for new talent across Canada, Davidson was hired by Sydney Newman in 1948 along with Colin Low, Roman Kroitor and Wolf Koenig. As a writer, editor and assistant director, he worked on the series "Canada Carries On" and "Eye Witness"; he researched for the television series "On the Spot", edited and scripted Douglas Wilkinson's **Arctic Saga** and was Roger Blais's assistant on the dramatic series "Horizon". In 1955 he left the NFB and began writing dramas for the new CBC drama department headed by Sydney Newman. He began producing the documentary series "Graphic" first as a staff member and later on a freelance basis when in 1956 he and Norman Klenman formed Klenman-Davidson Productions Ltd. This company also worked on CBC's "Close-Up" and "Montreal by Night", as well as a number of shorts and features — all directed by Davidson, written by Klenman and co-produced; the feature **Now That April's Here** is based on stories by Morley Callaghan. The company was dissolved in 1960 but Norman Klenman has since formed Galanty Productions in Vancouver with director Daryl Duke. Davidson rejoined the CBC in 1960 and became executive producer of Children and Youth Programs for the English network; he created and produced the series "Razzle Dazzle", "Roundup", "Time Out for Adventure" and "Time of Your Life", a variety-drama series hosted by Peter Kastner and highlighting young writers such as David French, Norman Skolnick and David Freeman. Davidson went on to produce the series "Forest Rangers" and "Starlost", and to create as well as produce the popular series "Adventures in Rainbow Country" of which Maxime Samuel was executive producer. Since 1968 Davidson has written over 125 scripts for educational films, including the series "Almost Home", "The Law and Where It's At", "Dusting Off Mythology" and "The Consumer Game". He has written a number of feature film scripts, including **Return to Rainbow Country**, **Charley, My Boy**, **The Life and Times of J. C. McRuer**, and **Never the Same Again** based on the series "Almost Home". Davidson returned to feature film production with **Lions for Breakfast** which had a screenplay by Martin Lager and music by Cliff Edwards and Black Creek.

Filmography (incomplete)

Country Auctioneer (1954). Prod: W. Davidson, NFB "Faces of Canada". 8 min. b&w.

Station Master (1954). Prod: NFB "Faces of Canada". 15 min. b&w.

Prepare for Advancement (1954). Prod: David Bairstow, NFB for the R.C.A.F. 45 min. b&w.

Alcoholism (1955). Prod: Jack Olsen, NFB "Eye Witness". 11 min. b&w.

Sally Ann — Fire and Blood Army (1955). Prod: Jack Olsen, NFB "Eye Witness". 11 min. b&w.

The Curlers (1955). Prod: Nick Balla, NFB. 27 min. b&w.

The Hoax (1955). Prod: Nick Balla, NFB. 27 min. b&w.

"Graphic" series (1956-7). Among others, **Tommy Has His Tonsils Out, The Liberace Fan Club, Honest Ed, Deacon Allen's Gym**. Prod: W. Davidson, CBC.

A Home of Their Own (1957). Prod: Norman Klenman, W. Davidson, Klenman-Davidson Prod. Ltd. 20 min. b&w.

"Graphic" series (1957-8). Among others, **The Cowboy from Cardston, Max Ferguson, Helen Creighton, Folk-song Collector, W. O. Mitchell, The Hills of Niagara**. Prod: N. Klenman, W. Davidson, Klenman-Davidson Prod. Ltd. for CBC.

Now That April's Here (1958). Prod: N. Klenman, W. Davidson, Klenman-Davidson Prod. Ltd. 90 min. b&w.

The Fast Ones or **Ivy League Killers** (1959). Prod: N. Klenman, W. Davidson, Klenman-Davidson Prod. Ltd. 75 min. b&w.

"Time of Your Life" series (1963-65). **Inside the Platinum Pad, Charley Love from Liverpool, The Sewer, Chinese Checkers, It's in the Bag, For France at Four, The Wonderful Winter, Ants Don't Leave Footprints, The Young Astronauts, Mystery at Loon Lake Lodge, The Kids and the Kidnappers, Hey, Murphey**. Prod: W. Davidson, CBC. 30 min. & 60 min. b&w.

Death Dance (1965). Prod: W. Davidson, A.S.P. Productions "Forest Rangers" series.

Panic in the Bush, Where the Wild Rice Grows, Milk Run (1968-70). Prod: W. Davidson, Manitou Productions, CBC, Associated British in series "Adventures in Rainbow Country".

Lions for Breakfast (1975). Prod: Tony Kramreither, Burg Productions Ltd. 98 min. col. Dist: Saguenay.

Feature films in progress: **In Council Rooms Apart** (co-scripted with John Craig from his novel of lthe same name); **Summer Rain** (from a script by Ratch Wallace).

Bibliography

Motion, May-June 1974, p. 14, "Bill Davidson: Interview", Peter Evanchuk; *That's Showbusiness*, no. 15 (July 30, 1975), on **Summer Rain**.

DEFALCO, MARTIN

When Martin Defalco joined the National Film Board in 1952 he trained as a sound recordist, becoming a picture editor with **Political Dynamite**, based on a story from W.O. Mitchell's *Jake and the Kid*. He began his directing career with government sponsored films, later moving into investigations of Canadian communities, such as that of the Japanese-Canadians in **Bird of Passage**. Defalco's fiction feature, **Cold Journey,** stars Johnny Yesno and Buckley Petawabano with songs by composer-musician-filmmaker Willie Dunn; this marks the second collaboration with Dunn on a film concerning native people. In 1968 Defalco was resident filmmaker at Stanford University and in 1973-74 president of the NFB artists' union, S.G.C.T.

Filmography

Bird of Passage (1966). Prod: Joe Koenig, NFB, 10 Min. b&w.
Northern Fisherman (1966). Prod: George Pearson, NFB for the Dept. of Fisheries. 24 min. col.
Trawler Fisherman (1966). Prod: John Kemeny, NFB for the Dept. of Fisheries. 22 min. col.
What in the World is Water? (1967). Prod: George Pearson, NFB. 12 min. col.
Charlie's Day (Les jeux de l'amour et de l'oxygène) (1967). Prod: George Pearson, NFB for the Dept. of Health and Welfare. 12 min. col.
Their Roots Run Deep (1968). Prod. NFB for the Dept. of National Defence. 17 min. col.
Don Messer: His Land and His Music (1971). Prod: George Pearson, NFB. 70 min. col.
The Other Side of the Ledger: An Indian View of the Hudson's Bay Company (1972). With Willie Dunn. Prod: George Pearson, NFB. 42 min. col.
The Great Little Artist (1973). Prod: David Bairstow, NFB. 30 min. col.
Cold Journey (1975). Prod: George Pearson, NFB. 76 min. col.
Work in Progress: distribution of **Cold Journey**.

Bibliography

Cinema Canada, no. 15 (August-September 1974), pp. 58-59, interview by Stephen Chesley; *Montreal Gazette,* June 5, 1971, "Buckley Petawabano had a Cold Journey", Dane Lanken; *Montreal Gazette,* April 12, 1973, "The Italian Community Gets into the Movies", Dane Lanken on **Great Little Artist;** *Toronto Star,* May 15, 1974, "Canada Through Indian Eyes Turned into a History Lesson", Peter Goddard.

DEVLIN, BERNARD

Born in Quebec City in 1923, Bernard Devlin entered the National Film Board in 1946 as an editor, writer and director. He has been particularly involved in a number of series for television — among them "On the Spot", a series of documentary reports which began in 1953. Moving from English to French television production in 1954, Devlin produced the French version of "On the Spot" ("Sur le vif") and collaborated with Léonard Forest, Fernand Dansereau and Louis Portugais on the series "Passe-partout" and "Panoramique". Devlin was the producer of the 18 films of the series "Les artisans de notre histoire" (produced in English by Julian Biggs). He was director of the French section of production and head of English production at the National Film Board before returning recently to active film direction. His feature, **A Case of Eggs**, for the "Filmglish" series has a scenario by Charles Israel.

Filmography (incomplete)

L'homme aux oiseaux (The Bird Fancier) (1952). Prod: Guy Glover, NFB. 30 min. b&w.

L'abatis (The Settler). (1953). With Raymond Garceau. Prod: Guy Glover, NFB. 16 min. b&w.

Strongman (1953). Prod: B. Devlin, NFB "On the Spot". 15 min. b&w.

Survival in the Bush (1954). Prod: Robert Anderson, NFB. 30 min. b&w.

L'abbé Pierre (1955). Prod: B. Devlin, NFB "Sur le vif". 15 min. b&w.

Night Children (1956). Prod: Julian Biggs, NFB "On the Spot". 29 min. b&w.

Les suspects (1957). Prod: Guy Glover, NFB "Passe-partout". 30 min. b&w.

Les brûlés (The Promised Land) (1958). Prod: Léonard Forest, Guy Glover, NFB "Panoramique". 114 min. b&w.

La misère des autres (Walk Down Any Street) (1960). Prod: Léonard Forest, NFB. 28 min. b&w.

Dubois et fils (1961). With Raymond Le Boursier. Prod: Léonard Forest, NFB. 59 min. b&w.

La soif de l'or (The Gold Seekers) (1962). With Raymond Garceau. Prod: R. Garceau, B. Devlin, NFB. 28 min. b&w.

David Thompson, the Great Mapmaker (David Thompson, cartographe) (1964). Prod: Guy Glover, NFB. 28 min. b&w.

The Voyageurs (Les voyageurs). Prod: Nicholas Balla, NFB. 20 min. col.

Octopus Hunt (Chasse à la pieuvre) (1965). Prod: Julian Biggs, NFB. 17 min. col.

A Question of Identity: War of 1812 (La guerre de 1812) (1966). Prod: NFB. 28 min. b&w.

Seniority Versus Ability (Ancienneté et compétence) (1968).
Prod: Guy Glover, NFB. 13 min. b&w.
A Matter of Survival (Une décision capitale) (1969). Prod: Bill
Brind, NFB, for Canada Department of Labour. 26 min. col.
The End of the Nancy J. (Le Nancy J ne pêchera plus) (1970).
Prod: B. Devlin, NFB, for the Department of Fisheries and
Forestry. 22 min. col.
A Case of Eggs (1974). Prod: Daisy de Bellefeuille, John N.
Smith, NFB "Filmglish" series. Four episodes, totalling 65 min.
col.
The Visit. Prod: Julian Biggs, NFB. 28 min. b&w.

Bibliography

Séquences, October 1962, pp. 13-21, a review and interview by
Pierre Théberge on Louis-Hippolyte Lafontaine (from the series,
"Les artisans de notre histoire"); *Montreal Star*, October 2, 1965,
"Charging Horsemen and Popping Pistols", Don Newnham (on
War of 1812), references in: *Jeune cinéma canadien, Le cinéma
canadien, Le cinéma québécois: tendances et prolongements,
Vingt ans de cinéma au Canada français*, and *Cinéma d'ici*.

DUCKWORTH, MARTIN

Born in Montreal in 1933, Martin Duckworth received an M.A. in
history from the University of Toronto and taught at Mount Allison
University. He joined the NFB in 1963 as assistant cameraman
and became a director in 1970. As a cameraman Duckworth shot
The Ernie Game, **Christopher's Movie Matinée**, **Niagara Falls**,
Angel, **A Film for Max**, **Pandora**, **Sad Song of Yellow Skin**, **La
richesse des autres**, **Les deux côtés de la médaille**, **Where are
You Going Company Town?**, **Vivre entre les mots**, **The New
Alchemists**, **Le bonhomme**, **Half Half Three Quarters Full**, **Un-
touched and Pure**, and the series "Il n'y a pas d'oubli".
Duckworth's **Cell 16** was scripted by playwright Peter Madden.

Filmography

Passing Through Sweden (En passant par la Suède) (1969).
Prod: Joe Koenig, NFB. 21 min. b&w.
The Wish (1970). Prod: Tom Daly, NFB. 28 min. col.
Cell 16 (1971). Prod: Colin Low, NFB "Challenge for Change". 14
min. col.
Accident (1973). With Pat Crawley. Prod: Tom Daly, NFB. 16
min. col.
Forget It, Jack (1974). With Jim Littleton, Judy Jackson, Service
Employees International Union. 20 min. b&w.
Temiscaming, Quebec (1976). Prod: Dorothy Hénault, NFB
Challenge for Change, 63 min. col.

Work in progress: **The Twenties in Cape Breton**, for the "Multi Media" program, NFB.

Bibliography

Screen, vol. 5, no. 2, pp. 11-12, 18-19, reviews of **Half Half Three Quarters Full** and **The Wish**; *The Canadian Magazine,* July 20, 1974, p. 2-4, 6, "Gasp...Sob...Hurray!! How Turning the Town's Troubles into a Movie Melodrama Helped Save Temiscaming", Barry Conn Hughes.

DUFAUX, GEORGES

Born in France in 1927, Georges Dufaux studied at the Ecole nationale de cinématographie before joining the National Film Board in 1956. As a cameraman he worked on two early drama series, "Passe-partout" and "Panoramique", made weekly by the NFB for French television. In 1958 he shot Colin Low's **City Out of Time** and the following year joined Koenig, Kroitor and Macartney-Filgate in the Candid Eye Unit, shooting the French section of **The Days Before Christmas**, Macartney-Filgate's **Blood and Fire** and **I Was a Ninety Pound Weakling**. Dufaux has shot many important films since his work in the unit: **Rose et Landry, Tiger Child, Le festin des morts, Fortune and Men's Eyes, Isabel, YUL 871, Les filles du roy, C'est pas Chinois, Des armes et les hommes, Taureau** and **Partis pour la gloire**. He has also co-directed a number of films, among them **C'est pas la faute à Jacques Cartier**, a musical comedy. **A votre santé** documents the work of a city hospital's emergency ward and his most recent features are concerned with the subject of old age.

Filmography

Bientôt Noël (1959). With Terence Macartney-Filgate, Wolf Koenig and Stanley Jackson. Prod: Koenig, Kroitor, NFB. 30 min. b&w.

I Was a Ninety Pound Weakling (1960). With Wolf Koenig. Prod: Roman Kroitor, Wolf Koenig, NFB. 24 min. b&w.

Les dieux (1961). With Jacques Godbout. Prod: Fernand Dansereau, NFB. 29 min. b&w.

Pour quelques arpents de neige (Strangers for the Day) (1961). With Jacques Godbout. Prod: Fernand Dansereau, NFB. 28 min. b&w.

36,000 Brasses (1962). Prod: Fernand Dansereau, NFB. 28 min. b&w.

Rencontres à Mitzic (1963). With Marcel Carrière. Prod: Fernand Dansereau, NFB. 27 min. b&w.

Caroline (1964). With Clément Perron. Prod.: Fernand Dansereau, NFB. 27 min. b&w.

A propos d'une plage (1964). Prod: Claude Nedjar, André Belleau, NFB/ORTF. 26 min. b&w.

Les départs nécessaires (Sudden Departure) (1965). Prod:

Marcel Martin, NFB. 35 min. b&w.

Precision (Précision) (1966). Prod: Jacques Bobet, NFB. 10 min. col.

Cinéma et réalité (1967). With Clément Perron. Prod: C. Perron, G. Dufaux, NFB. 58 min. b&w.

C'est pas la faute à Jacques Cartier. With Clément Perron. Prod: C. Perron and G. Dufaux, NFB. 72 min. col.

L'homme multiplié (1969). With Claude Godbout. Prod: Clément Perron, NFB. For split-screen cinema at Terre des hommes.

Deux ans et plus (Two Years or More) (1970). With Gilles Thérien. Prod: Marc Beaudet, NFB for the Canadian Penitentiary Services. 27 min. col.

A cris perdus (Cries From Within) (1972). With Marc Beaudet. Prod: François Séguillon, NFB. 45 min. col.

A votre santé (1974). Prod: Jean-Marc Garand, NFB. 116 min. col.

Au bout de mon âge (1976). Prod: Jean-Marc Garand, NFB. 90 min. col.

Les jardins d'hiver. Prod: Jean-Marc Garand, NFB. 90 min. col.

Bibliography

Liberté, vol. 8, no. 2-3 (March-June 1966), pp. 84-90, "Le fameux cinéma candide", an interview by Jean-Claude Labrecque on the Candid Eye Unit; *Dossiers du cinéma: 1* (Edition fides, 1968), review of **Caroline**; *Globe and Mail,* June 10, 1969, "Cinematic Poem", Dennis Braithwaite (also a review of **C'est pas la faute à Jacques Cartier**); *L'Action,* July 25, 1969, a review of **C'est pas la faute à Jacques Cartier**; *American Cinematographer,* July 1970, pp. 671, 680-681, "Filming **Tiger Child** in the World's Largest Film Format", Georges Dufaux (the entire issue is devoted to "Film at Expo '70"); *La Presse,* April 27, 1974, "Une salle d'urgence sous observation pendant cinq semaines", Serge Dussault; *Montréal-matin,* May 31, 1974, "...l'étonnante banalité de la souffrance et de la mort", H.D.R.; *Cinéma-Québec,* vol. 4, no. 1 (December 1974), pp. 25-27, "La renaissance du 'candid' québécois" Pierre Demers, on **A votre santé**; *How to Make or Not to Make a Canadian Film* (Cinémathèque canadienne, 1967), "Picture and Film", by Dufaux; references in: *Le cinéma canadien, Vingt ans de cinéma au Canada français, Jeune cinéma canadien, Cinéma d'ici,* and *L'aventure du cinéma direct.*

DUKE, DARYL

A native of Vancouver, Daryl Duke has more than 20 years of television drama and variety musicals to his credit in Canada and the United States. He graduated in English and philosophy from the University of British Columbia and joined the National Film Board in 1950 as a writer, film editor and assistant director. In 1953 he returned to Vancouver and to CBUT as supervising producer of the Vancouver Film Unit, working with Ron Kelly, Gene Lawrence and Allan King, among others. In Toronto from 1958 to 1964, Duke produced "Close-Up", "Explorations" and "Quest", leaving for the United States in 1964 to produce "The Steve Allen Show" and later "The Les Crane Show" for ABC. Since 1965 Duke has worked mainly in film and the following television series: "Telescope", "Document", "Sunday", and "Quentin Durgens" in Canada, and "The Senators", "The Psychiatrist" and "The Bold Ones" in the United States. Some of his well-known productions for CBC include **Thy Brother's Keeper**, **Chocolate Fudge with Walnuts**, and **The Road to Chaldea** for "Quentin Durgens", **The Spike in the Wall** for "Manipulators", and **West Coast On My Mind**. For CTV he made **Hollywood: The Canadians** in 1969 with Galanty Productions, the company he formed with Norman Klenman and Edgar Cowan in 1968. While Duke has made a number of features for television, **Payday** was his first theatrical feature, made in 1972 in the U.S.A.; it won the National Society of Film Critics Award the following year. Since then, Duke has directed several segments for the NFB's "West" series and has produced two half-hour comedy pilots for CBS and NBC. He lives in Vancouver. In 1976 Duke and his associate, Norman Klenman, opened the Vancouver television station, CKVU-TV.

Bibliography
Toronto Star, December 28, 1963, pp. 13, 20, "Star of the Year, TV Producer Daryl Duke", Bob Reguly; *Toronto Star,* October 20, 1966, "Daryl Duke Shatters Momentary CBC Calm", Roy Shields; *Vancouver Sun,* March 13, 1973, "Sordid Tale Makes Good Film", Les Wedman (on **Payday**); *Weekend Magazine,* July 17, 1976, pp. 16-19, "The Shadow of the Eagle" Martin Knelman.

EWING, IAIN
Novelist, actor, songwriter Iain Ewing was born in Ottawa in 1945; he attended the University of Toronto where he studied history and philosophy. Ewing worked on David Sector's **The Offering**, starred in David Cronenberg's **Stereo** and **Crimes of the Future**, and acted, sang and wrote music for Clarke Mackey's **The Only Thing You Know**. **Kill**, Ewing's first feature, is about three people who plan to kill the father of one of them; Ewing and Ian Carruthers devised the unscripted film and Ewing directed, recorded and edited it. Ewing travelled in India in 1971-72, where he shot **Silk Saris**. He produced and acted in Ed Hunt's **Diary of a Sinner** (1975) and another feature of Hunt's still in progress, and photographed Judy Steed's **It's Going to Be All Right**. In 1974 Ewing was assistant to producer Gerry Arbeid on **My Pleasure is My Business** and **Black Christmas.**

Filmography
Picaro (1967). Prod: Independent. 27 min. col.

A Short Film (1967). Prod: Independent. 3 min. b&w.
Kill (1969). Prod: Independent. 85 min. b&w.
Eat Anything (1970). Prod: Hallelujah Films Ltd. 84 min. col.
Bo Diddley's Back in Town (1972). Prod: Hallelujah Films Ltd. for CBC. 20 min. b&w.
Unity in Diversity (1975). Prod: I. Ewing, Anna Charles, Hallelujah Films Ltd. for Sivananda Yoga Vedanta Organization. 56 min. col.
Kew Beach (1975). Pro: Hallelujah Films Ltd. for CBC. 3½ min. col.
Autumn Trees (1975). Prod: Hallelujah Films Ltd. 4 min. col.
Temple Garlands (1975). Prod: Hallelujah Films Ltd. 4 min. col.
Silk Saris (1975). Prod: Hallelujah Films Ltd. 6 min. col.
The Mackenzie Valley (1975). With John Fyles. Prod: Hallelujah Films Ltd. 40 min. col.
Permafrost (1975). With Ross MacKay. Prod: Hallelujah Films Ltd. 35 min. col.
Work in progress: **The Berger Inquiry**. Prod: Hallelujah Films Ltd. 30 min. col.
A Film About My Father. Prod: Hallelujah Films Ltd. 30 min. col.

Iain Ewing's independent films are distributed by the Canadian Filmmakers' Distribution Centre.

Bibliography

Take One, vol. 2, no. 3, Ewing co-interviews Peter Fonda; *Montreal Gazette,* October 21, 1966, "Young Filmmaker Repelled by Plastic People", Marilyn Argue; *Globe and Mail,* November 19, 1966, p. 17, "Shoestring Productions Ltd.", Bruce Lawson; *Toronto Star,* December 13, 1968, "5 'Shot' at T-D Centre— That's Show Biz"; *Saturday Night,* February 1970, a review of **Kill** by Marshall Delaney; *Cinema Canada,* no. 15, pp. 75-77, reviews of **Diary of a Sinner,** Natalie Edwards and Robert Fothergill.

FERGUSON, GRAEME

Born in Toronto in 1929, Graeme Ferguson attended the University of Toronto where he was actively involved in the film society. He was a summer student at the National Film Board in 1950 and worked with the Swedish film director Arne Sucksdorff on **The Flute and the Arrow**, which was filmed in India. Ferguson has made a number of his films in the United States but returned to Canada in 1970 to set up Graeme Ferguson Films Ltd. and later, Multi-Screen Corporation with Roman Kroitor and Robert Kerr in Montreal and Galt, Ontario. This unit developed the revolutionary Imax system used at Ontario Place and many other recent installations in Canada and the United States. In 1975 Kroitor left the company which is now called Imax Entertainment. As well as producing Imax films, the company builds projectors and rents Imax cameras; they are also responsible for six Imax installations in theatres.

Filmography

The Legend of Rudolph Valentino (1961). Prod: Saul J. Turell, Paul Killiam for Wolper-Sterling. 60 min. b&w.
The Love Goddesses (1964). Prod: G. Ferguson, Saul J. Turell for Walter Reade-Sterling Inc. 83 min. b&w and col.
The Days of Dylan Thomas (1965). Prod: Rollie McKenna, Graeme Ferguson Films Ltd. 25 min. b&w.
Man and the Polar Regions (1967). Prod: G. Ferguson, Robert Kerr, Ferguson-Kerr Multi-Screen Ltd. for Expo '67. 18 min. col.
The Virgin President (1968). Prod: G. Ferguson, Severn Darden, James Hubbard, Graeme Ferguson Films Ltd. 85 min. b&w. Dist: New Cinema.
IBM Close-Up (1968). With Roman Kroitor. Prod: R. Kroitor, Multi-Screen Corp. for IBM.
North of Superior (1971). Prod: G. Ferguson, Multi-Screen Corp. for Ontario Place. 18 min. col.
The Question of Television Violence (1972). Prod: Colin Low, Len Chatwin, NFB Challenge for Change. 56 min. col.
Snow Job (1974). Prod: G. Ferguson, Multi-Screen Corp. for Ontario Place. 17 min. col
Man Belongs to the Earth (1974). Prod: G. Ferguson, R. Kroitor, Paramount Pictures for United States Pavilion, Expo '74. 23 min. col.

Bibliography

Globe and Mail, October 5, 1965, "Lack of Funds Curbs Filming in Canada", Frank Morriss (interview); *Montreal Star,* January 22, 1966, "Questions and Answers from Filmmaker Ferguson", Martin Malina (interview); *La Presse,* July 16, 1966, "Une galérie des grandes déesses du septième art", Michele Favreau (interview); *Montreal Star,* December 24, 196, "Eighteen Months for Eighteen Minutes", Dusty Vineberg (interview); *Cinema Canada,* no. 9, pp. 34-37, interview by Shelby M. Gregory and Phyllis Wilson; *Inner Views: Ten Canadian Film Makers,* J. Hofsess (McGraw-Hill Ryerson, 1975), pp. 91-100 (interview); *Films and Filming,* July 1, 1965, review of **The Love Goddesses**; *Toronto Star,* October 16, 1965, p. 20, "Fifty Years of Love Goddesses: Did Bara's Charms Pale Bardot's?", David Cobb; *Toronto Telegram,* October 23, 1965, "The Lovely Love Goddesses", Clyde Gilmour.

FORCIER, ANDRE

Born in 1947 in Montreal, André Forcier began his film career as a student with an 8mm short, **La mort vue par . . .** ; co-directed, it won top prize in a Radio-Canada competition. His first feature, **Le retour de l'Immaculate Conception**, was shown as part of the 1972 Museum of Modern Art Quebec film festival in 1972. Forcier's second feature, **Bar Salon**, received an honourable mention from the Association of Quebec Film Critics (AQCC) in 1974. **Bar Salon** was co-authored by Forcier and Jacques Marcotte, and François Gill was cinematographer; the three worked together on Forcier's third feature, **L'eau chaude, l'eau frette**.

Filmography

Chroniques labradoriennes (1966). Prod: André Forcier Inc. / Onyx Films Inc. 12 min. col.
Le retour de l'Immaculate Conception (1972). Prod: Les films André Forcier. 85 min. b&w. Dist. CQDC.
Night Cap (1974). Prod: Laurence Paré, NFB. 36 min. col.
Bar Salon (1974). Prod: Jean Dansereau, Les ateliers du cinéma québécois/Les films André Forcier. 84 min. b&w. Dist: ACPAC and New Cinema.
L'eau chaude, l'eau frette (1976). Prod: A. Forcier, Bernard Lalonde, ACPAC/Les films André Forcier. 94 min. col.

Bibliography

Séquences, no. 80 (April 1975), p. 47, "La poésie du réalisme" (interview), in the same issue, pp. 25-26, review of **Bar Salon** by Jannick Beaulieu; *Montreal Star,* August 23, 1975, "Opaquely transparent", Martin Malina (interview); *Cinéma-Québec,* vol. 3, no. 1 (September 1973), pp. 25-27, "André Forcier et **Le retour de l'Immaculate Conception**", P. Demers; *Cinéma-Québec,* vol. 4, no. 1 (December 1974), pp. 40-42, "Le retour des désoeuvrés", P. Demers; *La Presse,* February 22, 1975, "Le petit monde d'André Forcier", Luc Perreault; *Bar Salon*, a critique by Gilles Marsolais (Ottawa: CFI "Filmexpo", 1975), available in film study centres; *Cinema Canada,* no. 19, pp. 28-29, "The Film **Bar Salon**", D. John Turner, and pp. 30-31, "The Man André Forcier", M. Morisset; references in *Cinéma d'ici.*

FOREST, LEONARD

Born in Chelsea, Massachusetts in 1928 of Acadian parents,

Léonard Forest grew up in Moncton, New Brunswick. He first worked as a broadcaster and journalist and began his film career in Halifax. He moved to Toronto and Montreal to direct musical and information shows for Radio-Canada before joining the National Film Board in 1953. As a director and producer Forest has been involved in a number of television series — "Passe-partout", "Temps présent", "Panoramique", and "Profils et paysages"; the latter series, with direction by Bernard Devlin, Fernand Dansereau, Louis Portugais and Claude Jutra, marks the significant steps of the social and political evolution of French Canada. A published poet, Forest has written the scenarios for many films — among them, **Pêcheurs de Pomcoup**, **La vie est courte**, **Amitiés haïtiennes**, and **Mémoire en fête**. **Les Acadiens de la dispersion** is a feature documentary on the historical Acadians, with Edith Butler's folksongs adding to the power of their story. His innovative work with Société nouvelle includes **La noce n'est pas finie**, a fictional feature with historical dimensions, collectively written and acted by citizens in northeast New Brunswick. Forest became director of the French Program Committee of the National Film Board in 1973.

Filmography

La femme de ménage (The Charwoman) (1954). Prod: Roger Blais, NFB. 11 min. b&w.

Les aboiteaux (The Dikes) (1955). With Roger Blais. Prod: Roger Blais, NFB. 29 min. b&w.

Midinette (Needles and Pins) (1955). With Roger Blais. Prod: Roger Blais, NFB. 19 min. b&w.

Pêcheurs de Pomcoup (Fishermen of Pubnico) (1956). With Victor Jobin. Prod: Roger Blais, NFB. 25 min. b&w.

Le monde des femmes (1956). Prod: NFB. 30 min.

The Whole World Over — Mexican Episode (1957). Prod: Julian Biggs, NFB. 30 min. b&w.

Amitiés haïtiennes (1958). Prod: Guy Glover, NFB "Passe-partout". 30 min. b&w.

Mémoire en fête (Walls of Memory) (1964). Prod: Marcel Martin, NFB. 27 min. b&w.

A la recherche de l'innocence (In Search of Innocence) (1964). Prod: Jacques Bobet, Victor Jobin, NFB. 28 min. col.

Les Acadiens de la dispersion (1968). Prod: Clément Perron, NFB. 118 min. b&w.

Acadie libre (1969). Prod: François Séguillon, NFB. 22 min. b&w. A satellite film of **Les Acadiens de la dispersion**.

La noce n'est pas finie (1971). Prod: François Séguillon, NFB. 84 min. b&w.

Out of Silence (1972). Prod: Robert Verrall, Dorothy Courtois, NFB. 38 min. col.

Un soleil pas comme ailleurs (A Sun Like Nowhere Else) (1972). Prod: Jean-Marc Garand, NFB, Société nouvelle. 47 min. col.

Bibliography

La Presse, January 7, 1967, an article by Forest on **Les Acadiens de la dispersion,** and August 31, 1968, an interview with him concerning the same film; *Médium-média,* no. 1 (Autumn 1971), "Un film c'est une question", an interview with Forest on **La noce n'est pas finie**; *Challenge for Change: Access,* no. 10 (Autumn 1972), "Société Nouvelle Goes Back to Acadia" (interview); *Challenge for Change Newsletter,* no. 7 (Winter 1972), "Fiction Film as Social Animator" (interview); *Cinema Canada,* no. 15, pp. 30-31, "Léonard Forest: French Programming Committee", Ronald Blumer and Duncan Thorne (interview); *Objectif,* no. 31 (February-March 1965), "Travelling arrière", Christian Rasselet, a review of **Mémoire en fête**; "Psaumes pour un dieu préalable", poems by Léonard Forest in *Ecrits du Canada français,* no. 23 (1967); *Moncton Times,* New Brunswick, August 9, 1968, "Warm Reception for First Showing of Acadian Film", Sharon Saunders; Press clippings **Les Acadiens de la dispersion**, September 10, 1968, have been collected by the National Film Board and are available at their offices or at film study centres; *Liberté,* no. 9 (January-February 1969), pp. 69-70, "Un cinéaste à la recherche d'un film", by Forest; *Le Soleil,* Quebec, October 2, 1971, "Société nouvelle veut déranger", G. Rheault on **La noce n'est pas finie**; references in *Jeune cinéma canadien, Le cinéma québécois: tendances et prolongements, Vingt ans de cinéma au Canada français* and *Cinéma d'ici.*

FOURNIER, CLAUDE

Born in Waterloo, Quebec in 1931, Claude Fournier has been a journalist, a publicist, poet and photographer as well as a film-maker. As a cameraman Fournier shot many of the films that he directed or co-directed at the National Film Board, and in the U.S., films directed by Leacock, Drew and Pennebaker, whom he joined for eighteen months in 1962; among the latter are **Susan Star** and **Playboy Bunnies** by D. A. Pennebaker, **Nehru** by Richard Leacock and **Eddie Sachs at Indianapolis** by Robert Drew and Leacock. In 1963 he formed his own company in Montreal producing for a number of ORTF and Radio-Canada television series; among these are "Vingt ans express", "Cent millions de jeunes" and "Villes du Canada". The latter series was directed by Claude Sylvestre and shot by Fournier and Michel Brault. In 1966 he worked with Omega Productions and Crawley Films to produce a triple-screen production for the fifth theatre of the Canadian Pavilion at Expo '67. Fournier's talent as a humourist has made his features widely appealing to Quebec audiences.

Filmography

Télesphore Legaré, garde-pêche (1959). Prod: Léonard Forest, NFB. 29 min. b&w.

La France sur un caillou (1960). With Gilles Groulx. Prod: Jacques Bobet, NFB. 28 min. b&w.

Alfred Desrochers, poète (1960). Prod: Léonard Forest, Jean Roy, Victor Jobin, NFB. 28 min. b&w.

La lutte (Wrestling) (1061). With Claude Jutra, Michel Brault and Marcel Carrière. Prod: Jacques Bobet, NFB. 28 min. b&w.

Midwestern Floods (1962). Prod: Filmmakers/ Drew Associates. 20 min. b&w.

''Vingt ans express'' (1963-1964). Prod: Les films Claude Fournier for Radio-Canada. 20-28 min. each. b&w. The following were directed by Fournier: **Témoins de Jehova**, **Maliotenam**, **Les jeunes romanciers**, **Bohèmes '64**, **Les allelluyahs**, **Serge et Réal**, **Armageddon**.

Deux femmes (1965). Prod: Les films Claude Fournier for Radio-Canada, ''Cent millions de jeunes''. 28 min. b&w.

Londres (1966). Prod: Les films Claude Fournier. 28 min. b&w.

Ti-Jean (1966). Prod: Les films Claude Fournier for Radio-Canada, ''Cent millions de jeunes''. 28 min. b&w.

Tony Roman (1966). Prod: Les films Claude Fournier for Radio-Canada. 54 min. b&w.

Columbium (1966). Prod: Office du film du Quebec (OFQ) for Expo '67. 8 min. col.

Québec an 2000 (1966). Prod: OFQ for Quebec Pavilion, Expo '67. 5 min. col.

On sait où entrer Tony, mais c'est les notes (1966). Prod: Les films Claude Fournier. 30 min. b&w.

Sebring, la cinquième heure (1966). Prod: Les films Claude Fournier. 20 min. col.

Le dossier Nelligan (1968). Prod: Onyx-Fournier for OFQ. 90 min. col.

Hearts (Coeurs neufs) (1968). Prod: Les films Claude Fournier for OFQ. 19 min. col.

Trente-mille employés de l'état du Québec (1968). Prod: Les films Claude Fournier for Le conseil des syndicats nationaux. Six half-hour films.

Du général au particulier (1968). Prod: Les films Claude Fournier for OFQ. 28 min. col.

Deux femmes en or (Two Women in Gold) (1970). Prod: Onyx-Fournier/France Films. 108 min. col.

Les chats bottés (The Master Cats) (1971). With Marie-Josée Raymond. Prod: Onyx-Fournier/France Films. 100 min. col.

Alien Thunder (Tonnerre rouge) (1973). Prod: Marie-Josée Raymond, Onyx Films. 90 min. col. Dist: Mutuel and Ambassador.

La pomme, la queue et les pépins (The Apple, the Stem and the

Seeds) (1974). Prod: Marie-Josée Raymond, Rose Films/Cinepix
/Productions mutuelles. 90 min. col.
...Et Dieu créa l'été (1974). With Marie-Josée Raymond. Prod:
Jacques Parent, Rose Films Inc. for OFQ, for Ministère de
tourisme. 13 min. col.
Feature work in progress: **Je suis loin de toi Mignonne.** Prod:
Pierre David for Les productions mutuelles, Marie-Josée Ray-
mond for Rose Films Inc.

Bibliography

Le Devoir, May 23, 1970, "Claude Fournier par lui-même (ou pres-
que)", Christian Allegre (interview); *La Presse,* May 23, 1970,
"Claude Fournier, un gars qui ne se prend pas pour un autre",
Luc Perreault (interview);*Skoop,* Amsterdam, vol. 8, no. 8 (1973),
pp. 32-34, interview and article on **Alien Thunder** (in Dutch);
Soirée Claude Fournier (La cinémathèque canadienne, 1966), a
pamphlet with a filmography, critiques and an article by Fournier,
available only in film study libraries; *Le Devoir,* February 22,
1969, "Fallait-il nous tuer ce mythe?", Claude Nadon and André
Major, on **Le dossier Nelligan**: un procès jugé d'avance", Luc
Perreault; *La Presse,* March 15, 1969, "Protestation contre; *La
Presse,* March 1, 1969, "**Le dossier Nelligan**"; *Séquences,* April
1969, "Procès à Nelligan", Léo Bonneville on **Le dossier
Nelligan**; *Montreal Star,* May 23, 1970, "Film d'auteur? No",
Martin Malina on **Deux femmes en or**; *Montreal Gazette,* June
13, 1970, on **Deux femmes en or**; *Rélations,* no. 353 (October
1970), p. 281, "**Deux femmes...en or?**", Yves Lever; *Le
Devoir,* June 9, 1971, "Divertir en faisant 'miauler' de rire", Jean-
Pierre Tadros on **Les chats bottés**; *La Presse,* June 12, 1971,
"Claude Fournier a le succès amer", Luc Perreault on **Les chats
bottés**; *Québec-presse,* June 13, 1971, "**Les chats bottés**: des
vedettes connues des grosses farces, un film commercial", Carol
Faucher; *La Presse,* November 18, 1972, Un **Little Big Man** en
plus authentiqué", Luc Perreault on **Alien Thunder**; *Toronto Star,*
May 13, 1974, "It's Called Canada's Most Expensive Film but it's
No Triumph", Clyde Gilmour on **Alien Thunder**; *Saturday Night,*
July 1974, review of **Alien Thunder**; *Motion,* July-August 1974,
p. 52, review of **Alien Thunder** by Nat Shuster; *Le Jour,* August
28, 1974, "Retour de Claude Fournier 'sexy et aphrodisiaque'",
Jean-Pierre Tadros on **La pomme**; *Montreal Gazette,* August 31,
1974, "Rumbling Thunder and Weird Minds", Jack Kapica; *Le
Devoir,* September 14, 1974, "**La pomme** a ses premiers
pépins", Jean-Pierre Tadros; *Le Soleil,* November 12, 1974,
"Pour Claude Fournier, après le rosbif viendra le dessert", Claude
Daigneault; *Cinema Canada,* no. 14, pp. 73-74, reviews of **Alien
Thunder**, Mark Miller and Natalie Edwards; references in: *Vingt
ans de cinéma au Canada français, Le cinéma québécois: ten-*

dances et prolongements, Jeune cinéma canadien and *L'aventure du cinéma direct.*

FOURNIER, ROGER

Roger Fournier was born in St. Anaclet, Quebec in 1929 and studied at the University of Laval; he began his film career as a cameraman in 1954 for CFCM-TV and joined Radio-Canada in 1955 as a director of variety shows. In this capacity he collaborated on the 1959 ''Wayne and Shuster Hour''. As well as his numerous television assignments (notably the series ''Moi et l'autre''). Fournier has written scripts for Denis Héroux's **L'amour humain** and his own feature, **Pile ou face**; scenario for the latter film was written by Gérald Tassé, photography was by René Verzier and music by Stephanne Venne. Fournier has six novels to his credit including *Inutile et adorable* and *Mon corps, mon âme, Montréal.* He has also written a collection of short stories and the portrait *Gilles Vigneault, mon ami,* published by *La Presse,* 1972.

Filmography

''Moi et l'autre'' series (1971-1974). Prod: Radio-Canada. 30 min. each. col.

Pile ou face (Heads or Tails) (1971). Prod: Cinepix/Les productions Nouvelle-France. 94 min. col.

30 cadres-secondes (1972). Prod: Radio-Canada. 45 min. col.

Miroir de Gilles Vigneault (1972). Prod: Radio-Canada. 90 min. col.

Bye Bye 74 (1974). Prod: Radio-Canada. 60 min. col.

Pas de problème (1974). Prod: Radio-Canada. 60 min. col.

Les aventures d'une jeune veuve (1974). Prod: Pierre David, Les productions mutuelles/Cinémas unis/Le groupe Sogecor/Bellevue-Pathé/Productions Dominique Michel. 94 min. col.

Bibliography

Séquences, no. 64 (February 1971), p. 40, review of **Pile ou face** by Léo Bonneville; *Québec-presse,* February 21, 1971, ''**Pile ou face**: une tarte à la crème au visage du spectateur'', Carol Faucher; *Montreal Gazette,* January 20, 1973, ''**Heads or Tails**: It's Not Just Skin Deep'', Dane Lanken; *Le Soleil,* December 12, 1974, ''Roger Fournier: le divertissement plutôt que la satire'', Claude Daigneault; *La Presse,* December 28, 1974, ''Le boulot de Dodo'', S.D.

FOX, BERYL

Born in Flin Flon, Manitoba in 1931, Beryl Fox studied history at the University of Toronto and joined the CBC in 1961, working on a number of public affairs series — "The Critical Years", "Document" and "This Hour Has Seven Days". Fox received the Wilderness Award given for the best television documentary and the Woman of the Year Award in 1966 for her coverage of the Viet Nam war, **Mills of the Gods: Viet Nam**; she and Douglas Leiterman received their first Wilderness Award for **One More River**. After the demise of "Seven Days", Fox worked with CBS and is a director/producer with Hobel-Leiterman Productions Ltd. in Toronto, co-producing "Here Come the Seventies (Towards the Year 2000)", as well as freelancing. In 1973 Fox produced 13 half-hour shows in the series "Walrus" for OECA. In the NFB's move to regionalize production, Fox was named, in 1976, Regional Production Manager for Ontario.

Filmography

Balance of Terror (1962). With Douglas Leiterman. Prod: D. Leiterman, Talent Associates/Paramount. 60 min.

Servant of All (1962). With D. Leiterman. Prod: D. Leiterman, CBC "Document". 60 min.

Three on a Match (1963). With D. Leiterman. Prod: D. Leiterman, CBC "Document".

The Single Woman and the Double Standard (1963). Prod: B. Fox, CBC.

The Chief (1963). With D. Leiterman. Prod: D. Leiterman, CBC "Document". 60 min.

One More River (1964). With D. Leiterman. Prod: D. Leiterman, CBC "Intertel". 50 min. b&w.

Summer in Mississippi (1964). Prod: B. Fox, CBC "Seven Days". 27 min. b&w.

The Honourable René Lévesque (1964). Prod: D. Leiterman, CBC.

Youth: In Search of Morality (1965). Prod: D. Leiterman, CBC "Seven Days".

Mills of the Gods: Viet Nam (1965). Prod: B. Fox, CBC "Seven Days". 56 min. b&w.

Last Reflections on a War (1968). Prod: B. Fox, CBS.

Be a Man — Sell Out (1969). Prod: CTV "The Fabulous Sixties".

The Family: Life Styles of the Future, **Generic Opening**, **The Economy** (1971). Prod: Philip Hobel, Hobel-Leiterman Productions for "Here Come The Seventies". 30 min. each. col.

The Human Potential Movement, **Race Relations**, **Cinema: The Living Camera** (1972). Prod: Philip Hobel, Hobel-Leiterman Productions for "Here Come the Seventies". 30 min. each. col.

North with the Spring (1972). Prod: B. Fox, CTV for Xerox International. 60 min. col.

Jerusalem, Habitat 2000 (1973). Prod: Hobel-Leiterman Productions for CTV. 30 min. each. col.

"Travel and Leisure" series (1973). Prod: Hobel-Leiterman Productions. 30 min. each. col.

Man into Superman (1974). Prod: Hobel-Leiterman Productions for CTV. 30 min. col.

Wild Refuge (1974). Prod: Hobel-Leiterman Productions 30 min. col.

Take My Hand (1975). Prod: Hobel-Leiterman Productions for Children's Aid Society of Metropolitan Toronto. 30 min. col.

How to Fight with Your Wife (1975). Prod: CBC. 30 min. on VTR.

The Visible Woman (1975). Prod: B. Fox, The Federation of Women Teachers' Association of Ontario. 31 min. col.

Bibliography

CBC Times, October 1964, an article by Fox on **Summer in Mississippi**; *Toronto Star,* May 22, 1965, "TV's Ash-blonde Paradox from Out of the West", Marilyn Dunlop; *Star Weekly,* February 12, 1966, "Front Line Filmmaker", Margaret Steen; *Maclean's,* February 1966, "One Woman's War", by Fox; *Star TV Week*, Toronto, March 9, 1967, pp. 12, 34-35, "Beryl Fox", H.R.W. Morrison; references in *L'aventure du cinéma direct*.

FRAPPIER, ROGER

Born in 1945 in St. Joseph de Sorel, Roger Frappier received a degree in political science and studied at the London School of Film Technique. He worked as a film critic for a number of Montreal newspapers and edited film for La société général cinématographique and Radio-Canada before directing his first film; **Le grand film ordinaire**, written by Raymond Cloutier, is a document of Quebec life interwoven with a theatrical circus fable. Frappier succeeded in fusing music and poetry in **L'infonie inachevée**, a feature documentary with stereo sound; starring Raoul Duguay and Walter Boudreau with an appearance by Karlheinz Stockhausen, the film traces the musical evolution of Duguay's group. In 1973 Frappier was an assistant to Robert Altman on **Nashville**, and in 1975 was first assistant director on Gilles Carle's **La tête de Normande St-Onge**. Two segments of Jacques Leduc's **Chronique de la vie quotidienne** were directed by Frappier. He is a founding member of the Association coopérative de productions audio-visuelles in Montreal.

Filmography

Le grand film ordinaire or **Jeanne d'Arc n'est pas morte, se porte bien et vit au Québec** (The Great Ordinary Film) (1970). Prod: Independent. 79 min. b&w and col. Dist: Faroun.
Gaston Miron (1971). Prod: Jean-Claude Labrecque, Les films Jean-Claude Labrecque for OFQ "Ecrivains québécois". 59 min. col.
Alain Grandbois (1971). Prod: Jean-Claude Labrecque, Les films Jean-Claude Labrecque for OFQ "Ecrivains québécois". 28 min. col.
L'infonie inachevée (1973). Prod: Marc Daigle, R. Frappier, ACPAV. 85 min. col. Dist: Faroun.
La Gravure (1973). Prod: Via le monde Inc. for Radio-Canada. 30 min. col.
Xenakis (1974). Prod: Cinéfactorie for OFQ. 28 min. col.

Bibliography

Québec-presse, February 7, 1971, "J'ai appris le cinéma en faisant **Le grand film ordinaire**", Carol Faucher (interview); *Cinema,* Paris, no. 176 (May 1973), pp. 70-75, "Ronde table", interview by G. Langlois on the state of Quebec cinema with Jean Chabot, Guy Bergeron and Frappier; *Cinéma-Québec,* vol. 3, no. 2 (October 1973), pp. 20-26, "Un film portrait", Jean-Pierre Tadros (interview); *Cinema Canada,* no. 9, pp. 28-31, "Roger Frappier: **L'infonie inachevée**", interview by Á. Ibrányi Kiss and George Köller; *La Tribune,* Sherbrooke, December 12, 1970, "Du cinéma en tant que produit de culture et non de culture et non de consommation"; *Le Devoir,* February 2, 1971, "**Jeanne d'Arc** prise entre fanfares et matraques", Jean-Pierre Tadros; *Cinéma-Quebec,* vol. 2, no. 8 (May-June 1973), pp. 17-20, Michel Euvrard on **Alain Grandois**; *La Presse,* September 8, 1973, "Frappier et l'Fonie . . . en Californie", Axel Madsen; *Le Jour,* March 23, 1974, "Un film-portrait de Raoul Duguay infoniaque", Jean-Pierre Tadros; *La Presse,* April 6, 1974, "Roger Frappier: la critique inachevée, Serge Dussault; *Cinéma-Québec,* vol. 3, no. 6-7, pp. 68-69, review by Jean Leduc; references in *Cinéma d'ici.*

FRUET, BILL

Bill Fruet was born in Lethbridge, Alberta in 1933. He attended the Canadian Theatre School in Toronto on a Dominion Drama Festival scholarship, acting in a number of NFB films including its first feature, **The Drylanders**, which also starred Don Francks and Francis Hyland. In this period he wrote small dramas for television and worked as a photographer, directing short sponsored medical teaching films. In 1960 Fruet went to California, studied briefly at the film school at UCLA and worked on industrial and teaching films. He returned to Canada in 1965 and worked as a film editor for Don Haig's Film Acts, editing the CBC specials **Cuba** and **Voyage of the Phoenix**, and segments of the series "Wojeck" and "The Fabulous Sixties". As a writer, Fruet has made an important contribution to Canadian cinema both in terms of style and subject matter; Don Shebib's **Goin' Down the Road** and **Rip-Off**, David Acomba's **Slipstream** and his own **Wedding in White** were all scripted by Fruet. Based on his play set in the prairies of the 1940s, **Wedding in White** won the 1972 Etrog for the best feature film.

Filmography

Wedding in White (1972). Prod: John Vidette, Dermet Productions. 103 min. col. Dist: Cinepix.

Italy (1974). Prod: B. Fruet, CTV "Heritage". 57 min. col.

Bring Whisky and a Smile (1974). Prod: Ross McLean, CBC "Of All People". 28 min. col.

Death Weekend (1976). Prod: Ivan Reitman for Cinepix. 90 min. col.

Bibliography

Cinema Canada, no. 8 (June-July 1973), pp. 58-60, interview with Donald Pleasance on **Wedding in White** and Potterton's **Rainbow Boys**; *Toronto Star*, January 29, 1972, "Customers are Knocking on Screenwriter's Door", Urjo Kareda; *Cinema Canada*, no. 3 (August 1972), pp. 42-47, 57, "Bill Fruet's **Wedding in White**"; *Toronto Star*, October 21, 1972, "**Wedding in White** Tugs Powerfully at the Emotions", Clyde Gilmour; *Globe and Mail*, October 21, 1972, "**Wedding in White**: A Measure of Sensitivity but No Sense of Life", Martin Knelman; *Montreal Star*, October 21, 1972, review by Martin Malina; *Le Devoir*, November 11, 1972, "**Wedding in White** meilleur film canadien", Robert-Guy Scully; *Québec-presse*, November 12, 1972, p. 26, "Se dire cinéaste canadien, c'est un peu se donner le baiser de la mort", Robert Lévesque; *La Presse*, November 18, 1972, "Du marriage en blanc à la Cosa Nostra", Luc Perreault; *Le Droit*, November 20, 1972, "Avec le réalisateur de **Wedding in White**, Bill Fruet", Murray Maltais; *Saturday Night*, November 1972, "Getting Drunk is One Way of Getting Along", Marshall Delaney; *Maclean's*, November 1972, "Through a Clear Glass Darkly", John Hofsess on **Wedding in White**; *Cinéma-Québec*, vol. 2, no. 4 (December-January 1972-73), pp. 41-42, review by Richard Gay; *Séquences*, no. 71 (January 1973), pp. 29-30, review by Robert-Claude Bérubé; *Vancouver Sun*, February 7, 1973, "Canadian Movie

Makers Slapped", Les Wedman; *New York Times*, April 30, 1973, "**Wedding in White** Views a 40s Family", Vincent Canby; *Take One,* vol. 3, no. 7, pp. 29-31, reviews of **Wedding in White** by John Hudecki and Jean-Pierre Tadros; *Inner Views: Ten Canadian Film-makers*, J. Hofsess (McGraw-Hill Ryerson, 1975), p. 117-127.

GAGNON, CHARLES

Painter and experimental filmmaker Charles Gagnon was born in Montreal in 1934. He designed the Christian Pavilion at Expo '67, as well as creating the film for that exhibition, **The Eighth Day**. As a painter, Gagnon has exhibited in Canada, the United States and Europe. He has recently been studying the interface between video and cinema. Gagnon lives in Montreal and teaches film and photography in the Fine Arts Department at the University of Ottawa.

Filmography

The Eighth Day (Le huitième jour) (1967). Prod: C. Gagnon for the Christian Pavilion, Expo '67. 13 min. b&w.
The Sound of Space (Le son d'un espace) (1968). Prod: Independent. 27 min. b&w. Silent.
Pierre Mercure 1927-1966 (1966-70). Prod: Independent. 33 min. col.
R-69 — Two Years Later (1972-76). Prod: Independent. 75 min. col.

All Gagnon's films are distributed by the Coopérative cinéastes indépendants and the Canadian Filmmakers' Distribution Centre.

Bibliography

La Presse, March 8, 1969, "Le tableau est aussi le monde", Normand Theriault on Gagnon's work as a painter; *Artscanada,* April 1970, pp. 39-42, "Charles Gagnon, Painter, Filmmaker, 35 Years Old, Lives in Montreal", Danielle Corbeil; *Montreal Star,* October 2, 1971, "Zooming In. . .to Reach Out", Denis O'Brien, on the Communication Arts Department at Loyola College.

GARCEAU, RAYMOND

Born near Trois-Rivières in 1919, Raymond Garceau joined the National Film Board in 1945 after studying agriculture at Laval University. His work there included a series of pre-Challenge for Change films made for ARDA (Aménagement rural et développement agricole); under the production of Garceau and André Belleau, the people of the lower St. Lawrence and the Gaspé were encouraged to express their problems and awareness of rural development. One of the classical poets of Canadian cinema, Garceau has produced many dramatic portraits in his investigation of life in a rural setting. His first feature, **Le grand rock**, expresses the loss of innocence in the face of urban values. With financial assistance from Canada Council, Garceau travelled to Czechoslovakia in 1968 to work with Jan Kadar.

Filmography (incomplete)

Le bedeau (1952). Prod: Bernard Devlin, NFB. 6 min. b&w.

L'abatis (The Settler) (1952). With Bernard Devlin. Prod: Guy Glover, NFB. 16 min. b&w.

Monsieur le maire (Mister Mayor) (1953). Prod: Roger Blais, NFB. 11 min. b&w.

Referendum (Tempest in Town) (1953). Prod: Bernard Devlin, NFB. 13 min. b&w.

La drave (River of Wood) (1956). Prod: David Bairstow, NFB. 29 min. b&w.

Ti-Jean s'en va dans l'ouest (Ti-Jean Goes West) (1957). Prod: Léonard Forest, NFB. 25 min. col.

Une ile du St. Laurent (Crane Island) (1958). Prod: Léonard Forest, NFB. 11 min. b&w.

Rivière-la-paix (1961). Prod: Léonard Forest, NFB. 29 min. b&w.

La chaudière (Wayward River) (1961). Prod: Léonard Forest, NFB. 28 min. b&w.

L'homme du lac (Alexis Ladouceur, métis) (The Lake Man) (1962). Prod: Victor Jobin, Bernard Devlin, NFB. 28 min. b&w.

La soif de l'or (The Gold Seekers) (1962). With Bernard Devlin. Prod: R. Garceau, Bernard Devlin, NFB. 28 min. b&w.

Les petits arpents (The Little Acres) (1963). Prod: Fernand Dansereau, Victor Jobin, NFB. 24 min. b&w.

Une année à Vaucluse (1964) Prod: R. Garceau, NFB, "Temps présent". 28 min. b&w.

Travailleur forestier (1965). Prod: André Belleau, NFB, "ARDA No. 16". 22 min. b&w.

Diableries d'un sourcier (The Water Devil) (1966). Prod: Guy L. Côté, NFB. 21 min. col.

Le grand rock (1967). Prod: Guy L. Côté, NFB. 73 min. col.

Vive la France (1969). Prod: Laurence Paré, NFB. 80 min. b&w.

Et du fils (In the Name of the Son) (1971). Prod: Paul Gauvreau, NFB. 90 min. col.

Guérissez-nous du mal (1972). Prod: Paul Larose, NFB. 27 min. col.

Pris au collet (1974). With Pierre Magny. Prod: Paul Larose, NFB, "Toulemonde parle français". 38 min. col.

Les petits inventeurs (1975). Prod: Paul Larose, NFB. 60 min. col.

Work in progress: **Les petits inventeurs II**. 8 min. col.

Bibliography

Soirée Raymond Garceau (La cinémathèque canadienne, January 1966), a pamphlet including a filmography, interview and criticism, available at film study libraries; *La Presse,* March 1, 1969, p. 29, "Un film qui accroche le gros public", Luc Perreault (interview); *Séquences,* April 1969, pp. 44-45, (interview); *La Patrie,* Montreal, October 5, 1969, (interview); *Objectif* published "Les carnets d'un p'tit Garceau", a series by Garceau, in the following issues: no. 1 (May-June 1966), no. 2 (August 1966), no. 3 (November-December 1966), no. 4 (May 1967), and no. 5 (August-September 1967); *Objectif,* November-December 1966, pp. 36-38, "Bandes a part"; *La Presse,* August 8, 1967, "**Le grand rock**: un film de Raymond Garceau sur la déchéace d'une génération sacrif", Luc Perreault; press clippings collected by the NFB on **Le grand rock**, March 28, 1969, available only at film study libraries; *Cinéma-Québec,* vol. 2, no. 1 (September 1972), pp. 10-11, Garceau tells the background of **Et du fils**; *La Presse,* September 22, 1972, "Le dur pays où les manoirs brûlent", Luc Perreault; *Québec-presse,* September 24, 1972, "L'Ile aux Grues au printemps", Robert Lévesque; *Montreal Gazette,* September 26, 1972, "**Et du fils**, a Sparse Tragedy", Jack Kapica; *Le Devoir,* September 26, 1972, "Voir deux beaux films...d'endehors de la ville", Robert-Guy Scully; *Séquences,* no. 70 (October 1972), pp. 25-26, review of **Et du fils** by Jean-René Ethier; *Cinéma-Québec,* vol. 2, no. 6/7 (March-April 1973), pp. 57-58, review of **Guérissez- nous du mal** by Pierre Demers; short reviews in: *Jeune cinéma canadien, Essais sur le cinéma québécois, Le cinéma québécois: tendances et prolongements, Vingt ans de cinéma au Canada français, Le cinéma canadien, Cinéma d'ici,* and *L'aventure du cinéma direct.*

GENTLEMAN, WALLY

Born in Middlesex, England in 1926, Wally Gentleman received his engineer's technician degree before joining Technicolor Ltd. as an assistant cameraman in 1942. He left Technicolor two years later and joined the British Army. Gentleman continued his career as cameraman and special effects man with J. Arthur Rank (now Pinewood Studio) and the MGM company in England. He became a director of special effects for National Film Board in 1957. In his eight years with NFB, Gentleman designed special effects for the Board's most popular film, Colin Low's **Universe**. From his work in space effects at NFB, Gentleman went on to design effects for Kubrick's **2001: A Space Odyssey**. **Labyrinth**, NFB's Expo '67 film, also had special effects designed by Gentleman. In 1965 he founded SPEAC (Special Photographic Effects and Allied Crafts Ltd.). He now has his own group of students and lectures on

special effects in various universities and schools, including
McGill and York University. Although based in Montreal, Gentleman travels around the world to work on various films. He has
served on committees with the Canadian Society of Cinematographers, Directors' Guild of Canada and the CFDC. He is past
president of the Canadian Society of Filmmakers.

Bibliography

Take One, vol. 1, no. 2, "Inside **2001**" (interview); *Globe and
Mail,* January 24, 1970, "Why a Cinematic Master Came to
Canada", Kaspars Dzeguze; *Montreal Gazette,* December 12,
1970, "The Man Who Made **2001** Fly Has a Little Shop in a Mon-
treal Suburb . . .and He's Very Outspoken About Canadian Film",
Dane Lanken; *Pot pourri,* July 1972, an entire issue dedicated to
special effects with articles by Gentleman, Colin Low, Pierre
L'Amare and Sidney Goldsmith; *Special Effects* by Wally
Gentleman, an illustrated paper surveying special effects opera-
tions and covering a few basic principles, 16 pp., available from
Pot pourri; Cinema Canada, no. 19, pp. 24-26, "Notes on an
Italian Venture", W. Gentleman.

GODBOUT, JACQUES

Jacques Godbout has distinguished himself as a man of letters. As
well as publishing numerous collections of poetry and several
novels, Godbout founded and edited the literary review, *Liberté.*
After studying at the University of Montreal, Godbout taught in
Ethiopia. In 1958 he joined the National Film Board as a scriptwriter, later becoming a director and in 1970, director of French
production. His acclaimed musical-comedy, **IXE-13**, tells of the
exploits of the Canadian espionage agent IXE-13, popularized in
serial novels by Pierre Saurel published during the 1950s;
François Dompierre and Godbout collaborated on the music and
lyrics. Dompierre also composed the music for **La gammick**, Godbout's fourth feature, which is about a petty underground figure
and his link in the crime chain. **La gammick** was scripted by
Pierre Turgeon, with camera by Jean-Pierre Lachapelle.

Filmography

Les dieux (1961). With Georges Dufaux. Prod: Fernand
  Dansereau, Victor Jobin, NFB. 28 min. b&w.
Pour quelques arpents de neige (Strangers for a Day) (1962).
  With Georges Dufaux. Prod: Fernand Dansereau, NFB. 28 min.
  b&w.
A Saint Henri, le 5 septembre (September Five at Saint Henri)
  (1962). Prod: Fernand Dansereau, NFB. 42 min. b&w.

Rose et Landry (1963). With Jean Rouch. Prod: Fernand Dansereau, NFB. 28 min. b&w.

Paul Emile Borduas (1963). Prod: Fernand Dansereau, NFB. 21 min. col.

Le monde va nous prendre pour des sauvages (People Might Laugh at Us) (1964). With Françoise Bujold. Prod: André Belleau, NFB. 9 min. col.

Fabienne sans son Jules (Fabienne) (1964). Prod: Jacques Bobet, NFB. 27 min. b&w.

Huit témoins (1965). Prod: André Belleau, NFB. 58 min. b&w.

YUL 871 (1966). Prod: André Belleau, NFB. 71 min. b&w.

Vivre sa ville (Vivre sa ville) (1967). Prod: André Belleau, NFB, for Central Housing and Mortgage Corporation. 17 min. col.

Kid Sentiment (1968). Prod: Clément Perron, NFB. 88 min. b&w.

Les vrais cousins (1970). Prod: Paul Larose, ORTF and NFB. 53 min. b&w.

IXE-13 (1971). Prod: Pierre Gauvreau, NFB. 113 min. col.

La gammick (1974). Prod: Marc Beaudet, NFB. 86 min. col.

Les "troubbes" de Johnny (1974). Prod: Marc Beaudet, NFB "Toulmonde parle français". 21 min. col.

Aimez-vous les chiens (1975). Prod: Paul Larose, NFB. 57 min. col.

Bibliography

Parti-pris, no. 7 (April 1964), an interview on the series, "Temps présent"; *Objectif,* no. 38 (May 1967), pp. 35-42, interview with Godbout on **YUL 871**; *Séquences,* no. 52 (February 1968), pp. 22-23, "Le récit cinématographique: dialogue avec Jacques Godbout" (interview); *Le Devoir,* June 1, 1968, an interview on **Kid Sentiment**; *Cinéastes du Québec No. 9: Jacques Godbout,* (C-QDC, 1972), interviews, criticism and complete filmography; *Cinema Canada* no. 7 (April-May 1973), pp. 36-39, "Jacques Godbout: **IXE-13**", George Köller (interview); *Séquences,* no. 78 (October 1974), pp. 4-6, interview by Léo Bonneville; *Cinéma-Québec,* vol. 4, no. 1 (December 1974), pp. 33-36, "Jacques Godbout **La gammick**, ou comment les gangsters québécois sont aussi victimes de l'impérialisme américain", Richard Gay (interview); *Liberté,* vol. 8, no. 2-3 (March-June 1966), article by Godbout; *Montreal Star,* August 1, 1966, p. 26 "City Film Snags Explained" (on **YUL 871**); *Objectif,* May 1967, pp. 35-42, on the production of **YUL 871**; *La Presse,* March 24, 1968 "Godbout nous dit comment est né son film **Kid Sentiment**"; *La Presse,* March 30, 1968, "Les jeunes évoluent-ils vers la confusion des sexes?"; *La Presse,* March 30, 1968, "Un film vrai sur la jeunesse d'aujourd'hui"; *Le Soleil,* September 7, 1968, "Jacques Godbout: Il est impensable d'établir une industrie du cinéma dans le schème capitaliste du Québec actuel", Claude Daigneault; *Canadian*

Literature, no. 46 (Autumn 1970), pp. 84-89, "Le temps: la poésie du cinéma", by Jacques Godbout in symposium entitled "Write Me a Film?"; *Québec-presse,* July 4, 1971, "**IXE-13** arrivera-t-il a temps?"; *Le Devoir,* July 29, 1971, "Le retour d'**IXE-3**, l'as des espions canadiens", Jean-Pierre Tadros; *Le Devoir,* January 22, 1972, "Les aventures de l'agent **IXE-13** à l'écran: le retour des petites obsessions d'antan", Jean-Pierre Tadros; *Le Devoir,* January 29, 1972, "**IXE-13** à l'écran: une féérie de couleurs et de notes", Jean-Pierre Tadros; *La Presse,* February 12, 1972, p. C-9, "Ces mythes qui nous ont faits", Luc Perreault (on **IXE-13**); *Montreal Gazette,* February 19, 1972, "Move Over James Bond, **IXE-13** est arrivé", Dane Lanken; *Séquences,* no. 69 (April 1972), pp. 39-40, review of **IXE-13** by Robert-Claude Bérubé; *Performing Arts,* vol. 10, no. 2 (Summer 1973), p. 32, "En français: cinéma from Québec", Ben Shek (discussion of **IXE-13**); *Le Devoir,* February 14, 1974, "André Major souligne l'exemplaire liberté de Jacques Godbout", Jacques Thériault; *Séquences,* no. 78 (October 1974), pp. 29-30, review of **La gammick** by Janick Beaulieu; *Le Jour,* March 1, 1975, "Une petite pègre à notre image", Jean-Pierre Tadros on **La gammick**; *Le Devoir,* March 1, 1975, "**La gammick**; un brillant film québécois", André Leroux; *Cinéma-Québec,* vol. 4, no. 5, pp. 36-37, review of **Aimez-vous les chiens** by Pierre Demers; *How to Make or Not to Make a Canadian Film,* (La cinémathèque canadienne, 1967), "A Trap: the Script", by Godbout; *Essais sur le cinéma québécois,* review of **Kid Sentiment**; references in: *Le cinéma québécois: tendances et prolongements, Le cinéma canadien, Vingt ans de cinéma au Canada français, Jeune cinéma canadien, Cinéma d'ici* and *L'aventure du cinéma direct;* fifteen songs from **IXE-13** have been recorded by Louise Fmrestier and Les cyniques (Gamma Records, GS-148).

GOSSELIN, BERNARD

Born in Drummondville, Quebec in 1934, Bernard Gosselin studied printing at Ecole des arts graphique and worked as a printer before joining the title department at the National Film Board in 1956. Gosselin worked as an assistant editor, location manager and assistant cameraman; he assisted Brault in shooting **Pour la suite du monde** and Labrecque in his **60 Cycles**. Perrault's **Un pays sans bon sens, Le règne du jour** and **Les voitures d'eau**, Godbout's **Huit témoins**, Brault's **Entre la mer et l'eau douce**, Lamothe's **Les bûcherons de la Manouane** and Groulx's **Voir Miami** were all shot by Gosselin. His more recent camera work includes **Claude Gauvreau, poète, Sous le vent** and a series of films about the James Bay Crees, directed by Pierre Perrault.

Gosselin's feature, **Le Martien de Noël**, is a Christmas story for children.

Filmography

Le jeu de l'hiver (The Joy of Winter) (1962). With Jean Dansereau. Prod: Tom Daly, NFB. 15 min. b&w.

Le beau plaisir (Beluga Days) (1968). With Pierre Perrault. Prod: Jacques Bobet, Guy L. Côté, NFB. 15 min. col.

Capture (Capture) (1969). Prod: Marc Beaudet, NFB. 17 min. col.

Passage au nord-ouest (1970). Prod: François Séguillon, NFB. 27 min. col.

Odyssée du Manhattan (Manhattan Odyssey) (1970). Prod: François Séguillon, NFB. 8 min. col.

Le Martien de Noël (The Christmas Martian) (1971). Prod: Faroun/Les cinéastes associés inc. 66 min. col.

César et son canot d'écorce (Cesar's Bark Canoe) (1972). Prod: Paul Larose, NFB. 50 min. col.

Les raquettes des Atcikameg (1974). Prod: Paul Larose, NFB. 33 min. col.

Jean Carignan, violoneux (1975). Prod: Paul Larose, Louise Carré, NFB. 88 min. col.

Work in progress: **La veillée, les veillées**.

Bibliography

La Presse, March 14, 1970, and October 7, 1971, "Bernard Gosselin estime que les films pour enfants sont malhonnêtes" (interviews); *Le Soleil*, Quebec, August 6, 1971, "**Le Martien de Noël**: cinéma", Paul Roux; *La Presse*, August 7 1971, p. B-4, "Un rêve de jeunesse réalisé", Luc Perreault; *Le Devoir*, August 7, 1971, "Le premier film québécois pour toute la famille", Jean-Pierre Tadros; *Le Jour*, June 21, 1975, "Aux fêtes nationales, un film de Bernard Gosselin **Jean Carignan, violoneux**"; *La Presse*, August 21, 1975, "L'ignorance crasse du monde me chicote"; *Cinéma-Québec*, vol. 3, no. 1, pp. 47-48, review of **César et son canot d'écorce** by Pierre Demers; references in *Le cinéma québécois: tendances et prolongements, Cinéma d'ici* and *L'aventure du cinéma direct*.

GROULX, GILLES

Born in Montreal in 1931, Gilles Groulx started his cinematic career as a newsreel editor and director for Radio-Canada before joining the National Film Board in 1956 to work with Michel Brault, Marcel Carrière, Claude Fournier and Louis Portugais; his first film, **Les raquetteurs**, was co-directed with Michel Brault. Wolf

Koening and Roman Kroitor of the Candid Eye Unit introduced **Les raquetteurs** to Mrs. Robert Flaherty during her search for material for the 1958 Flaherty Seminar. The critical recognition awarded to the film as a result of the Seminar marked the beginning of the French Unit at the National Film Board. Groulx's first feature, **Le chat dans le sac**, reflected and gave coherence to Quebec's political and cultural awakening. Today that film stands as a watershed in Quebec cinema. Groulx's fourth feature, **24 heures ou plus**, was denied release by the NFB.

Filmography

Les raquetteurs (1958). With Michel Brault. Prod: Louis Portugais NFB. 28 min. b&w.

Normetal (1959). Prod: Louis Portugais, NFB. 17 min. b&w. Unsigned.

La France sur un caillou (1960). With Claude Fournier. Prod: Jacques Bobet, NFB. 28 min. b&w.

Golden Gloves (1961). Prod: Fernand Dansereu, Victor Jobin, NFB. 28 min. b&w.

Voir Miami (1962). Prod: Fernand Dansereau, NFB. 28 min. b&w.

Un jeu si simple (1963). Prod: Jacques Bobet, NFB. 30 min. col. and b&w.

Le chat dans le sac (The Cat in the Bag) (1964). Prod: Jacques Bobet, NFB. 80 min. b&w.

Québec...? (1966). With Michel Brault. Prod: Les Cinéastes associés inc. for Office du film du Québec 30 min.

Où êtes-vous donc? (1969). Prod: Guy L. Côté, NFB. 95 min. col.

Entre tu et vous (1969). Prod: Jean-Pierre Lefebvre, NFB. 65 min. b&w.

24 heures ou plus (1973). Prod: Paul Larose, NFB. 115 min. col. Not released.

Place de l'équation (1973). Prod: Les films Jean-Claude Labrecque inc. for OFQ. 35 min. b&w.

Bibliography

Montreal Star, November 22, 1969, "Gilles Groulx — an interview with M. Paskal"; *Cinéastes du Québec 1:* Gilles Groulx, (CQDC, 1969), includes criticism, an interview, a filmography, bibliography, and an article by Robert Daudelin (translated into English in *Second Wave,* edited by Robin Woods, pp. 120-123, Praeger, N.Y., 1970); *Le Devoir,* December 16, 1972, "L'affaire Gilles roulx: 's'impliquer: le droit du creatéur'", Jean-Pierre Tadros (interview); *Cinéma-Québec,* vol. 2, no. 5 (January- February 1973), pp. 35-36, "Gilles Groulx et l'affaire **24 heures ou plus**", Jean-Pierre Tadros and Luc Perreault (interview); *Motion,* May-

June 1974, p. 17, interview with Groulx by Peter Evanchuk;
Cahiers du cinéma in English, no. 4, "10 Questions to 5 Canadian
Filmmakers" (interview); *Dossiers de cinéma: 1,* (Editions fides
1968), review of **Un jeu si simple**; *Eléments pour un nouveau
cinéma,* Louis Marcorelles, (Paris: UNESCO, 1970); *Gilles
Cinéma Groulx: le lynx inquiet,* edited by Patrick Straram and
Jean-Marc Piotte (Cinémathèque québécoise/Editions
québécoises, 1971, available from Diffusion-Québec, 3611 St.
Denis, Montreal, Cinémathèque québécoise, 360 McGill Street,
Montreal); *Presqu'Amérique,* vol. 1, no. 5 (March 1972), p. 32,
"Aspects marxistes dans l'oeuvre de Groulx", Jean-Marc Piotte;
Québec-presse, September 30, 1973, p. 29, "L'affaire **24 heures
ou plus**: l'ONF refuse de vendre son film à Gilles Groulx", Robert
Lévesque, with letter by Groulx; several reviews in: *Le cinéma
québécois: tendances et prolongements, Vingt ans de cinéma au
Canada français, Essais sur le cinéma québécois, Jeune cinéma
canadien, Cinéma d'ici* and *L'aventure du cinéma direct.*

HALDANE, DONALD

Born in Edmonton, Alberta in 1914, Don Haldane studied drama at
Yale University and later directed in theatres in the United States
and western Canada. He became involved in industrial filmmaking
before joining the NFB as a freelance director in 1954 to work on
the television series "Perspective". Subsequently, Haldane
directed shows for a number of television series — including
"Forest Ranger" and "RCMP" — which produced highly trained
film crews. The first English feature produced by the NFB, **The
Drylanders**, was directed by Haldane, with a script by M. Charles
Cohen that dramatized prairie settlement. In 1961, Haldane formed Westminster Films in Toronto with Lee Gordon; with staff
editor Arthur Campus and creative designer Keith Harley, they
concentrate most of their efforts in producing industrial documentaries. Haldane also freelances as a director. He has worked on a
number of series for CBC and CTV, including CTV's "Swiss Family
Robinson".

Filmography (incomplete)

Who is Sylvia?, Saskatchewan Traveller (1956). Prod: Julian
  Biggs, NFB "Perspective". 30 min. each. b&w.
Crossroads, Joe and Roxy, Howard, Embassy (1957). Prod:
  Julian Biggs, NFB "Perspective". 30 min. each. b&w.
The Gifted Ones (1959). Prod: David Bairstow, NFB. 30 min.
  b&w.
Mystery in the Kitchen (1959). Prod: Guy Glover, NFB. 23 min.
  col.
Eternal Children (1960). Prod: David Bairstow. 30 min. b&w.

Nikki, Wild Dog of the North (1961). With Jack Couffer. Prod:
Lee Gordon, Disney Productions. 100 min. col. Dist: Bellevue.
Fires of Envy or **Political Dynamite** (1962). Prod: Donald
Ginsberg, NFB. 26 min. b&w.
The Drylanders (Un autre pays) (1963). Prod: Peter Jones, NFB.
70 min. b&w.
"Forest Ranger" (13 of the series) (1965). Prod: Maxine Samuels,
CBC. 30 min. each.
Rye on the Rocks (1969). Prod: Westminster Films for Interna-
tional Nickel. 14 min. col.
The Reincarnate (1971). Prod: Nat Taylor, Meridian Films. 101
min. col. Dist: International Film Distributors.
Checkpoint (1972). Prod: D. Haldane, Westminster Films for the
Canadian Cancer Society. 14 min. col.
The Winning of Nickel (1973). Prod: Westminster Films for Inter-
national Nickel. 33 min. col.
Beyond All Reasonable Doubt (1974). Prod: Richard Gilbert,
CBC "The Collborators". 60 min. col.
Rape, The Rebellion of Bertha MacKenzie (1975). Prod: Brian
Walker, CBC "Sidestreets". 60 min. each. col.

Bibliography

Canadian Cinematography, May-June 1962, pp. 3-4, "Special Ef-
fects Ease Problems on **Drylanders**", John Gunn; *Star Weekly,*
August 31, 1963, pp. 2-4, 6-7, **Drylanders**: Wide Screen Saga of
the West", Bill Stephenson; *Toronto Telegram,* October 5, 1963,
"A Drama of the Canadian West", Clyde Gilmour; *Toronto*
- *Telegram,* January 14, 1964, "Honest Dust-bowl Drama", Clyde
Gilmour; *La Presse,* Montreal, May 9, 1964, p. 17, "**Un Autre
Pays**: les aléas du blé gras et ingrat", Alain Pontaut; *Canadian
Film Digest,* April 1971, pp. 36-38, review of **The Reincarnate**.

HAMMOND, ARTHUR

Born in London, England in 1930, Arthur Hammond received his
Honours B.A. in English Literature from the University of London.
He arrived in Canada in 1955, and for three years he was editor of
Quill & Quire, the Canadian publishing industry's trade magazine.
Hammond was also writing children's books and freelancing for
CBC radio and television in Toronto. In 1964 he joined the National Film Board as a writer-researcher and worked on such films
as **Memorandum, Never a Backward Step** and **The New World
of Leisure**, a multi-screen presentation for the CNE in 1965. After
directing the "Corporation" series, a six-part study of business using Steinberg's supermarket as a model, Arthur Hammond was appointed to a two year term as Director of Programming for
English production at the NFB.

Filmography

Never a Backward Step (La presse et son empire) (1967). With
 Donald Brittain and John Spotton. Prod: Guy Glover, NFB. 57
 min. b&w.
The Choice (1967). Prod: Nick Balla, NFB for the Department of
 Citizenship and Immigration. 20 min. col.
This Land (1968). Prod: Cecily Burwash, NFB. 57 min. b&w.
"Corporation" series (1973): **Bilingualism**, **Growth**, **Interna-
 tional Operations**, **The Market**, **Motivation**, **Real Estate**.
 Prod: A. Hammond, NFB. 29 min. each. b&w.
After Mr. Sam (1974). Prod: A. Hammond, NFB "Corporation".
 78 min. b&w.

Bibliography

Financial Post, November 24, 1973, "Cinéma Vérité at the Check-
out Counter", Raoul Engel; *Montreal Star,* December 11, 1973,
"The Film That Everyone Wants to See", Michael Shelton; *Pot
pourri,* December 1973, issue dedicated to the "Corporation"
series; *Time,* January 14, 1974, "True to Sam", Geoffrey James;
Globe and Mail, January 21, 1974, "Steinberg's Supermarkets the
Star of NFB's 6-part Study", Betty Lee; *Screen,* vol. 7, no. 2,
"The Corporation Series" and "Living in a Corporate World",
Terry Ryan.

HART, HARVEY

Born in Toronto in 1928, Harvey Hart, with Norman Jewison,
Sydney Newman, Arthur Hiller, Paul Almond and Robert Allen,
formed one of the first production units of the CBC. After appren-
ticing in New York, Hart directed and produced drama for CBC's
"Festival" series, including **The Luck of Ginger Coffey**, **The
Quare Fellow**, and **The Wild Duck**, as well as live drama. While
working in the United States from 1963 to 1971, he directed
episodes for several television series, including "Mannix" and
"Alfred Hitchcock Presents", and worked on such features as
Bus Riley's Back in Town, **The Dark Intruder** and **The Sweet
Ride**. Hart returned to Canada to direct John Herbert's drama of
prison life, **Fortune and Men's Eyes**, and **The Pyx**, an adaptation
of the novel by Montrealer John Buell, with Maxime Samuel as executive producer.

Recent Filmography

Fortune and Men's Eyes (Aux yeux des hommes) (1971). Prod:
 Lester Persky, Lewis Allen, Donald Ginsberg, MGM/Cinemex.
 100 min. col. Dist: Bellevue.

Mahoney's Estate (1972). Prod: Alexis Kanner, Topaz Productions. 105 min. col.

The Pyx (1973). Prod: Julian Roffman, Host Productions Quebec Ltd. 107 min. col. Dist: Cinepix.

Bibliography

Montreal Star, February 13, 1971, "The Wheel of Fortune", Martin Malina, (interview); *Cinema Canada,* no. 10/11, pp. 56-59, "Harvey Hart's Back in Town" (interview with Kiss/Köller); *Toronto Star,* February 28, 1959, "An Open Letter to Nathan Cohen from Harvey Hart"; *Globe and Mail,* February 3, 1965, "Hart Leaves CBC", Frank Morriss; *Globe and Mail,* January 9, 1971, "Hebert's Fortune in Quebec Jail", Martin Knelman; *Montreal Gazette,* February 6, 1971, "A Fortune for an Apostle", Dane Lanken; *Québec-presse,* Montreal, October 17, 1971, "**Fortune and Men's Eyes**: un film à la Hollywood..."; *Séquences,* no. 67, December 1971, pp. 34-35, review by Patrick Schupp; *Cinéma-Québec,* vol. 1, no. 5, 1971, p. 30, review of **Fortune and Men's Eyes** by Richard Gay; *Image et son,* Paris, no. 262, June-July 1972, pp. 89-90, "Des prisons et des hommes", Danielle Sauvaget; *Montreal Star,* September 18, 1972, "Take Your **Pyx**", Charles Lazarus; *Montreal Gazette,* September 29, 1973, "Harvey Hart Wants Good Movies, Not Just 'Canadian' Movies", Jay Newquist; *Globe and Mail,* October 5, 1973, "**The Pyx** Avoids the Well-worn Track", Betty Lee; *Le Devoir,* October 10, 1973, "Quand Satan se fait diablotin", Jean-Pierre Tadros; *Le Soleil,* November 17, 1973, p. 41, "Le cinéma canadien-anglais clopine encore", Claude Daigneault; *Séquences,* no. 75, January 1974, pp. 25-27, review of **The Pyx**; *Cinema Canada,* no. 10/11, p. 71, review of **The Pyx**.

HEROUX, DENIS

Born in Montreal in 1940, Denis Héroux studied history at the University of Montreal where he directed his first film with Denys Arcand and Stephane Venne; **Seul ou avec d'autres** was the first feature film to be made on the university circuit. (Larry Kent's **Bitter Ash** and David Secter's **Winter Kept Us Warm** soon followed.) Formerly a writer and director for Radio-Canada, Héroux has since directed a number of popular features, including **Sept fois par jour**, an Israeli-Canadian co-production written by Ted Allan, who also worked on Jan Kadar's **Lies My Father Told Me**. At Expo '67, Héroux conceived the audio-visual material for the Quebec and the agricultural pavilions. He has taught history and written two books, a history manual and a study of the unionized worker in Quebec. The musical feature on Jacques Brel was shot by cameraman René Verzier.

Filmography

Seul ou avec d'autres (1962). With Denys Arcand and Stephane Venne. Prod: Denis Héroux, Association générale des étudiants de l'Université de Montréal. 65 min. b&w.

Jusqu'au cou (1964). Prod: AGEUM. 90 min. b&w.

Pas de vacances pour les idoles (1965). Prod: Claude Héroux, Onyx Films/Latino Films Ltd. 80 min. b&w. Dist: France Film.

Mais où sont les Anglais d'antan? (1967). Prod: Radio-Canada. 30 min. b&w.

Cent ans déjà (1967). Prod: Radio-Canada. 30 min. b&w.

Une ville à vivre (1967). Prod: Radio-Canada. 60 min. b&w.

Valérie (1968). Prod: André Link, John Dunning, Cinepix Inc. 95 min. b&w.

L'initiation (The Initiation) (1969). Prod: John Dunning, André Link, Cinepix Inc. 91 min. col.

L'amour humain (The Awakening) (1970). Prod: John Dunning, André Link, Claude Héroux, Cinepix Inc./Les productions Héroux. 90 min. col.

Sept fois par jour (Seven Times a Day) (1971). Prod: John Kemeny, Claude Héroux, Les productions Héroux/Minotaur Film Productions/France Film/Steiner Films. 98 min. col.

La fille du roi, **Les Acadiens** (1971). Prod: Onyx Films for the series "La feuille d'érable", co-produced by Radio-Canada and the national television networks of France, Belgium, Switzerland and Germany. Both 60 min. col.

Un enfant comme les autres (A Child Like Any Other) (1972). Prod: John Kemeny, Cinévidéo/Bellevue-Pathé/Famous Players. 88 min. col.

Quelques arpents de neige (The Rebels) (1972). Prod: Claude Héroux, Cinévidéo. 94 min. col.

J'ai mon voyage (Inof iz inof) (1973). Prod: Pierre David, Claude Héroux, Cinévidéo/Kangourou films. 89 min. col.

Y a toujours moyen de moyenner (1973). Prod: Claude Héroux, Cinévidéo/Les films du nouveau monde. 92 min. col.

Jacques Brel is Alive and Well and Living in Paris (1974). Prod: Claude Héroux, Cinévidéo/Paul Marshall /Libellule. 97 min. col.

Pousse mais pousse égal (1974). Prod: Claude Héroux, Cinévidéo. 93 min. col.

La vallée-jardin (1974). With Justine Bouchard. Prod: Jacques Parent, Cinévidéo for Ministère du tourisme. 12 min. col.

Born for Hell (Né pour l'enfer) (1975). Prod: Pierre David/Claude Héroux, Cinévidéo/Les productions mutuelles/Cinerama Tit/Filmel France.

The Strikebreaker (1975). Prod: Brian Walker, CBC "Sidestreet". 60 min. col.

Feature work in progress: **The Outcry**. Prod: Claude Héroux, Cinévidéo. Written by Pierre Lesou.

Bibliography

Objectif, no. 36, August 1966, "Les 101 questions sur le cinéma canadien" (interview); *La Presse*, May 3, 1969, "Denis Héroux: jouer le jeu de la mythologie", Luc Perreault (interview); *La Presse*, January 31, 1970, "L'indépendance pour quoi faire?", Luc Perreault (interview); *Actualité*, November 1970, "Denis Héroux et le déculottage des défroqués", Jean-Louis Morgan (interview); *Cinéma-Québec*, vol. 2, no. 4 (December-January 1972-1973), pp. 23-26, "Denis Héroux à la recherche de cadres nouveaux", Jean-Pierre Tadros (interview); *Séquences*, no. 71 (January 1973), pp. 4-10, interview with Léo Bonneville; *La Presse*, February 24, 1973, "Le nouveau Denis Héroux", Luc Perreault (interview); *Le Droit*, February 24, 1973, "Denis Heroux nous parle de lui de ses **Quelques arpents de neige**", Murray Maltais (interview); *Rélations*, no. 342 (October 1969), p. 281, "**Valérie**, film antiquébécois", Yves Lever; *La Presse*, January 31, 1970, p. 35, "L'ambition de Cinepix", Luc Perreault; *Le Devoir*, October 16, 1970, p. 10, "Comment atteindre tous les publics...et ne rien dire", Jean-Pierre Tadros; *Montreal Gazette*, October 17, 1970, p. 43, "Denis Héroux Plans His Films to Generate Family Discussion"; *Le Devoir*, October 16, 1972, "**Quelque arpents**...de moins", Robert Guy Scully; *Journal de Montréal*, December 30, 1972, "D'une rare beauté...", Claude Jasmin; *Séquences*, no. 71 (January 1973), pp. 28-29, review of **Quelques arpents de neiges** by Patrick Schupp; *Montreal Star*, January 3, 1973, "Héroux Film Naive in its Anti-English Bias", Martin Malina; *La Tribune*, January 30, 1973, "**Quelques arpents de neige**...un film où les héros ne sont que les figuronts", René Berthiaume; *Cinéma-Québec*, vol. 2, no. 5 (January-February 1973), pp. 38-40, review of **Quelques arpents de neiges** by Jean Leduc; *La Presse*, February 24, 1973, "De bon goût et pas trop mauvaise au goût", Luc Perreault on **J'ai mon voyage**; *Montreal Star*, February 27, 1973, "Bad Ethnic Jokes Flaw Farce", Martin Malina; *Québec-presse*, March 4, 1973, "**J'ai mon voyage**: du nationalisme à l'eau de rose", Robert Lévesque; *Séquences*, no. 72 (April 1973), pp. 27-28, review by Jean-René Ethier; *Le Devoir*, October 1, 1973, "Le dernier Héroux est-il décevent...ou déprimant?", Robert Guy Scully; *Séquences*, no. 74 (October 1973), p. 30, review of **Moyen** by Robert-Claude Bérubé; *Motion*, January-February 1974, pp. 24-25, "The Sense of Comedy", Alexander Hausvater; *Variety*, January 29, 1975, review of **Jacques Brel**; *Le Soleil*, February 8, 1975, "Denis Héroux: le Patof du cinéma québécois", Claude Daigneault; *La Presse*, February 15, 1975, "Du cinéma à la va comme je te pousse"; *Montreal Star*, February 15, 1975, "Alive, Well and Prospering," Nettie Harris; *Montreal Star*, February 22, 1975, "Alive But Not Well", Myron Galloway; *Le Jour*, February 24, 1975, "Quand Denis Héroux se mesure à **Brel**", Jean-Pierre Tadros; *New York Times*, February

25, 1975, "American Film Theater's **Jacques Brel is Alive**...",
Vincent Canby.

HOWE, JOHN

Born in Toronto in 1926, John Howe became involved in theatre
while attending the University of Toronto. As an actor and director, his theatre work took him to the Juniper Theatre, the New
Play Society in Toronto and the Canadian Repertory Theatre in Ottawa. Joining the CBC in Ottawa in 1954, he produced "Exploring
Minds" and "Press Conference", CBOT's first network contributions. Moving to the NFB in 1955, Howe worked as a director and
producer of, among others, **The Hundredth Summer**, **Where
Mrs. Whalley Lives** and **Labour College**; in 1964-65 he directed
a number of pilots and episodes for American television. Howe
wrote both the music and lyrics for his "Filmglish" musical, **A
Star is Lost**. He has served as president of the Society of Filmmakers and of the Syndicat général du cinéma et de la télévision.

Filmography

"Artic Essay" series (1956): **North of 60**, **Invasion from the
   South**, **Our Northern Neighbour**. Prod: Grant McLean, NFB.
   b&w.
The Sceptre and the Mace (Le sceptre et la masse) (1957).
   Prod: Nick Balla, NFB. 29 min. col.
Canada's Air Defence (1957). Prod: Nick Balla, NFB.
"The Commonwealth of Nations", 13-part series (1958). Director
   of live segments.
Down North (Un fleuve à découvrir) (1958). Prod: J. Howe, NFB.
   29 min. col.
The Queen's Plate (Le centième trophée) (1959). Prod: J. Howe,
   NFB. 21 min. b&w.
The St. Lawrence Seaway (La voie maritime du Saint-Laurent)
   (1959). With Isobel Kehoe. Prod: J. Howe, NFB. 29 min. col.
   and b&w.
Robert Baldwin – A Matter of Principal (Robert Baldwin – une
   question de principe) (1960). Prod: Julian Biggs, NFB "The
   History Makers". 32 min. b&w.
Canada on Stage (1960). Prod: Nick Balla, NFB. 11 min. b&w.
Summary Trials (1969). Prod: Stanley Clish, NFB.
Lord Durham (Lord Durham) (1961). Prod: Julian Biggs, NFB.
   "The History Makers". 28 min. b&w.
Yukon Old – Yukon New (Le Yukon – passé et présent) (1961).
   Prod: Nick Balla, NFB. 20 min. b&w.
The Test (1961). Prod: Nick Balla, NFB. 29 min. col. and b&w.
Mathematics at Your Fingertips (Les mathématiques: un jeu
   d'enfant) (1961). Prod: Joe Koenig, NFB. 29 min. col.

Georges-Etienne Cartier – The Lion of Québec (Georges-Etienne Cartier – le lion de Québec) (1962). Prod: Julian Biggs, NFB "The History Makers". 28 min. b&w.

Vote for Michalski (L'expédition Michalski) (1962). Prod: Nick Balla, NFB. 35 min. b&w.

"World War II" series (1962). Dramatized live-action segments. Prod: Stanley Clish, NFB.

"Comparisons" series (1963): **Three Apprentices, Three Grandmothers, The Head Man, Portrait of the Artist, Wedding Day**. Co-director of Nigeria segments, NFB. 28 min. each. b&w.

Gone Curling (Curling, quand tu nous tiens) (1963). Prod: J. Howe, NFB. 10 min. b&w.

David and Hazel: A Story in Communication (1963). Prod: Nick Balla, NFB. 28 min. b&w.

Jamie: The Story of a Sibling (1964). Prod: Nick Balla, NFB. 28 min. b&w.

Ducks, Of Course (Des canards, bien sûr) (1966). With William Carrick. Prod: Peter Jones, NFB. 14 min. col.

Long Ways to Go (1966). Prod: David Bairstow, NFB. 28 min. col.

Canadians Can Dance (Les Canadiens savent danser) (1967). Prod: J. Howe, NFB. 22 min. col.

Do Not Fold, Staple, Spindle or Multilate (Prière de ne pas plier) (1967). Prod: Robert Baylis, NFB. 50 min. b&w.

Why I sing (Je chante pour . . .) "Adieu alouette" (1973). Prod: Ian McLaren, NFB. 56 min. col.

A Star is Lost (1974). Prod: Daisy de Bellefeuille, John N. Smith, NFB "Filmglish". (Four segments or complete version.) 75 min. col.

Why Rock the Boat (1974). Prod: William Weintraub, NFB. 112 min. col.

Feature film in progress (1976).

Bibliography

Motion, September-October 1974, pp. 32-34, interview with Anthony Maulucci; *Canadian Labour*, November 1967, "International Film Festival", Linc Bishop (on **Do Not Fold, Staple, Spindle or Mutilate**); *Edmonton Journal*, July 2, 1968, "Another Disappointing Collaboration", Barry Westgate (on **Do Not Fold, Staple, Spindle or Multilate**); *Montreal Star*, February 7, 1973, "Tonight's Intimate NFB Film on Gilles Vigneault is a Must", Joan Irwin on **Adieu alouette**; *Le Devoir*, February 7, 1973, "Vigneault à travers ses chansons", Jean-Pierre Tadros on "Adieu alouette". *Montreal Star*, November 17, 1973, "Gloria (That's the Blonde) Teaches English", Martin Malina on **A Star is Lost**; *Toronto Star*, December 8, 1973, "A Star is Born – Just Maybe in Spoof of Movie Musicals", Marci McDonald on **A Star is Lost**; *Montreal*

Star, September 28, 1974, "Films in Doldrums Despite Debuts",
Martin Malina on **Why Rock the Boat**; *Le Devoir,* September 30,
1974, "**Why Rock the Boat** de Howe: le monde journalistique
des années 40"; *Globe and Mail,* October 12, 1974, "**Why Rock
the Boat** has Winning Ways, Even When it Doesn't Work", Martin
Knelman; *Séquences,* no. 78, review of **Why Rock the Boat** by
Robert-Claude Bérubé; *Cinéma-Québec,* vol. 4, no. 1, review of
Why Rock the Boat by Michel Buvrard; *Cinema Canada,* no. 17,
pp. 74-76, review of **A Star is Lost** by Laurinda Hartt and Robert
Fothergill.

JACKSON, DOUG

Born in Montreal in 1938, Doug Jackson graduated from McGill
University in 1956 and began his film career as a writer; two of
his dramas, **Power to Destroy** and **The Mistake of His Life**, were
produced by CBC-TV in 1960. Joining the National Film Board in
1962, he assisted on such films as **The Drylanders** and **Coronet
at Night**. His children's film, **The Huntsman**, was based on a
short story by David Lewis Stein, with an original score by Eldon
Rathburn. Jackson's drama, **The Sloane Affair**, won awards for
best director, best television drama and best screenplay (for
Jackson and Alvin Goldman) in the 1972 Canadian Film Awards.
Jackson's first feature film script was **The Heatwave Lasted
Four Days** for the "Filmglish" series, with camera by Douglas
Kiefer and music by Ben Low.

Filmography

Eclipse at Grand'mère (1963). Prod: Walford Hewitson, NFB
  "Televisits". 9 min. col.
"Penitentiary" series (1964): **Control of Inmates**, **Custodial Pro-
  cedures**, **Attitude in Supervision**. Prod: NFB for Canadian
  Penitentiary Services. 30 min. each. b&w.
Crafts of My Province (Artisans du Nouveau-Brunswick) (1964).
  With Kirk Jones. Prod: Peter Jones, NFB. 13 min. col.
Lacrosse (La crosse) (1964). Prod: D. Jackson, Walford Hewit-
  son, NFB. 14 min. col.
Learning Lacrosse (Une leçon de crosse) (1965). Prod: D.
  Jackson, Walford Hewitson, NFB. Part I, 18 min. Part II, 10
  min. b&w.
Benoit (1965). Prod: D. Jackson, NFB. 12 min. b&w.
"Penitentiary" series (1966-67).
Reception (1967). Prod: D. Jackson, NFB "Penitentiary" series.
  30 min. b&w.
Danny and Nicky (1969). Prod: Tom Daly, NFB. 56 min. col.
Norman Jewison, Filmmaker (1971). Prod: D. Jackson, NFB. 50
  min. col.

The Huntsman (1972). Prod: D. Jackson, NFB. 16 min. col.
The Sloane Affair (L'affaire Sloane) (1972). Prod: D. Jackson,
Tom Daly, NFB for Department of National Revenue. 53 min.
col.
La gastronomie (1973). Prod: Ian McLaren, NFB "Adieu
alouette". 27 min. col.
The Heatwave Lasted Four Days (1975). Prod: D. Jackson, NFB
"Filmglish" series. 72 min. plus 4 episodes totalling 80 min.
col.
Work in progress: script research with Gordon Pinsent on **John
and the Missus**.

Bibliography

Ottawa Citizen, March 5, 1973, "Fine Eating in Quebec Works Out
for Director; *La Presse,* March 6, 1973, "Entre la poire et le
fromage", Francoise Kayler; *Motion,* May-June 1974, pp. 30-31,
"Filmglish", Alexander Hausvater; *Globe and Mail,* August 7,
1975, "NFB Goes Commercial with Thriller", Blaik Kirby.

JAWORSKI, TADEUSZ

Born in 1926 in Poland, Jaworski achieved considerable stature in
his native country as a maker of documentary and feature films.
Of his 50 major films, 16 are based on his travels in Africa and
Asia over a ten-year period. (He has also published books on
Ghana and Guinea.) Jaworski won national and international
awards for his film work, most notably for his features **The Boys**
(Chlopcy) and **The Cry in the Emptiness of the World**. His films
were banned in Poland in 1968 and a year later Jaworski
emigrated to Canada. In 1972 **Selling Out**, which he also produced and co-scripted (with dramatist Jack Winter), won both an
Etrog for best documentary and an Academy Award nomination. In
1975 he received a Senior Canada Council grant. Now a Canadian
citizen, Jaworski lives in Toronto and teaches film at York University and Humber College.

Selected Filmography

Medical Care in Ontario (1970). Prod: ETV. 17 min. col.
"Canadian Artists" series (1971): **Art Carvings by Barac, De
Niverville, Morrisseau-Ojibway Artist, Merton Chamber's
Batik, Spiers and Fulford — Sculptors, Michael Hayden —
Vibrations, Ceramic by Rothschild**. Prod: Tadeusz Jaworski,
Art Productions. 45 min. col.
Selling Out (1972). Prod: Unit Productions. 30 min. col.
The Search for Solutions (1972). Prod: Ontario Housing Cor-
poration. 30 min. col.

Leonard Oesterle (1973). Prod: T. Jaworski, CBC. 12 min. col.
Italo (1974). Prod: CBC "The Seekers". 30 min. col.
Italian Herigage (1974). Prod: T. Jaworski, YSA. 60 min. col.
"Design for Change" series (1974). Prod: David Piper, Design for
Change Inc. 13 hour-long films.
Tamara's Tapestry World (1975). Prod: T. Jaworski for CBC
"Arts '75". 25 min. col.
Among the People (1975). Prod: T. Jaworski for CBC "This
Land". 30 min. col.
Work in progress: **Dead End.** 120 min. col. **Who Killed Jesus
Christ?** A six-part series for TV Ontario.

Bibliography

Film, July 23, 1967, "Nie Chcé Robić Filmów z Byle Czego",
Jaworski on **The Boys** (interview); **Ekran,** April 2, 1967,
"Chlopcy...telewizyjna przsygoda"; *Kino,* May 1967, no. 5 (17),
pp. 56-59, "Na tropach wielkiego tematu", Zbigniew Klaczński;
Film, April 21, 1968, "*Pacyfik 68* i inne filmy"; *Globe and Mail,*
Toronto, February 2, 1972, "Film on 'Sellout' of Prince Edward
Island Moving and Disturbing", Blaik Kirby.

JODOIN, RENE

René Jodoin was born in Hull, Quebec in 1920 and graduated from
Montreal's L'Ecole des Beaux-Arts. He began work for the Na-
tional Film Board in 1943 as an animator and left four years later
to travel through Mexico. After his return he worked with Audio
Pictures in Toronto and as artistic director of Current Publications
Ltd. He rejoined the NFB in 1954 to direct animation programing
for scientific and educational films. In 1963 Jodoin became NFB's
director of science programs and director of French animation.
Jodoin has directed over 20 animated films, including the series
"Let's All Sing Together", "Radio Navigation" and "Antenna Fun-
damentals", two scientific series, and the well-known **An Introduction to Jet Engines** (Comment fonctionne le moteur à jet).
Dance Squared, an introduction to the beauty of mathematics,
and **Notes on a Triangle** were animated to music by Maurice
Blackburn. **Spheres**, a collaboration with Norman McLaren, grew
out of Jodoin's work on the unfinished **Chalk River Ballet**. As a
producer, Jodoin has worked on numerous films, including the
series "Chansons contemporaines" in which Quebec songs by
popular performers were animated by Pierre Moretti (**Cerveau
gelé**), Laurent Coderre (**Les fleurs de macadam**), Viviane
Elnécavé (**Notre jeunesse en auto-sport**), Roland Stutz (**Taxi**),
Bernard Longpré (**Tête en fleurs**), André Leduc (**Tout écartillé**)
and Jean Bedard (**La ville**). Jodoin also produced André Leduc's

La baque de tout nu and Leduc and Bernard Longpré's live- action fantasy, **Monsieur Pointu**, Longpré's **Nebule** and Ken McCready's **Glaciation** and **Among Fish**. Peter Foldes' **La faim**, with music by Pierre F. Brault, won the Palme d'or for animation at the 1974 Cannes Film Festival; a computer animated film, **La faim**, was produced by Jodoin for the National Research Council of Canada. Ron Tunis' **Le vent**, Co Hoedeman's **Maboule**, Pierre Moretti's **A Child in His Country**, Kaj Pindal's **Un cheval à toute vapeur** (with music by Pierre F. Brault) and Normand Gregoire's experimental films, **Série 4**, **Passage** and **Horizon** were all produced by Jodoin. Jodoin is a member of the executive council of the International Association of Animators (ASIFA.)

Bibliography

Pot pourri, April 1972, an issue dedicated to NFB's animators which includes an interview with Réné Jodoin; *La Tribune,* March 6, 1968, review of **Notes on a Triangle**; *Box Office*, April 15, 1968, review of **Notes on a Triangle**; *Cinema Canada,* vol. 2, no. 15 (August-September 1975), p. 57, "French Animation", Laurinda Hartt; references in *Le cinéma canadien*.

JUTRA, CLAUDE

Born in Montreal, 1930, Claude Jutra was still a medical student when he made his first short films with the collaboration of Michel Brault. As an actor, Jutra worked with Norman McLaren on **A Chairy Tale** and starred in his own **A tout prendre**, **Mon Oncle Antoine**, **Pour le meilleur et pour le pire** and Thomas Vamos' feature, **La fleur aux dents**. He has worked extensively within the National Film Board, joining Claude Sylvestre and Brault on the television series "Images en boîte" and involving himself in many of the seminal films produced by the French Unit. In his collaboration with French filmmaker- anthropologist Jean Rouch in documenting the Niger Republic, Jutra was instrumental in the cross-fertilization of documentary and cinéma-vérité techniques. Jutra's fictional work is marked by a warm attentiveness to his characters; he has been assisted in his efforts by Clément Perron and Anne Hébert, who, with Jutra, co-scripted **Mon Oncle Antoine** and **Kamouraska**, respectively. With script by Jutra, **Pour le meilleur et pour le pire** chronicles a long day in the life of a married couple (played by Jutra and Monique Miller); Alain Dostie was cameraman. Jutra has won numerous national and international awards; he has been honoured with a retrospective at the Cinémathèque québécoise in 1973 and received the Prix Victor-Morin from the Saint Jean Baptist Society in 1972. Jutra was the founding president of L'Association professionnelle des cinéastes.

Filmography

Le dément du Lac Jean Jeune (1947).
Mouvement perpétuel (1949). Prod: Independent. 15 min. b&w.
Pierrot des bois (1956). Prod: Independent. 11 min. b&w.
Les jeunesses musicales (1956). Prod: Roger Blais, NFB. 44 min. b&w.
A Chairy Tale (Il était une chaise) (1957). With Norman McLaren. Prod: Tom Daly, NFB. 10 min. b&w.
Les mains nettes (1958). Prod: Guy Glover, Léonard Forest, NFB. 75 min. b&w.
Fred Barry, comédien (1958). Prod: Léonard Forest, NFB. 30 min. b&w.
Anna la bonne (1959). Prod: François Truffaut, Les films du Carosse, Paris. 10 min. b&w.
Félix Leclerc, troubadour (1959). Prod: Léonard Forest, NFB "Profils". 30 min. b&w.
Le Niger — jeune république (1961). Prod: Bernard Devlin, NFB. 58 min. b&w.
La lutte (Wrestling) (1961). With Michel Brault, Claude Fournier and Marcel Carrière. Prod: Jacques Bobet, NFB. 28 min. b&w.
Québec-USA or **L'invasion pacifique** (Visit to a Foreign Country) (1962). With Michel Brault. Prod: Fernand Dansereau, NFB. 28 min. b&w.
Les enfants du silence (1963). With Michel Brault. Prod: Fernand Dansereau, Victor Jobin, NFB. 24 min. b&w.
Petit discours de la méthode. With Pierre Patry, Prod: Fernand Dansereau, Victor Jobin. NFB. 27 min. b&w.
A tout prendre (Take It All) (1963). Prod: Les films cassiopée/Orion Films. 110 min. b&w. Dist: Faroun.
Comment savoir (Knowing to Learn) (1966). Prod: Marcel Martin, NFB. 70 min. b&w.
Rouli-roulant (The Devil's Toy) (1966). Prod: Les films cassiopée for NFB. 14 min. b&w.
Wow (1969). Prod: Robert Forget, NFB. 95 min. col.
Au coeur de la ville (1969). Prod: OFQ. 5 min. col.
Marie-Christine (1970). Prod: OFQ. 10 min. col.
Mon Oncle Antoine (1970). Prod: Marc Beaudet, NFB/Gendon Films Ltd. 100 min. col. Dist: Astral/Columbia.
Kamouraska (Kamouraska) (1972). Prod: Pierre Lamy, Mag Bodard, Les productions Carle-Lamy/Société parc film. 118 min. col. Dist: Cinepix.
Pour le meilleur et pour le pire (1975). Prod: Pierre Lamy, Les productions Carle-Lamy ltée. 110 min. col. Dist. Cinepix.
Pennies for My Chocolate (1976). Prod: Ralph Thomas, CBC "For the record". 58 min. col.
Dream Speaker (1976). Prod: Ralph Thomas, CBC "For the record". 58 min. col.

Bibliography

Objectif, no. 3 (December 1960), pp. 3-16, "Michel Brault et Claude Jutra racontent Jean Rouch", Robert Daudelin and Michel Patenaude (interview); *Cinéastes du Québec 4: Claude Jutra* (C-QDC, 1970), critique by Jean Chabot, interview, filmography and bibliography; *Cinéma 73,* Paris, no. 172 (January 1973), pp. 64-68, "Claude Jutra: une exploration dans une morale pathologique", Gérard Langlois (interview); *La Presse,* March 31, 1973, "A la recherche de l'enfance", Luc Perreault (interview on **Kamouraska**); *Cinéma-Québec,* vol. 2, no. 6-7 (March-April 1973), pp. 11-19, "Un espèce de joie dans la création", Jean-Pierre Tadros (interview), also an interview with Geneviève Bujold by Michel Euvrard; *Cinema Canada,* no. 7 (April-May 1973), pp. 42-50, interviews with Bujold, Brault and Jutra on the making of **Kamouraska**; *Cinema Canada,* no. 23, pp. 30-34, interview with Köller and Peter Wronski; *Cahiers du Cinéma,* no. 113 (November 1960), pp. 32-43, no. 115 (January 1961), pp. 23-33, and no. 116 (February 1961) pp. 39-44; *La Presse,* July 16, 1966, p. 6, "Claude Jutra ou les confidences d'un professeur de cinéma", Michèle Favreau; *McGill Medical Journal,* vol. 38 (December 1969), "Dr. Claude Jutra: Filmmaker", Ronald Blumer; *Le Devoir,* October 11, 1971, p. 13, "A la découverte de Claude Jutra, acteur", Jean-Pierre Tadros; *Montreal Star,* November 13, 1971, p. C-11, "Jutra's Stock Goes Up", Martin Malina; *La Tribune,* Sherbrooke, January 4, 1972, "**Mon Oncle Antoine**, un film miraculeux", René Berthiaume; *Saturday Night,* January 1972, p. 41, "Coming of Age in Quebec: Jutra Tells How It Was", Marshall Delaney; *New Yorker,* April 22, 1972, "Story of a Man Who is a Foreign Body in His Life", Penelope Gilliatt; *Canadian Forum,* April 1972, review of **Mon Oncle** by David Beard; *Sunday Times,* London, August 20, 1972, review of **Mon Oncle** by Dilys Powell; *New York Times,* September 10, 1972, and *Globe and Mail,* September 11, 1972, "Obsolete Human Scale", Russell Baker; *Nouvelles littéraires,* Paris, December 11, 1972, "Un monde qui bascule" (on **Mon Oncle Antoine**); *Cinema 73,* Paris, no. 1972 (January 1973), pp. 116-118, review of **Mon Oncle Antoine** by Jacques Grant; *Le Devoir,* March 31, 1973, "L'oeuvre de notre grande bourgeoisie", Robert-Guy Scully; *Montreal Star,* March 31, 1973, "Probably the Most Polished Picture Ever Made in This Country", Martin Malina; *Le Soleil,* March 31, 1973, "Fallait-il faire **Kamouraska**?", Claude Daigeault; *Jutra,* (La cinémathèque québécois, 1973), booklet published on the occasion of Jutra retrospective, March 1973, available for reference at the Centre de documentation cinématographique, Montreal; *Le Devoir,* May 5, 1973, "Documentaires solides et fiction vivante: vive le cinéma québécois!", Michel Regnier; *Le Devoir,* May 12, 1973, "Les critiques face à **Kamouraska**", Pierre Vallières; *Rélations,* no. 382 (May 1973), pp. 157-158, review of **Kamouraska** by Yves

Lever; *Globe and Mail,* October 6, 1973, "Jutra's Latest, A Stunning Portrayal of Tragedy in Quebec", Betty Lee; *Cinéma- Québec,* vol. 2, no. 9 (1973), "A pied? à joual?...ou en ski- doo?", Claude Jutra; *Globe and Mail,* October 11, 1975, "Marriage in Quebec: The Sly Humour of Claude Jutra"; *How to Make or Not to Make a Canadian Film* (La Cinémathèque canadienne, 1967), "How Not to Make a Canadian Film", Claude Jutra; *Cahiers du cinéma in English,* no. 4, p. 45, "10 Questions to 5 Canadian Filmmakers"; *L'écran,* Montreal, no. 2, pp. 7-15, "Entretien de deux cinéastes" (Brault and Jutra talk about Jean Rouch and Norman McLaren); *Cinéma-Québec,* vol. 4, no. 8, pp. 11-14, "Claude Jutra et la vie de couple: le pour et le contre", Richard Gay and Francine Laurendeau; references in *Le cinéma québécois: tendances et prolongements, Le cinéma canadien, Jeune cinéma canadien, Essais sur le cinéma québécois, Cinéma d'ici, L'aventure du cinéma direct* and *Inner Views: Ten Canadian Film-makers* (McGraw-Hill Ryerson, 1975).

KACZENDER, GEORGE

George Kaczender was born in Budapest, Hungary in 1933 and worked as an assistant director in Hungary before joining the National Film Board in 1957. At the NFB he worked as an editor on numerous films, including **Nahanni**; he continues to edit all his own films. As a scriptwriter, Kaczender authored **Phoebe** and **You're No Good**; with Timothy Findlay he co-authored his first feature, **Don't Let the Angels Fall**, which was the first Canadian film selected for in-competition showing at the 1969 Cannes Film Festival. From a script by Doug Bowie, Kaczender's second feature, **U-Turn**, was photographed by Miklos Lente and scored by composer Neil Chotem. He co-founded International Cinemedia Center Ltd. in 1969 and George Kaczender Productions Ltd. in 1971.

Filmography

Ballerina (Margaret Mercier, ballerine) (1963). Prod: Nicholas Balla, NFB. 28 min. b&w.
City Scene (1963). Prod: Gordon Burwash, NFB. 28 min. b&w.
Phoebe (Sylvie) (1964). Prod: Julian Biggs, NFB. 28 min. b&w.
You're No Good (Eddie) (1965). Prod: John Kemeny, NFB. 28 min. b&w.
The World of Three (1966). Prod: Nicholas Balla, NFB, 28 min. b&w.
The Game (1966). Prod: John Kemeny, NFB. 28 min. b&w.
Little White Crimes (1967). Prod: John Kemeny, NFB. 28 min. b&w.

Sabre and Foil (Sabre et Fleuret) (1967). Prod: John Kemeny, NFB. 7 min. b&w.

To Track a Shadow (Suivre une piste) (1967). Prod: William Canning, NFB for the RCMP. 18 min. col.

Don't Let the Angels Fall (Seul les enfants étaient présents) (1968). Prod: John Kemeny, NFB. 99 min. b&w.

Freud: The Hidden Nature of Man (1969). Prod: International Cinemedia Center Ltd. 27 min. col.

Marxism (1969). Prod: International Cinemedia Center Ltd. 27 min. col.

Newton: The Mind that Found the Future (1970). Prod: International Cinemedia Center Ltd. 20 min. col.

The Story of a Peanut Butter Sandwich (1971). Prod: G. Kaczender, International Cinemedia Center Ltd. 13 min.

Brown Wolf (1971). Prod: International Cinemedia Center Ltd. 28 min. col.

U-Turn (1973). Prod: George Kaczender Productions, Ltd. 97 min. col. Dist: Cinepix.

Women Want... (1975). Prod: Don Duprey, International Cinemedia Center Ltd. 30 min. col.

They Don't Build Them Like They Used To (1975). Prod: Don Duprey, International Cinemedia Center Ltd. 20 min. col.

Bibliography

Motion, May-June 1974, p. 18, interview by James McLarty; *Cinema Canada,* no. 10-11, pp. 50-53, "To Chase the Elusive", George Köller (interview); *Saturday Gazette,* May 3, 1969, p. 29, "Kaczender on Tape on Kaczender on Film or **Don't Let the Angels Fall** and Other Filmic Events", Jacob Siskind; *Cinema Canada,* September-October 1969, pp. 18, 24, "NFB Feature Wins Accolades at Cannes", Gerald Pratley; *Globe abd Mail,* October 24, 1969, p. 24, review of **Don't Let the Angels Fall**; *La Presse,* November 1, 1969, "What DO the Angels Want?", Luc Perreault; *Montreal Star,* February 21, 1970, "Rita, Say Hi to George", Carol Pascoe; *Montreal Gazette,* August 17, 1973, "The Cast is Strong...But the Story is Weak", Dane Lanken; *Montreal Star,* August 18, 1973, review of **U-Turn** by Martin Malina; *Le Devoir,* Montreal, August 18, 1973, review by Robert-Guy Scully; *Toronto Star,* October 8, 1973, "Movie **U-Turn** Offers 100 Minutes of Drawn-out Dream Chasing That Wears Somewhat Thin", Kent Potter; *Séquences,* no. 74 (October 1973), pp. 29-30, review by Robert-Claude Bérubé; *Saturday Night,* January 1974, review by Marshall Delaney; *Cinema Canada,* no. 10-11, p. 72, review by Bob Fothergill; *Take One,* vol. 3, no. 11, p. 33, review by Bruce Berman.

KELLY, RON

Born in Vancouver in 1929, Ron Kelly was a painter before joining the CBC in 1954 to become part of the famed Vancouver Film Unit; his film, **A Bit of Bark,** inaugurated the production of dramatic films by the CBC. He also pioneered the dramatic use of the handheld camera for the modern retelling of the Easter story in **Open Grave**. Winner of one Wilderness Award for **The Thirties: A Glimpse of a Decade**, Kelly captured a second for **The Last Man in the World.** His most impressive work has evolved from his dramatic insight into historical events; Kelly wrote the scripts for both **Springhill** and **Megantic Outlaw**. He won a third Wilderness Award in 1971 for **Megantic Outlaw**, which also was voted best film drama in the 1970 Canadian Film Awards. His feature, **Waiting for Caroline,** was co-produced by the CBC and the National Film Board. **King of the Grizzlies**, made at Disney, was based on Ernest Thompson Seton's novel *The Biography of a Grizzly*. Ron Kelly is currently freelancing and working on two one-hour films on aboriginal rights for OECA.

Filmography (incomplete)

Spanish Village (1957). Prod: Ron Kelly, CBC. 29 min. b&w.
Dark Gods (1958). Prod: Ron Kelly, CBC. 28 min. b&w.
The Lacondonnes (1958). Prod: Ron Kelly, CBC. 29 min. b&w.
A Bit of Bark (1959). Prod: CBC. 30 min. b&w.
Object Matrimony (1959). Prod: CBC. 30 min. b&w.
The Seeds (1959). Prod: CBC. 45 min. b&w.
Back of the Sun (1960). Prod: BBC. 30 min.
The Tearaways (1961). Prod: BBC. 30 min.
Montreal (1962). Prod: CBC. 60 min. b&w.
So This is Life (1963). Prod: CBC. 60 min.
Caio Maria (1963). Prod: CBC. 60 min.
The Thirties: A Glimpse of a Decade (1964). Prod: Thom Benson, CBC. 50 min. b&w.
The Open Grave (1964). Prod: Ron Kelly, CBC for "Horizon" series. 50 min. b&w.
The Gift (1965). Prod: Ron Kelly, CBC. 60 min.
Quo Vadis Mrs. Lum (1965). Prod: Peter Jones, NFB. 28 min. b&w.
Such is Life (1966). Prod: Winston Hibbler, CBC. 60 min. b&w.
Valley in a River (1966). Prod: William Canning, NFB for the Canada Emergency Measures Organization. 28 min. b&w.
Waiting for Caroline (1967). Prod: Walford Hewitson, NFB/CBC. 84 min. col.
Centennial Travellers (Voyageurs du centenaire) (1967). Prod: Ron Kelly, Walford Hewitson, NFB for the Centennial Commission. 53 min. b&w.

The Last Man in the World (1968). Prod: Ronald Weyman, CBC "Wojeck". 50 min. b&w.

King of the Grizzlies (Le roi des grizzlys; El rey de los osos) (1969). Prod: Disney Productions. 90 min. col.

Megantic Outlaw (1970). Prod: R. Kelly, CBC. 90 min. col.

Springhill (1971). Prod: R. Kelly, CBC. 90 min. col.

The Atlantic and **The Shield** (1973). Prod: Ron Kelly, CTV "Canada: Five Portraits". Each 50 min. col.

Japan and **Ireland** (1974-1975). Prod: Ron Kelly, CTV "Heritage". Each 50 min. col.

Bibliography

Canadian Photography, June 1974, pp. 13-14, "Ron Kelly Tells of the Excitement and Frustration of Theatrical Films", Dean Walker (interview); *Toronto Telegram,* August 22, 1964, p. 7, "The Revolution-maker", an interview by Jon Ruddy; *The Film and Ron Kelly,* from the Canadian Filmography Series, no. 102 (Canadian Film Institute, 1965), includes an interview with Kelly by Charlotte Gobeil and a filmography current to publication date (out-of-print, available at film study centres); *Canadian Cinematography,* March-April 1964, pp. 11-14, "Film Features Hand-held Camera" (on **Open Grave**); *Canadian Cinematography,* November-December 1965, pp. 11-14, "Conversations on Film with Ron Kelly"; *Montreal Star* January 14, 1967, pp. 2-3," '**Caroline**' Seems to be Worth Waiting For", Dusty Vineberg; *Star Weekly Magazine,* September 23, 1967, pp. 18-23, "One Girl's Struggle with the Eternal Triangle, Canadian Style"; *Variety,* January 8, 1970, p. 17, review of **King of the Grizzlies**; *How to Make or Not to Make a Canadian Film* (La Cinémathèque canadienne, 1967), "Hello '**Caroline**', Goodbye", article by George Robertson, who wrote **Waiting for Caroline**; references in: *Le cinéma canadien* and *Hommage to the Vancouver Film Unit* (La Cinémathèque canadienne).

KENT, LARRY

Born in South Africa in 1938, Larry Kent emigrated to Vancouver in 1957 where he worked as a printer and studied theatre and psychology at the University of British Columbia. While a student at UBC he wrote a play, **The Africaaner**, and directed his first film, **Bitter Ash**, one of the first films to be shot and distributed on the university circuit. (A year earlier students at the University of Montreal had produced **Seul ou avec d'autres**.) Kent presently lives in Montreal where he has taught, directed features and the children's film, **Cold Pizza**, and appeared in Lefebvre's **Q-bec My Love**. **Three Against the Wilderness** is based on the adventure-autobiography of Eric Collier.

Filmography

Bitter Ash (1963). Prod: Lawrence L. Kent Prod. 83 min. b&w.

Sweet Substitute or **Caressed** (1964). Prod: Lawrence L. Kent
  Prod. 81 min. b&w.
When Tomorrow Dies (1965). Prod: Lawrence L. Kent Prod. 91
  min. b&w.
High (1967). Prod: Lawrence L. Kent Prod. 84 min. b&w. and col.
Facade (1968). Prod: Lawrence L. Kent Prod. 80 min. col.
Saskatchewan — 45° Below (1969). Prod: Tom Daly, NFB. 14
  min. col.
The Apprentice (Fleur-bleue) (1971). Prod: Donald Brittain, Pot-
  terton Productions. 85 min. col.
Cold Pizza (1972). Prod: Mike Rubbo and Tom Daly, NFB. 30
  min. col.
Keep It in the Family (Les cocus) (1973). Prod: John Dunning,
  André Link, DAL Productions. 99 min. col. Dist: Cinepix.
Work in progress: **Three Against the Wilderness**.

Kent's independent films are distributed by the Coopérative
cinéastes indépendants in Montreal.

Bibliography
Touchstone, no. 2 (September 1965), pp. 7-14, "Larry Kent: On
Film in Canada" (interview); *Objectif,* no. 37 (November-
December 1966), "101 questions sur le cinéma canadien" (inter-
view); *Toronto Telegram,* January 13, 1968, "If I'm Going to Show
Nudity", interview by Noah James; *Motion,* May-June 1974, p.
19, interview by James McLarty; *Take One,* vol. 1, no. 4, "The
Triumph and Trials of Larry Kent" (interview); *Toronto Telegram,*
November 27, 1965, Gerald Pratley (on **When Tomorrow Dies**);
Toronto Telegram, August 9, 1967, Gordon Sheppard (on **High**);
La Presse, November 2, 1968, "Un film canadien qui risque d'être
fort contesté", Luc Perreault (on **High**); *The Georgian,* Sir George
Williams University, Montreal, November 5, 1968, "Larry Kent
Talks with Peter Bors"; *Point de mire,* vol. 1, no. 11 (September
1970), pp. 32-36, "Tout le monde aime Larry Kent. . .et vous?"
(on **Fleur-bleue**); *La Presse,* September 10, 1971, "Une fleur
déjà fanée", Luc Perreault; *Québec-presse,* September 19, 1971,
Fleur-bleue: un film politique raté", Carol Faucher; *Montreal
Star,* October 14, 1972, "The Respectable Mr. Kent", Martin
Malina; *Montreal Gazette,* April 7, 1973, "Veteran Filmmaker
Determined to Make Canadians Laugh", Dane Lanken; *La Presse,*
Montreal, April 14, 1973, "**Les cocus** de Westmount"; *Montreal
Star,* April 17, 1973, "Film Fills Bill as Romantic Farce", Martin
Malina; *Cinéma-Québec,* vol. 2, no. 8, pp. 48-49, review of **Les
cocus** by Richard Gay; *Cinema Canada,* no. 10/11, review by
Natalie Edwards.

KING, ALLAN
Born in Vancouver in 1930, Allan King began his career with the

CBC Vanvouver Film Unit, founded in 1953 by Stan Fox, Jack Long and Arla Saare. King's early documentary style was influenced by, and in turn influenced the Candid Eye productions at the NFB. The fictional-documentary style which King has since evolved in **Warrendale** and **A Married Couple** has opened up an innovative structure for feature films. **A Bird in the House**, based on the story by Margaret Laurence, won Canadian Film Awards in 1975 for best supporting actress (Patricia Hamilton), best screenplay (Patricia Watson), best television drama and best cinematography (Ken Greggs). Canadian playwright Carol Bolt adapted her play, *Red Emma,* for King's film (also titled **Red Emma**), and **Six War Years** was scripted by Norman Klenman from Barry Broadfoot's book. King is currently working with scripts for dramas based on the life of Norman Bethune, on Carol Bolt's *The Fidelity Quartet,* and on W.O. Mitchell's *Who Has Seen the Wind?*

Filmography (incomplete)

Skid Row (1956). Prod: A. King, CBC. 38 min. b&w.

Pemberton Valley (1957). Prod: A. King, CBC. 59 min. b&w.

Rickshaw (Rickshaw Boy) (1960). Prod: A. King, CBC "Closeup". 28 min. b&w.

A Matter of Pride (1961). Prod: A. King, CBC. 57 min. b&w.

Dreams (1961). Prod: A. King, CBC "Quest". 28 min. b&w.

Bjorn's Inferno (1964). Prod: A. King, CBC "Document". 53 min. b&w.

Running Away Backwards or **Coming of Age in Ibiza** (1964). Prod: A. King, CBC "Document". 60 min. b&w.

Warrendale (1967) Prod: A. King, Allan King Associates for CBC "Document". 100 min. b&w.

A Married Couple (1969). Prod: A. King, Allan King Associates for Aquarius Films Ltd. 112 min. col.

The Jewish Question (1971). Prod: David Peddie, CBC "To See Ourselves". 30 min. col.

Delilah (1972). Prod: David Peddie, CBC "To See Ourselves". 30 min. col.

Come On Children (1973). Prod: A. King, Allan King Associates. 92 min. col.

Can I Count You In? (1963). Prod: David Peddie, CBC "To See Ourselves". 30 min. col.

A Bird in the House (1974). Prod: Ronald Weyman, CBC "Anthology". 60 min. col.

Pity the Poor Piper (1974). Prod: David Peddie, CBC "To See Ourselves". 30 min. col.

Baptizing (1975). Prod: David Peddie, CBC "Performance". 60 min. col.

Six War Years (1975). Prod: Robert Sherrin, CBC "Performance". 60 min. col.

Red Emma (1976). With Martin Kinch. Prod: A. King for CBC "Performance". 60 min. col.
Work in progress: **Who Has Seen the Wind?**

Bibliography

Canadian Cinematography, vol. 4, no. 4 (May-June 1965), pp. 11-14, "Conversations on Film with Allan King" (interview); *Les lettres françaises,* May 20, 1970, pp. 19, 24, "Propos sur la croisette", Gérard Langlois (interview); *Allan King,* from Canadian Filmography Series, no. 105, Canadian Film Institute, includes an interview by Bruce Martin and complete filmography (revised edition, 1971); *Film Quarterly,* Summer 1970, pp. 9-23, "The Fictional Documentary: Interview with the Makers of **A Married Couple**", Alan Rosenthal (also published in Rosenthal's *The New Documentary in Action,* University of California Press, 1971); *Canadian Film Digest,* January 1973, p. 10, "Allan King Ponders", Lloyd Chesley (interview); *Globe and Mail,* March 24, 1973, "You May Have Difficulty Seeing Allan King's Latest Movie", Martin Knelman (interview on **Come On Children**); *The Reel Thing,* vol. 1, no 1, The Ontario Film Association, "An Interview with Allan King", Wayne Cunningham; *Objectif,* no. 61, October 1961, pp. 21-22, "Dix-sept artisans du cinéma canadien"; *An Allan King Retrospective* (La cinémathèque canadienne), a 30-page brochure, available for reference at La bibliothèque nationale, Montreal; *Positif,* no. 100 (December 1968-January 1969), pp. 83-87, "Les journées de 'Positif'"; *Globe and Mail,* November 1, 1969, p. 23, "A Moviemaker Gets Personal", Martin Knelman; *Montreal Gazette,* November 15, 1969, p. 14, "**A Married Couple** Emasculated", Herbert Aronoff; *Saturday Night,* September 1971, pp. 30-32, "A Director Hoping for a Miracle", Morris Wolfe; *La Tribune,* August 18, 1972, p. 9, "Le cinéma: un moyen de se mieux connaître", Victor Stanton; *Cinéma-Québec,* vol. 2, no. 6/7 (March-April 1973), pp 54-55, review of **Come On Children** by André St.-Jacques; *Cinema Canada,* no. 9 (August-September 1973), pp. 70-71, review of **Come On Children** by Natalie Edwards; *Take One,* vol. 4, no. 3 (May 1974), p. 38, review of **Come On** by John Stuart Katz; *Warrendale,* a booklet on the making of the film, available from Warrendale's successor, Browndale, Oakridges, Ontario; *How to Make or Not to Make a Canadian Film* (La cinémathèque canadienne, 1967), "Canadian-Cinema-Vancouver", article by King on his early work; *Take One,* vol. 1, no. 5, "The Director as Pilgrim"; *Inner Views: Ten Canadian Film-makers,* (McGraw-Hill Ryerson, 1975), pp. 55-65; *Maclean's,* November 1, 1976, p.42, "Day of the Gopher", David Cobb on the making of **Who Has Seen the Wind**. references in: *Le cinéma canadien, Jeune cinéma canadien, Non-fiction Film: A Critical History* by Richard M. Barsam, and *L'aventure du cinéma direct.*

KOENIG, WOLF

Animator, cameraman, editor, scriptwriter, director and producer, Wolf Koenig has proved himself to be an inventive, creative and influential filmmaker. Born in Germany in 1927, he joined the National Film Board in 1948. From Koenig's original idea, based on the spirit of Cartier-Bresson's photography, the Candid Eye Unit created many remarkable documentary portraits for television between 1957 and 1960; produced by Roman Kroitor and Wolf Koenig, the Unit operated within Tom Daly's Unit B. Koenig went on to produce live action and animated material in Studio A; he was involved in **Man the Polluter** (Don Arioli), **King Size** (Kaj Pindal), **What on Earth** (Kaj Pindal and Les Drew), **Exeter** (Gerald Budner), **The Family That Dwelt Apart** (Yvon Malette), **The House That Jack Built** (Ron Tunis), **The Innocent Door** (Ken Mc-Cready), **Ten—The Magic Number** and **Propaganda Message** (Barrie Nelson), **Standing Buffalo** (Joan Henson), **To See or Not to See** (Bretislav Pojar), **The Great Toy Robbery** (Jeff Hale), **Hot Stuff** (Zlatko Grgic), **Pictures Out of My Life** (Zino Heczko), **Satellites of the Sun** (Sidney Goldsmith) and **Who Are We**. In 1972 Koenig was appointed executive producer of English animation. As executive producer he has been involved with the Artic Workshops in Frobisher Bay and Cape Dorset; two films are available as a result of these workshops — **Animation of Cape Dorset** and **Natsik Hunting.** Within Koenig's aegis are "The Canadian Poetry Series", a series produced by Guy Glover, a chapter of Richler's **The Street**, animated by Carolyn Leaf, **The Token Gesture**, a comment on International Women's Year, directed by Micheline Lanctot, and Blake James's **Through a Broken Pane.**

Filmography

The Romance of Transportation in Canada (Sports et transports) (1952). With Colin Low and Robert Verrall. Prod: Tom Daly, NFB. 11 min. col.

Structure of Unions (1955). Prod: Tom Daly, NFB. 11 min. col.

It's a Crime (C'est criminel) (1957). With Gerald Potterton. Prod: Tom Daly, NFB for the Department of Labour. 13 min. col.

City of Gold (Capitale de l'or) (1957). With Colin Low. Prod: Tom Daly, NFB. 22 min. b&w.

The Days Before Christmas (Bientôt Noël) (1958). With Terence Macartney-Filgate, Stanley Jackson and Georges Dufaux. Prod: R. Kroitor, W. Koenig, NFB. 30 min. b&w.

Glenn Gould—Off the Record (Glenn Gould) 1959). With Roman Kroitor. Prod: R. Kroitor, W. Koenig, NFB. 29 min. b&w.

Glenn Gould—On the Record (Glenn Gould) (1959). With Roman Kroitor. Prod: R. Kroitor, W. Koenig, NFB. 29 min. b&w.

I Was a Ninety Pound Weakling (1960). With Georges Dufaux.
Prod: R. Kroitor, W. Koenig, NFB. 24 min. b&w.
Festival in Puerto Rico (1961). With Roman Kroitor. Prod: R.
Kroitor, W. Koenig, NFB. 28 min. b&w.
Lonely Boy (Paul Anka) (1962). With Roman Kroitor. Prod: R.
Kroitor, NFB. 27 min. b&w.
Stravinsky (1965). With Roman Kroitor. Prod: R. Kroitor, NFB. 49
min. b&w.
Steeltown (1967). With Rex Tasker. Prod: Walford Hewitson,
NFB. 56 min. col.

Bibliography

Objectif, vol. 2, no. 5-6 (1962), an interview by Michel Patenaude
(on **Lonely Boy**, **The Days Before Christmas** and the Candid Eye
Unit); *Canadian Film — Past and Present* (La cinémathèque canadienne, 1967), article by Marcel Carrière on the filming of **Stravinsky** (available for reference at film study libraries and reprinted in
Eléments pour un nouveau cinéma, Louis Marcorelles, UNESCO,
Paris, 1970); *Dossiers de cinéma: 1* (Fides, 1968), reviews of
Lonely Boy and **City of Gold***; Objectif,* 61, pp. 21-22, "Dix-sept
artisans du cinéma canadien", criticism and a filmography; *How
to Make or Not to Make a Canadian Film* (La cinémathèque canadienne, 1967), "A Note on 'Candid Eye'", by Wolf Koenig;
references in *Jeune cinéma canadien, Le cinéma canadien,
Cinéma d'ici* and *L'aventure du cinéma direct.*

KOHANYI, JULIUS

Born in 1936 in Kelowna, British Columbia, Julius Kohanyi spent
his early years in Hungary before returning to Canada. Largely
self-taught, Kohanyi first began to film people and events around
his Toronto home — and all his films retain this sense of community. Much of Kohanyi's work has evolved out of his interest in
art — he made **Little Monday** from John Gould's drawings,
Tevye from Saul Field's work and directed a short on the
sculpture of Henry Moore. **Games** was a fiction film about a child
accidentally locked in the Royal Ontario Museum. Kohanyi produced CBC's Canadian filmmakers series, "Sprockets", in 1974-75,
which featured innovative, experimental and abstract films. He
lives in Toronto where he makes independent films and teaches
his craft.

Filmography

Requiem for a City Block (1960). Prod: Independent. 30 min.
b&w.
The Softness of Concrete (1961). Prod: Independent. 30 min.
b&w.

The Herring Belt (1963). Prod: Independent. 23 min. b&w.
The Artists' Workshop (1964). Prod: Independent. 26 min. b&w.
Little Monday (1965). Prod: Independent. 17 min. b&w.
Teddy (1967). Prod: Victor Solnick, Group Film Productions. 30 min. b&w.
Henry Moore (1968). Prod: Independent. 26 min. col.
Tevye (1969). Prod: Haida Films. 17 min. col.
Images (1970). Prod: Harold Levy, Empire Films Ltd. 10 min. col.
Eight Short Films on Art (1971). J. Kohanyi, CBC. Each 3-8 min. col.
Rodin (1972). Prod: Independent. 30 min. col.
Gates of Hell (1972). Prod: Independent. 10 min. col.
Games (1974). Prod: Stephen Sobot, Macmillan of Canada Ltd. 19 min. col.
H—A (1974). Prod: J. Kohanyi. 8 min. col.

Mr. Kohanyi's films are distributed by the Canadian Filmmakers' Distribution Centre, Toronto.

Bibliography

Cinema Canada, no. 14, pp. 38-40, "Short Games", interview by George Köller; *Globe and Mail,* December 16, 1965, "Auto Repair Shop Keeps Film Rolling", Frank Morriss; *Montreal Gazette,* April 17, 1967, p. 18, "A Look at a Promising Young Film Director"; *Montreal Star,* April 22, 1967, "The Customers' Cars Will Have to Wait Until He's Finished the Movie"; *Globe and Mail,* December 6, 1967, "Kohanyi Makes Film of Moore"; *Performing Arts in Canada,* vol. 5, no. 3-4 (1968), pp. 26-31, "**Henry Moore**", Jean Bruce; *Cinema Canada,* no. 4 (November 1972), p. 29, review of **Rodin**.

KOTCHEFF, TED

Ted Kotcheff, the director of **The Apprenticeship of Duddy Kravitz** (L'apprentissage de Duddy Kravitz), studied English Literature and later directing (under Robert Gill of Hart House) at the University of Toronto; his first job at the newly-opened CBC television station in 1952 was as a stagehand. Kotcheff soon became a director under producer Sydney Newman, and they later worked together in England for ABC-TV's "Armchair Theatre". Among his feature films in England are **Tiara Tahiti** (1962), **Life at the Top** (1965), with screenplay by novelist Mordecai Richler, **Edna, the Inebriate Woman** (1972), **Two Gentlemen Sharing**, which represented Britain at the 1969 Venice Film Festival. In United States Kotcheff directed **The Human Voice** and **Of Mice and Men** for television; with producer Norman Jewison, he directed **Billy Two Hats** in Israel, and

Outback in Australia, which was that country's official entry at the 1971 Cannes Film Festival. The Richler screenplay of **The Apprenticeship of Duddy Kravitz** marks the second collaboration of Richler and Kotcheff. The feature period-piece (set in Montreal in the '40s) was produced by John Kemeny, International Cinemedia Center Ltd., and won the 1974 Film of the Year, awarded at the Canadian Film Awards.

Bibliography

Cinema Canada, no. 14, pp. 42-50, series of interviews with Kotcheff and three actors in **Duddy Kravitz**; *Cinema Canada,* no. 20, pp. 60-63, "Kotcheff: An Interview by John Katz"; *Saturday Night,* March 1974, pp. 17-24, "How Duddy's Movie Brings Us All Back Home", Martin Knelman; *Le Jour,* April 13, 1974, "Le Canada entre mythologie et réalité", Jean-Pierre Tadros; *Le Devoir,* April 20, 1974, "**Duddy** tout en os", R.G.S.; *Cinéma-Québec,* vol. 3 (April-May 1974), pp. 43-44, "Il était une fois dans l'est — **The Apprenticeship of Duddy Kravitz**: Le représentation d'une milieu donné", J. Leduc; *Books in Canada,* vol. 3, no. 5, pp. 8-9, "How Duddy Makes a Pip of a Film", Douglas Marshall; *Take One,* vol. 4, no. 3, pp. 32-33, review of **Duddy** by Joe Medjuck; *Cinema Canada,* no. 14, pp. 72-73, reviews of **Duddy** by N. Edwards and M. Miller.

KROITOR, ROMAN

Born in Yorkton, Saskatchewan, in 1926, Roman Kroitor joined the National Film Board in 1949. As a director-producer in the Candid Eye Unit, Kroitor worked closely with Wolf Koenig, Stanley Jackson, Terence Macartney-Filgate, Colin Low and Georges Dufaux. With Koenig, Kroitor went on to make two fascinating portraits of public figures, **Stravinsky** and **Paul Anka**, using the "Candid Eye" technique. The National Film Board's **Labyrinth** project at Expo '67 was headed by Kroitor, and in 1967 he joined Robert Kerr and Graeme Ferguson in founding Multi-Screen Corporation, which produced **Tiger Child** (directed by Donald Brittain) for the Fuji Group Pavilion at Expo '70 in Osaka and, as Imax Entertainment, **Man Belongs to the Earth**, co-produced by Kroitor for the United States Government Pavilion at the 1974 World Fair in Spokane, Washington. Kroitor returned to the National Film Board in 1974 as producer of the Drama Development Program and in 1975 was appointed executive producer of the Drama Studio.

Filmography

Paul Tomkowicz, Street-Railway Switchman (Paul Tomkowicz, nettoyeur d'aiguillages) (1954). Prod: Tom Daly, NFB. 9 min. b&w.

Farm Calendar (L'année à la ferme) (1955). Prod: Tom Daly,
NFB. 44 min. b&w.
The Great Plains (Les grandes plaines) (1956). Prod: Tom Daly,
NFB. 24 min. b&w.
Glenn Gould—Off the Record (Glenn Gould) (1959). With Wolf
Koenig. Prod: R. Kroitor, W. Koenig, NFB. 29 min. b&w.
Glenn Gould—On the Record (Glenn Gould) (1959). With Wolf
Koenig. Prod: R. Kroitor, W. Koenig, NFB. 29 min. b&w.
Universe (Notre univers) (1960). With Colin Low. Prod: C. Low,
R. Kroitor and Tom Daly, NFB. 26 min. col.
The Living Machine (La machine à penser) (1961). Prod. R.
Kroitor, NFB. Parts 1 and 2, each, 28 min. b&w.
Festival in Puerto Rico (1961). With W. Koenig. Prod: R.Kroitor,
W. Koenig, NFB. 28 min. b&w.
Lonely Boy (Paul Anka) (1962). With Wolf Koenig. Prod: R.
Kroitor, NFB. 27 min. b&w.
Above the Horizon (Par-dela les nuages) (1964). With Hugh
O'Connor. Prod: R. Kroitor, Hugh O'Connor, Tom Daly, NFB for
the American Meteorological Society. 21 min. col.
Stravinsky (1965). With Wolf Koenig. Prod: R. Kroitor, W.
Koenig, NFB. 49 min. b&w.
Labyrinth (1967). With Colin Low and Hugh O'Connor. Prod: NFB
for Expo '67.
IBM Close-up (1968). With Graeme Ferguson. Prod: R. Kroitor,
Multi-Screen Corp. for IBM.
Code Name Running Jump (1972). Prod: R. Kroitor, Multi-
Screen Corp. for Department of National Defence. 17 min. col.
Exercise Running Jump II (1972). Prod: R. Kroitor, Multi-Screen
Corp. for Department of National Defence. 75 min. col.
Circus World (1974). Prod: R. Kroitor, Imax Entertainment for
Ringling Bros. 25 min. col.

Bibliography

La Presse, July 1, 1967, "Le *Labyrinthe* de l'Expo, cinéma de
l'avenir" (interview), reprinted in *Dossiers de cinéma: 1; Objectif,*
no. 61, "Dix-sept artisans du cinéma canadien" (interview);
Dossiers de cinéma: 1 (Fides, 1968) (on **Lonely Boy**; *Montreal
Gazette,* February 8, 1969, "From **Labyrinth** to Multiscreen",
Dane Lanken; *American Cinematography,* July 1970, "Film at Ex-
po '70", discussion with Kroitor, Brittain and Dufaux on the pro-
duction of **Tiger Child**; *Terence Macartney-Filgate,* Canadian
Filmography Series no. 104, The Canadian Film Institute, "On
Terence Macartney-Filgate, the Candid Eye and Filmmaking",
Roman Kroitor (out-of-print, available at film study centres);
references in *Jeune cinéma canadien, Le cinéma canadien,
Cinéma d'ici* and *L'aventure du cinéma direct.* For further informa-
tion on the Candid Eye Unit, see WOLF KOENIG and INTRODUC-
TION TO CANADIAN FILM.

LABRECQUE, JEAN-CLAUDE

Labrecque was born in Quebec City in 1938. Since 1964 he has been directing his own films documenting life in Quebec. **Les vautours**, a feature drama set in the last months of the Duplessis era with camerawork by Alain Dostie, was chosen to appear in "La Quinzaine des réalisateurs" festival running out of Cannes in 1975. Labrecque worked with a team of filmmakers recording Quebec's preparations for the 1976 Olympics. As a cameraman, Jean-Claude Labrecque has been involved with many of Canada's most important films. His camera credits include: **A tout prendre** (Jutra), **Le chat dans le sac** (Groulx), **The Hundredth Summer** (Macartney-Filgate), **A Great Big Thing** (Till), **Notes for a Film About Donna and Gail** and **The Ernie Game** (Owen), **La vie heureuse de Leopold Z** (Carle), **Les maudits sauvages** (Lefebvre), **Un jeu si simple** (Groulx), **Mémoire en fête** (Forest), **Antonioni** (Gian-Franco Minguzzi, Italy), **De mère en fille** (with François Séguillon, for Poirier), **The Apprentice** and **Fleur-bleu** (Kent), **Bingo** (Lord), **Les corps célestes** (Carle), and **La conquête** (Jacques Gagné).

Filmography

60 cycles (1964). Prod: Jacques Bobet, NFB. 17 min. col.

La guerre des pianos (1965). With Jean Dansereau. Prod: Jacques Bobet, NFB. 35 min. b&w.

Intermède (Feux follets) (1966). Prod: Jacques Bobet, NFB. 9 min. col.

La visite du Général De Gaulle au Québec (1967). Prod: Les films Jean-Claude Labrecque for Office du film du Québec. 28 min. col.

Canada — pays vaste (Canada — The Land) (1968). With Rex Tasker. Prod: John Kemeny, Robert Baylis, NFB for Expo '70, Osaka. 8 min. col.

La vie (1968). Prod: Les films Jean-Claude Labrecque. 60 min. b&w.

L'hiver en froid mineur (Easy Winter) (1968). Prod: OFQ for Office of Information and Publicity. 17 min. col.

Les canots de glace (Ice Rally in Quebec) (1969). Prod: Les films Jean-Claude Labrecque for OFQ. 15 min. col.

Come to Quebec, Get the Feeling (1969). Prod: OFQ for Ministry of Tourism. 5 min. col.

Essai à la mille (1970). Prod: Les films Jean-Claude Labrecque. 7 min. col.

La nuit de la poésie (1970). With Jean-Pierre Masse. Prod: Marc Beaudet, NFB. 111 min. col.

Hochelaga (1972). Prod: Jacques Parent, Les films Jean-Claude Labrecque for OFQ. 9 min. col.

Les smattes (1972). Prod: Les films Jean-Claude Labrecque/Les

productions Carle-Lamy/Cinak. 90 min. col. Dist: Faroun.
Images de la Gaspésie (1972). Prod: Les films Jean-Claude Labrecque for OFQ. 10 min. col.
Université du Québec (1972). Prod: Les films Jean-Claude Labrecque. 10 min. col.
L'entreprise de toute une vie (with Jacques Gagné) and **Les notes de la vie,** both forming parts of "Analyse critique de l'éducation du français au secondaire" (1973). Prod: Les films Jean-Claude Labrecque for OFQ. Each 32 min. b&w.
Claude Gauvreau, poète (1974). Prod: Marc Beaudet, ONF. 57 min. col.
Les vautours (1975). Prod: Louise Ranger, Les films Jean-Claude Labrecque. 91 min. col. and b&w. Dist: Ciné-Art.
Work in progress: **L'été d'avant** or **Le Québec se rechauffe**. Prod: Jacques Bobet, NFB.

Bibliography

Cinema Canada, September 1968, p. 11, interview by Gerald Pratley; *Québec-presse*, August 16, 1970, interview and review of **La nuit de la poésie**; *La Presse*, January 23, 1971, "Une trêve avant la guerilla", Luc Perreault (interview); *Point de mire*, vol. 3, no. 10 (December 18, 1971), "Autour de Jean-Claude Labrecque et des smattes" (interview); *Cinéastes du Québec No. 7: Jean- Claude Labrecque*, CQDC, 1971, a collection of criticism, interview, editing plan for **60 Cycles**, filmography and bibliography; *Séquences*, no. 69 (April 1972), pp. 4-9, "Rencontre avec Jean- Claude Labrecque", Léo Bonneville (interview); *Cinéma-Québec*, vol. 1, no. 9 (1972), pp. 22-25, "Intégrer le véçu à la fiction", Luc Perreault (interview); *Cinéma-Québec*, vol. 1, no. 10, pp. 33-35, "L'amertume et la révolté", Michel Euvrard on **Les smattes**; *Image et son*, Paris, no. 267 (January 1973), pp. 18-23, "Propos de Jean-Claude Labrecque", Guy Gauthier (interview); *Motion*, January-February 1974, pp. 26-27, "Labrecque: An Image", Alexander Hausvater (interview); *Take One*, vol. 1 no. 2, pp. 13-16 (interview); *Liberté*, vol. 8, no. 2/3 (March-June 1966), pp. 84-90, "Le fameux cinéma candide"; *Dossiers de cinéma: 1*, (Edition fides, 1968) on **60 Cycles**; *Presqu'Amérique*, vol. 1, no. 3 (December 1971-January 1972), p. 20, "Retrospective des réalisateurs québécois", Tremblay; *Séquences*, no. 69 (April 1972), pp. 9-11, review of **Les smattes** by Léo Bonneville; *Québec-presse*, April 16, 1972, "Au Québec, tout ce qu'on touche devient politique", Robert Lévesque on **Les smattes**; *Montreal Star*, April 22, 1972, "Quebec Movie **Les smattes** Falls Flat", Martin Malina; *Le Soleil*, April 22, 1972, "Entre la réalité et la fiction", G.R.; *Les lettres françaises*, Paris, no. 1438 (May 31, 1972), p. 16, "Un auteur: Jean-Claude Labrecque", Gérard Langlois; *Le nouvelliste*, March 8, 1975, "**Les vautours**: un portrait de nous- mêmes", Réné Lord; *Le Soleil*, March 8, 1975, "Le noir et bleu de la mélancolie", Claude Daigneault; *Le Devoir,* March 15, 1975, "Labrecque et Bunuel: des phantasmes fanés", André Leroux; *Cinéma-Québec,* vol. 4, no. 3, pp. 15-22, "Des personnages qui me sont chers", J.-C. Labrecque, also "**Les vautours**: Pour continuer l'exorcisme du Duplessisme", Yves Lever, and "**Claude Gauvreau, poète**: profil d'un poète méconnu", Gaston Imbeau; references in: *Vingt ans de cinéma au Canada français, Jeune cinéma canadien, Essais sur le cinéma québécois, Le cinéma canadien, Le cinéma québécois: tendances et prolongements, Language of Change, Cinéma d'ici,* and *L'aventure de cinéma direct.*

LAMOTHE, ARTHUR

Born in France in 1928, Arthur Lamothe studied agriculture in France and economics at the University of Montreal. As a journalist and critic, he wrote for *Cité Libre,* co-founded *Images* and wrote a Royal Commission report on Canada's economic prospects. Lamothe joined the National Film Board in 1962 as a researcher and writer for Gilles Carle's **Manger** and **Dimanche d'Amérique**; more recently he collaborated on Carle's scripts of **La mort d'un bûcheron** and **Les corps célestes**. Although Lamothe has directed a fiction feature (**Poussière sur la ville**, from a story by André Langevin), most of his work has involved the reality of labour and its social and political significance. Lamothe has been active as a writer and critic of cinema; one of the founding members of Connaissance du cinéma (now La Cinémathèque québécoise) and of L'Association professionnelle de cinéastes, he created his own production house, La Société générale cinématographique (SGC), in 1965 and in 1972 Les ateliers audio-visuels du Québec (AVQ).

Filmography

Les bûcherons de la Manouane (Manouane River Lumberjacks) (1962). Prod: Fernand Dansereau, Victor Jobin, NFB. 28 min. b&w.

De Montréal à Manicouagan (Montreal-Manicouagan) (1963). Prod: Fernand Dansereau, NFB. 28 min. b&w.

La neige a fondu sur la Manicouagan (1965). Prod: Marcel Martin, NFB. 58 min. b&w.

Poussière sur la ville (1965). Prod: Pierre Patry, Jean Roy, Coopératio Inc./SGC. 95 min. b&w.

La moisson (Harvesting) (1966). Prod: Guy L. Côté, Marcel Martin, NFB. 10 min. col.

Le train du Labrador (1967). Prod: Société nouvelle des établissements Gaumont. 28 min. b&w.

Ce soir-là, Gilles Vigneault... (1967). Prod: SGC/Omniart. 70 min. col.

Pour une éducation de qualité (1969). Prod: SGC, for La corporation des enseignants du Québec. Series of six films, each 30 min.

Au-delà des murs (1969). Prod: SGC, for OFQ. 28 min. col.

Le mépris n'aura qu'un temps (1970). Prod: SGC for Le conseil des syndicats nationaux (CSN). 95 min. bçw & col. Dist: DEC Films.

La machine à vapeur — physique et rationalité (1970). Prod: SGC for OFQ "Revolution Industrielle". 35 min. col.

Le technicien en arpentage minier (1970), Prod: SGC for OFQ. 30 min. col.

Conflit scolaire St-Léonard (1971). Prod: SGC. 12 min. b&w.

Un homme et son boss (1971). Prod: SGC. 7 min. b&w.

La machine à vapeur — esthétique par Henri Jones (1971). Prod: SGC for OFQ "Revolution Industrielle". 35 min. col.

Le monde de l'enfance (1971). Prod: SGC for Corporation des enseignants du Québec. 30 min. b&w.

Techniques minières (1971). Prod: SGC for OFQ. 14 min. col.

La route de fer (1972). Prod: AVQ. 10 min.

Les gars de Lapalme (1972). With François Dupuis. Prod: AVQ. for CSN.

Special Delivery (1972). With François Dupuis. Prod: AVQ.

A bon pied, bon oeil (1972). Prod: AVQ. 12 min. col.

"Le systeme de la langue française", a series of seven short films (1972). Prod: AVQ for OFQ.

Tu promenes-tu souvent sur un lapin? (1973). Prod: AVQ for OFQ. 35 min. b&w.

"A propos de méthodes", a series of five short films (1973). Prod: AVQ for OFQ.

La chasse aux montagnais (1974) Prod: AVQ. 15 min. col.

Mistashipu (La grande rivière) (1974). Prod: AVQ. 79 min. col. Dist: Faroun.

Pakuashipu (1974). Prod: AVQ. 54 min. col. Dist: Faroun.

Netsi Nana Shepen (On dirait que c'était notre terre) (1975). Prod: AVQ. Three parts totalling 4 hours. col. Dist: Faroun.

Work in progress: **Carcagoua et le péril blanc**.

Bibliography

La Patrie, Montreal, January 7, 1968, an interview on **Ce soir-là, Gilles Vigneault**...; *Le Soleil,* Québec, June 8, 1968, p. 41, an interview by Claude Daigneault; *Cinéastes du Québec 6: Arthur Lamothe,* CQDC, 1971, analysis of **Le mépris n'aura qu'un temps**, also includes interview, criticism, bibliography and a filmography; *Travelling,* Zurich, no. 32 (July-August 1972), pp. 32-36, interview with Lamothe by Robert Daudelin and Yvan Patry; *Take One,* vol. 1, no. 2, pp. 13-16, "Canadian Filmmakers: Arthur Lamothe and Jean-Claude Labrecque" (interview); *Cahiers du cinéma in English,* no. 4, "10 Questions to 5 Canadian Filmmakers" (interview); *Séquences,* no. 53, pp. 19-24, interview by Léo Bonneville; *Dossiers de cinéma: 1* (Edition fides, 1968), on **Les bûcherons de la Manouane**; *Le Soleil,* April 3, 1971, p. 48, "Cinéma québécois/la S.G.C.: le temps des indépendants", Paul Roux; *Cinéma-Québec,* vol. 1, no. 1 (May 1971), pp. 10-18 (on **Le mépris n'aura qu'un temps**); *Champ libre,* no. 2 (1971), pp. 82-90, "L'utilization du **Mépris n'aura qu'un temps**"; *Champ libre,* no. 4 (1973) pp. 68-75, reviews of **Le mépris** and **Les gars de Lapalme**; *Le Devoir,* June 8, 1974, "Dans ce temps-la, les indiens n'avaient pas peur", Pierre Vallières on **Mistashipu**; *Le Soleil,* June 15, 1974, "Pour découvrir un moins beau visage des québécois, voir le dernier film d'Arthur Lamothe", Claude Daigneault; *Québec-presse,* June 16, 1974, "Nous devons plus que des terres aux indiens", Gérald Godin; *La Presse,* July 20, 1974, "Regards blancs sur la question amérindienne", Luc Perreault, and "C'est pour partir le monde", Charles Binamé; *Take One,* vol. 1, no. 10, pp. 32-33, reviews of **Poussière sur la ville** and **Ce soir-là, Gilles Vigneault** by Gabriel Breton; *How to Make or Not to Make a Canadian Film* (La cinémathèque canadienne, 1967), "The Actor and Film", by Lamothe; references in: *Jeune cinéma canadien, Essais sur la cinéma québécois, Vingt ans de cinéma au Canada français, Le cinéma québécois: tendances et prolongements, Cinéma d'ici* and *L'aventure du cinéma direct.*

LARKIN, RYAN

Born in Montreal in 1943, Ryan Larkin graduated from Montreal's Museum of Fine Arts' School of Art and Design and studied at the Ecole des Beaux-Arts. He joined the National Film Board in 1964 as a painter and inker, completing a two-minute experimental film, **Cityscape**, in a training course conducted by Norman McLaren. Larkin's early work includes a number of loops for a mathematics series, an animated pastel, **Burning Fox**, for the Department of Lands and Forests and a clip for the Department of Health and Welfare, **ABC of First Aid. Syrinx**, released in 1965, extended his work in animated charcoal drawings. In **Walking** (1968), Larkin's colour-wash figures explode into movements on white space. While completing **Street Musique** (1972), Larkin worked as an animation teacher at the Vancouver School of Art; since then he has taught in numerous schools and universities, most notably at U.B.C. where he assisted in a video production entitled **Cartoon Thinking**. He has also worked with art and dance groups to produce music-film performances. Larkin was associate director and animation artist on Mort Ransen's musical feature, **Conflict Comedy. Street Musique** received the Grand Prix at the

1972 Melbourne Film Festival and Animation First Prize at the
1972 Oberhausen Festival.

Bibliography

Montreal Gazette, September 13, 1969, "Ryan Larkin: Painting on
Film to Stir the Minds of Old and Young", Mark Slade; *Perspectives,* January 31, 1970, pp. 16-17, "Les dessins fantastiques
de Ryan Larkin", Pol Chantraine; *Artscanada,* April 1970,
"Nine Animators Speak", Guy Glover, and "Six Filmmakers in
Search of an Alternative", Terry Ryan; *Positif,* no. 117 (June
1970), review of **Walking**.

LAVOIE, RICHARD

Born in 1937, Richard Lavoie studied music and assisted his
father, Herménégilde Lavoie, a pioneer in Quebec film history.
The elder Lavoie worked in public service first as assistant director of the Quebec Office of Tourism from 1933 to 1949 and returned to government service in 1964 until 1969. In his private work,
Herménégilde Lavoie founded Les documentaires Lavoie, which
produced 50 industrial, tourist and religious films. The company
became Les films Lavoie in 1962 and later, in 1969, Richard
Lavoie Inc. In recent years Richard Lavoie has gathered together
a small company of filmmakers including Marielle Frenette, Yves
Saint-Jean, Oscar Marcoux, Claude Lavoie, Georges Gardin and
Thérèse Gagnon, who have all been involved in a number of children's films, including **La cabane** and **La guitare. Itarnitak**,
Opération survie and **La maternelle esquimaude de Fort-Chimo** were originally filmed with an Eskimo soundtrack.

Filmography

One Heart and One Soul (1956). Prod: Independent. 30 min.
col.

Stop (1957). Prod: Quebec Minister of Transport and Communications. 25 min. col.

"Cézar" series (1958). Prod: Radio-Canada. Each 90 min.

Old Quebec, Gateway to Canada's New Wealth (1959). Prod:
Le soleil ltée. 25 min. col.

Itarnitak (1960). Prod: T. Beaudin, Independent. 19 min. b&w.

Opération survie (Struggle for Existence) (1960). Prod: T.
Beaudin, Les films Lavoie inc. 17 min. col.

Franciscaines Missionnaires de Marie (1961). Prod: Independent. 30 min. col.

Dialogue avec la terre (Men and Earth) (1962). Prod: OFQ for the
Minister of Natural Resources. 26 min. col.

L'exposition provinciale de la ville de Québec (1964). Prod: La ville de Québec. 20 min. col.

Noël a l'Ile aux Grues (1964). Prod: Les films Lavoie inc. 27 min. col.

Le prix de l'eau (The Waste of Waters) (1964). Prod: OFQ for the Minister of Natural Resources. 27 min. col.

Champs d'action (1965). Prod: Hydro-Québec. 15 min. col.

Les cobayes (1965). Prod: Les films Lavoie inc. 20 min. b&w.

Diary of a Quebecer (1965). Prod: Jack Zolov, CBC "Diary" series. 27 min. b&w.

La maternelle esquimaude de Fort-Chimo (1966). Prod: OFQ for the Minister of Natural Resources. 15 min. col.

L'Ile aux Oies (1966). Prod: Les films Lavoie inc. 20 min. col.

Les néo-québécois (1967). Prod: OFQ for the Quebec Pavilion, Expo. 3 min. b&w.

Te retrouver Québec (1967). Prod: La ville de Québec. 20 min. col.

Le repas a l'école (1967). Prod: OFQ for the Minister of Health. 20 min. col.

Rencontre dans l'invisible (1968). Prod: Les films Lavoie inc. 20 min. col.

Le poste de la baleine (1968). Prod: OFQ for the Minister of Natural Resources. 30 min. b&w.

Pourquoi c'est faire (What's That For?) (1968). Prod: Les 4/4. 25 min. col. Dist: Faroun.

Catamaran (1970). Prod: Richard Lavoie Inc./Marine industries de Sorel. 14 min. cl.

On ne fera pas rire de nos autres (1970). Prod: OFQ. 30 min. col.

L'avale-mots (1970). Prod: OFQ for L'office de la langue française. 10 min. col.

Pathologie et linguistique (1970). Prod: OFQ for L'office de la langue française. 9 min. col.

Atelier de travail sur la gestion scolaire Parts 1 and 2 (1971). Prod: OFQ for SGME. 28 min. each b&w.

Place Royale — première étape (Place Royale — Part One) (1971). Prod: OFQ for the Minister of Cultural Affairs. 14 min. col.

Katak et Kuktuk se racontent et chantent (1971). Prod: Richard Lavoie Inc. for SGME. 24 min. col.

"L'enfer blanc" ("White Inferno") (1972). Prod: Richard Lavoie Inc./Ontario Minister of Education. Series of 4 films, each 15 min. col.

Au Grand Théâtre de Québec (1972). Prod: OFQ for the Minister of Cultural Affairs. Two films totalling 18 min. col.

"La carte de crédit" (1973). Prod: Richard Lavoie Inc. for the Consumer Protection Bureau. Series of 5 films totalling 28 min. col.

"Dew" (1973). Prod: Richard Lavoie Inc. Series of 30 television
  clips. Each 3 min. col.
La cabane (The Shack) (1973). Prod: Richard Lavoie Inc. 45 min.
  col.
La guitare (1974). Prod: Richard Lavoie Inc. 80 min. col. Dist:
  Faroun.
Franc jeu (1975). Prod: OFQ for the Minister of Cultural Affairs.
  112 min. col.
Work in progress: a feature film entitled **Les beautés de mon
  pays**, and a film on the work of his father, **Le regard du pion-
  nier du cinéma québécois: Herménégilde Lavoie**.

Bibliography

Le Soleil, February 4, 1967, "L'avenir du cinéma canadien repose
sur les jeunes", Christiane Brunelle-Garon; *Le Soleil,* June 2,
1973, "Tous les enfants ont une cabane dans leur tête", Marie
Clermont, and "Explorer d'abord la vie humaine, globalement,
simplement (Lavoie)", Jacques Dumais; *Le Soleil,* August 25,
1973, "Tribulations d'un cinéaste aux prises avec les éléments",
Claude Daigneault; *Le Soleil,* July 27, 1974, "Un film tourné pour
et par des enfants, **Guitare**, du cinéaste Richard Lavoie", Michel
Lambert; *Le Jour,* September 18, 1974, "Un genre oublié: le
cinéma pour enfants", Jean-Pierre Tadros; *La Presse,* February
8, 1975, "Le grand jeu de la francophonie", Luc Perreault; *Le
Jour,* February 13, 1975, "Au son des tam-tams de la Superfran-
cofête", Jean-Pierre Tadros; *Cinéma-Québec,* vol. 3, no. 1, pp.
45-46, review of **La Cabane** by Pierre Demers.

LAVUT, MARTIN

Actor, screenwriter and director, Martin Lavut was born in 1937 in
Toronto, where he now freelances and teaches film-writing at York
University. As an actor, Lavut performed the role of Duddy in
CBC's adaptation of Richler's **The Apprenticeship of Duddy
Kravitz** and toured with the satirical troupe, Second City. His
screenplay, **Jenny**, was filmed by George Bloomfield in 1970.
Lavut directed numerous television commercials, segments for
variety programs, and a series of radio movies for the blind in
1970, using archival sounds from television and radio. His feature
documentary, **Orillia: Our Town**, is a fascinating portrait of
Stephen Leacock's hometown.

Filmography

Leni Riefenstahl (1965). Prod: CBC "Tuesday Night". 30 min.
  b&w.

Marshall McLuhan (1965). Prod: CBC "Other Voices". 30 min. b&w.

At Home (1968). Prod: M. Lavut, Allan King Associates. 14 min. b&w.

The Life Game (1970). Prod: Jesse Nishihata, CBC. 57 min. b&w.

Don Messer's Funeral, Blondie's Daddy's Dead and **John Max** (1973). Items for CBC "Weekend".

Without A Hobby, It's No Life (1974). Prod: M. Lavut, CBC. 60 min. col. Dist: New Cinema.

Requiem for Porkchop and **The Whistler** (1974). Prod: Ross McLean, CBC "Of All People".

Orillia: Our Town (1975). Prod: Jesse Nishihata, CBC. 90 min. col.

Melony (1975). Prod: Jerry Mayer, CBC. 30 min. col.

Middlegame (1975). Prod: Julian Roffman, CBC. 60 min. col.

Work in progress: feature film script, **Frankie and Johnny**, with Arnie Gelbert.

Bibliography

Toronto Telegram, May 23, 1970, p. 51, "Martin Lavut is No Longer a Nut, Maybe Just a Little Disorganized", Pat Annesley (interview); *Toronto Star,* October 10, 1969, Martin Knelman on **At Home**; *Globe and Mail,* September 22, 1970, Blaik Kirby on **The Life Game**; *Miss Chatelaine,* vol. 8, no. 4 (August 10, 1971), "Let's Hear It for Don & Morley & Martin & Ivan & Sylvia & Eric...", Kay Armatage; *Cinema Canada,* no. 19, pp. 61-62, review of **Orillia** by Á. Ibrán/ -Kiss; *New York Times,* June 26, 1974, "TV: The Joy of Hobbies", John J. O'Connor.

LEDUC, JACQUES

Born in Montreal in 1941, Jacques Leduc studied art at Collège Bourget and earned a B.A. from Collège St-Denis; he joined the National Film Board in 1962 as an assistant cameraman and worked on **Comment savoir, Le festin des morts, 60 Cycles** and **Nobody Waved Goodbye**. Leduc shot four of Lefebvre's films — **Il ne faut pas mourir pour ça, Mon amie Pierrette, Mon oeil**, and **Ultimatum** — and worked as assistant director on Godbout's **YUL 871**. **On est loin du soleil** is a delicate tale which revolves around the social and religious spirit of Brother André, founder of Montreal's St. Joseph Oratory; **La tendresse ordinaire**, made with Esther Auger and Luce Guilbeault on Quebec's north shore, reveals the feelings of a married couple through the common gestures of their daily lives.

Filmography

Chantal: en vrac (1967). Prod: Guy L. Côté, NFB. 50 min. col.
Nominingue...depuis qu'il existe (1968). Prod: Guy L. Côté, NFB. 73 min. col. and b&w.
Là ou ailleurs (1969). With Pierre Bernier. Prod: Guy L. Côté, NFB. 10 min. col.
Ça marche (1970). With Arnie Gelbart. Prod: NFB for the Minister of Labour and the Minister of Immigration. 16 min. col.
Cap d'Espoir (1970). Prod: Pierre Maheu, NFB. 60 min. col. Not released.
On est loin du soleil (1971). Prod: Paul Larose, NFB. 79 min. b&w.
Je chante à cheval avec Willie Lamothe (1971). With Pierre Bernier, Lucien Menard, Alain Dostie, Suzanne Demers. Prod: Paul Larose, NFB. 58 min. col.
La tendresse ordinaire (Ordinary Tenderness) (1973). Prod: Paul Larose, NFB. 82 min. col.
Alegria (Alegria) (1973). Prod: François Séguillon, NFB. 28 min. col.
Work in progress: **Chronlque de la vie quotidienne**. Prod: Jacques Bobet, NFB.

Bibliography

Québec-presse, November 21, 1971, "Quand je fais une tournée au Québec avec un film québécois, j'ai l'impression de faire du cinéma clandestin", Carol Faucher (interview); *Québec-presse*, December 26, 1971, "Nous sommes tous des frères André", Robert Levésque (interview); *Le Soleil*, June 10, 1972, "A contre-courant du cinéma d'auteur", Ghislaine Rheault (interview); *Séquences*, no. 73 (July 1973), pp. 4-9, interview by Léo Bonneville; *Motion*, May-June 1974, p. 21, interview by Peter Evanchuk; *Objectif*, August 1967, Pierre Hébert on **Chantal: en vrac**; *Montréal-matin*, September 26, 1971, pp. 6-7, review of **On est loin du soleil** by François Piazza; *Point de mire*, vol. 2, no. 33 (September 17, 1971), pp. 40-41, review of **On est loin du soleil**; *Cinéma-Québec*, November 1971, pp. 6-8, "L'evidence mise a nue", review of **On est loin du soleil** by André Leroux; *Séquences*, no. 68 (February 1972), pp. 38-39, review of **On est loin du soleil**; *La Tribune*, Sherbrooke, April 4, 1973, review of **La tendresse ordinaire** by René Berthiaume; *Québec-presse*, April 6, 1973, "Un film anti-spectacle", review of **La tendresse ordinaire** by R.L.; *Le nouvelliste*, April 18, 1973, "Jacques Leduc et Alain Dostie parlent de **Tendresse ordinaire**"; *Le Devoir*, June 23, 1973, "L'échec de **La tendresse ordinaire**", Robert-Guy Scully; *Séquences*, no. 73 (July 1973), pp. 12-13, review of **Tendresse** by Robert-Claude Bérubé; *La voix de l'est*, January 29, 1975, "Un document de l'ONF a irrité au plus haut point les particpantes", review of **La tendresse ordinaire**; *Jacques Leduc: essai de travail d'équipe,* by Jean-Pierre Bastien and Pierre Veronneau, "Cinéastes du Québec" no. 12, Conseil québécois pour la diffusion du cinéma; references in: *Essais sur le cinéma québécois, Le cinéma canadien,* and *Cinéma d'ici.*

LEFEBVRE, JEAN-PIERRE

Born in Montreal in 1941, Lefebvre is Quebec's most prolific filmmaker. Poet and critic (Lefebvre was a staff writer on the now-defunct cinema review, *Objectif*), he creates visual poems with his films; his sense of humour and irony give his work warmth and poignancy. He has worked primarily as an independent, forming his own company, Cinak, which has co-produced Arcand's **La maudite galette** and Labrecque's **Les smattes**. While head of the Fiction Studio at the National Film Board, Lefebvre produced "Premières oeuvres", a series which included the first feature films of Jean Chabot, André Théberge, Michel Audy, Yvan Patry and Fernand Bélanger. In 1973 Lefebvre was honoured by La cinémathèque québécoise with a retrospective of his work. Lefebvre was president of association des réalisateurs de films du Québec in 1974.

Filmography

L'homoman (1964). Prod: Les films Jean-Pierre Lefebvre. 24 min. b&w.
Le révolutionnaire (1965). Prod: Les films Jean-Pierre Lefebvre. 74 min. b&w.
Patricia et Jean Baptiste (1965). Prod: Les films Jean-Pierre Lefebvre. 83 min. b&w.
Mon oeil (My eye) (1965). Prod: Les films Jean-Pierre Lefebvre. 90 min. b&w.
Il ne faut pas mourir pour ça (Don't Let It Kill You) (1967). Prod: Les films Jean-Pierre Lefebvre. 75 min. b&w.
Mon amie Pierrette (1967). Prod: Clément Perron, NFB. 68 min. col.
Jusqu'au coeur (Straight to the Heart) (1968). Prod: Clément Perron, NFB. 93 min. col. and b&w. Dist: Colum/Astral in English Canada.
La chambre blanche (House of Light) (1969). Prod: Cinak. 80 min. b&w.
Un succès commercial or **Q-bec My Love** (1970). Prod: Cinak. 83 min. b&w.
Les maudits sauvages (Those Damned Savages) (1971). Prod: Cinak. 90 min. col.

Les dernières fiançailles (1973). Prod: Marguerite Duparc, Bernard Lalonde, Cinak. 91 min. col.

Ultimatum (1973). Prod: Laurence Paré, Cinak. 140 min. col. and b&w.

On n'engraisse pas les cochons à l'eau claire (Pigs are Seldom Clean) (1973). Prod: Marguerite Duparc, Claude Godbout, Cinak. 120 min. b&w.

L'amour blessé (Les confidences de la nuit) (1975). Prod: Marguerite Duparc, Cinak. 78 min. col.

Lefebvre's films are distributed by Faron and Disci.

Bibliography

Le Devoir, Montreal, April 16, 1969, interview on **La chambre blanche**; *Culture vivante,* no. 13 (May 1969), pp. 38-45, ''Jean-Pierre Lefebvre: révolutionnaire **Jusqu'au coeur**'', Huguette O'Neill (interview); *Cinéastes du Québec 3: Jean-Pierre Lefebvre,* CQDC, 1970, collection of criticisms, an interview, extracts of dialogue from **Q-bec My Love**, filmography and complete bibliography; *Jean-Pierre Lefebvre,* Ronald Bérubé and Yvan Patry, eds. (Les presses de l'Université du Québec, 1971, C.P. 250, Station N, Montreal, Canada), includes critiques, interviews, documents and filmography; *Cinema Canada,* vol. 2, no. 3 (August 1972), p. 58 (interview), pp. 14-17, filmography; *Cinema 72,* Paris, no. 171 (1972), pp. 80-99, ''**Q-bec My Love**'', interview by M. Hamill, filmography; *Jean-Pierre Lefebvre retrospective —* November 1973, booklet, includes filmography and interview (La cinémathèque québécoise, available at film study centres); *La Presse,* February 15, 1974, ''Lefebvre: un film est une sonde'' (interview); *Séquences,* no. 176 (April 1974), pp. 2, 5-18, ''Lettre ouverte'', and interview by J. Beaulieu; *Ecran,* Paris, no. 30 (November 1974), pp. 63-64, review of **Les dernières fiançailles** and interview by Marcel Martin; *La Presse,* January 31, 1975, ''La maturation d'un cinéaste intransigeant'', Luc Perreault (interview); *Cahiers du cinéma in English,* no. 4, ''10 Questions to 5 Canadian Filmmakers'', article by and interview with Lefebvre; *Cahiers du cinéma,* no. 186, pp. 56-61, ''Le coup de dès'', Michel Delahaye and Patrick Straram (interview); *Toronto Telegram,* August 2, 1967, ''How to Resist the Yanks'', a talk with Lefebvre and Clyde Gilmour; *Le Devoir,* February 1, 1969, ''Jean-Pierre Lefebvre: 'Il faut fire des témoignages''', Claude Nadon; *Le Devoir,* February 8, 1969, p. 17, ''Godard et Lefebvre, quand le cinéma devient des fables-témoignages'', Claude Nadon; *Second Wave,* Robin Wood, ed. (Praeger, N.Y., 1970) ''Jean-Pierre Lefebvre'', Jean Chabot; *Cinéma-Québec,* vol. 1, no. 3 (September 1971), pp. 20-23, review of **Les maudits sauvages** by André Leroux; *Québec-presse,* October 31, 1971, p. 25, ''**Les maudits sauvages** de la colonie aux communes'', Carol Faucher; *Cinéma-*

Québec, vol. 3, no. 4 (December 1973), pp. 24-27, "Deux pôles d'une même sensibilité", Michel Brûle on **On n'engraisse pas** and **Les dernières fiançailles**; *La Presse,* December 22, 1973, "Les anges dans nos campagnes" (on **Les dernières fiançailles**); *Séquences,* no. 76 (April 1974), "Lettre ouverte à Jean-Pierre Lefebvre", Léo Bonneville; *Le nouvel observateur,* Paris, September 30, 1974, "Deux visages de la mort", Jean-Louis Bory; *La Presse,* January 31, 1975, "Et mourir de betise", Luc Perreault on **On n'engraisse pas**; *Les dernières fiançailles — film de Jean-Pierre Lefebvre,* Gilles Marsolais Collection "Le cinématographe" (Editions de l'Aurore, Montreal, 1976); *Objectif* has several of Lefebvre's own critical articles; *How to Make or Not to Make a Canadian Film* (La cinémathèque canadienne, 1967), "Technique is Absurd", by Lefebvre; *Take One,* vol. 1, no. 7, pp. 10-13, "The Gentle Revolutionary", Graham Fraser; *Sept jours,* no. 199, "Le grand bluff de l'art au Québec", Claude Jasmin; references in *Essais sur le cinéma québécois, Jeune cinéma canadien, Vingt ans de cinéma au Canada français, Le cinéma canadien, Le cinéma québécois: tendances et prolongements, Cinéma d'ici,* and *L'aventue du cinéma direct.*

LEITERMAN, RICHARD

Leiterman was born in northern Ontario in 1935. After studying with Stan Fox of the Vancouver Film Unit, he began his career as a cameraman, shooting news for the CBC in Vancouver. Later he went to London, England, where he was involved in news and documentary filming. In 1961 he joined Allan King in his London office to form Allan King Associates. Leiterman returned to Canada in 1966, where he has worked as a cameraman on many important films. Leiterman has also done camerawork for the NET network in the United States. The stylistic freedom and facility which has developed from his experience in cinéma-vérité style television documentaries also marks his recent work on a number of feature films. Leiterman was associate director (with Allan King) as well as cinematographer for **A Married Couple**. He directed **Germany** (CBC "Heritage", 1965), **Good News, Bad News** (Marshall Prod., 1972), **Winter Sports** (Hobel-Leiterman, 1972), **There's More To It** (NFB, 1973) and **Walrus** (NFB, 1973). Leiterman is currently a partner in Hobel-Leiterman Productions. In 1976 he received a Canada Council travel grant to visit film studios in Europe.

Among his cinematographic credits are: **In Search of the Real Che Guevara** (Bonner); **Hamlet** (Bonnière); **Catskinner Keen** and **Cavendish Country** (Brittain); **El Salvador** and **Niger** (Carney); **Summer in Mississipi** and **Cinema: The Living**

Camera (Fox); **One More River** (Fox and Douglas Leiterman);
Italy and **Wedding in White** (Fruet); **Running Away Backwards**
or **Coming of Age in Ibiza**, **The New Woman,** and **A Married
Couple** (King); **Operation Running Jump** (Kroitor); **Recommendation for Mercy** (Markowitz); **Christopher Plummer**
(Macartney-Filgate); **Horse Latitudes** (Rowe); **Thunderbirds in
China** (Rose); **Goin' Down the Road**, **Rip-Off**, **Paul Bradley**,
and **Between Friends** (Shebib); **The Far Shore** (Wieland); and
High School (Frederick Wiseman). He also shot Allan King's first
dramatic feature based on the W.O. Michell novel, *Who Has Seen
the Wind?*

Bibliography

Film Quarterly, Summer 1970, pp. 9-23, "The Fictional Documen-
tary: Interviews with the Makers of **A Married Couple**", Alan
Rosenthal, (reprinted in Rosenthal's *The New Documentary in Ac-
tion,* University of California Press, 1971); *Cinema Canada,*
Second Edition, no. 1 (March 1972), interview by George Köller;
Motion, May-June 1974, pp. 21-22, interview by Trevor D. Davies;
Cinema Canada, no. 12, pp. 14-16, "Leiterman in China", George
Köller (interview); *Armies of the Night* (General Publishing, 1968),
Part IV, "Saturday Night and All of Sunday", Norman Mailer, in-
cludes a portrait of Leiterman in action; *Toronto Star,* November
8, 1969, "It's Said This Man Was Born With a Camera in His
Hands", Dorothy Mikos; *Montreal Star,* March 13, 1971, "Optim-
ism: Leiterman's Forecast", Carole Clifford.

LORD, JEAN-CLAUDE

Born in Montreal in 1943, Jean-Claude Lord obtained his B.A. in
1963 and that same year began his apprenticeship in the cinema
as a collaborator on Coopératio, a group that produced six
features in Quebec from 1963 to 1966. Lord co-authored and
acted as assistant director on Pierre Patry's **Trouble-fête** (the
Canadian entry at Cannes in 1964) and assisted Patry in the direction of two other features, **La corde au cou** and **Cain**, and a
short, **Il y eut un soir, il y eut un matin**. Since then Lord has
been assistant director on a number of features, including Arthur
Lamothe's **Poussière sur la ville**, Michel Brault's **Entre la mer et
l'eau douce** and Eric Till's **A Great Big Thing**, and was production manager on Roger Fournier's **Pile ou face**. Since 1967 Lord
has been part-time director of the Vaudreuil Cultural Centre, a film
critic on a weekly television show and a film columnist for a Montreal weekly. Lord writes the scenarios for his own films and is
presently preparing a feature script entitled **Panique**.

Filmography

Délivrez-nous du mal (1965). Prod: Pierre Patry, Coopératio. 82 min. b&w.

Les colombes (The Doves) (1972). Prod: Pierre Patry, Coopératio. 82 min. b&w. Dist: France Film, Faroun, Mutual.

Bingo (Bingo) (1974). Prod: Pierre David, J.-C. Lord, Les productions mutuelles, 116 min. col. Dist: Mutual.

Work in progress: **Parlez-moi d'amour**, a feature film, with script by Lord and Michel Tremblay.

Bibliography

La Presse, September 16, 1972, "Rejoindre le grand public", Luc Perreault (interview); *Le Droit,* April 6, 1974, interview by Murray Maltais; *Cinema Canada,* no. 18, pp. 30-31, interview by Stephen Chesley; *Le Devoir,* July 7, 1969, review of **Délivrez-nous du mal** by Jean Chabot; *Séquences,* no. 70 (October 1972), pp. 22-23, review of **Les colombes** by Léo Bonneville; *Le Jour,* March 16, 1974, "Un surprenant tourbillon d'événements mais une réalité à peine effleurée", Jean-Pierre Tadros; *Globe and Mail,* August 10, 1974, "A Movie Exposé Worth Exposing: Why Do Quebeckers Love **Bingo**?", Martin Knelman; *Bingo,* Michel Capistran (Editions de l'Aurore, 1975), a novel based on the filmscript; *Cinéma-Québec,* vol 2, no. 1, pp. 9-10, Lord talks about **Les colombes**; *Cinéma-Québec,* vol. 2, no. 3, pp. 28-29, "Une mythologie québécoise toujours à déchiffrer", Jean Leduc; *Cinéma-Québec,* vol. 3, no. 6-7, pp. 31-38, **Bingo** sur une foire de confusion", Pierre Vallières, "Critique de Gauche ou critique gauche", Jacques Godbout, and "**Bingo** à Joliette", Pierre Forest.

LOW, COLIN

Colin Low was born in Cardston, Alberta in 1926, and in 1945, at Norman McLaren's request, he joined the National Film Board as an animator. Later, as director of animation, Low produced Derek Lamb's **I Know an Old Lady Who Swallowed a Fly** and Gerald Potterton's **My Financial Career** and **The Ride**. Low's films are poetic investigations of our relationship with the past and, although his work in the Challenge for Change unit from 1967 to 1972 was innovative in structure, it was also concerned with traditions. As film director for the Fogo Island project (undertaken in conjunction with Newfoundland's Memorial University Extension Service, the project produced 28 short films which were used as tools for community discussion), Low was involved in the process of solving problems within a community. Low was guest producer with the Office of Economic Opportunity in the United States and produced a number of films there on community development. He co-produced and co-directed **Labyrinth** with Roman Kroitor for Expo '67. As head of the NFB's Challenge for Change Unit, Low had an important and far-reaching effect on Canadian cinema; for this work he received the Grierson Award at the 1972 Canadian Film Awards. The same year he was appointed executive producer for the new Unit C, and was charged with developing inter-disciplinary films to explore the social, economic and political aspects of environmental problems. As producer and executive producer, Colin Low has recently been involved with the following films: **Kainai, Cree Hunters of Mistassini, In Search of the Bowhead Whale, Musicanada, Los Canadienses: The Mac-kenzie-Papineau Battalion, Descent** and **Blackwood**. Dr. Low received an honourary L.L.D. from Memorial University in 1968 and another from the University of Calgary in 1972.

Filmography

Cadet Rousselle (1946). With George Dunning. Prod: NFB. 8 min. col.

Time and Terrain (Le temps et la terre) (1947). Prod: NFB. 11 min. col.

Up, Right and Wrong (Le Baron Munchausen) (1947). With George Dunning. Prod: T.V. Cartoons (London). 10 min. col. Finished in 1965 with soundtrack by Norman McLaren.

Age of the Beaver (L'âge du castor) (1951). Prod: Tom Daly, NFB. 17 min. b&w.

The Romance of Transportation in Canada (Sports et transports) (1953). With Wolf Koenig and Robert Verrall. Prod: Tom Daly, NFB. 11 min. col.

Corral (Corral) (1953). Prod: Tom Daly, NFB. 12 min. b&w.

The Jolifou Inn (L'auberge Jolifou) (1954). Prod: Tom Daly, NFB. 10 min. col.

Gold (L'or) (1955). Prod: Tom Daly, NFB. 11 min. b&w.

City of Gold (Capitale de l'or) (1957). With Wolf Koenig. Prod: Tom Daly, NFB. 22 min. b&w.

City Out of Time (Ville intemporelle) (1959). Prod: Tom Daly, NFB. 16 min. col.

Universe (Notre univers) (1960). With Roman Kroitor. Prod: C. Low, R. Kroitor and Tom Daly, NFB. 26 min. col.

Circle of the Sun (Le soleil perdu) (1960). Prod: Tom Daly, NFB. 29 min. col.

The Days of Whisky Gap (1961). Prod: Roman Kroitor, Wolf Koenig, NFB. 28 min. b&w.

The Hutterites (Les Huttérites) (1963). Prod: Tom Daly, Roman Kroitor, NFB. 28 min. b&w.

Labyrinth (1967). With Roman Koritor and Hugh O'Connor. Prod: NFB for Expo '67.

The Winds of Fogo (1969). Prod: Tom Daly, Challenge for Change, NFB. 20 min. col.

Bibliography

Images, vol. 1, no. 3 (April 1956), interview by Arthur Lamothe; *Séquences*, no. 24 (February 1961), pp. 29-30, "Un cinéaste canadien: Colin Low" (interview); *Objectif* 63, no. 23/24 (October-November 1963), pp. 24-38, "Colin Low, poète de la survivance", Jean-Pierre Lefebvre (interview); *Séquences*, no. 50 (October 1967), pp. 22-23, "La création cinématographique: dialogue avec Colin Low" (interview); *Objectif* 61, no. 4 (January 1961), pp. 21-25, "A la recherche du soleil", Michel Regnier; *Montreal Star*, November 9, 1968, "How Film May Help the Fogo Islanders", Boyce Richardson; *Dossiers de cinéma: 1* (Edition fides, 1968), reviews of **Corral** and **City of Gold**; *St. John's Evening Telegram*, April 14, 1970, review of **Winds of Fogo** by Michael Cook; *How to Make or Not to Make a Canadian Film* (La cinémathèque canadienne, 1967), "Will Story Film Use Multi-screen?", by Low; *Editions*, no. 174 (published by Institut des hauts études cinématographiques, Paris) extensive review of **City of Gold** (compiled by the Canadian filmmaker, Jean-Pierre Masse); references in *Jeune cinéma canadien, Le cinéma canadien, Cinéma d'ici* and *L'aventure du cinéma direct.*

LYNCH, PAUL

Born in Liverpool, England in 1946, Paul Lynch came to Canada in 1960 and worked in advertising agencies and as a cartoonist for the *Toronto Star;* he has also been a photographer for *Maclean's, The Canadian* and *Toronto Life*. His first film, **Teenage Marriage**, grew out of a photographic story he had undertaken. Lynch's first feature, **The Hard Part Begins**, was written by John Clifford Hunter who also co-produced the film. As well as preparing a feature film script, Lynch continues his work as a graphic designer in Toronto for the *Calendar Magazine* group.

Filmography

Teenage Marriage (1968). Prod: Glen Sarty, CBC "Take Thirty". 15 min. b&w.

Be Not Too Hard (1969). Prod: Leo Rampen, CBC "Man Alive". 30 min. b&w.

Charlie (1969). Prod: Don Elder, CBC. 30 min. col.

What's You Gonna Be, Boy, What's You Gonna Do? (1970). Prod: David Peddie, CBC "To See Ourselves". 30 min. col.

A Handy Guy Like Sandy (1970). Prod: Sam Levine, CBC "Telescope". 30 min. col.

Choice (1970). Prod: Don Elder, CBC, Schools and Youth Department. 30 min. col.

Big Bus Going to Nashville (1971). Prod: Sam Levine, CBC "Telescope". 30 min. col.

The Late Man (1972). Prod: Paddy Sampson, CBC "Program X". 30 min. col.

The Hard Part Begins (1973). Prod: John Clifford Hunter, Derrett G. Lee, Odyssey Films Ltd. 91 min. col. Dist: Cinepix.

The Stock Car Boys (1973). Prod: Sam Levine, CBC "Gallery". 30 min. col.

The Painted Door (1973). Prod: David Peddie, CBC "To See Ourselves". 30 min. col.

Guccione (1974). Prod: Hugh F. Curry, Hupa Productions. 30 min. col.

Bibliography

Saturday Night, August 1974, "On the Road With a Middle-Aged Loser", Marshall Delaney; *Globe and Mail,* September 14, 1974, "**The Hard Part** Catches the Flavour of Ontario's Nowhere Towns", Martin Knelman; *Toronto Star,* September 21, 1974, review of **The Hard Part Begins** by Clyde Gilmour; *Time,* September 30, 1974, "Last Hoedown in Paris", Mark Nichols; *Motion,* September-October 1974, p. 38, review of **The Hard Part Begins**; *Maclean's,* October 1974, "Showing Canada As It Is, **The Hard Part Begins**" John Hofsess; *La Presse,* November 23, 1974, "Lynch et Hunter sont sobres. . .trop!", S.D.; *Séquences,* no. 79 (January 1975), p. 33, review of **The Hard Part Begins** by Robert-Claude Bérubé; *Cinema Canada,* no. 18; pp. 56-60, review of **The Hard Part Begins** by Mark Miller.

MACARTNEY-FILGATE, TERENCE

Born in England in 1924, Terence Macartney-Filgate joined the NFB as a scriptwriter in 1954 and became a key member of the Candid Eye Unit between 1957 and 1960. The sense of actuality and ability to adapt readily to ongoing situations which were developed in the unit have had reverberating effects, not only within the NFB but in *cinéma-vérité* everywhere. Since leaving the NFB, Filgate has spent time in the United States working with Leacock and Maysles, produced film in Lebanon, taught at UCLA and, most recently, has been freelancing out of the CBC in Toronto. Filgate is an active cameraman on all of his films and shot the live-action sequences for Potterton's **Pinter People**. Eldon Rathburn wrote scores for the films on Montgomery and Grenfell.

Filmography (incomplete)

The Days Before Christmas (Bientôt Noël) (1958). With Wolf

Koenig, Georges Dufaux and Stanley Jackson. Prod: Roman Kroitor, Wolf Koenig, NFB. 30 min. b&w.

Blood and Fire (1958). Prod: Roman Kroitor, Wolf Koenig, NFB. 30 min. b&w.

Police (1958). Prod: Wolf Koenig, Roman Kroitor, NFB. 29 min. b&w.

Pilgrimage (1958). Prod: Wolf Koenig, NFB. 29 min. b&w.

The Back-breaking Leaf (La feuille qui brise les reins) (1959). Prod: Roman Kroitor, Wolf Koenig, NFB. 29 min. b&w.

End of the Line (1959). Prod: Roman Kroitor, Wolf Koenig, NFB. 30 min. b&w.

The Cars in Your Life (1959). Prod: Roman Kroitor, Wolf Koenig, NFB. 29 min. b&w.

Emergency in Morocco (1960). Prod: United Nations/NFB. 16 min. b&w.

Pilot X-15 (1960). Prod: Time Broadcasting Inc. 30 min. b&w.

Robert Frost: A Lover's Quarrel (1962). (Director and cameraman for Vermont sequences.) Prod: WGBH/NET. 60 min. b&w.

Inside the Movie Kingdom (1963). Prod: NBC. 60 min. b&w.

South Africa Essays (1964). Prod: NET. 60 min.

The Hundredth Summer (Le centième été) (1964). Prod: T. Macartney-Filgate, NFB. 52 min. col.

Vladimir Nabokov (1965). With Robert Hughes. Prod: NET "Creative Persons". 30 min. b&w.

Composers U.S.A.: The Avant-Garde (1966). Prod: NET "Creative Persons". 30 min. b&w.

Portrait of Karsh (1966). Prod: CBC "Telescope". 30 min. col.

Marshall McLuhan (1967). Prod: CBC "Telescope". 30 min. col.

Christopher Plummer (1967). Prod: CBC, "TBA". 30 min. b&w.

Woody Allen (1967). Prod: CBC. 20 min. b&w.

Up Against the System (1969). Prod: George C. Stoney, NFB, Challenge for Change. 20 min. b&w.

A.Y. Jackson: A Portrait (1970). Prod: CBC "Man at the Centre". 30 min. col.

Henry David Thoreau: The Beat of a Different Drummer (1972). Prod: T. Macartney-Filgate, CBC. 60 min. col.

The Time Machine (1973). Prod: T. Macartney-Filgate, CBC "Man at the Centre". 60 min. col.

Indian Music at York University (1974). Prod: T. Macartney-Filgate, CBC "Arts Magazine". 15 min. col.

Lucy Maud Montgomery: The Road to Green Gables (1975). Prod: T. Macartney-Filgate, CBC. 90 min. col.

Grenfell of Labrador (1976). Prod: T. Macartney-Filgate, CBC. 90 min. col.

Work in progress: **In the Steps of Norman Bethune**. Prod: CBC.

BIBLIOGRAPHY

Terence Macartney-Filgate: The Candid Eye, Canadian Filmography Series no. 104 (Canadian Film Institute, Ottawa, 1966). Has an interview by Sarah Jennings, comments by Gilles Gascon and Georges Dufaux, discussions with Roman Kroitor and Jean-Claude Labrecque on Filgate and the Candid Eye Unit, and a filmography. (Now out of print. Available at film study centres.); *Sight and Sound,* vol. 34, no. 1 (Winter 1964-65), pp. 19-23, "The Innocent Eye — An Aspect of the Work of the National Film Board of Canada", Peter Harcourt; *Image et Son,* April 1965, Louis Marcorelles; *Montreal Star,* June 26, 1965, "Apartheid Documentary Shot Cloak-and-Dagger Style", Raymond Heard; *Books in Canada,* vol. 4, no. 10 (October 1975), pp. 5-6, "Arts and the Women", Catherine L. Orr; references in *Cinéma d'ici* and *L'aventure du cinéma direct.*

McCOWAN, GEORGE

George McCowan was born in Winnipeg in 1931. After graduating from the University of Toronto he spent four years acting and directing at Stratford, Ontario. He directed many films for the CBC, including **Twelfth Night**, **Mother Courage**, **Feast of Lupercal** and **A Suitable Case for Treatment**, as well as numerous episodes of "Seaway", "The Forest Ranger" and "Wojeck" before going to Hollywood in 1967. There McCowan made programs for various television serials and directed seven 90-minute films for ABC's "Movie of the Week". His first feature was **Face-Off** (1971); it was followed by **Frogs** (1972), a horror movie; **The Magnificent Seven Ride** (1972); and **The Inbreaker** (1974), set in British Columbia. **To Kill the King** (1974) was made originally on videotape and then filmed. McCowan lives in Toronto and Los Angeles.

Bibliography

Toronto Star, February 20, 1965, "Hedonist Reaches End of His Tether", David Cobb; *Le petit journal,* November 18, 1971, "**Face-Off** du hockey au cinema"; *Montreal Gazette,* November 20, 1971, "**Face-Off** . . . Fair Sports Movie — Disastrous as a Love Story", Dave Billington; *Time,* November 22, 1971, p. 16, "Hockey Night at the Movies", Mark Nichols; *Maclean's,* December 1971, review of **Face-Off** by John Hofsess; *Saturday Night,* January 1972, p. 41, review of **Face-Off**; *Motion,* September-October 1974, p. 7, review of **Inbreaker** by Marta Farevaag; *Globe and Mail,* December 17, 1974, "**Inbreaker** a Failure with Good Intentions", L.O.T.

MACKEY, CLARKE

Born 1950 in Port Colbourne, Ontario, Clarke Mackey studied acting at the Toronto School of Drama and the University of Toronto, making his first 8mm film after working with filmmakers David Sector and Julius Kohanyi. He had worked as a film editor at the CBC and edited a number of films by Dick Ballentine. As a cameraman he shot Iain Ewing's **Picaro**, **Kill** and **Eat Anything**, and more recently **As We Are**, a film on handicapped children directed by Marty Gross; this film, on which Mackey collaborated, won the 1973 Grand Prix at the Oberhausen documentary film festival. Mackey's feature **The Only Thing You Know** won two Etrogs in the 1971 Canadian Film Awards for best first feature and best actress (Ann Knox). Mackey has taught filmmaking at the Toronto Film Coop, Artists' Workshop, Sheridan College and York University. In 1972 he worked with Margot Cronis on the Regent Park Film Workshop and in 1975 they produced **The Edge**, directed by prison inmates.

Filmography

On Nothing Days (1967). Prod: Independent. 25 min. b&w.

Ruins (1967). Prod: Independent. 10 min. col.

Grass (1968). Prod: Independent. 45 min. col. Dist: International Telefilm.

Mihi P. (1969). Prod: Independent. 28 min. b&w.

The Only Thing You Know (1971). Prod: Clarke Mackey Films. 82 min. col. Dist: New Cinema.

Indian Handicrafts (1974). With Margot Cronis. Prod: Angus McLelland, CTV "W5". 10 min. col.

Gulf Oil in Angola (1974). With Margot Cronis. Prod: CBC "Weekday" 6 min. col.

The Workman's Compensation Board (1974). With Margot Cronis. Prod: Hans Pohl, CBC "Weekday". 17 min. col.

Live With Lea-Anne (1974). Prod: Ross McLean, CBC "Of All People". 15 min. col.

Fight Night (1975). Prod: Gerald Mayer, CBC "Peep Show". 30 min. col.

Bibliography

Pot pourri, December 1971, an interview by Pat Thorvaldson; *Toronto Citizen,* vol. 2, no. 16 (August 16, 1971), interview by Bruce Leaux; *Toronto Telegram,* October 9, 1971, "Fame's Reward Selling Books", Sid Adilman, and August 14, 1971, "The Young Canadian Filmmaker's First Feature Tonight", also by Adilman; *Maclean's,* November 1971 and January 1972 — both articles by John Hofsess; *Take One,* vol. 2, no. 12, pp. 20-21, Bob Fothergill; *Globe and Mail,* June 2, 1972, "**Only Thing You Know**: Pleasing Growing Pains", Robert Martin.

McLAREN, NORMAN

Born in Scotland, Norman McLaren studied at the Glasgow School of Art where he made his first animated films. John Grierson, at that time head of the British General Post Office (GPO) Film Unit, invited McLaren to join them in 1937; there he made **Book Bargain**, **News for the Navy** and **Love on the Wing**. From 1939 to 1941 McLaren worked in New York, independently and for the Museum of Non-Objective Art, before joining the National Film Board in 1941. There he first made animated films to support the war effort: **Mail Early**, **V for Victory**, **Five for Four**, **Dollar Dance** and **Keep Your Mouth Shut**. Much of McLaren's early work involved painting directly on film, but in 1952 with the anti-war film, **Neighbours**, he developed a process of animating live actors called "pixillation". McLaren went on to work with actors in many other films: **A Chairy Tale** starring Claude Jutra and a chair that felt oppressed; **Opening Speech: McLaren** featuring McLaren himself and a microphone which refuses to stand still; and more recently his dance films, **Pas de deux** and **Ballet Adagio**. McLaren's involvement with music resulted in **A Phantasy** (1952) with music for saxophones and synthetic sound by Maurice Blackburn; **Canon**, an animated musical explication; and **Pen Point Percussion** and **Synchromy**, both visualizing sound which has been drawn directly onto the film.

McLaren has had a long collaboration with Evelyn Lambart who has since retired from the NFB. Ms Lambert joined the National Film Board in 1942 after studies at the Ontario College of Art; with McLaren she collaborated on **Begone Dull Care**, **Short and Suite**, **Lines Vertical**, **Lines Horizontal**, **A Chairy Tale** and **Mosaic**.

Bibliography

Séquences, no. 42 (October 1965), pp. 52-55, "Entretien avec Norman McLaren"; *McGill Reporter*, vol. 1, no. 35 (April 28, 1969), pp. 3-5, "Talking to a Great Film Artist", Don McWilliams (interview); *Dots and Loops: The Story of a Scottish Film Cartoonist, Norman McLaren*, Hardy Forsyth (Edinburgh, 1951), available for reference at film study centres; *Tamarack Review*, Autumn 1957, pp. 42-53, "Norman McLaren", Germaine Warkentin; *Film Culture*, no. 25 (Summer 1962), pp. 46-47, "Mc et Moi: A Spiritual Portrait of Norman McLaren", Gretchen Weinberg; *The Quarterly of Film, Radio and Television*, vol. 8, no. 1, "Norman McLaren: His Career and Techniques", William E. Jordan, includes a short biography, a filmography to 1964 and an appreciative study of his techniques, also available as a pamphlet reprint from National Film Board offices; *Canadian Art*, no. 97 (May-June 1965), "The Unique Genius of Norman McLaren", May Ebbitt Cutler; *Perspectives*, no. 43 (October 23, 1965), pp. 28-30,

"Le cinéaste sans camera"; *The National Film Board of Canada: The War Years,* Peter Morris, ed., Canadian Film Archives, Canadian Filmography Series, no. 3 (Ottawa: Canadian Film Institute, 1965), available for reference at film study centres; *Norman McLaren* (La Cinémathèque québécoise, 1965), published on the occasion of a Norman McLaren retrospective, containing testimonials by André Martin, Alexandre Alexeieff, John Grierson, John Hubley, Dusan Vukotic, Robert Benayoun, Maurice Blackburn, Colin Low, Len Lye, George Dunning and Grant Munro, among others. A detailed filmography to 1965 and an inventory of techniques developed or used by McLaren in specific films are also included. Available in film study centres; *Fundamental Education: A Quarterly Bulletin,* vol. 1, no. 4, UNESCO, "Cameraless Animation", Norman McLaren. Technical information with plans for setting up a work table and procedures for cameraless animation. Also available as a reprinted pamphlet in English and French from the National Film Board; *Take One,* vol. 1, no. 1, pp. 18-23, "Multi-McLaren"; *Film Quarterly,* Fall 1968, pp. 36-41, "Pixillation", Don Burns; *Le Soleil,* December 12, 1970, "McLaren: 'je suis un miniaturiste'", G. Rheault; *Film Culture,* no. 48-49 (1970), pp. 41-48, "The Synthesis of Artificial Movements in Motion Picture Projection", Norman McLaren and Guy Glover; *Montreal Gazette,* March 4, 1972, "The Graphic Side of Norman McLaren", Michael White; *Séquences,* no. 82 (October 1975), 20th Anniversary issue, "Norman McLaren"; *The Drawings of Norman McLaren,* Norman McLaren (Montreal: Tundra Books, 1975), 560 drawings with a bilingual text; *Norman McLaren,* Maynard Collins (Canadian Film Institute, 1975); *Cinema Canada,* no. 9, pp. 42-49, "The Career of Norman McLaren", includes a filmography and bibliography; *The Eye Hears The Ear Sees* is a hour-long exposition, on film, of McLaren's work and a tribute to him. Made by the BBC, it is available for loan from the National Film Board.

MANKIEWICZ, FRANCIS

Born in Shanghai in 1944, Francis Mankiewicz became a Montrealer a year later. He attended McGill and the University of Montreal where he received a degree in geology. After graduation Mankiewicz worked as a translator, photographer and journalist, and in 1965 wrote a critical analysis of the war in Viet Nam for a Paris newspaper. His film career began in England with studies at the London School of Film Technique, working as a cameraman and as director-actor in a professional acting studio. He returned to Montreal in 1968 where he directed, produced and shot six short industrial documentaries, "CN 68". As a cameraman he worked on Tom Fletcher's study of a Windsor black community, Alain Laury's **McGill français** and Jutra's **Marie-Christine**. As assistant director he has worked on **Love in a Four Letter World**, **Cold Journey** and **L'amour humain**. His own feature, **Le temps d'une chasse**, was the official selection at the 1972 "Critique section", Festival of Venice, and at the 1972 Canadian Film Awards it won best photography, best sound recording and special jury prize awards; the screenplay was written by Mankiewicz, with editing by Werner Nold and photography by Michel Brault.

Filmography

Le temps d'une chasse (Hour of the Hunt) (1972). Prod: Pierre Gauvreau, NFB. 92 min. col.

Valentin (1973). Prod: Bertrand Viard and René Avon, Projex for ORTF, Radio-Canada "Témoignage". 30 min. col.

Un procès criminal and **Une cause civile** (1973). Prod: Donald Duprey, International Cinemedia Centre, for OFQ for Quebec Department of Education. 20 min. each. b&w.

L'orientation (1974). Prod: Donald Duprey, Cinemedia for Quebec Department of Education. 30 min. col.

Work in progress: A feature with script by Marc Gélinas.

Bibliography

La Presse, October 7, 1972, "Mankiewicz: une fiction parente du documentaire", Yves Leclerc (interview); *Séquences,* no. 70 (October 1972), pp. 21-22, interview by Léo Bonneville and pp. 4-8, review of **Le temps** by Janick Beaulieu; *Cinema Canada,* no. 7 (April-May 1973), pp. 64-67, interview by Kiss/Köller: *Motion,* May-June 1973, pp. 16-19, "The Idea of Life and Death" (interview); *Image et son,* France, no. 287 (September 1974), pp. 91-93, interview by Guy Gauthier and critique of **Le temps**; *Take One,* vol. 3, no. 7, review of **Le temps** by Barbara Godard; *La Presse,* October 7, 1972, "La fin de l'innocence", Luc Perreault; *Gazette,* October 7, 1972, "Excellent Fare From the NFB", Jacob Siskind; *Le Soleil,* October 14, 1972, "Le premier film, soigné, appliqué, et sans bavure, de Francis Mankiewicz", Pierre Desrosiers; *Cinéma-Québec,* vol. 2, no. 3 (November 1972), pp. 20-24, "Pas tout à fait une oeuvre", Michel Euvrard on **Le temps**; *Globe and Mail,* March 10, 1973, "Québécois Mankiewicz and His Subtle Study", Martin Knelman.

MARKOWITZ, MURRAY

Born in Toronto in 1945, Murray Markowitz majored in psychology at the University of Waterloo. He studied law before making his first films as a student in still-photography and film at Ryerson Polytechnical Institute. His first feature, **More Than One**, is a study of the relationships among three retarded people. Markowitz has written or collaborated on the scripts of all his films. The subject of his latest feature, **Recommendation for Mercy**, shot by Richard Leiterman, is the trial of a 14-year-old boy for the rape and murder of a young girl. In addition to his work in film, Markowitz has studied drawing, worked as a doorman and usher at Bank Theatres in London, published photographs and a book of drawings and prose (*Drawings by a Jewish Boy Who Loved a German Girl,* Coach House Press, 1970).

Filmography

Ode to Blake (1969). Prod: Independent. 7 min. b&w.
Ode to Mom and Dad (1969). Prod: Independent. 7 min. b&w.
More Than One (1970). Prod: Independent. 64 min. b&w.
August & July (1973). Prod: M. Markowitz, Paradise Films Ltd. 92 min. col. Dist: New Cinema.
Recommendation for Mercy (1975). Prod: James P. Lewis, M. Markowitz, Paradise Films Ltd. 92 min. col. Dist: Astral.
Feature work in progress: **Cruel** (working title).

Bibliography

Saturday Night, July 1971, "Soul to Soul", review of **More Than One** by Marshall Delaney; *Saturday Night,* February 1973, review of **August & July**; *Cinema Canada,* no. 6 (February-March 1973), pp. 54-61 (interview); *Globe and Mail,* April 7, 1973, "Weary Characters, Inane Dialogue. Two Lesbians in Search of Canada"; *Globe and Mail,* May 4, 1973, "A Glossy Loser, a Wacky Winner", Natalie Edwards on **August & July**; *Montreal Gazette,* December 1, 1973, "Boring Claptrap in the Bullrushes" (on **August & July**); *Montreal Gazette,* December 15, 1973, "Putting Real People on Film", Jay Newquist; *Le Droit,* Ottawa, February 23, 1974, "Chronique (lesbienne) d'un amour d'été"; *Take One,* vol. 3, no. 9, "**August & July**", Robert Fothergill; *Cinema Canada,* no. 19 (May-June 1975), pp. 40-41, "Murray Murders a Memory and Calls It **Recommendation for Mercy**", Natalie Edwards; *Cinema Canada,* no. 20 (July-August 1975), pp. 46-48, "A Reply to Hofsess, a Challenge to Shebib and a **Recommendation for Mercy**", Robert Fothergill; *Take One,* vol. 4, no. 9, pp. 29-30, "Humanity and Power", Robert Fothergill on **Recommendation for Mercy**.

MARKSON, MORLEY

Designer, photographer, inventor and teacher Morley Markson created the Kaleidoscope pavilion at Expo '67; as well as designing the three-chambered pavilion, Markson directed the films and produced the colour, movement and sound interior within a mirror projection system. Intensely personal, Markson's films deal with the convolutions of individual and social expression when passing through different media. His two feature films, **The Tragic Diary of Zero the Fool** and **Breathing Together: Revolution of the Electric Family**, won first prizes at the Ann Arbor Film Festival in 1970 and 1971. His latest feature, **Monkeys in the Attic: A Tale of Exploding Dreams**, was scripted by John Palmer and Markson, shot by Henri Fiks and stars Toronto actress Jackie Burroughs; it received the "Prix Khalimer" for best foreign film at the 1974 Toulon Film Festival. Markson lives and works in his native city, Toronto.

Filmography

Man and Color (1967). Prod: M. Markson for Kaleidoscope Pavilion, Expo '67. 12 min. col.

Zero (1968). Prod: Independent. 8½ min. b&w.

America Simultaneous: The Electric Family (1968). Prod: Independent. A multi-screen sound spectacle.

Electrocution of the Word (1968). prod: Independent. 4 min. col.

Eyebang (1968). Prod: Independent. 5 min. b&w.

The Tragic Diary of Zero the Fool (Zéro le fou) (1970). Prod: Morley Markson and Associates Ltd. 72 min. b&w. Dist: New Cinema.

Breathing Together: Revolution of the Electric Family (Vivre ensemble: la famille électrique) (1971). Prod: Morley Markson and Associates Ltd. 84 min. b&w. Dist: New Cinema.

Kaleidoscope '73 (1973). Prod: Morley Markson and Associates Ltd. for Ontario Place. 12 min. col.

Monkeys in the Attic: A Tale of Exploding Dreams (Les singes au grenier) (1974). Prod: Morley Markson, K.T. Productions Inc. 85 min. col. Dist: Ambassador.

Bibliography

Cinema Canada, no. 16, pp. 38-41, interview with Markson by Á. Ibrányi-Kiss; *CIL Oval,* vol. 35, no. 4 (Winter 1966), "Expo's Potent Color Show — Kaleidoscope", Joy Carroll; *Architecture Canada,* October 1967, "Psychedelic Experience Without LSD"; *Toronto Star,* January 17, 1969, "Are You Beginning to See the Light?", Martin Knelman; *Saturday Night,* February 1970, "Movie Review", Marshall Delaney; *Artscanada,* no. 142-43 (April 1970), pp. 50-51, "New Film in Toronto", Douglas Pringle on **Tragic**; *Jeune Cinema,* no. 56 (June-July 1971), p. 34, review of **Breathing Together**; *Positif,* no. 130 (September 1971), pp. 14-15, review of **Breathing Together**; *Le Soleil,* October 30, 1971, "On ne connait pas l'issue du combat", review of

Breathing Together; *Image et son,* no. 252 (1971), p. 30, review of **Breathing Together**; *Filmmakers Newsletter,* N.Y., vol. 4, no. 7, p. 49, review of **Breathing Together**; *Les lettres françaises,* no. 1439 (June 8, 1972), p. 16, "Morley Markson: respirons, conspirons", Gerald Langlois; *Motion,* January-March 1975, p. 26, review of **Monkeys** by Ian McBride; *Cinema Canada,* no. 16 (February 1975), pp. 68-70, reviews of **Monkeys** by Robert Fothergill and George Köller; *Globe and Mail,* Toronto, March 1, 1975, review of **Monkeys** by Martin Knelman; *Toronto Star,* March 5, 1975, review of **Monkeys** by Clyde Gilmour.

MASON, BILL

Bill Mason was born in Winnipeg in 1929. He was a painter and commercial artist before moving into animation. While working with Crawley Films he portrayed the canoeist in Christopher Chapman's **Quetico** and shot a variety of films, among them **On the Top of a Continent** and **The Voyageurs**. Mason's love of the bush encouraged him to bring a storyline to his still photography, and as a conservationist, he has touched the popular imagination. His most charming film, **Blake**, has as hero, animator Blake James; James also stars in **The Rise and Fall of the Great Lakes**. Veteran writer Stanley Jackson supplied commentary for **Death of a Legend**. Mason is currently making four films on canoeing, including **Basic**, **White Water** and **Canoe Camping**. Mason works out of the National Film Board.

Filmography

Wilderness Treasure (1965). Prod: Wilber Sutherland, Intervarsity Christian Fellowship. 20 min. col.
Paddle to the Sea (Vogue-à-la-mer) (1966). Prod: Julian Biggs, NFB. 28 min. col.
The Rise and Fall of the Great Lakes (1968). Prod: Joseph Koenig, NFB. 17 min. col.
Blake (Blake) (1969). Prod: Douglas Jackson, NFB. 19 min. col.
Death of a Legend (La fin d'un mythe) (1971). Prod: Barrie Howells, NFB. 51 min. col.
Cry of the Wild (Le chant de la forêt) (1972). Prod: Bill Brind, NFB. 88 min. col.
In Search of the Bowhead Whale (1974). Prod: Bill Brind, Colin Low, NFB. 49 min. col.
Face of the Earth (1975). Prod: Wolf Koenig, NFB. 20 min. col.

Bibliography

Pot pourri, September 1971, interview by Pat Thorvaldson,

reprinted in *Sight Lines,* November-December 1971, pp. 4-8;
Saturday Citizen, Ottawa, January 24, 1970, "Big Bad Wolf:
Wright Family Filming in 'Secret'", review of **Death of a Legend**
by Burt Heward; *Ottawa Citizen,* September 25, 1971, "Film
Probes 'Bad Guy' Reputation of Wolves", review of **Death of a
Legend** by Gordon Stoneham; *Québec-presse,* October 3, 1971,
"Les loups ne sont pas si méchants qu'on le dit...", review of
Death of a Legend by Carol Faucher; *Le grand journal illustré,*
October 11-17, 1971, p. 24, "La fin d'un mythe...les loups ren-
dus sympathiques", review of **Death of a Legend** by Benoit
L'Herbier; *Montreal Gazette,* September 9, 1972, "The Man Who
Found a Sheep in Wolf's Clothing", review of **Death of a Legend**
by Dane Lanken; *Time,* February 25, 1974, "Lone Wolf", review
of **Cry of the Wild**; *Globe and Mail,* March 2, 1974, "Canada's
Cry of the Wild Booms But Not in Its Own Country", Betty Lee;
Montreal Gazette, March 9, 1974, "**Cry of the Wild**: The Wolf in
Retreat", Dave Billington; *Séquences,* no. 76 (April 1974), pp.
32-33, review of **Cry of the Wild** by Michael Vanasse; *Cinéma-
Québec,* vol. 3, no. 6-7, pp. 72-73, review of **Cry of the Wild** by
Richard Gay; *Pot pourri,* February 1975, pp. 17-18, review of **In
Search of the Bowhead Whale** by Paul Hennig.

MAY, DEREK

Painter and filmmaker Derek May was born in London, England in
1932. He joined the National Film Board as an assistant editor in
1965, and acted in Don Owen's **Notes For a Film About Donna
and Gail** and **The Ernie Game**; he was also art director for the
latter production. May's own films can be described as personal,
very much in the tradition of the London, Ontario artist-filmmaker
Jack Chambers. May worked in video with the Challenge for
Change Unit and in 1972 travelled and painted on a Canada Council grant. In 1975 he worked in West Africa for the United Nations
project, Habitat '76.

Filmography

Angel (1967). Prod: Guy Glover, NFB. 7 min. col.
Niagara Falls (1968). Prod: Tom Daly, NFB. 28 min. col.
McBus (1969). Prod: Tom Daly, NFB. 15 min. col.
A Film for Max (1971). Prod: Tom Daly, NFB. 80 min. col. and
   b&w.
Pandora (1971). Prod: Tom Daly, NFB. 6 min. col.
Sananquagat: Inuit Masterworks (1974). Prod: Tom Daly, NFB
   and the Department of Indian Affairs and Northern Develop-
   ment. 25 min. col.
Work in progress: **National Gallery**.

Bibliography

Pot pourri, September 1973, pp. 11-15 (interview); *Montreal Gazette,* September 27, 1969, "Derek May: A Cosmic Weatherman", Terry Ryan; *Artscanada,* April 1970, p. 26, "Six Filmmakers in Search of an Alternative", Terry Ryan; *Le Nouvelliste,* Trois-Rivières, May 18, 1968, p. 173, on **Angel**; *Screen,* vol. 5, no. 2, pp. 15-17, on **Pandora**; *Pot pourri,* November 1974, pp. 18-19, review of **Sananquagat** by Dan Driscoll; *Language of Change,* by Mark Slade, reference to May on p. 173.

MELANÇON, ANDRE

André Melançon was born in 1942 in Rouyn-Noranda, and studied psychology at the Université de Montréal after working for a year in Peru. Upon graduation he worked as a psychologist and an educator; he also played the title role in Clément Perron's **Taureau** and acted in **Partis pour la gloire**, also directed by Perron. He directed his first film, **Charles Gagnon**, working with cameramen Guy Borreman and Jean-Claude Labrecque. **Des armes et les hommes** surrealistically combines classroom demonstrations of guns used on live subjects and interviews with convicted criminals about the use of guns.

Filmography

Charles Gagnon (1970). Prod: A. Melançon. 50 min. b&w.
L'enfant et les mathématiques (1971). Prod: Les Cinéastes associés for OFQ "Mathématiques à l'élémentaire". 12 min. b&w.
Le professeur et les mathématiques (1971). Prod: Les cinéastes associés for OFQ. 12 min. col.
Des armes et les hommes (1973). Prod: Jean-Marc Garand, NFB. 58 min. col.
"Les oreilles" mène l'enquête (1974). Prod: Jacques Bobet, NFB, "Toulmonde parle français". 22 min. col.
Les tacots (1974). Prod: Jacques Bobet, NFB "Toulmonde parle français". 22 min. col.
Le violon de Gaston (1974). Prod: Paul Larose, NFB "Toulmonde parle français". 22 min. col.

Bibliography

Actualité, March 1973, "Un acteur pas ordinaire: André Mélançon", Emmanuel Cocke (interview); *Motion,* May-June 1974, p. 22, interview by James McLarty; *Cinéma-Québec,* vol. 3, no. 4 (December 1973), pp. 10-11, "**Des armes et les hommes** - d'André Melançon: une fascinante réussite", Pierre Demers.

MOREAU, MICHEL

Born in Joigny, France in 1931, Michel Moreau studied at the Ecole métiers d'art in Canada and earned his master's degree in psychology at the Université de Québec. He worked for several advertising agencies before joining the NFB in 1962; in 1964 he founded the Educational Film Unit with Jacques Parent and Robert Forget, pioneering the Canadian use of 8mm film loops and producing and directing countless teaching films. In 1967 he also worked as a consultant for the TEVEC and BAEQ projects; the latter resulted in a series of scripts for adult education on economic problems. In 1969, Moreau became a member of the Société générale cinématographique where he directed a number of films on the psychology of the child and on modern teaching techniques. He founded Educfilm in 1972 with Edith Fournier, Yves Sauvageau and Louis Daviault.

Selected Filmography

Geology series of 11 colour loops (1965). Prod: NFB.
"Jeu des propositions" series of ten colour loops (1966). Prod: NFB.
Vocabulary series of 12 loops (1967). Prod: NFB.
"Trois lecteurs en difficulté" (1968). Prod: NFB. Four films totalling 56 min. b&w.
"Mathématique à l'élémentaire" (1970). Prod: OFQ for the Quebec Ministry of Education. Approximately 20 min. each. b&w.
"Sensibilisation aux moyens d'enseignement" (1970). Prod: OFQ for SGME. Series includes: **Lucille**, 24 min. b&w; **Bonjour Monsieur Turgeon**, 14 min. b&w; **Audiovision no. 17**, 23 min. b&w; **La géographie et 5 média**, 16 min. col.; **Communication à 13 ans**, 33 min. b&w.
Comment trouver un emploi (1971). Prod: OFQ. 20 min. col.
"L'enfance inadaptée", series of nine films, one film loop and two audio-visual simulations (1971-72). Prod: OFQ for SGME. Among these were the films **Le mal de parler** and **Quatre jeunes et trois boss**, produced by Les ateliers audio-visuels du Québec.
A l'aise dans ma job (1973). Prod: Robert Millet, Educfilm for OFQ for SGME. 29 min. col.
La leçon des Mongoliens (1974). Prod: Jacques Parent, OFQ/Educfilm for SGME. 82 min. col.
"Le combat des sourds" (1974). Prod: OFQ for SGME. Series consists of: **Le combat des sourds**, 29 min. b&w. **Expériences d'une famille**, 9 min. b&w; **Le jeu des priorités**, 6 min. b&w; and **Premiers contacts,** 11 min. b&w.

Bibliography

Le Devoir, July 31, 1971, "A la découverte du film pedagogique", Jean-Pierre Tadros; *Cinéma-Québec,* vol. 3, no. 1 (September 1973), pp. 46-47, on **Au seuil de l'opératoire** by Jean-Claude Boudreault; *Cinéma-Québec,* vol. 2, no. 8, pp. 21-23, "Des cinéastes à reconnaître", Jean-Claude Boudreault on educational cinema, particularly Michel Moreau and Jacques Parent; *La Presse,* "Perspective", July 19, 1975, pp. 12-15, "Michel Moreau, cinéaste des enfants pas comme les autres", Nicole Charest on **Leçon des mongoliens**.

MUNRO, GRANT

Grant Munro was born in Winnipeg in 1923. He attended the Winnipeg School of Art and the Ontario College of Art before joining the National Film Board in 1944 as an animator of titles and special effects in the series "Canada Carries On" and "World in Action". Munro has animated a number of films and worked with the NFB as a director, producer, editor and actor. He animated the "Let's All Sing" and "More We are Together" series, and worked with Norman McLaren as an actor and editor for the Academy Award-winning film **Neighbours**, on **Two Bagatelles**, and on **Canon** which he also helped to write. Munro designed the storyboard and was co-animator of Potterton's **My Financial Career**, and was co-animator of **Christmas Cracker**. He wrote, directed and, with Ron Tunis, animated **The Animal Movie**, and produced, animated and directed **Toys**, a powerful anti-war film. His anti-smoking clips for television include **Ashes of Doom**. In 1970 Munro was sent to Cuba to work with animators at the Cuban film board and has taught film workshops in many Canadian and American colleges. He produced and directed **Tour en l'air** (1973), a documentary about Canadian dancers David and Anne-Marie Holmes, and is currently working on a documentary **Homage to Nijinska**. **Boo Hoo** (1974) is a documentary on a cemetary and crematorium in Saint John, New Brunswick.

Bibliography

Pot pourri, April 1974, p. 12, review of **Tour en l'air** by Diane Grant; "Toys", a critical pamphlet in the package *Study of the Film,* P.A. Schreivogel, (Dayton, Ohio: Geo. A. Pflaum).

NEWMAN, SYDNEY

Sydney Newman first joined the National Film Board in 1941 as a film editor after working in Toronto as a commercial artist and photographer. His first directing assignments included Armed Forces training films and war information shorts; by 1945 Newman was producing the "Canada Carries On" series under John Grierson's commissionership. In 1952 Newman joined the CBC as director of features and outside broadcasts, producing not only the first National Hockey League games but dramatic series for "General Motors Theatre" and "Ford Theatre". In 1958 he joined ABC-TV in England where he produced "The Avengers" and "Armchair Theatre" series including plays by Alun Owen and Harold Pinter. In 1963 Newman became head of the Drama Group at the BBC-TV where he commissioned the series "The Forsythe Saga" and supervised over 720 separate drama programs a year until 1969 when he became executive producer with the Associated British Picture Corporation; the company was unable to invest in feature films and Newman returned to Canada in 1970 as advisor to Pierre Juneau and the Canadian Radio-Television Commission. The same year he was appointed Government Film Commissioner and Chairman, National Film Board, an office which he held until 1975 when he was appointed Special Advisor on films to the Secretary of State. Under Newman's direction, the NFB opened regional production offices in Halifax and Winnipeg and began plans for production in Toronto; a long sought working arrangement with the CBC began with the airing of the series "Adieu alouette", "West", "Pacificanada" and 'Atlanticanada". Michel Brault's **Les ordres** was vetoed as a possible NFB production and Denys Arcand's **On est au coton** and Gilles Groulx' **24 heures ou plus** were banned.

Bibliography

Revue du cinéma international, no. 17 (May 1971), pp. 8-9, an interview by André Lafrance; *Montreal Star,* January 13, 1973, "Reflections on the NFB", Charles Lazarus (interview); *Films and Filming,* vol. 20, no. 9 (June 1974), "Rhythm 'n' truths", article and interview by D. Elley; *Cinema Canada* no. 15 (August-September 1974), pp. 42-46, "Sydney Newman: Government Film Commissioner", George Köller (interview); *Montreal Star,* August 22, 1970, "I Don't Know What I'm Going to be Fighting For", Dusty Vineberg; *Gazette,* January 27, 1973, "NFB's Newman: Censor or Saviour", Dane Lanken; *La Presse,* February 21, 1973, "Nous ne saurons pas qui nous sommes si nous n'avons pas d'artistes pour nous le dire", James Nelson; *Québec-presse,* May 6, 1973, "Le 'boss' de l'ONF parle à coeur ouvert de ses cinéastes québécois", Robert Levesque; *Globe and Mail,* January 18, 1975, "This Time NFB's Newman Won't Say No", Martin Knelman.

NOLD, WERNER

Born at St. Moritz, Switzerland in 1933, Werner Nold studied photography in his native land before coming to Canada in 1955. He worked first as a cameraman on two television series for the Quebec Film Board and later as cameraman and editor for Nova Films in Quebec City. In 1960 he joined the National Film Board as an editor, working on Gilles Carle's earliest films. One of the few editors of features films in Canada, Nold received a Canada Council grant in 1972 for further study of his craft in film centres. Nold has also directed a short, **Préambule**, with camerawork by Michel Brault, and conceived as well as edited the 35mm split-screen production **L'eau** for the Quebec Pavilion at Expo '67.

A partial list of Nold's editing credits includes: **Dimanche d'Amérique, Patinoire, Solange dans nos campagnes** and **La vie heureuse de Léopold Z** (Gilles Carle); **Le temps perdu, Entre la mer et l'eau douce**, and **La fleur de l'âge** (Michel Brault); **Pour la suite du monde** (Pierre Perrault); **Champlain** and **La route de l'ouest** (Denys Arcand); **The Indian Speaks, Avec tambours et trompettes, Episode, Saint-Denis dans le temps...**, and **OK...Laliberté** (Marcel Carrière); **A tout prendre, Comment savoir, Rouli-roulant**, and **Marie-Christine** (Claude Jutra), **IXE-13** and **La gammick** (Jacques Godbout); **60 cycles** (Jean-Claude Labrecque); **Un fait accompli** (André Théberge), **Le temps d'une chasse** (Francis Mankiewicz); **La fleur au dents** and **L'exil** (Thomas Vamos).

Bibliography

La Patrie, January 5, 1969, "Un géant qui s'appelle Werner Nold", André Bertrand; *Le cinéma québécois: tendances et prolongements,* p. 122, article by Yvan Patry; references in *L'aventure du cinéma direct* and in *Michel Brault,* "Cinéastes du Québec", no. 11.

OWEN, DONALD

Born in Toronto in 1934, writer and poet Don Owen began his film career writing for Westminster Films and the National Film Board. His first directed work, **Runner**, shows the early promise of Owen's intimate portraiture and fluid style; with commentary by W.H. Auden, **Runner** is a poetic film, an interior drama of an ancient ritual. **Nobody Waved Goodbye**, which began as a short document, became an inspired feature receiving critical acclaim wherever it was shown. **The Ernie Game** won an Etrog in 1968 as best film. Recently Owen has been investigating a more formalized style in **Gallery, A View of Time** and **Cowboy and Indian** which nevertheless retain the intimacy of his early work. **Ontario Towns and Villages** uses the recorded voices of old people as the narrative for a series of architectural documents. **Not Far From Home** is a personal narrative about living in the country. His latest feature, **Partners**, was scripted by Owen and Norman Snider. He lives and works in Toronto.

Filmography

Runner (Le coureur) (1962). Prod: Tom Daly, NFB. 11 min. b&w.

Toronto Jazz (1963). Prod: Roman Kroitor, NFB. 27 min. b&w.

Nobody Waved Goodbye (Départ sans adieux) (1964). Prod: Roman Kroitor, D. Owen, NFB. 80 min. b&w.

You Don't Back Down (1965). Prod: Joe Koenig, NFB. 28 min. b&w.

High Steel (Charpentier du ciel) (1965). Julian Biggs, NFB. 14 min. col.

Notes For a Film About Donna and Gail (1966). Prod: Julian Biggs, NFB. 49 min. b&w.

Ladies and Gentlemen: Mr. Leonard Cohen (1966). With Donald Brittain. Prod: John Kemeny, NFB. 41 min. b&w.

A Further Glimpse of Joey (1967). Prod: Ross McLean, NFB. 28 min. b&w.

The Ernie Game (Ernie) (1967). Prod: Gordon Burwash, CBC/NFB co-production. 88 min. col.

Gallery, A View of Time (1969). Prod: Albright-Knox Gallery, Buffalo, N.Y. 14 min. col.

Snow in Venice (1970). Prod: Fletcher Markle, CBC "Telescope". 30 min. b&w.

Cowboy and Indian (1972). Prod: Tom Daly, NFB. 45 min. col.

Ontario Towns and Villages, series of film clips (1972-73). Prod: Independent. 2 to 4 min. each. col.

Not Far From Home (1973). Prod: D. Owen. 30 min. col.

The St. Lawrence (1973). Prod: D. Owen, CTV "Canada, Five Portraits". 50 min. col.

A Little Something for the Old Age, **Dreams and Things**, and **Undercover** (1974). Prod: René Bonnière, CBC "The Collaborators". 60 min. each. col.

Partners (1976). Prod: D. Owen, G. Chalmers Adams, Clearwater Films Ltd. 95 min. col. Dist: Astral.

Work in Progress: **Green House Blues**.

Bibliography

Objectif, October-November 1964, pp. 47-49, "Bandes à part", and August-September 1965, pp. 30-33, both interviews; *Objectif*, no. 37 (November-December 1966), pp. 31-35, "101 questions à

Don Owen sur **Nobody Waved Goodbye**" (interview); *Canadian Cinematography*, no. 30 (January-February 1967), pp. 11-14, "Conversation on Film with Don Owen"; *Revue internationale du cinéma*, Brussels, no. 110 (April 1967), p. 13, "Don Owen: Réponses globales" (interview); *Séquences*, no. 50 (October 1967), pp. 24-26, "Dialogue avec des cinéastes canadiens, la création cinématographique" (interview); *Take One*, vol. 1, no. 2 (interview); *Canadian Cinematography*, May-June 1964, pp. 6, 7 and 16, "New Film Features Improvisation", by John Spotton, cameraman on **Nobody Waved Goodbye**; *L'Action*, Quebec, August 28, 1964, "Cinéaste de la spontanéité", André Paquet; *Objectif 63*, vol. 2, no. 10, pp. 31-32, "A pied ou en Bentley", Jacques Leduc on **Toronto Jazz**; *The Canadian*, January 6, 1966, "Going Places by Staying in Canada", Robert Miller; *Le petit journal*, March 5, 1967, "Don Owen: il est très sûr de lui, et il a raison", Danielle Sauvage; *Montreal Gazette*, November 4, 1967, "The Rules for Don Owen's **Ernie Game**", Mark Slade; *Take One*, vol. 1, no. 6 (1967), pp. 4-6, "Adrift in a Sea of Mud", Owen; *Montreal Star*, December 14, 1968, "Tip-toe Through the Sculpture — on Film", Denise Kalette, **Gallery: A View of Time**; *Globe and Mail*, December 21, 1968, "Don Owen: Meditation with Film", Martin Malina; *Dossiers de cinéma: 1* (Fides, 1968), on **Runner** and **High Steel**; *Image et son*, no. 230-231 (September-October 1969), pp. 111-112, on **The Ernie Game**; *Cinema Canada*, no. 8 (June-July 1973), pp. 30-38 and 47-48, "Who's Don Owen? What's He Done and What's He Doing Now?", Natalie Edwards; various articles in: *Le cinéma québécois: tendances et prolongement*, *Jeune cinéma canadien*, *Essais sur le cinéma québécois*, and *Le cinéma canadien;* references in *Language of Change: Moving Images of Man* and *L'aventure du cinéma direct*.

PEARSON, PETER

Born in Toronto in 1938, Peter Pearson studied political science and economics at the University of Toronto, advanced television production at Ryerson and graduated from the Centro Sperimentale di Cinematografia in Rome. In 1961 he worked as a journalist, reporting for the *Daily Press* in Timmins; from 1964 to 1966 he directed and produced items for CBC's "This Hour Has Seven Days" and "Document". **The Best Damn Fiddler from Calabogie to Kaladar**, with screenplay by Joan Finnegan, marked Pearson's move into fiction; the film received awards for best film and best director in the 1968 Canadian Film Awards. **Paperback Hero**, a finely controlled feature, written by Les Rose and Barry Pearson and shot by Don Wilder, received CFA honours for cinematography, research and editing in 1973. In 1972 Pearson was President of the Director's Guild of Canada and, in 1973, Chairman of the Council of Canadian Filmmakers.

Filmography

Sex in Advertising (1965). With Ron Mulholland. Prod: CBC "Seven Days". 4 min. b&w.

Mastroianni (1965). Prod: CBC. 30 min. b&w.

This Blooming Business of Bilingualism (1966). Prod: CBC "Eight Stories Inside Quebec". 30 min. b&w.

What Ever Happened to Them All? (1966). Prod: CBC. 30 min. b&w.

"Northern Development Films" (1966). Co-dir./Prod: David Bairstow, NFB for the Department of Indian and Northern Affairs.

Inmate Training (La formation des détenus), Parts I & II (1967). Prod: Douglas Jackson, NFB. 29 and 31 min. b&w.

Saul Alinsky Went to War (1968). With Donald Brittain. Prod: John Kemeny, NFB. 57 min. b&w.

The Best Damn Fiddler from Calabogie to Kaladar (1968). Prod: Barry Howells, NFB. 49 min b&w.

The Dowry (1969). Prod: William Canning, NFB. 20 min. col.

If I Don't Agree, Must I Go Away? (1969). Prod: P. Pearson, CBC/NET. 60 min. b&w.

Roar of the Hornet (1969). Prod: Bill Davidson, Manitou Productions "Adventures in Rainbow Country". 30 min.

Long Tough Race (1969). Prod: Bill Davidson, Manitou Productions "Adventures in Rainbow Country". 30 Min.

Seasons in the Mind (1971). With Michael Milne. Prod: Milne-Pearson Productions Ltd. for Ontario Place. 22 min. col.

"The Beachcombers" (1973). Prod: CBC. Two episodes, each 27 min. col.

Paperback Hero (1973). Prod: James Margellos, John F. Bassett, Agincourt Productions. 93 min. col. Dist: New Cinema.

1000 Miles of Highway (1974). Prod: International Cinemedia. 13 min. col.

Only God Knows (1974). Prod: Larry Z. Dane, Canart Films Ltd. 92 min. col.

Along These Lines (1975). Prod: P. Pearson, Inmedia Inc. for Bell Canada. 16 min. multi-screen. col.

The Insurance Man from Ingersoll (1976). Prod: Ralph Thomas, CBC "Performance". 58 min. col.

Kathy Karuks is a Grizzly Bear (1976). Prod: Ralph Thomas, CBC "Performance". 58 min. col.

Bibliography

Cinema Canada, no. 10/11 (October-January 1973), pp.42-47,

"Fellini's Not Bad, Bergman's Okay, But How About Me?, A. Ibranyi-Kiss and George Csaba Köller (interview); *Village Voice,* April 24, 1969, "Modest Quest", Stephanie Harrington (on **If I Don't Agree, Must I Go Away?**); *Montreal Star,* October 11, 1969, pp. 43-44, "Judgment on Film and Directors in Canada", Marc Gervais; *Toronto Telegram,* October 11, 1969, "Good Reasons for Being an Angry Young Man", Sid Adilman; *American Cinematographer,* March 1971, "Cinesphere at Ontario Place"; *Canadian Photography,* June 1971, "How Milne-Pearson Productions Made Film for Ontario Cinesphere"; *Edmonton Journal,* October 2, 1973, "**Paperback Hero** Powerful in Its Own Way", Barry Westgate; *Toronto Star,* October 11, 1973, "Gorgeous Hunk of Film", George Anthony; *Globe and Mail,* October 16, 1973, "Hero: Canadian Obsession with Losers", Betty Lee; *Toronto Star,* October 22, 1973, "**Paperback Hero** Shows Signs of Making It at Box Office", Doug Fetherling; *Saturday Night,* November 1973, p. 29, "On the Danger of Taking Women Seriously", Marshall Delaney; *Canadian Forum,* February 1974, pp. 33-36, "**Paperback Hero:** Three Canadian Films", Robert Fothergill; *Saturday Gazette,* Montreal, April 13, 1974, "A Haunting Prairie Metaphor", Jay Newquist; *Le Jour,* April 13, 1974, p. V-5, "Le Canada entre mythologie et réalité", Jean-Pierre Tadros, *Séquences,* no. 77 (July 1974), pp. 28-29, review of **Paperback Hero** by Robert-Claude Bérubé; *Globe and Mail,* September 16, 1974. "**Only God Knows** Yet Another Hackneyed Caper", Martin Knelman; *Cinema Canada,* no. 16 (October-November 1974), p. 69, review of **Only God Knows** by Mark Miller.

PERRAULT, PIERRE

Born in Montreal in 1927, Perrault studied in Montreal, Paris and Toronto and practiced law in Montreal until 1956, when he joined Radio-Canada. A poet and dramatist as well as a lawyer, Perrault added a visual dimension to his observations of the inhabitants of the north shore of the St. Lawrence. He wrote and produced a series of 13 half-hour films, directed by Réne Bonnière, entitled "Au pays de Neuve-France" and then extended his investigation with an award-winning film trilogy — **Pour la suite du monde**, **Le règne du jour**, **Les voitures d'eau** — which revolves around Marie and Alexis Tremblay, a couple strongly tied to their land. Through Perrault's poetic images we discover the source and strength of their roots. Extremely popular in France, these films have reinforced the French people's identification with the Québécois. Perrault's political awareness is expressed in **L'Acadie, l'Acadie** made with Michel Brault, and **Un pays sans bon sens**; the latter film was made at the request of the English

Unit to explain Quebec's attitudes. Since 1971 Perrault has been working on a series of 11 films about the James Bay region.

Filmography

Pour la suite du monde (Moontrap) (1963). With Michel Brault and Marcel Carrière. Prod: Jacques Bobet, Fernand Dansereau, NFB. 105 min. b&w.

Le règne du jour (1966). Prod: Jacques Bobet, Guy L. Côté, NFB. 118 min. b&w.

Les voitures d'eau (River Schooners) (1969). Prod: Jacques Bobet, Guy L. Côté, NFB. 110 min. b&w.

Le beau plaisir (Beluga Days) (1969). With Bernard Gosselin. Prod: Jacques Bobet, Guy L. Côté, NFB. 15 min. col.

Un pays sans bons sens (Wake Up, mes bons amis!!!) (1970). Prod: Tom Daly, Guy L. Côté, Paul Larose, NFB. 117 min. b&w.

L'Acadie, l'Acadie (Acadia, Acadia) (1971). With Michel Brault. Prod: Guy L. Côté, Paul Larose, NFB. 117 min. b&w.

Tickets, s.v.p. (1973). Prod: Wolf Koenig, Tom Daly, NFB. 9 min. col.

Un royaume vous attend (1975). Prod: Paul Larose, NFB. 120 min. col.

Bibliography

Cahiers du cinéma, no. 165 (April 1965), pp. 32-41, "L'action parlée", interview by Michel Delahaye and Louis Marcorelles with postscript by Michel Brault; *Le Devoir,* March 22, 1969, "Pierre Perrault: contre le mépris", Jean Chabot (interview); *Châtelaine,* September 1969, pp. 26-27 "Pierre Perrault le plus célèbre de nos cinéastes", Alice Parizeau (interview); *Cinéastes du Québec: Pierre Perrault,* CQDC, 1970, includes criticism, interview, filmography and a complete bibliography; *Cahiers du cinémathèque,* France, no. 6 (Spring 1972), pp. 72-76, "La parole est à Perrault", interview at the Festival of Avignon in 1971 by Mireille Basset; *Le Devoir,* August 10, 1974, "Un entretien avec Pierre Perrault", Louis Marcorelles; *Le Devoir,* May 24, 1975, "Le Québec de Pierre Perrault", Robert-Guy Scully (interview); *Image et son,* no. 256, devoted almost entirely to Perrault's work, with an interview and articles by Louis Marcorelles, Yves Lacroix and Guy Gauthier; *Portulan,* poetry by Pierre Perrault (Montreal: Beauchemin, 1961); *Au coeur de la rose,* a three-act play by Pierre Perrault (Beauchemin, 1964); *Saturday Night,* November 1968, pp. 24-28, "Marie and Alexis Tremblay, Movie Stars", Graham Fraser; Transcriptions of **Le règne du jour** and **Les voitures d'eau** (Montreal: Editions Lidec, 1968 and 1969, respectively); *Le Devoir,* November 28, 1970, on **Un pays sans bon sens**; *Téléciné,* France, no. 168 (March-April 1971), pp. 2-20,

"Libre cours: Pierre Perrault", Nicole Alson and Jean Aizac; *Cinéma-Québec,* vol. 1, no. 1, May 1971, "Se donner des outils de réflexion", Pierre Perrault, much of this issue is devoted to **Un pays sans bon sens**; *Actualité,* May 1971, pp. 44-45, "Pierre Perrault, un cinéaste. . .**Un pays sans bon sens**", Huguette O'Neil; *Village Voice,* February 24, 1972, p. 67, "**Les voitures d'eau** at the MOMA", Jonas Mekas; *Séquences,* no. 69 (April 1972), pp. 36-38, review of **L'Acadie** by Janik Beaulieu; *Canadian Forum,* December 1972, pp. 34-35, "Two French-Canadian Films", Gwen Matheson on **L'Acadie** and **Un pays sans bon sens**; *Un pays sans bon sens, ou Wake Up, mes bons amis,* filmscript by Pierre Perrault, Bernard Gosselin, Yves Leduc and Serge Beauchemin (Montreal: Editions Lidec Inc., 1972); *Parti pris,* 1973, "L'art et l'état", Pierre Perrault in collaboration with Robert Roussil, Denys Chevalier and André Laplante; *Le Monde,* June 20, 1974, "Un cinéaste et son pays: Pierre Perrault récrit l'histoire du Québec", Louis Marcorelles; *Montreal Star,* October 11, 1974, "**Au coeur de la rose** Ruined by Tight Budget, Poor Staging", Lawrence Sabbath; *La Presse,* October 12, 1974, "La parole du créateur n'est pas ecoutée", Martial Dassylva on **La coeur**; *Le Jour,* October 17, 1974, "**Au coeur de la rose**. . .et de bien d'autres choses", Michel Bélair; *Pierre Perrault ou un cinéma national* by Michel Brûlé (Montreal: Les Presses de l'Université de Montréal, 1974), 160 pp.; *Le cinéma québécois: tendances et prolongements,* "Pierre Perrault et la découverte d'un langage", Maximilien Laroche; "Film and Reality" by Perrault in *How to Make or Not to Make a Canadian Film* (La Cinémathèque canadienne, 1967); *Culture vivante,* no. 1, pp. 19-36, "Discours sur la parole", Pierre Perrault, reprinted in *Cahiers du cinéma,* no. 191, pp. 26-33; *Take One,* vol. 1, no. 5, "The Director as Pilgrim"; references to Perrault's work in: *Eléments pour un nouveau cinéma, Cinéma et société québécoise, Jeune cinéma canadien, Essais sur le cinéma québécois, Cinéma d'ici,* and *L'aventure du cinéma direct.*

PERRON, CLEMENT

Born in Quebec City in 1929, Clément Perron studied at the University of Laval and the Sorbonne before joining the National Film Board in 1957. As a scriptwriter he worked with Jean-Claude Labrecque on **Les smattes**; Perron wrote the scripts for his own **Taureau**, **Partis pour la gloire**, **Jour après jour** and **Caroline**, and for Jean Beaudin's **Stop**. His childhood experiences provided the story for his scenario for Jutra's **Mon Oncle Antoine**. Perron was executive producer in French Production at the NFB in 1968, and has produced many films, among them **Les Acadiens de la dispersion** (Forest), **Kid Sentiment** (Godbout), **Jusqu'au coeur** and **Mon amie Pierrette** (Lefebvre). Perron has worked closely with Georges Dufaux, co-directing the delightful comedy **C'est pas la faute à Jacques Cartier**. Jean Cousineau wrote the music for **Taureau** and François Dompierre for **Partis pour la gloire**.

Filmography

Georges-P. Vanier, soldat, diplomate, gouverneur-général (Georges-P. Vanier) (1960). Prod: Léonard Forest, NFB. 28 min. b&w.

Les loisirs (1961). With Pierre Patry. Prod: Bernard Devlin, NFB. 28 min. b&w.

Les bacheliers de la cinquième (1961). With François Séguillon. Prod: Bernard Devlin, Victor Jobin, NFB. 28 min. b&w.

Jour après jour (Day After Day) (1962). Prod: Fernand Dansereau, Hubert Aquin, Victor Jobin, NFB. 28 min. b&w.

Marie-Victorin (1963). Prod: Victor Jobin, Fernand Dansereau, NFB. 25 min. col.

Caroline (1964). With Georges Dufaux. Prod: Fernand Dansereau, NFB. 27 min. b&w.

Salut Toronto! (Bonjour Toronto!) (1965). With Marc Beaudet. Prod: Marcel Martin, NFB. 28 min. b&w.

Cinéma et réalité (1967). With Georges Dufaux. Prod: G. Dufaux, C. Perron, NFB, 58 min. b&w.

C'est pas la faute à Jacques Cartier (1967). With Georges Dufaux. Prod: G. Dufaux, C. Perron, NFB. 72 min. col.

Taureau (The Bull) (1973). Prod: Marc Beaudet, NFB. 97 min. col.

Partis pour la gloire (1975). Prod: Marc Beaudet, NFB. 103 min. col. Dist: Mutuel.

Bibliography

Séquences, no. 30 (October 1962), pp. 49-52, ''Rencontre avec Clément Perron'', Léo Bonneville (interview); *Séquences,* no. 51 (December 1967) ''Dialogue avec des cinéastes canadiens, le travail'', Maryse Grandbois (interview); *La Presse,* March 18, 1972, ''La Beauce mise à nu'', Luc Perrault (interview) (on **Mon Oncle Antoine** and **Taureau**); *Cinéma-Québec,* vol. II, no. 5 (January-February 1973), pp. 30-34, ''Clément Perron affrontant les images de son enfance'', interview with Jean-Pierre Tadros and p. 29, ''**Taureau**: le drame de l'intolérance'', by Perron; *Montreal Gazette,* February 3, 1973, ''Author-Director Clément Perron: The Characters are in My Heart'', Dane Lanken (interview); *Séquences,* no. 72 (April 1973), pp. 4-10, interview with Léo Bonneville; *Séquences,* no. 31 (December 1962), pp. 17-19, ''Réflexion d'un scènartiste canadien'', by Perron; *Parti-pris,* no. 7 (April 1964), pp. 16-17, ''Un témoignage'', by Perron; *Objectif,* August-September 1964, pp. 3-17, ''Petit éloge des grandeurs et des misères de la colonie française de l'Office national du film", Jean-Pierre Lefebvre; *Dossier de cinema: 1* (Fides, 1968), reviews of **Caroline** and **Jour après jour**; *Le Droit*, Ottawa, December 24, 1971, "Avec Clément Perron, cinéaste qui n'a pas voulu devenir 'metaphysicien et niaiseaux", Murray Maltais; *La Tribune*, Sherbrooke, December 31, 1971, "Du cinéma québécois en tant que. . . 'carte d'identité", René Berthiaume; *Québec-presse*, March 12, 1972, p. 26, "**Taureau** ou l'intolérance d'un village de la Beauce"; *Montreal Star*, February 3, 1973, "Write on, Perron", Martin Malina; *Rélations*, no. 380 (March 1973), p. 90, review of **Taureau** by Yves Lever; *Cinéma-Québec*, vol. 2, no. 6-7 (March-April 1973), pp. 50-51, "A la recherche du père et d'un film", Jean-Pierre Tadros; *Motion*, May-June 1973, p. 36, review of **Taureau** by Nat Shuster; *Cinema Canada*, no. 8 (June-July 1973), pp. 64-65, review of **Taureau** by Natalie Edwards; *Le Jour*, October 18, 1975, "**Partis pour la gloire** de Perron: un regarde timide sur notre réalité", Jean-Pierre Tadros; *La Presse*, October 18, 1975, "La guerre, no sir!" (on **Partis**); *Le Soleil*, October 18, 1975, "La conscription vue de la Beauce par Clément Perron", Claude Daigneault; *Cinéma-Québec*, vol. 4, no. 8, pp. 22-23, "Pour saluer la parente", Yves Lever; reviews in *Jeune-cinéma canadien, Le cinéma québécois: tendances et prolongements, Vingt ans de cinéma au Canada français, Essais sur le cinéma québécois, Le cinéma canadien,* and *Cinéma d'ici.*

POIRIER, ANNE-CLAIRE

Born in St. Hyacinthe, Quebec in 1932, Anne-Claire Poirier studied law at the University of Montreal and, later, theatre at the Conservatoire d'art dramatique de la province de Québec. She freelanced as a writer and interviewer for Radio-Canada and in 1960 joined the NFB, assisting on such productions as **Quebec-USA**, **Voir Miami** and **Jour après jour** (which she edited). Her first feature, **De mère en fille**, with camera by François Séguillon and Jean-Claude Labrecque, is based on diaries kept during her own pregnancy. Under the series title "En tant que femmes", Poirier produced her own **Les filles du roy**, Mireille Dansereau's **J'me marie, J'me marie pas**, Aimée Danis' **Souris, tu m'inquiètes** and Susan Gibbard's **A qui appartient ce gage**. More recently, she produced Hélène Girard's **Les filles c'est pas pareil** and became executive producer of Unit B (including Société nouvelle program). Ms. Poirier was Canada's representative at the creation of "Film Women International" and was elected a member of the executive committee; the organization grew out of a symposium held in Italy in 1975 sponsored by UNESCO.

Filmography

Stampede (Nomades de l'ouest) (1961). With Claude Fournier.
  Prod: Jacques Bobet, NFB. 27 min. b&w.
30 Minutes, Mister Plummer (1962). Prod: Jacques Bobet,
  NFB. 28 min. b&w.
La fin des étés (1964). Prod: Jacques Bobet, NFB. 28 min. b&w.
Les ludions (1965). Prod: Jacques Bobet, NFB. 23 min. b&w.
De mère en fille (Mother To Be) (1968). Prod: Guy L. Côté, NFB.
  75 min. b&w.
Impôt et tout...et tout (1968). Prod: Anne-Claire Poirier, NFB
  for the Department of National Revenue. Five films, each 5 min.
  col.
Le savoir-faire s'impose (1971). Prod: Anne-Claire Poirier, NFB
  ˙for the Department of National Revenue. Six films, each 5 min.
  col.
Les filles du roy (1974). Prod: Anne-Claire Poirier, NFB, Société
  nouvelle, "En tant que femmes". 56 min. col.
Le temps de l'avant (1975). Prod: Anne-Claire Poirier, NFB,
  Société nouvelle. 90 min. col.
Work in progress: **Spiritualité**, with script by Marthe Blackburn.

Bibliography

Chatelaine, November 1966, "Women in Canada" (interview);
Cinema Canada, no. 15, pp. 52-54, an interview with Poirier on
the series "En tant que femmes" by Laurinda Hartt; Press clippings on **De mère en fille**, collected by the NFB, March 31, 1969,
are available at film study centres or any NFB office; *Femmes
d'aujourd'hui,* Belgium, no. 1283 (December 3, 1969) pp. 64,
66-67, "Que fait-on pour les femmes au Canada?"; *Médium-
Média,* January 1973, this issue is devoted to the series "En tant
que femmes"; *Dimanche matin,* April 28, 1974, "**Les filles du
roy** : un tableau faussé et dangereux!", Josette Bourdonnais;
Relations, no. 392 (April 1974), p. 126, Yves Lever discusses the
series; *Maintenant,* November 1974, pp. 28-30, Richard Gay
on"En tant que femmes"; *La Presse,* September 22, 1975, "Une
série dont on parlera longtemps...", Lysiane Gagnon.

POTTERTON, GERALD

Born in London, England in 1931, Gerald Potterton trained at the
Hammersmith School of Art and later served in the R.A.F. On his
release he worked as an assistant animator on **Animal Farm**,
Halas and Batchelor's animated feature based on George Orwell's
novel. In 1954 Potterton came to Canada and the National Film
Board and worked in animation and live action; with Grant Munro

he directed Stephen Leacock's **My Financial Career** and the
"Star" episode of **Christmas Cracker**. Potterton acted the role of
the chauffeur in **The Ride** and directed Buster Keaton in **The
Railrodder**. In 1968 he formed Potterton Productions which pro-
duced live-action and animation features such as **The Apprentice**
(Larry Kent), **Child Under a Leaf** (Bloomfield), **The Rainbow
Boys** (Potterton) and, in animation, **The Happy Prince** (Mike
Mills), **The Little Mermaid** and **The Selfish Giant** (Peter
Sanders); the company also produced **The Remarkable Rocket**,
The Christmas Messenger and **Tiki Tiki**. Potterton directed
segments of **Yellow Submarine** and live and animated segments
for series "Cool McCool", "Sesame Street", and "Let's Call the
Whole Thing Orff". Potterton has written many scripts, including
Superbus, **The Rainbow Boys** and a script on leisure for
U.S.I.A. Gerald Potterton is now freelancing, most recently work-
ing on Richard Williams' animated and live-action musical, **Rag-
gedy Ann and Andy.**

Filmography

Huff and Puff (1955). Prod: NFB for RCAF. 8 min. col.

Fish Spoilage Control (Le poisson se mange frais) (1956). Prod:
   David Bairstow, NFB for Department of Fisheries. 9 min. col.

It's a Crime (1957). Prod: NFB for Department of Labour. 11
   min. col.

Follow that Car (1958). Prod: Halas & Batchelor for Shell Oil. 10
   min. col.

The Energy Picture (1958). Prod: Halas & Batchelor for B.P. Oil.
   15 min. col.

My Financial Career (Ma carrière financière) (Minha Carreira
   Financeira) (1962). With Grant Munro. Prod: Colin Low, Tom
   Daly, NFB. 7 min. col.

The Ride (La course) (1963). Prod: Colin Low, Tom Daly, NFB. 7
   min. col.

Napoleon Clip (1963). Prod: Montreal Film Festival. 2 min. b&w.

Centennial Clips (1964). Prod: John Fisher, NFB for the Centennial Commission. Six 1 min. clips. col.

Money to Burn (1964). Prod: NFB for the Department of
   Fisheries. 1 min. col.

The Railrodder (1965). Prod: Julian Biggs, NFB. 25 min. col.

The Quiet Racket (Le campeur décampe) (1966). Prod: Guy
   Glover, NFB. 7 min. col.

The Trade Machine (1968). Prod: Potterton Productions for Place
   Bonaventure. 10 min. col.

Superbus (1969). Prod: G. Potterton, Potterton Productions for
   Canadian Pavilion, Expo '70, Osaka, Panavision, 5½ min. col.

Pinter People (1969). Prod: G. Potterton for NBC. 60 min. col.
   Dist: Marlin Motion Pictures.

The Charge of the Snow Brigade (1970). Prod: G. Potterton, Potterton Productions. 6 min. col.

Tiki Tiki (1971). With Jack Stokes. Prod: Potterton, Potterton Productions, Cinemascope. 75 min. col. Dist: Faroun.

Rainbow Boys (1973). Prod: Anthony Robinow, Potterton Productions. 90 min. col. Dist: Mutuel.

Bibliography

Cinema Canada, no. 8 (June 1963), pp. 56-62, interview by Laurinda Hartt on **Rainbow Boys** with Potterton, Donald Pleasance and Pierre David; *Positif,* Paris, no. 134 (January 1972), pp. 41-44, interview with Potterton by J. Niogret and J.-P. Török; *Montreal Gazette,* January 8, 1973, "That Empty Feeling Just Means Potterton Has Been a Busy Man", Dane Lanken (interview); *Montreal Star,* January 8, 1973, "Visions of Disaster Haunted Filmmaker", Lou Seligson (interview); *Objectif 62,* August 1962, pp. 68-69, review of **My Financial Career**; *Montreal Star,* March 29, 1969, "Potterton's **Pinter People**", Boyce Richardson; *Time,* April 18, 1969, review of **Pinter People**; *Montreal Star,* March 14, 1970, "A Funny Thing Happened on the Way to the Kremlin", Martin Bronstein; *Positif,* Paris, no. 130 (September 1971), pp. 34-35, on **Tiki Tiki**; *Montreal Star,* November 26, 1971, "Wilde's Fairy Tale a Beauty", Michael Ballantyne (on **The Selfish Giant**); *Montreal Star,* January 15, 1972, "Potterton People: How to Manufacture Dreams and Make Money", Doris Giller; *Montreal Gazette,* December 30, 1972, "**Tiki Tiki** a Complicated Delight", Dane Lanken; *Le Devoir,* January 6, 1973, review of **Tiki Tiki** by Robert-Guy Scully; *Vancouver Province,* March 28, 1973, "Pleasance Surprise at End of **Rainbow**", Michael Walsh; *Toronto Star,* March 31, 1973, "**Rainbow Boys** Fail to Find Pot of Gold", Clyde Gilmour; *Montreal Gazette,* April 3, 1973, "Crazy Search for Gold Highlights **Rainbow Boys**", Dane Lanken; *Globe and Mail,* Toronto, April 5, 1973, "A Tired Retread of Treasure Hunt Tale", Martin Knelman; *Time,* April 16, 1973, "Gold Rush", Geoffrey James; *Globe and Mail,* Toronto, May 4, 1973, review of **Tiki Tiki**; *Saturday Night,* May 1973, p. 49, "Born Losers and Home-Grown Porn", Marshall Delaney (on **Rainbow Boys**).

RADFORD, TOM

See also: Filmwest Associates.

Co-founder of Film Frontiers Ltd., Tom Radford joined Barnyard Films International Ltd. to form Filmwest Associates in 1971. Radford's training in film began with photography, and in this capacity he exhibited at the Edmonton Art Gallery in 1972 and at The National Gallery in 1973; his studies in history at the University of

Alberta prepared him for his investigations of the historical west. **Ernest Brown: Pioneer Photographer**, done with Filmwest, won the Golden Sheaf Award and the best documentary award at the 1973 Yorkton International Film Festival and best film at the 1974 Alberta Film Festival. Original music for this film was composed and played by Bruce Cockburn. Since 1973 Radford has been freelancing with the National Film Board's regional production units in Vancouver and Winnipeg. **Sakaw Timmajohen**, a bilingual Cree-English film shot in northern Alberta by Tony Westman, won awards for best director and best cinematography at the 1975 Alberta Film Festival.

Filmography

The Country Doctor (1972). Prod: Glen Sarty, CBC "Take 30"/Filmwest. 28 min. col.
Ernest Brown: Pioneer Photographer (1972). Prod: Filmwest for Northwestern Utilities. 54 min. col.
Every Saturday Night (1973). Prod: John Taylor, NFB "West". 28 min. col.
A Slow Hello (1974). Prod: John Taylor, NFB "Pacificanada". 30 min. col.
Sakaw Timmajohen (Man Who Chose the Bush) (1975). Prod: Peter Jones, NFB/Government of Alberta. 30 min. col.
The Forests and Vladimir Krajina (1976). Prod: Roman Bittman, NFB. 60 min. col.
Museum (1976). Prod: Jerry Krepakevich, NFB. 30 min. col.
Feature film scripts in progress: **Music at the Close** with Jim DeFelice; **Wooden Hunters** with Matt Cohen.
Work in progress: **The Last Best West** with script by Radford; **Chester Ronning**.

Bibliography

Pot pourri, June 1974, pp. 14-17, on "West" series by Carl Lauppe; *The Western Producer*, July 18, 1974, "I Didn't Know It Was That Good" (on **Ernest Brown**).

RANSEN, MORT

Freelance actor, director and writer, Mort Ransen joined the National Film Board in 1961 and worked on a number of films in conjunction with other filmmakers. His dramatic documentaries include a film on and by young people, **Christopher's Movie Matinée**, and on drug addiction, **The Circle**, starring Don Francks. Ransen collaborated with the Indian crew at the Board on the film **You are on Indian Land** and has been involved in the training of actors for film work. His musical, **Running Time**, was

written, edited and has lyrics by Ransen; Bill Brooks wrote the
music and Jean-Pierre Lachapelle was on camera. Ransen was
born in Montreal in 1933.

Filmography

John Hirsch: A Portrait of a Man and a Theatre (1965). Prod:
Julian Biggs, NFB. 28 min. b&w.
No Reason to Stay (Pour un bout de papier) (1966). Prod: John
Kemeny, NFB. 28 min. b&w.
The Circle (1967). Prod: John Kemeny, NFB. 57 min. b&w.
Christopher's Movie Matinée (1968). Prod: Joseph Koenig,
NFB. 87 min. col.
Falling From Ladders (1969). Prod: John Kemeny, Joseph
Koenig, NFB. 9 min. b&w.
Untouched and Pure (1970). With Christopher Cordeaux and Mar-
tin Duckworth. Prod: Tom Daly, John Kemeny, NFB. 46 min.
b&w.
Running Time (1976). Prod: George Pearson, Tom Daly, NFB. 80
min. col.

Bibliography

Ransen was interviewed on the CBC-TV series "New Film-
makers", April 23, 1969 (executive producer, Roslyn Farber, CBC
Toronto); *Toronto Star,* February 1, 1969, "A Movie About Kids
Only Kids are Seeing", Martin Knelman (on **Christopher's Movie
Matinée**); *Globe and Mail,* February 22, 1969, p. 22, "**Movie
Matinée** Hidden from Movie Houses", Melinda McCracken; *Satur-
day Night,* June 1969, pp. 44-45, "Once Upon a Time the Flower
Children Said They Were Going to Liberate Us All. But that, Alas,
Was in the Distant Past: 1967", review of **Christopher's Movie
Matinée** by Marshall Delaney; *Vie des arts* no. 63 (Summer
1969), "A Cinema of Wandering", Dominque Noquez (review of
Matinée with reference to other films on youth); *No Reason to
Stay: A Study of the Film,* Paul A. Schreivogel (Dayton, Ohio:
Geo. A. Pflaum Publisher, Inc., 1969) 19 pp.

REGNIER, MICHEL

Born in France in 1934, Michel Régnier spent three years in
Senegal and on the Ivory Coast as a ethnological photographer.
He came to Canada in 1957 and worked for the National Film
Board, private film companies and prepared a number of
photographic books and exhibitions. As a cameraman, Régnier
shot Lefebvre's **Mon oeil**, **Patricia et Jean-Baptiste** and **Le
révolutionnaire**, Fernand Dansereau's **Saint-Jérome** and
Maurice Bulbulian's **La p'tite Bourgogne**. As a continuation of his
two important series on urban life, Régnier spent six months in

1975-76 in Africa as a film producer for the NFB; the project, "Habitat '76", was sponsored by the United Nations.

Filmgraphy (incomplete)

"X . . . raconte" series of 26 children films (1959). Prod: Nova for Radio-Canada.
La pauvreté (1960). Prod: Fernand Rivard, Radio-Canada. 24 min. b&w.
"Ports of Call" series of children's films (1963). Prod: Allan Wargon, Pied Piper Films Ltd.
"L'Afrique noire d'hier à demain" series of 13 films (1964). Prod: Radio-Canada. Each 28 min. b&w.
Memoire indienne (Indian Memento) (1967). Prod: André Belleau, Robert Forget, NFB for the Minister of Indian Affairs and Northern Development. 18 min. col.
Tatoo 67 (Tatoo 67) (1967). With Yves Leduc. Prod: Clément Perron, NFB for the Department of National Defence. 20 min. col.
L'école des autres (1968). Prod: Robert Forget, NFB. 153 min. b&w.
L'homme et le froid (Below Zero) (1970). Prod: M. Régnier, Janic Abenaim, NFB for the Minister of Indian Affairs and Northern Development. 107 min. col.
"Urbanose", 15 films in series (1972): **Les taudis, Griffintown, Concordia I & II, L'automobile, Rénovation urbaine, Réhabilitation des habitations, Les rives, Locataires et propriétaires, Le sol urbain, Le labyrinthe, Où va la ville? I & II, L'attitude néerlandaise, Entretien avec Henri Lefebvre**. Prod: Normand Cloutier, NFB Challenge for Change/Société nouvelle. Each 27 min. b&w.
"Urba 2000", 10 films in series (1974): No. 1 **Montréal: retour aux quartiers**, No. 2 **Saskatoon: la mesure**, No. 3 **New York: Twin Parks Project-TV Channel 13**, No. 4 **Sapporo: croissance planifiée**, No. 5 **Bologne: une ville ancienne pour une société nouvelle**, No. 6 **Düsseldorf: équilibre urbain**, No. 7 **Basingstoke-Runcorn: villes nouvelles britanniques**, No. 8 **et piétons**, No. 10 **Varsovie-Québec: comment ne pas détruire une ville**. Prod: Nicole Chamson, Jean-Marc Garand, NFB Challenge for Change/Société nouvelle. Each 57 min. except No. 7, 87 min. and No. 8, 117 min. col.

Bibliography

Objectif 61, October 1961, pp. 9, 10, 21, 22, "Dix-sept artisans du cinéma canadien"; *Québec, 1967* and *Québec, une autre Amérique,* "Michel Régnier, l'editeur officiel du Québec"; *La Presse,* December 7, 1968, "Michel Régnier opte pour un cinéma fonctionnel", review of **L'école des autres**; *Le Devoir,* June 17, 1972, "'Urbanose'. . . le cinéma au service de la ville", Jean-

Pierre Tadros: *Champ libre,* no. 4 (Spring 1973), pp. 126-127
(review); *Le Devoir,* October 11, 1973, "Le Village Olympique:
Jean Drapeau doit reconnaître son erreur", Michel Régnier; *Le
Devoir,* October 30, 1974, "'Urba 2000': améliorer la qualité de la
vie urbaine . . . en dix films de l'ONF", Pierre Vallières; *La
Presse,* Nov. 1, 1974, "'Urba 2000': comment soigner la
cité moderne malade", Luc Perreault; *Le Soleil,* December 7,
1974, "Le cinéma-outil de Michel Régnier", Claude Daigneault;
Médium-média, scrapbook issue, p. 25, letter from Michel
Régnier; references in *Le cinéma canadien* and *Jeune cinéma
canadien.*

REID, BILL

Bill Reid's **Coming Home**, which starred his own family, won the
1973 Canadian Film Award for best non-fiction feature film. Reid
joined the National Film Board in 1969 as a production assistant
and editor after freelancing for CBC radio in documentary and
journalistic programs. He had studied English and philosophy at
the University of Western Ontario and began his doctorate program in political science at McGill. His film, **Occupation**, deals
with political action taken by McGill students. A former high
school teacher, Bill Reid was born in Toronto in 1941.

Filmography

Challenge for Change (1968). Prod: John Kemeny, NFB
Challenge for Change. 24 min. b&w.
Occupation (1970). Prod: B. Reid, George C. Stoney, NFB
Challenge for Change. 47 min. b&w.
Coming Home (1973). Prod: Tom Daly, Colin Low, NFB. 84 min.
col.
Script in progress with playwright Peter Madden: **The Bag Lady**
(1976).

Bibliography

Pot pourri, April 1974, pp. 2-10, an interview with Bill Reid, review
of **Coming Home**, and a report on public reactions to the
film; *Toronto Star,* March 18, 1974, "Film Bares Family Power
Struggle", Helen Worthington; *Globe and Mail,* March 23, 1974,
"NFB Film Looks at Family Conflict With Unposed Honesty", Bet-
ty Lee; *Cinema Canada,* no. 15, pp. 74-75, review of **Coming
Home** by Harris Kirshenbaum; *Screen,* vol. 7, no. 2, "On the
Road With **Coming Home**", Terry Ryan.

REITMAN, IVAN

Born in Ontario in 1947, Ivan Reitman made his first film while attending the National Film Board's Summer Institute. With Peter Rowe and John Hofsess, Reitman was involved in the McMaster Film Board where he directed, wrote, photographed, edited and composed the music for **Orientation** which received nation-wide theatrical distribution. A Bachelor of Music, Reitman scored many of his films. He has produced a number of films, including **Columbus of Sex**, **Shivers** and **Death Weekend**, which was directed by Bill Fruet. Reitman was also producer of "The National Lampoon Show" and "The Magic Show" on Broadway and produced **The National Lampoon Movie**. He is currently working with Cinepix as a producer.

Filmography

Guitar Thing (1967). Prod: Independent. 7 min. col.
Orientation (1968). Prod: Ivan Reitman, McMaster Film Board. 25 min. col.
Freak Film (1968). Prod: Ivan Reitman, McMaster Film Board. 7 min. b&w.
Foxy Lady (1971). Prod: Ivan Reitman, Ivan Reitman Productions. 88 min. col.
Cannibal Girls (1972). Prod: Dan Goldberg, Ivan Reitman, Scary Pictures Corp. 88 min. col.

Bibliography

Take One, vol. 3, no. 10, pp. 23-29, "The Makers of **Cannibal Girls**", interview by Joe Medjuck; *Saturday Night,* August 1970, pp. 11-16, "The Witchcraft of Obscenity", John Hofsess; *Maclean's,* November 1970, p. 93, "The Magic and Decidedly 'Ungroovy' Garden of Filmmaker Ivan Reitman", John Hofsess; *Toronto Telegram,* September 1, 1971, "Moviemaker Must Hustle, Says Newcomer Reitman", Sid Adilman; *Maclean's,* June 1973, p. 90, "Making It Big By Being Truly Awful", John Hofsess.

RIMMER, DAVID

Born in 1943 in Vancouver, David Rimmer has worked there independently and with video in 1971-72 in New York. An experimentalist, Rimmer explores the possibilities of the film medium. He has an uncanny ability to take a film cliché, often in the form of a stockshot, as in **Variations on a Cellophane Wrapper**, **The Dance** and **Surfacing on the Thames**, and discover, through spatial and temporal manipulation, a fresh and wonderful image. His work has a precision that is infused with a droll sense of humour. Rimmer won numerous awards at the 1969 Vancouver International Film Festival and has had showings at the Museum of Modern Art, the National Film Theatre in England, and at many experimental and avant-garde film festivals.

Filmography

Know Place (1967). With Sylvia Spring. Prod: Independent. 11 min. b&w.

Square Inch Field (1968). Prod: Independent. 13 min. col.

Migration (1969). Prod: Stan Fox, CBC "New World". 11 min. col.

Headend (1970). Prod: Independent. 2 min. col.

Variations on a Cellophane Wrapper (1970). Prod: Independent. 8 min. col.

The Dance (1970). Prod: Independent. 4 min. b&w.

Surfacing on the Thames (1970). Prod: Independent. 5 min. col.

Blue Movie (1970). Prod: Independent. 5 min. col.

Landscape (1970). Prod: Independent. 11 min. col.

Real Italian Pizza (1971). Prod: Independent. 12 min. col.

Seashore (1971). Prod: Independent. 12 min. col.

Treefall (1971). Prod: Independent. 5 min. b&w.

Fracture (1973). Prod: Independent. 10 min. col.

Watching for the Queen (1973). Prod: Independent. 11 min. b&w.

Canadian Pacific, Part I (1974). Prod: Independent. 11 min. col. Two screen projection.

Canadian Pacific, Part II (1975). Prod: Independent. 11 min. col. Two screen projection.

Mr. Rimmer's films are distributed by the Canadian Filmmakers' Distribution Centre, Pacific cinémathèque pacifique and the Coopérative cinéastes indépendants.

Bibliography

Vancouver Sun, September 12, 1969, p. 29, "And the Camera Betrays the Hand and Eye", Charlotte Townsend; *Artscanada,* April 1970, pp. 7-13, "The New Canadian Cinema: Images from the Age of Paradox", Gene Youngblood; *Vancouver Province,* July 31, 1970, "Simple Genius", Andreas Schroeder; *Village Voice,* April 6, 1972, reprinted in *Film Library Quarterly,* vol. 5, no. 3 (Summer 1972), pp. 28ff, "The Films of David Rimmer: Artist of the Avant-Garde Explores the Levels of Reality", Kristina Nordstrom; *New York Times,* October 8, 1972, p. 17 (Entertainment Section), "Quick — Who are David Rimmer and James Herbert?", Roger Greenspun; *Take One,* vol. 2, no. 11, "Vancouver Letter", Kirk Tougas.

ROBERTSON, GEORGE

A key member of the Vancouver CBC Film Unit, George Robertson began his career as a radio producer, joining the Unit as a writer in 1957; from 1957-60 he wrote a number of scripts directed by Allan King: **Where Will They Go**, **Pemberton Valley** and **Rickshaw**. While a producer at CBC Vancouver, Robertson wrote all the films he directed, including **Sports Day** which won the 1966 Wilderness Award. **Caroline**, a feature film directed by Ron Kelly, was co-scripted by Kelly and Robertson. In 1968 Robertson received a Canada Council grant to write, and in 1969 he moved to Ottawa as executive-producer of public affairs programming where he produced "Something Else". Living in Toronto since 1971, he has been executive-producer of "Weekend", producer of the series "Images of Canada" and "The Great Canadian Culture Hunt".

Filmography

Victoria 100 (1961). Prod: G. Robertson, CBC. 30 min. b&w.
Through the Eyes of Children (1962). Prod: G. Robertson, CBC. 30 min. b&w.
Class of '39 (1963). Prod: G. Robertson, CBC. 30 min. b&w.
Sports Day (1964). Prod: G. Robertson, CBC "The Seven O'Clock Show". 20 min. b&w.
"Remembrance of Lowry" Part I: **To the Volcano**; Part II: **The Forest Path** (1964). Prod: G. Robertson, CBC "Explorations". 30 min. b&w.
Shawinigan (1964). Prod: G. Robertson, CBC 30 min. b&w.
Running to India (1965). Prod: G. Robertson, CBC. 60 min. b&w.
The Journey (1965). Prod: G. Robertson, CBC "Good Friday Special". 60 min. b&w.
The Islanders (1967). Prod: G. Robertson, CBC. 30 min. b&w.
Felicia is Happy (1968). Prod: G. Robertson, CBC. 30 min. col.
Barriada (1968). Prod: G. Robertson, CBC. 30 min. col.
The Trouble with Fred (1968). Prod: G. Robertson, CBC. 30 min. b&w.
Joyceville (1971). Prod: Robert Clark, CBC "Tuesday Night". 60 min. b&w.
The Craft of History (1972). Prod: G. Robertson, CBC "Images of Canada". 60 min. col.
Heroic Beginnings (1973). Prod: G. Robertson, CBC "Images of Canada". 60 min. col.
Citizen Baroness (1976). Prod: G. Robertson, CBC. 60 min. col.
The Politics of Culture (1976). Prod: G. Robertson, CBC "The Great Canadian Culture Hunt". 60 min. col.

Bibliography

Homage to the Vancouver CBC Film Unit (La Cinémathéque canadienne, 1964), available in film study centres; *How to Make or Not to Make a Canadian Film* (La Cinémathèque canadienne, 1967), "Hello, 'Caroline', Goodbye'', George Robertson on the script for **Caroline**.

ROFFMAN, JULIAN

Born in Montreal in 1919, Julian Roffman attended McGill University, studied film at New York and Columbia Universities and became an independent producer in the United States. Between 1934 and 1938 he directed for the "March of Time" series and produced a series of consumer films entitled "Getting Your Money's Worth". He returned to Canada and to the NFB in 1940 at John Grierson's request; Roffman was a producer in charge of the "Armed Service Production Program". In New York he was co-founder of Pioneer TV Films (now Screen Gems Inc.), producing television series, documentaries and commercials. Back in Canada, Roffman founded Meridian Productions with Ralph Foster (former Deputy Film Commissioner), and later Taylor-Roffman Productions Ltd. with Nathan Taylor. Roffman has directed hundreds of films, including **The Mask**, a 3-D horror story which is viewed through 3-D glasses. As a producer for ABC, CBS and NBC, many of his "movies of the week" later had theatrical release. In 1973 he wrote and produced **A Knife for the Ladies** (Warner Bros.) and in 1971 Roffman was executive-producer for John Hirsch on the NFB "Anthology" drama series. He produced **The Pyx** in 1973.

Filmography (incomplete)

"March of Time" series (1934-38): **Men of Medicine**, **The Father Devine Story**, **Bootleg Coal**, **The Huey Long Story**, **The Disinherited**.
"Getting Your Money's Worth" series (1935-36). For Consumer Union Reports.
And So They Live (1940). (co-dir.) For the Sloan Foundation.
A Report to the People (1940). For President Roosevelt.
"Armed Services Production Program" series (1941-45): **Battle is Our Business**, **Up From the Ranks**, **Thirteen Platoon**, **The Proudest Girl in the World**, **So Proudly She Marches**. Prod: NFB.
"United Nations" series (1950-52): **United Nations Patrols**, **Israel**, **United Nations Magazine**.
"Korean War Reports", "The Inner Sanctum", "The Big Story", "The Search" (1953-54). All series for American television.
Freedom to Read (1953-54). For Columbia University Bi-centennial.

Canadian Grocer, **Toronto Symphony** (1954-59). For NFB.
Here and There, **Pour le sport** (1954-59). For CBC "Tips", a
series for the J. Arthur Rank Organization.
The Bloody Brood (1959). Prod: J. Roffman, Key Films Produc-
tions for Allied Artists Inc. 80 min.
The Mask or **Eyes of Hell** (1961). Prod: Nat Taylor, J. Roffman,
Taylor-Roffman Productions. 83 min. col. Dist: International
Film Distributors.
Work in progress: **Far East**, a theatrical feature.

Bibliography

Toronto Star, May 20, 1961, "Interview with Roffman", Blaik
Kirby; *Canadian Sponsor,* October 19, 1959, "Blueprint for TV
Expansion"; *Toronto Star,* October 26, 1961, "Canadian Film in
N.Y. Premiere"; *Globe and Mail,* December 27, 1969, "Launch-
ing the Canadian Feature Film into Orbit — with a U.S. Booster",
Kaspars Dzeguze.

ROWE, PETER

Peter Rowe started his film career in 1966 with the McMaster Film
Board in Hamilton as cameraman on "Palace of Pleasure". In
1967 he became an assistant editor at the CBC and the following
year joined Allan King Associates, where he worked as assistant
editor on King's **The New Woman** and assistant cameraman and
editor on Martin Lavut's **At Home**. In 1971 Rowe directed his first
feature, **Neon Palace**, for ETV, a happy piece of nostalgia about
the 50s and 60s. As well as working as production manager and
assistant director on **Between Friends** and **The Supreme Kid**,
Rowe has written comedy scripts for Don Harron's "Shh! It's the
News" and his own **Horse Latitudes**. In 1975 he formed Rosebud
Films with art director Tony Hall. Born in Winnipeg in 1947, Rowe
works out of Toronto.

Filmography

Buffalo Airport Visions (1967). Prod: McMaster Film Board. 19
min. b&w.
Golly Shit Sounds Like Something Andy Warhol Would Do
(1968). Prod: Independent. 3 min. b&w.
Neon Palace: A Fifties Trip, **A Sixties Trip** (1970). Prod: P.
Rowe, Tony Hall, Jim Lewis, Acme Idea & Sale. 90 min. col.
Dist: New Cinema.
Good Friday in Little Italy (1972). Prod: F.R. Crawley, Crawley
Films. 14 min. col.
Six television commercials for the Department of Travel, Province
of British Columbia (1974). Each 1 min. col.

Susan (1975). Prod: Jerry Mayer, CBC "The Peep Show". 30
  min. col.

Haiti (1975). Prod: Tony Hall, P. Rowe, Rosebud Films. 30 min.
  col.

Backlot Canadiana (1975). Prod: Martyn Burke, Sam Levine,
  CBC. 20 min. col. and b&w.

Horse Latitudes (1976). Prod: Tony Hall, Chalmers Adams,
  Rosebud Films. 60 min. col. Dist: Viking Films.

Work in progress: **The Hostage Drama**. 90 min. special for CBC.

Bibliography

Toronto Telegram, June 21, 1971, "Rowe Not a Putdowner",
Clyde Gilmour (interview); *Toronto Star*, October 27, 1969, "Three
Shoot on a Shoestring", Martin Knelman (on Cronenberg, Shebib
and Rowe); *Montreal Gazette*, October 17, 1970, "Youth Looks
Back to the 1950s with Nostalgic Eagerness", Marilyn Becker (on
Neon Palace); *Hamilton Spectator*, November 13, 1970,
"Cinematic Scrapbook of 20 years Basically Fun in the **Neon
Palace**"; *Globe and Mail*, January 9, 1971, "Rowe's Got Promise
— and an Etrog to Prove It", Betty Lee; *Maclean's*, March 1971,
p. 76, on **Neon Palace**; *Miss Chatelaine*, vol. 8, no. 4 (August
10, 1971), "Let's Hear it for Don & Morley & Martin & Ivan &
Sylvia & Eric. . .", Kay Armatage; *Take One*, vol. 2, no. 10, pp.
32-34, Bruce Pittman on **Neon Palace**; *Cinema Canada*, no. 19,
pp. 61-62, reivew of **Backlot Canadiana**, A.I.K.

RUBBO, MICHAEL

Born in Melbourne, Australia in 1938, Michael Rubbo studied
anthropology at Sydney University and travelled extensively in
Asia. A painter and still photographer, Rubbo prepared an exhibition of photographs on village life in India for an Australian direct
aid organization in 1962. He joined the National Film Board in
1965 after studying film at Stanford University. His success in
improvised work with young people led to his appointment as the
first head of the NFB's Films for Children Department. **Sad Song
of Yellow Skin**, a document of life in war-torn Saigon, won the
1971 Flaherty Award. Rubbo travelled to Asia again in 1972-73 to
make **The Man Who Can't Stop** about an amateur environmental-
ist in Sydney, and visited Cuba to make **Waiting for Fidel** and **I
Am an Old Tree**. In 1975, he worked in Southeast Asia on the
UN's Habitat '76 project.

Filmography

True Source of Knowledge (1965). Prod: Independent. 30 min.
  b&w.

The Long Haul Men (1966). Prod: John Kemeny, NFB. 17 min. col.

Adventures (Escapade) (1968). Prod: Nicholas Balla, NFB. 10 min. col.

That Mouse (1968). Prod: Nicholas Balla, NFB. 14 min. col.

Mr. Ryan's Drama Class (1969). Prod: Tom Daly, Cecily Burwash, NFB. 35 min. b&w.

Sir! Sir! (1969). Prod: T. Daly, Cecily Burwash, NFB. 20 min. b&w.

Here's to Harry's Grandfather (1969). Prod: M. Rubbo, NFB. 58 min. col.

Summer's Nearly Over (1970). Prod: M. Rubbo, NFB. 30 min. col. (A shortened version of **Here's to Harry's Grandfather**.)

Sad Song of Yellow Skin (Le jaune en péril) (1971). Prod: M. Rubbo, NFB. 58 min. col.

Persistent and Finagling (1971). Prod: M. Rubbo, NFB. 58 min. b&w.

Wet Earth and Warm People (1972). Prod: M. Rubbo, NFB. 59 min. col.

OK...Camera (1973). Prod: Ian McLaren, NFB "Adieu Alouette". 27 min. col.

The Streets of Saigon (1973). Prod: Tom Daly, NFB. 28 min. col. (Abridged version of **Sad Song of Yellow Skin**.)

Jalan, Jalan: A Journey in Sudanese Java (1973). Prod: Tom Daly, NFB. 20 min col. (Abridged version of **Wet Earth and Warm People**.)

The Man Who Can't Stop (1974). Prod: Tom Daly, Richard Mason, NFB Film Australia. 50 min. col.

Waiting for Fidel (1974). Prod: Tom Daly, M. Rubbo, NFB. 58 min. col.

I Am an Old Tree (1975). Prod: Tom Daly, M. Rubbo, NFB. 57 min. col.

Work in progress: **Save Montreal** and **Loghouse**. Prod: Roman Bittman, NFB "Environment Studio".

Bibliography

Lumière, Melbourne, April 1973, pp. 8-15, "D.B. Jones on Rubbo" and "The Man in the Picture", (interviews); *Montreal Star*, March 24, 1971, p. 70, "**Sad Song** Showed an Absorbing View of Saigon Life", Joan Irwin; *Pot pourri*, June 1971, p. 8, review of **Here's to Harry's Grandfather** by Dan Driscoll; *Film News*, N.Y., vol. 28, no. 4 (1971), p. 10, on **Sad Song of Yellow Skin**; *New York Times*, January 8, 1972, "*Rubbo's* **Sad Song of Yellow Skin**", Roger Greenspun; *Screen*, vol. 5, no. 2, pp. 6-7 and pp. 23-27, on **Sad Song of Yellow Skin**; *Take One*, vol. 1, no. 7, "Love and Life in Children's Films", Michael Rubbo.

SAARE, ARLA

Born in Finland in 1915, Arla Saare came to Canada in 1924 and graduated from the Vancouver School of Art. In 1942 she joined the NFB where she began as a negative cutter and later headed the optical and special effects department. When television started in Toronto, Saare landed the single editing job available, and in 1953 she moved to Vancouver to co-found, with Jack Long and Stan Fox, CBC's Vancouver Film Unit. Since 1963, Saare has been a freelance editor in Toronto. She directed as well as edited **West Coast Painters**, and **Ma Murray** (CBC "Take 30"). Saare won CFA awards for her editing for **The Canadian Shield** (Kelly) and **Next Year in Jerusalem** (Rasky), and received a Wilderness Award for her work on **The Wit and World of George Bernard Shaw** (Rasky). For CBC's "Telescope" series she edited **Maureen Forrester**, **Brian MacDonald**, **Georges Simenon**, **Glenn Gould** and **Gracie Fields**. Saare also edited the "History of the Olympics" series, and, for the "Images of Canada" series, she worked on **Heroic Beginnings**, **Peace, Order and Prosperity**, **Journey Without Arrival**, and **A Personal Point of View from Northrop Frye**.

A Partial list of her editing credits includes: **The Arctic Islands: A Matter of Time** (Archibald); **Gratien Gélinas** and **Alex Colville** (Bonnière); **At the Moment of Impact: Flight 831** (Carney); **Backyards of Canada** (Duke); **Journey into Summer** (Fox); **Italy** (Fruet); **Cathedrals of Europe** (Peter Kelly); **A Bit of Bark**, **The Thirties: A Glimpse of a Decade** and **Open Grave** (Ron Kelly); **Skid Row**, **Pemberton Valley**, **A Married Couple** and **Come On Children** (King); **Germany** (Richard Leiterman); **Portrait of Karsh** and **Marshall McLuhan** (Macartney-Filgate); **Seasons in the Mind** (Pearson and Milne); **Chagall** and **Tennessee Wilder's South** (Rasky); **Joyceville** and **Heroic Beginnings** (Robertson) and four episodes in "The National Dream" series.

Bibliography

Film Quarterly, Summer 1970, pp. 9-23, "The Fictional Documentary: Interviews with the Makers of **A Married Couple**", Alan Rosenthal, reprinted in Rosenthal's *The New Documentary in Action* (University of California Press, 1971); *Hommage to the Vancouver Film Unit* (La Cinémathèque canadienne), on a series of showings in 1964, available from film study libraries.

SHANDEL, THOMAS

Born in St. Boniface, Manitoba in 1938, Tom Shandel studied

theatre at the University of British Columbia and film at Stanford University. Actor, broadcaster and writer, Shandel wrote **Dr. Glass** for CBC's "Festival", **Yukon**, a feature documentary produced by Alaska Safari Productions, and **The Activators**, a documentary produced by the National Film Board's Challenge for Change Unit. He has also scripted most of the films he has directed. In 1970 he represented Canada, along with Gerald Potterton and Michel Brault, in an exchange of film showings with The Russian Filmmakers' Institute (Moscow and Leningrad) and La Cinémathèque canadienne. Shandel's first feature, **Another Smith for Paradise**, was photographed on the west coast by Michael Lente. In recent years Mr. Shandel has been involved with Werner Aellen, William Nemtin and Ray Hall in the resource organization, Image Flow Centre Ltd.; they produced a multi-media pavilion at the 1974 Pacific National Exhibition on alternate energy. In 1974 Shandel also produced a video report, **Pacific Reach**, an examination of how individuals of different cultures contact one another.
Potlatch: A Strict Law Bids Us Dance, directed by Vancouverite Dennis Wheeler, was produced by Shandel in 1975.

Filmography

El Diablo (1968). Prod: CBC "The Enterprise". 4 min. col.
Superfool (1968). Prod: CBC "The Enterprise". 15 min. col.
Nitobe (1968). Prod: CBC. 12 min. col.
Hum Central (1968). Prod: CBC "New World Series". 25 min.
 b&w.
Generations (1969). Prod: CBC. 60 min. b&w.
Community (1969). Prod: CBC. 30 min. b&w.
Shall We Gather at the River (1970). Prod: Independent. 30 min.
 b&w.
Another Smith for Paradise (1972). Prod: Jim Margellos,
 Another Smith Productions Ltd. 101 min. col.
We Call Them Killers (1972). Prod: Peter Jones, NFB. 16 min.
 col.
Community Action Theater on Tour (1973). Prod: Barrie
 Howells, NFB, Challenge for Change. 24 min. col.
Birth Control: Five Effective Methods (1973). Prod: Werner
 Aellen, Informedia Productions. 10 min. col.
"First Aid for Survival" (1973). Prod: Workers' Compensation
 Board of B.C. Two films, each 8 min.
Work in progress: **Life Support Systems**. Prod: Image Flow Centre Ltd.

Bibliography

La Presse, November 30, 1968, p. 30, "Un hippie-cinéaste qui aime vivre à Vancouver", Luc Perreault; *Vancouver Province*, December 14, 1968, Morrie Ruvinsky on **Nitobi**; *The Gazette*,

March 22, 1973, "Filmmaker Helps His Troubled Film", Dane
Lanken; *Daily Colonist,* June 29, 1973, "Whale Talk Recorded by
Filmer", Don Gain; *Georgia Straight,* January 3, 1974, "The
Whales", Dyan Roiko; *Take One,* vol. 2, no. 4, "The Night *The
Plastic Mile* Lost 500 Feet", an article by Shandel on the censor-
ing of Ruvinsky's **The Plastic Mile** at the Vancouver Film
Festival; *Take One,* vol. 3, no. 5, p. 22, review of **Another Smith**
by John Hofsess.

SHANNON, KATHLEEN

Born in western Canada in 1930, Kathleen Shannon has been instrumental in the development of films by women in Canada; her
series "Working Mothers" came after a long apprenticeship as an
editor of music, sound and image with Crawley Films and the National Film Board (which she joined in 1956). She worked on the
sound editing of **Circle of the Sun**, **Universe** and **Lonely Boy**
and as picture editor on **You are on Indian Land**, **The Summer
We Moved to Elm Street** and **Pikangikum**. In 1974 Shannon was
appointed executive producer of Studio D where she is producing
films by women and on co-operative housing. Her productions include **The Spring and Fall of Nina Polanski**, directed by Louise
Roy and Joan Hutton; **My Friends Call Me Tony** and **My Name
is Susan Yee**, directed by Beverly Schaffer in the series "Canadian Children"; **Co-op Housing: Getting it Together** and **Co-op
Housing: The Best Move We Ever Made** directed by Laura Sky;
and "Just a Minute", a series of one-minute films teaching women
how to make films. As executive producer, Shannon has been involved in **Great Grand Mothers** by Anne Wheeler and Lorna
Rasmussen and **Maud Lewis: A World Without Shadows**
directed by another regional filmmaker, Dianne Beaudry-Cowling.
Work in progress includes **Grierson's Dames**, to be directed by
Margaret Westcott; this material was shot during the "4 Days in
May" gathering in 1975. A biography of Agnes MacPhail, and interviews with American feminists (directed by Nicole Brassard and
Luce Guilbeault) are also in the works.

Filmography

I Don't Think it's Meant for Us (1971). Prod: Colin Low, George
    C. Stoney, NFB, Challenge for Change. 33 min. b&w.
Extensions of the Family (1974). Prod: K. Shannon, NFB
    "Working Mothers", Challenge for Change. 14 min. col.
It's Not Enough (1974). Prod: K. Shannon, NFB "Working
    Mothers", Challenge for Change. 16 min. col.
Like the Trees (1974). Prod: K. Shannon, NFB "Working
    Mothers", Challenge for Change. 15 min. col.

Luckily I Need Little Sleep (1974). Prod: K. Shannon, NFB
"Working Mothers", Challenge for Change. 8 min. col.
Mothers are People (1974). Prod: K. Shannon, NFB "Working
Mothers", Challenge for Change. 7 min. col.
They Appreciate You More (1974). Prod: K. Shannon, NFB
"Working Mothers", Challenge for Change. 15 min. col.
Tiger on a Tight Leash (1974). Prod: K. Shannon, NFB "Working
Mothers", Challenge for Change. 8 min. col.
Would I Ever Like to Work (1974). Prod: K. Shannon, NFB
"Working Mothers", Challenge for Change. 9 min. col.
And They Lived Happily Ever After (1975). Prod: K. Shannon,
NFB. 15 min. col.
Goldwood (1975). Prod: K. Shannon, NFB. 21 min. col.

Bibliography

See also: *Women in Film*
Pot pourri, June 1974, pp. 2-6, interview by Pat Thorvaldson on
"Working Mothers" series; *Vancouver Sun,* August 14, 1974,
"Plight of the Working Mother", Kayce White; *Access,* no. 14
(Spring 1975), the issue is dedicated to the series "Working
Mothers", with a discussion on how it was distributed in animated
groups; *Cinema Canada,* no. 15, p. 55, on "Working Mothers"
series.

SHEBIB, DON

Born in Toronto in 1938, Don Shebib graduated in sociology from
the University of Toronto before enrolling at UCLA as a student of
cinematography. Shebib served a long apprenticeship in television
and at the National Film Board before making his first feature,
Goin' Down the Road, a controlled fiction-documentary which
touched the Canadian collective consciousness; it was the first
Canadian film to be seen in the Soviet Union cinemas, the result
of a deal made at Cannes in 1971. **Goin' Down the Road** and
Rip-Off were scripted by Bill Fruet; Claude Harz scripted the
critically acclaimed **Between Friends**.

Filmography

Train Ride (1961). Prod: UCLA. 13 min. b&w.
The Duel (1962). Prod: UCLA. 8 min. b&w.
Joey (1962). Prod: D. Shebib, UCLA. 18 min. b&w.
Surfin' (1963). Prod: Ross McLean, CBC. 25 min. b&w.
Revival (1964). Prod: UCLA. 10 min. b&w.
A Search for Learning (1966). Prod: Joseph Koenig, NFB. 13
min. b&w.
Satan's Choice (1966). Prod: Tom Daly, NFB. 28 min. b&w.

Christalot Hanson (1966). Prod: Dick Ballentine, CTV "This Land is People". 14 min. b&w.

The Everdale Place (1966). Prod: Dick Ballentine, CTV "This Land is People". 22 min. b&w.

David Secter (1966). Prod: Dick Ballentine, CTV "This Land is People". 14 min. b&w.

Alan (1966). Prod: Ross McLean, CBC, "T.B.A.". 24 min. b&w.

Basketball (1967). Prod: Ross McLean, CBC "T.B.A.". 21 min. b&w.

San Francisco Summer 1967 (1968). Prod: CBC. col.

Unknown Soldier (1968). Prod: Ross McLean, CBC. 4 min. b&w.

Good Times, Bad Times (1969). Prod: Ross McLean, CBC. 33 min. b&w.

Goin' Down the Road (En roulant ma boule) (1970). Prod: D. Shebib, Evdon Productions. 90 min. col. Dist: New Cinema.

Rip-Off (1971). Prod: Bennett Fode, Phoenix Films. 90 min. col. Dist: New Cinema.

Paul Bradley (1972). Prod: Sam Levine, CBC "Telescope". 26 min. b&w.

Between Friends (Between Friends) (1973). Prod: Chalmers Adams, Clearwater Films Ltd. 100 min. col. Dist: New Cinema.

We've Come a Long Way Together (1974). Prod: Lew Aurebach, OECA. 60 min. col.

Deedee (1974). Prod: René Bonnière, CBC "The Collaborators". 60 min. col.

A Long Time Ago in Genarro (1974). Prod: René Bonnière, CBC. 48 min. col.

Mrs. Gray (1974). Prod: Ross McLean, CBC "Of All People". 24 min. col.

Winning is the Only Thing (1975). Prod: Sam Levine, CBC. 48 min. col.

The Canary (1975). Prod: Chalmers Adams, CBC "Performance". 45 min. col.

Second Wind (1976). Prod: Jim Margellos, Les Weinstein, Olympic Films. 100 min. col. Dist: Ambassador Films.

Feature film script in progress with Claude Harz: **Death on the Ice**.

Bibliography

La Presse, August 15, 1970, p. 31, "Réponse torontoise au défi québécois", Luc Perreault (interview); *Globe and Mail,* October 31, 1970, "It's the Same Don Shebib Despite **Road**", Betty Lee (interview); *New Yorker,* November 21, 1970, *"About Town",* Eleanor Ross (interview); *Skoop,* Amsterdam, vol. 8, no. 2 (1972), pp. 32-37, "Going Down the Roads of Canadian Cinema: Conversations with Don Shebib", André Pâquet; *Cinema Canada,* no. 10/11 (October 1973/January 1974), pp. 32-36, "Just Between Friends: Don Shebib Talks with Sandra Gathercole" (interview);

Take One, vol. 1, no. 10, "Toronto Letter", an interview by Joe Medjuck and Allan Collins; *Inner Views: Ten Canadian Film-makers* (McGraw-Hill Ryerson, 1975), J. Hofsess, pp. 67-79; *Montreal Star,* August 15, 1970, "The Underdogs Get Their Own Day", David Allnutt; *Séquences,* no. 62 (October 1970), pp. 36-37, on **Goin' Down the Road**; *Time,* October 4, 1971, "Status Seekers", Mark Nichols (On **Rip-Off**); *Saturday Night,* November 1971, "It's Not the Inherent Grace, It's the Money", Marshall Delaney; *Montreal Gazette,* February 12, 1972, "Shebib Turns to Youth Cult for His Latest Film", Dane Lanken; *Le Devoir,* February 12, 1972, Jean-Pierre Tadros on **Rip-Off**; *Montreal Star,* February 12, 1972, "**Rip-Off:** More Polish but Less Shine", Martin Malina; *Canadian Film Digest,* January 1973, p. 8, "Don Shebib Goes to Battle Again", Lloyd Chesley; *Globe and Mail,* October 13, 1973, "Shebib's Debut into Front Ranks", Betty Lee on **Between Friends**; *Cinema Canada,* no. 10/11 (October 1973-January 1974), pp. 68-69, reviews of **Between Friends** by Laurinda Hartt and Natalie Edwards; *Saturday Night,* November 1973, "On the Danger of Taking Women Seriously", Marshall Delaney; *Canadian Forum,* February 1974, pp. 33-36, "**Paperback Hero**: Three Canadian Films", Robert Fothergill discusses **Between Friends**; *Film Culture,* N.Y., no. 58-60 (1974), pp. 268-292, discussion of **Between Friends** by S. Stern in article "Filmexpo and the New English Canadian Cinema"; *Take One,* vol. 4, no. 1, p. 31, review of **Between Friends** by Joe Medjuck; *Cinema Canada,* no. 25 (February 1976), pp. 53-54, review of **Second Wind** by Clive Denton; *Cinema Canada,* no. 28 (May 1976), pp. 22-23, "The Soap Opera Route", review of **Second Wind** by John Reeves.

SHEPPARD, GORDON

Born in Montreal in 1937, Gordon Sheppard worked as a newspaper, television and radio journalist in Montreal and Toronto. In 1961 he and Richard Ballentine formed Inter-Video Productions Ltd., producing a number of short films for public affairs programs, including **The Most**, a witty study of Hugh Hefner and the Playboy empire. In 1963 Sheppard was appointed Special Assistant to the Secretary of State and until 1966 was a special consultant on the arts. He has written a song, "Mr. Plum", for Charlebois and published a children's book, *The Man Who Gave Himself Away.* Sheppard's first feature, **Eliza's Horoscope**, was photographed by Michel Brault, Paul Van der Linden and Jean Boffety.

Filmography

The Forum (1962). Prod: G. Sheppard, Richard Ballentine, Inter-Video Productions Ltd. 10 min. b&w.

The Grey Cup (1962). Prod: G. Sheppard, Richard Ballentine, Inter-Video Productions Ltd. for CBC. 10 min. b&w.

Strip Clubs in London (1962). Prod: G. Sheppard, Richard Ballentine, Inter-Video Productions Ltd. for CBC "Close-Up". b&w.

The Most (1962). Prod: G. Sheppard, Richard Ballentine, Inter-Video Productions Ltd. 28 min. b&w.

JKF and Mr. K. (1963). Prod: G. Sheppard, Richard Ballentine, Inter-Video Productions Ltd. 8 min. b&w.

Dream Girl (La femme des rêves) (1964). Prod: G. Sheppard, Richard Ballentine, Inter-Video Productions Ltd. for CBC. 28 min. b&w.

Fifty Bucks a Week (1967). Prod: G. Sheppard, The Wild Oats. 10 min. b&w.

Love (1967). Prod: G. Sheppard, The Wild Oats. 5 min. Tinted.

Dallegret (1967). Prod: G. Sheppard, The Wild Oats. col.

The Marriage (1967). Prod: G. Sheppard, The Wild Oats. 5 min. col.

The Liberal Party in Ontario (1968). Prod: G. Sheppard, Richard Ballentine, Inter-Video Productions Ltd. for the Ontario Liberal Party. Two films, each 15 min. b&w.

Eliza (1969). Prod: G. Sheppard, O-Zali Films Inc. 10 min. col.

Eliza's Horoscope (1975). Prod: G. Shepard, O-Zali Films Inc. 120 min. col. Dist: O-Zali Films Inc.

Bibliography

Toronto Star, September 8, 1962, "**The Most** is Also the First"; *Canadian Cinematography*, July-August 1963, Richard Ballentine on the making of **The Most**; *Toronto Star*, April 18, 1970, p. 89, "A Lucky Horoscope for Canadian Filmmaker", Margaret Penman on **Eliza's Horoscope**); *Montreal Star*, July 25, 1970, pp. 4 and 34, "Montreal Will Be a Hectic Summer Film Setting", Dusty Vineberg on the making of **Eliza's Horoscope**; *Cinema Canada*, no. 25 (February 1976), pp. 44-45, review of **Eliza's Horoscope** by Stephen Chesley.

SNOW, MICHAEL

Painter, sculptor, musician and filmmaker, Michael Snow was born in Toronto in 1929, and graduated from the Ontario College of Art in 1953. He began his filmmaking career working as an animator for George Dunning in the late '50s. Some of his early film work was done in New York, sustained by Jonas Mekas' Filmmakers' Cinematheque and the critical atmosphere. The Canadian entry for the 1970 Venice Biennale was dedicated to Snow's multimedia works; Don Owen shot **Snow in Venice** for the CBC

"Telescope" series at this festival. In 1970-71 Snow was Professor of Advanced Film, Yale University, and later in 1971 visiting Artist-Filmmaker at the Nova Scotia College of Art. **Wavelength**, which won first prize at the Fourth International Festival of Experimental Film in Belgium in 1968, has received much critical attention in Europe and North America. Snow lives and works in Toronto. In the 1976 Edinburgh International Film Festival he was an honoured guest for the Avant-Garde Symposium.

Filmography

A-Z (1956). Prod: Independent. 4 min. col. Silent.
New York Eye and Ear Control (1964). Prod: Independent. 34 min. b&w.
Short Shave (1965). Prod: Independent. 4 min. b&w.
Wavelength (1966-67). Prod: Independent. 45 min. col.
Standard Time (1969). Prod: Independent. 8 min. col.
Dripping Water (1969). With Joyce Wieland. Prod: Independent. 10 min. b&w.
One Second in Montreal (1969). Prod: Independent. 26 min. b&w. Silent.
↔ or **Back and Forth** (1968-69). Prod: Independent. 52 min. col.
Side Seat Paintings Slides Sound Film (1970). Prod: Independent. 20 min. col.
La région centrale (Central Region) (1970-71). Prod: Independent. 180 min. col. Designer of special movie equipment: Pierre Abbeloos.
Rameau's Nephew by Diderot (Thanx to Dennis Young) by Wilma Schoen (1974). Prod: M. Snow. 285 min. col.
Breakfast (1976) Prod: M. Snow. 20 min. col.

Snow's films are distributed by the Canadian Filmmakers' Distribution Centre.

Bibliography

Artscanada, February-March 1971, "Converging on **La région centrale**", Charlotte Townsend (interview); *Film critica,* Italy, vol. 23, no. 228 (October 1972), pp. 318-323, interview (in Italian); *Form and Structure in Recent Film,* Dennis Wheeler, catalogue of an exposition at the Vancouver Art Gallery, October 29-November 5, 1972, includes an interview by Köller, and notes on **La région centrale** in Snow's article on Barry Gerson, available from the Gallery; *Cinema Canada,* no. 4 (October-November 1972), pp. 50-55, interview by George Csaba Köller; *Michael Snow Retrospective,* March 1975, published by La Cinémathèque québécoise on the occasion of their retrospective, includes interview, filmography and bibliography; *Take One,* vol. 3, no. 3, a complete filmography, interview, and criticism by Jonas Mekas

and Bob Cowan; *Toronto Star,* January 3, 1968, "The Latest
News of Andy and Mike", Robert Fulford (on **Wavelength**); *Film
Culture,* N.Y., no. 46 (1968), pp. 1, 3 and 4, "Conversation with
Michael Snow", P. Adams Sitney, and "Letter from Michael
Snow"; *Michael Snow/Canada,* The National Gallery of Canada
(Queen's Printer, 1970), for the 25th International Biennial Exhibi-
tion of Art, Venice, June 24-October 31, 1970; *Michael Snow/A
Survey,* by Michael Snow (The Art Gallery of Ontario and Isaacs
Gallery, 1970), with "Michael Snow's Cinema", an article by P.
Adams Sitney; *Expanded Cinema,* Gene Youngblood (E.P. Dut-
ton & Co., 1970), references and reviews; *Film Culture,* N.Y., no.
52 (Spring 1971), pp. 58-63, "**La région centrale**"; *Artforum,*
N.Y., vol. 9, no. 10 (June 1971), pp. 30-37, "Toward Snow: Part
I", Annette Michelson; *Experimental Cinema: A Fifty-year Evolu-
tion,* David Curtis (Studio Vista, London, 1971), references and
reviews; *Negative Space: Manny Farber on the Movies,* Manny
Farber (Praeger Publications Inc., 1971), references and reviews;
Village Voice, January 27, 1972, p. 65, an article by Jonas Mekas
in his "Movie Journal"; *Cinéma Canada,* no. 6 (February/March
1973), pp. 63-65, "Snow Storms Italy"; *Film Culture,* no. 56/57
(Spring 1973), pp. 81-89, "A Casing Shelved", A. Hayum; *The Vi-
sionary Film,* P. Adams Sitney (Oxford University Press, 1974), in-
cludes 12 pages on **Wavelength**, *Cinema Canada,* no. 19 (May-
June 1975), pp. 34-36, "Snow's Sin(ema) Souffle", Á. Ibrányi-
Kiss; the soundtrack of **New York Eye and Ear Control,** by
Albert Ayler, Don Cherry and others, has been issued by ESP,
Disk 1016.

SPOTTON, JOHN

Born in Toronto in 1927, John Spotton worked as an assistant
cameraman with a small company (Shelly Films in Toronto) before
joining the National Film Board in 1949. At NFB he worked as a
cameraman and editor on the television series "Eyewitness" and
"On the Spot", and later in Unit B with Tom Daly, Wolf Koenig
and Roman Kroitor, among others. Some of the films on which
Spotton assisted in this period include Colin Low's **The Days of
Whisky Gap**, **Circle of the Sun** and **The Hutterites**, Koenig and   nd
Kroitor's **Lonely Boy** and Macartney-Filgate's **The Back-breaking
Leaf**; he filmed Gordon Sheppard's **The Most** with John Foster,
and Don Owen's **Runner**, **High Steel** and **Nobody Waved Good-
bye,** as well as editing the latter. As a director, Spotton was involved in the Manitoba Centennial film, **Of Many People**, and has
worked on assignments for the United States Information Agency
and Canadian National Railways. In 1970 Spotton joined Potterton
Productions where he investigated projects. He returned to the
NFB in 1972 and became involved in 3-D technology; a 70mm

demonstration film was directed and shot by Spotton and Ernie McNabb. Spotton serves as a member of the NFB Program Committee.

Filmography

Buster Keaton Rides Again (Avec Buster Keaton) (1965). Prod: Julian Biggs, NFB. 55 min. b&w.
The Forest (Nôtre forêt canadienne) (1966). Prod: Tom Daly, NFB. 21 min. b&w.
Memorandum (Pour mémoire) (1966). With Donald Brittain. Prod: John Kemeny, NFB. 58 min. b&w.
Never a Backward Step (La presse et son empire) (1967). With Arthur Hammond and Donald Brittain. Prod: Guy Glover, NFB. 57 min. b&w.
Activator One (1970). Prod: Barrie Howells, NFB. 58 min. b&w.
The People's Railroad (1973). With Donald Brittain. Prod: D. Brittain, Potterton Productions for CNR. 60 min. col.
Work in progress: **Portrait of an Adman**. Prod: NFB.

Bibliography

Canadian Cinematography, May-June 1964, pp. 6, 7 and 16, "New Film Features Improvisation", John Spotton (on the filming of **Nobody Waved Goodbye**); *Film Quarterly,* Britain, Winter 1966-67, pp. 57-59, Henry Breitrose on **Memorandum**; references in *Le cinéma canadien.*

SPRY, ROBIN

Born in Toronto in 1939, Robin Spry spent his childhood in England. While there, he was involved in the organizational side of theatre; he continued this involvement in Canada with the founding of classes on film acting technique given at the National Film Board. Spry began his film career at Oxford and the London School of Economics where he made a number of short, dramatic films. He first joined the Board in 1964 as a summer student, and in 1965 he began to work full-time with John Spotton as an assistant editor. He was later assistant director on Don Owen's films, **High Steel** and **The Ernie Game**. His feature film, **Prologue**, was the first Canadian feature to be accepted at the main festival in Venice. **Action** and **Reaction**, two feature-length documentaries on the October crisis, explore, respectively, the explosive events which took place in Montreal and the reaction of Montreal's English-speaking population. **Action** is built upon television footage, including newsclips from the years preceding 1970, edited together with Spry's own footage from October of that year.

For **Action**, Spry won a 1975 Etrog as best director of a non- fiction feature film.

Filmography

Change in the Maritimes (Métamorphoses dans les Maritimes) (1966). Prod: Joseph Koenig, NFB. 13 min. col.

Miner (Une place au soleil) (1966). Prod: John Kemeny, NFB. 19 min. col.

Level 4350 (4350 pieds sous terre) (1966). Prod: John Kemeny, NFB. 10 min. col..

Illegal Abortion (1967). Prod: Guy Glover, NFB. 25 min. b&w.

Ride for Your Life (Mourir champion) (1967). Prod: John Kemeny, NFB. 10 min. col.

Flowers on a One-way Street (1968). Prod: Joseph Koenig, NFB. 57 min. b&w.

Prologue (1969). Prod: R. Spry, Tom Daly, NFB. 88 min. b&w.

Action: The October Crisis of 1970 (Les événements d'octobre 1970) (1973). Prod: Tom Daly, Normand Cloutier, R. Spry, NFB. 87 min. col.

Reaction: A Portrait of a Society in Crisis (1973). Prod: Tom Daly, R. Spry, Normand Cloutier, NFB. 58 min. col.

Downhill (1973). Prod: Tom Daly, R. Spry, NFB. 36 min. col.

Face (1975). Tom Daly, R. Spry, NFB. 17 min. col. and b&w.

Work in progress: **One Man** (a feature). Prod: NFB.

Bibliography

Le Devoir, February 21, 1970, interview by Jean-Pierre Tadros on **Prologue**; *Séquences,* no. 61 (April 1970), pp, 60-66, ''Entretien avec Robin Spry'' (interview); *Jeune cinema,* France, no. 53 (March 1971), pp. 3-5, interview by André Tournes; *Cinema Canada,* no. 15, pp. 28-29, interview by Á. Ibrányi-Kiss; *La Presse,* September 11, 1969, and February 21, 1970, ''Prelude à un monde nouveau'', Luc Perreault; *Télécine,* France, December 1969, ''Au contact des hippies, je suis devenu plus optimiste''; *Montreal Star,* January 24 1970, ''Chicago Confrontation'', Dusty Vineberg; *Le Devoir,* February 21, 1970, ''Les dilemmes de Robin Spry'', Jean-Pierre Tadros; *Montreal Gazette,* March 7, 1970, ''**Prologue**: A Today Film'', Peter Ohlin; *Ciné & Medios,* Argentina, no. 4 (1970), ''**Prologo:** Canadienses alertas''; *Le Jour,* September 25, 1974, ''Un film historique sur les événements d'octobre'', Jean-Pierre Tadros; *Time,* October 17, 1974, ''Night of the Garbage Bags'', Geoffrey James; *Le Soleil,* January 18, 1975, ''Comment Robin Spry a montré les événements d'octobre 1970'', Claude Daigneault; *La Presse,* January 31, 1975, ''Le point de vue officiel sur la crise d'octobre'', Luc Perreault; *Pot pourri,* March 1975, p. 17, review of **Action** by Philip Marchand; *Rélations,* no. 405 (June 1975), pp. 185-187, critique of **Action** and

Reaction by Yves Lever; *News Clips/Revue de presse,* has the NFB's collection of the review of **Prologue**, available at film study libraries; *Cinéma-Québec,* vol. 4 no. 5, pp. 10-15, "Une histoire à suivre: Octobre 70 dans le cinéma québécois", Yves Lever; references in *L'aventure du cinéma direct.*

THEBERGE, ANDRE

André Théberge was born in 1945 in Saint-Eluthère, Kamouraska. After receiving his B.A. and M.A. in literature from the University of Montreal, he wrote film criticism for *Objectif* and *Parti pris.* He assisted Jean-Pierre Levebvre on three features, **Patricia et Jean-Baptiste, Mon oeil,** and **Il ne faut pas mourir pour ça.** Théberge also worked on Denys Arcand's **Québec: Duplessis et après**, researching stock shots. He received a Canada Council grant in 1971 to script **Les allées de la terre**; Réo Gregoire did the camerawork. Théberge has taught film and written scripts for himself and others. In 1974 he worked as consulting director on the first of the two shootings of Joyce Wieland's **The Far Shore**; he co-scripted **Les vagues** with Francis Mankiewicz in 1975. He is currently preparing a half-hour video program; Théberge began working in video in 1968 at the University of Montreal, where he directed and wrote shorts made with a porta-pak for the student television network.

Filmography

Teréleur (1967). Prod: Independent. 13 min. b&w.
L'ile trébuchante ou On a tout le temps (1967). Unfinished feature. Prod: Independent. b&w.
Question de vie (A Matter of Life) (1970). Prod: NFB. 66 min. b&w.
Les allées de la terre (1972). Prod: Jean-Marc Garand, NFB. 71 min. col.
La dernière neige (1973). Prod: Jacques Bobet, NFB "Toulmonde parle français". 46 min. col.
Un fait accompli (1974). Prod: Paul Larose, NFB "Toulmonde parle français". 23 min. col.
Close Call (1975). Prod: Allan King. CBC. 30 min. col.
Work in progress: **L'hazard et la nécessité** (feature script).

Bibliography

La Presse, February 13, 1971, p. D-9, "André Théberge" (interview); *Le Soleil,* February 13, 1971, "Le cinéma, une chose simple", Paul Roux (interview); *Québec-presse,* February 14, 1971, "**Question de vie**: de la manufacture à l'asile..." (interview); an interview by Gerard Langlois on **Les allées de la terre** is printed in the NFB pressbook on the film, available at film study centres; *Variety,* May 19, 1971, p. 24, on **Question de vie**; *Télécine* 181, September 1971, p. 19, "Nouveau cinéastes québécois", G. Langlois; *Québec-presse,* July 1, 1973, "**Les allées de la terre** ou l'art de ne rien dire", C.L.; *Séquences,* no. 74 (October 1973), pp. 28-29, review of **Les allées** by Janick Beaulieu; references in: *Cinéma et société québécoise* and *Cinéma d'ci.*

TILL, ERIC

Born in England in 1929, Eric Till came to Canada in 1954 as manager of the National Ballet Company of Canada. Like Paul Almond, Till began his film career with CBC's dramatic series "Festival"; he directed such memorable films as **Great Expectations, Pale Horse, Pale Rider, The Offshore Islands, Diary of a Scoundrel, The Master Builder, Miss Julie** and **Glenn Gould**. His first feature film, **A Great Big Thing**, was produced by Martin Rosen, Argofilms and Pierre Patry with the assistance of the Montreal company, Coopératio. Since 1968 Till has been working in England and the United States as well as in Canada. In 1968 he made **Hot Millions** for MGM, and **The Walking Stick** for the same company in 1970. Under his own company, Coquihala Films Ltd., Till directed his fourth feature, **A Fan's Notes**, for Warner Bros. Till co-directed with James Murray the CBC series "The National Dream" ("Un grand défi"), based on Pierre Berton's book, and produced as well as directed **Freedom of the City** for the CBC in 1974, with a script by playwright Brian Friel. In 1975 Eric Till directed the stage production of "Pygmalion" at the Shaw Festival and directed the feature **All Things Bright and Beautiful** for Talent Associates, U.S.

Work in progress: **The First Night of Pygmalion**. Prod: CBC.

Bibliography

Toronto Star, September 23, 1972, "How to Make a Film, Lose Friends", Marci McDonald (interview); *Toronto Star,* November 14, 1964, "The Television Labors of Eric Till", Antony Ferry; *Toronto Star,* October 4, 1965, "Eric Won't be Happy till He's Directing *The Fox* in Move Away from TV"; *Globe and Mail,* October 11, 1968, "Fantasies in a Bargain Grab-bag", Wendy Michener; *La Presse,* January 31, 1970 "Le cinéma maudit se porte bien", Luc Perreault; *Motion,* July-August 1973, p. 31, review of **Fan's Notes** by Nat Shuster; *Maclean's,* March 1974, pp. 30-31, "The Second Last Spike", John Hofsess; *Take One,* vol. 3, no. 7, p. 32, review of **Fan's Notes** by Joe Medjuck.

TRENT, JOHN

Born in London, England in 1935; John Trent worked as a
magazine writer both there and later in Toronto, where he now
lives. A writer, producer and director, he has made approximately
700 films for American and Canadian television, including
episodes for "Wojeck", "Quentin Jurgens" and the "Whiteoaks of
Jalna". His eight features have been made with international
casts and settings. Trent has served as president of the Directors'
Guild of Canada and as a member of the Industries Advisory
Board to the CFDC. He formed Quadrant Films with producer
David Perlmutter in 1971.

Filmography (incomplete)

The Bushbaby (1968). Prod: MGM. 100 min. col.
Homer (1969). Prod: Terry Dene, Steve North, Palomar/Cinema
   Centre Films. 90 min. col.
The Heart Farm (1970). Prod: Terry Dene, Palomar Pictures. 88
   min. col.
"The Whiteoaks of Jalna" (1972). Prod: J. Trent, CBC. 13 epid-
   sodes, each 60 min. col.
Sunday in the Country (1974). Prod: David Perlmutter, Quadrant
   Films Ltd. 90 min. col.
It Seemed Like a Good Idea at the Time (1975). Prod: Quadrant
   Films Ltd. 106 min. col.
Find the Lady (1975). Prod: J. Trent, David Main,Quadrant Films
   Ltd. 90 min. col.

Bibliography

Toronto Telegram, August 1, 1970, "John Trent: The Top-notch
Unknown", Sid Adilman (interview); *Motion,* vol. 1, no. 1 (Novem-
ber-December 1972), pp. 34-37, "John Trent Director" (inter-
view); *New York Times,* December 6, 1970, "Why Do They Dig
Easy Rider and Ignore **Homer**?", Stephen Farber; *Performing Arts
in Canada,* vol. 9, no. 1 (Spring 1972), p. 7, on "Whiteoaks";
Montreal Gazette, September 13, 1975, "Forget If It's Canadian or
Not, **Good Idea** Offers Dandy Comedy"; *Montreal Star,*
September 13, 1975, "**It Seemed Like a Good Idea** . . .", Martin
Malina; *Cinema Canada,* no. 22, p. 45, review of **Good Idea** by
Natalie Edwards.

VAMOS, THOMAS

Thomas Vamos was born in Budapest in 1938, and studied film
there before coming to Canada in 1965. He worked as camera-

man on many dramatic films, including **Kid Sentiment, Jusqu'au coeur, Où êtes-vous donc, Le chambre blanche, Mon enfance à Montréal, Vive la France, IXE-13, OK Laliberté, Françoise Durocher, waitress, La dernière neige** and **Les "troubbes" de Johnny**, and on the documentaries **Acadié libre, Bozarts** and **Saint-Denis dans le temps**. Vamos has directed two features; **La fleur aux dents**, based on Gilles Archambault's novel about the quiet revolution, was adopted for screen by Pierre Turgeon.

Filmography

9 minutes (1967). With Jacques Bobet. Prod: T. Vamos, Jacques Bobet, NFB. 9 min. col.
L'exil (1971). Prod: Pierre Gauvreau, NFB. 95 min. col. Dist: Faroun.
La fleur aux dents (1975). Prod: Marc Beaudet, NFB. 85 min. col.

Bibliography

Le Devoir, August 17, 1971, "**L'exil** ou de la relativité du bonheur"; *Québec-presse*, January 20, 1972, "Thomas Vamos a tourné **L'exil**: un film qu'il a voulu menaçant", Robert Lévesque; *Le Devoir*, February 19, 1972, "Les mésaventures du camping à deux", Jean-Pierre Tadros; *La Presse*, February 26, 1972, "Vamos: on est pogné" and "Une fuite inutile", Luc Perreault; *Rélations*, no. 370 (April 1972), review of **L'exil** by Yves Lever; *Séquences*, no. 69 (April 1972), p. 41, review of **L'exil** by Jean-René Ethier; *La Presse*, December 7, 1974, "Porte au cinéma que sera le roman d'Archambault?", Serge Dussault.

VERRALL, ROBERT A.

With Evelyn Lambart, Robert Verrall was one of the original members of the National Film Board's animation department set up by Norman McLaren. Born in Toronto in 1928, Verrall studied at the Ontario College of Art and worked with Arthur Lismer and his Children's Art Centre. Joining the NFB in 1946, he created maps, diagrams and titles and worked on **Three Blind Mice, Family Tree** and **Teamwork Past and Present**. He directed his first film, **Breadmaking in the Middle Ages**, in 1947 and co-directed, with Colin Low and Wolf Koenig, the classic, **The Romance of Transportation in Canada**. Other significant films directed by Verrall include **A is for Architecture, Energy and Matter** and **The Structure of Unions**. Working as an art director under Koenig's directorship, Verrall became Director of English Animation in 1967; during that time he produced **Valley of the**

Moon, George Geerston's **The Men in the Park,** Donald Winkler's **Doodle Film,** **Around Perception** by Pierre Hébert and **In a Box**. Verrall has co-produced numerous films including Les Drew and Kaj Pindal's witty **What on Earth,** Jeff Hale's **The Great Toy Robbery,** Eva Szasz's **Cosmic Zoom, To See or Not to See, The Half-masted Schooner,** directed by Bruce Mackay, **Hot Stuff,** Les Drew's **The North Wind and the Sun,** and Hugh Foulds' **The Bear's Christmas**. As an executive-producer, Verrall has been involved with **Man: The Polluter,** a Yugoslavian-Canadian co-production, and **Exeter,** directed by Gerald Budner. In 1972 Verrall was appointed Director of English Production at the National Film Board.

Bibliography

Pot pourri, April 1972, an interview with Verrall; *Cinema Canada,* no. 15, pp. 32-34,"Robert Verrall, English Production", Laurinda Hartt (interview).

VITALE, FRANK

Frank Vitale was born in the United States and came to study at McGill, graduating in 1967 with a degree in science. He co-directed his first film, **Country Music,** in 1971 in Montreal, but he began his film career as assistant cameraman on numerous NET documentaries in Washington and New York, as unit manager on the feature **Joe,** and as associate-producer on **Cry Uncle. Montreal Main** is an improvised feature with the principal character played by Vitale.

Filmography

The Metropolis Organism (1971). Prod: F. Vitale. 5 min. b&w. Dist: Carmen Educational Associates.
Country Music (1971). With Allan Moyle. Prod: F. Vitale, Allan Moyle. 27 min. b&w. Dist: Faroun and Canadian Film-makers' Distribution Centre.
Hitchhiker — Auto: Train: New York State Police (1972). 3 b&w videotapes totalling 45 minutes. Dist: Vidéographe.
Montreal Main (1974). Prod: F. Vitale, Allan Moyle, President Film, Montreal. 88 min. col. Dist: Faroun and New Cinema.
Penny and Ann (1974). Prod: Harry Gulkin for Lethbridge Rehabilitation Centre. 18 min. col.
East End Hustle (1976). Prod: F. Vitale, President Films/Cinepix Ltd. 90 min. col. Dist: Cinepix.
Friday Night Adventure (1976). Prod: Stephen Patrick, CBC "Tele-play". 30 min. col.

Bibliography

Inner Views: Ten Canadian Filmmakers (McGraw-Hill Ryerson, 1975), pp. 103-114 (interview); *Hitchhike: Montreal, New York/Montreal, Jacksonville,* Frank Vitale (Vehicle Press, 1973); *New York Times,* March 8, 1974, review of **Montreal Main** by A.H. Weiler; *Maclean's,* May 1974, p. 96, "A Plucky Dance in the Face of Adversity", J. Hofsess (review of **Montreal Main**); *Film Culture,* N.Y., nos. 58-60 (1974), pp. 268-292, "Filmexpo and the New English Canadian Cinema", Seymoure Stern; *Cinema Canada,* no. 13, p. 33, "**Montreal Main**: An Appreciation", David Beard; *Take One,* vol. 4, no. 4, pp. 30-31, review of **Montreal Main** by William Kuhns; *Cinema Canada,* no. 15, p. 78, review of **Montreal Main** by Natalie Edwards; *Take One,* vol. 5, no. 2, pp. 50-52, "Making **Cindy**", Elizabeth Wajnberg.

WAXMAN, ALBERT

Born in Toronto in 1935, Waxman studied acting at the Neighbourhood Playhouse in New York and with Lee Strasberg. (His most recent film role was in Paul Almond's **Isabel**. In 1962 he attended the London School of Film and worked largely in television drama before making his first feature in 1971. Waxman produced a number of commercials on recycling for the Toronto Recycling Action Committee (TRAC)and stars in CBC's "King of Kensington" series. Waxman is currently producing a feature based on John Hunter's **Night of the Tiger**. He lives and works in Toronto.

Filmography

Master of the House (1968). Prod: Kirk Jones, CBC "Quentin Durgens M.P.". 60 min. col.

Tviggy (1968). Prod: A. Waxman, Tobaron Productions. 13 min. col.

Kid from Spanish Harlem (1969). Prod: Bill Davidson, Manitou Productions and CBC "Adventures in Rainbow Country". 30 min. col.

Black Phoenix (1969). Prod: Ron Weyman, CBC "Anthology". 60 min. col.

Walk, Do Not Run (1969). Prod: Ron Weyman, CBC "McQueen". 30 min. col.

Father and Son (1970). Prod: Ron Weyman, CBC "Canadian Short Stories". 30 min. col.

The Crowd Inside (L'univers de Christina) (1971). Prod: A. Waxman, January One Films Ltd. 103 min. col. Dist: Warner Bros.

The Collector and **The Philatelist** (1973). Prod: CBC "Of all People". Each 15 min. col.

My Pleasure is My Business (1974). Prod: Gerry Arbeid, August Films. 93 min. col. Dist: International Film Distributors.

Bibliography

Ottawa Citizen, January 19, 1970, on **Black Phoenix**; *Variety,* January 28, 1970, on **Black Phoenix**; *Toronto Telegram,* July 3, 1970, "**The Crowd Inside** Movie Set in Toronto", Pat Annesly; *Toronto Star,* September 5, 1970, "Toronto Filmmaking is all Agony and Frustration", Urjo Kareda; *Financial Post,* October 10, 1970, "Want to be a Movie Angel?", Arnold Edinborough; *Globe and Mail,* October 17, 1970, "The House of Waxman: Ordeals of a Movie Maker", Kaspars Dzeguze; *Montreal Gazette,* April 17, 1971, "Big Al's Dream Comes True — His First Feature Film", Dane Lanken; *Maclean's,* September 1975, p. 80, "Get Out There, Al, and Make 'Em Laugh", Ron Base on "Kensington"; *Euro cinéma,* Paris, no. 28 (October 1975), pp. 73-77, **My Pleasure is My Business**, review by Tina Morello.

WEINTRAUB, WILLIAM

Writer-director-producer, William Weintraub was born in Montreal in 1926. After graduating from McGill University, he worked as a reporter for the *Gazette* in Montreal and as staff writer on *Weekend Magazine.* His novel, *Why Rock the Boat,* chronicles the exploits of a young reporter during the '40s; Weintraub later wrote the scenario and produced the film of the same title. Joining the National Film Board in 1955, Weintraub has been a commentary writer for a large number of important films, including **Nahanni**, **The Drylanders**, and the series, "Struggle for a Border". As a scriptwriter he worked on **A Matter of Fat**, **Vote for Michalski**, the series "Between Two Wars", and **Anniversary**; this latter film (which he also produced) is edited footage of Hollywood films starring Canadians, Walter Huston, Walter Pidgeon and Norma Shearer, among others. Weintraub's fascinating film on weight problems, **A Matter of Fat**, won the 1970 Canadian Film Award for the best full-length documentary. For six months in 1975-76, Weintraub worked in Nairobi as producer on the Habitat '76 project for the United Nations.

Filmography

A Matter of Fat (Qui perd gagne) (1969). Prod: Desmond Dew, NFB. 99 min. col.

Challenge for the Church (1972). Prod: Ian McLaren, NFB "Adieu Alouette". 30 min. col.

The Aviators of Hudson Strait (1973). Prod: W. Weintraub, NFB for the Department of National Defence. 28 min. b&w.

Bibliography

Montreal Star, February 23, 1974, "Newsmen, Then" (interview); *Globe and Mail,* October 12, 1974, "A Movie With a History of False Starts, But a Happy Ending", Martin Knelman (interview); *Cinema Canada,* no. 15, pp. 18-19, interview by Stephen Chesley; *Why Rock the Boat,* William Weintraub (McClelland and Stewart, 1968); *Canadian Literature,* no. 46 (Autumn 1970), pp. 74-78, "Uneasy Riders", William Weintraub in the symposium "Write Me a Film?"; *Canadian Magazine,* January 16, 1971, pp. 28-29, "The Man who Starved Himself to Death", Barry Conn Hughes; *Globe and Mail,* January 8, 1972, "Diet Show Feasts on One Man's Famine", Blaik Kirby; *Le Devoir,* January 18, 1973, "Une information sur l'église, dans une forme peu originale", Jean-Pierre Proulx; *Maclean's,* November 1974, p. 112, "**Why Rock the Boat**: The Best Canadian Movie of the Year", John Hofsess.

WIELAND, JOYCE

Born in Toronto in 1931, artist Joyce Wieland worked as an animator for George Dunning's Graphic Films and as a camera-woman for Shirley Clarke's film, **Vosnesensky**, in 1967. Although much of her work is personal in its subject and execution, her later films reflect her involvement with the New York movement of structural cinema. Recently, Wieland has been working on the dramatic feature film, **The Far Shore**, inspired by the story of Canadian painter Tom Thomson. **The Far Shore** uses art objects made specifically for the film in Wieland's continuing dialogue between films and other art forms.

Filmography

Larry's Recent Behaviour (1963). Prod: Independent. 18 min. col.

Peggy's Blue Skylight (1964). Prod: Independent. 17 min. b&w.

Patriotism (Part One) (1964). Prod: Independent. 15 min. col.

Patriotism (Part Two) (1964). Prod: Independent. 5 min. col.

Water Sark (1964-65). Prod: Independent. 14 min. col.

Sailboat (1967-68). Prod: Independent. 3⅓ min. Printed on colour stock.

1933 (1967-68). Prod: Independent. 4 min. col.

Hand-tinting (1967-68). Prod: Independent. 4 min. b&w. Hand-tinted.

Catfood (1968). Prod: Independent. 13 min. col.

Rat Life and Diet in North America (1968). Prod: Independent. 14 min. col.

La raison avant la passion (Reason over Passion) (1968). Prod: Independent. 90 min. col.

Dripping Water (1969). With Michael Snow. Prod: Independent. 10 min. b&w.
Pierre Vallières (1972). Prod: J. Wieland. 33 min. col.
Solidarity (1973). Prod: J. Wieland. 11 min. col.
The Far Shore (1976). Prod: Pierre Lamy, Judy Steed, J. Wieland, Far Shore Inc. 104 min. col. Dist: New Cinema.
Work in progress: **Birds at Sunrise** and **Wendy and Joyce**, with the late Wendy Michener.

Joyce Wieland's independent films are distributed by the Canadian Filmmakers' Distribution Centre.

Bibliography

True Patriot Love/Véritable amour patriotique, Joyce Wieland (Ottawa: The National Gallery of Canada, 1971), interview by Pierre Théberge interpreted by Michael Snow (also includes Regina Cornwall's article reprinted in English and French); *Take One,* vol. 3, no. 2, "Kay Armatage Interviews Joyce Wieland", a feature article in the women's issue; *Motion,* vol. 5, no. 2 (March 1976), pp. 32-33, "**The Far Shore**", an interview with Joyce Wieland by Brian Charent, Peter Harcourt and Margo Blackell; *Globe and Mail,* August 7, 1976, p. E-1, an interview with Wieland and Celine Lomez by Robert Martin; *Artforum,* February 1970, "Joyce Wieland", Manny Farber; *Artscanada,* April 1970, pp. 43-45, "There is Only One Joyce", P. Adams Sitney; *Film Culture,* no. 52 (Spring 1971), pp. 64-73, includes a selection from a film outline of "True Patriot Love" (working title of **The Far Shore**);*Ottawa Citizen,* July 10, 1971, "Joyce Wieland — Her Romantic Nationalism and Work", Robert Fulford; *Time,* July 12, 1971, "Whimsy over Passion", Geoffrey James; *Artscanada,* August-September 1971, pp. 17-27, "Wieland: An Epiphany of North", Hugo McPherson; *Artforum,* vol. 10, no. 1 (September 1971), pp. 36-40, "*True Patriot Love:* The Films of Joyce Wieland", Regina Cornwall; *Films and Filming,* February 1973, pp. 65-66, review of **Reason over Passion**; *Communiqué,* May 1975, pp. 36-39, "Women in Arts in Canada" issue, "Myth in Many Media: Joyce Wieland", Anne Montagnes; *Cinema Canada,* no. 23, pp. 41-43, "A Glimpse of **The Far Shore**", Michele Moses: *Canadian Forum,* September 1975, pp. 70-71, "Films: Joyce Wieland's Vision" Debby Magidson; *Art Magazine,* December-January 1976, pp. 6-11, "In Celebration: Joyce Wieland: Filmmaker. **The Far Shore**/In Progress", Bill Auchterlonie; *Cinema Canada,* no. 27 (April 1976), pp. 20-23, "**The Far Shore**: A Film about Violence, A Peaceful Film about Violence" Barbara Halpern Martineau; *Take One,* vol. 5, no. 2 (May 1976), pp. 63-64, "Joyce Wieland's **The Far Shore**" Peter Harcourt; *Saturday Night,* vol. 91, no. 3 (May 1976), pp. 76-77, "Movies: Wielandism: A Personal Style in Full Bloom", a review of **The Far Shore** by Marshall Delaney.

WILLIAMS, DONALD S.

Don Williams was born in Stony Plain, Alberta in 1938. His varied background in radio, television and theatre has led to unusual and fruitful combinations. In 1967 he won the Centennial Commission Playwright Award for his play, *Danny*. As artistic director of the Hatrack Theatre, a small company set up in Winnipeg to produce original Canadian works, Williams has funnelled its talents into television drama. In 1971 he filmed a cinemascope background for the Royal Winnipeg Ballet's version of George Ryga's *The Ecstasy of Rita Joe* and later filmed the ballet for CBC. William's interest in local history has produced a dramatized documentary on Manitoban naturalist Ernest Thompson Seton and a dramatized study of Mennonite history; **Cornet at Night** is based on a short story by Sinclair Ross and **Raisins and Almonds** on the book of the same title by Fredelle Bruser Maynard. Don Williams won Wilderness Awards for **Death of a Nobody** and **Nis'ku** and a 1974 Canadian Film Award for **The Trial of Polly Upgate**, which was voted the best scholastic film.

Filmography

A Bucket of Tears for a Pound of Jam (1967). Prod: D. Williams, CBC Winnipeg. 30 min. b&w.

Death of a Nobody (1968). Prod: D. Williams, CBC Winnipeg. 30 min. col.

Who? Me? Never! (1969). Prod: D. Williams, Manitoba Department of Education and Manitoba Department of Health. 30 min. b&w.

One Upsville (1969). Prod: D. Williams, CBC Winnipeg. 30 min.

I Run the Mile I Walked (1970). Prod: D. Williams, CBC Winnipeg for "Twenty-Four Hours". 40 min. col.

A Gift for Maggie (1970). Prod: D. Williams, CBC Network. 60 min. col.

Nis'ku (1970). Prod: D. Williams, CBC Winnipeg. 60 min. col.

Independence Day (1972). Prod: Philip Keatley, CBC "The Beachcombers". 30 min. col.

The Highliners (1972). Prod: Philip Keatley, CBC "The Beachcombers". 30 min. col.

Every Night at 8:30 (1972). Prod: D. Williams, CBC Winnipeg and Edmonton. 30 min.

Jerry Potts and 74's (1972). Prod: D. Williams, CBC "This Land". 60 min. col.

Portrait of a Pig (1972). Prod: D. Williams, CBC Winnipeg. 55 min. col.

La légende de vent (1973). Prod: D. Williams, Radio-Canada. 60 min. col.

St. Laurent Speaks (1973). Prod: David B. Dueck, Dueck Productions for the Government of Manitoba. 28 min. col.

The Ecstasy of Rita Joe (1974). Prod: D. Williams, CBC. 50 min. col.

Coronet at Night (1974). Prod: D. Williams, CBC "To See Ourselves". 30 min. col.

Raisins and Almonds (1974). Prod: David Ruskin, CBC "Performance". 60 min. col.

Seton's Manitoba (1974). Prod: D. Williams, CBC, 60 min. col.

"Indian Arts and Crafts" series of film clips (1974). Prod: D. Williams for the Department of Indian Affairs.

"The Industrial Revolution Trilogy" (1974): **The Trial of Polly Upgate, The Trial of Will Upgate, The Judgement of Jeremiah Upgate**. Prod: D. Williams for the Manitoba Department of Education. 28 min. each. col.

Three to Get Ready (1975). Prod: D. Williams, Winnipeg Bible College. 37 min. col.

Menno's Reins (1975). Prod: David B. Dueck, Dueck Productions. 60 min. col.

Winterpeg (1975). Prod: D. Williams, CBC "Musicamera". 36 min. col.

"The Beachcombers" series (1975): **Big Tow, The Fugitive, Treasure Hunt**. Prod: CBC. 30 min. col.

"Commercials" series of nine (1975). Prod: D. Williams, Manitoba Liquor Commission.

Bibliography

Toronto Telegram, September 24, 1970, p. 63, "Film on Geese a Labor of Love", Roy Shields; *Winnipeg Free Press,* December 19, 1970, p. 15, "**A Gift for Maggie**" (review); *Winnipeg Free Press,* March 6, 1971, p. 21, "Amateur Theatre in Winnipeg", Peter Crossley; *Winnipeg Free Press,* July 3, 1971, "Camera Rolls for Rita Joe Ballet", Karen Lerch; *Ottawa Citizen,* July 24, 1971, "Rita Joe Comes to Life Again in New Impressionistic Ballet", Gordon Stoneham; *Winnipeg Free Press,* January 5, 1974, "French Opera on National TV"; *Vancouver Sun,* December 23, 1974, Lisa Hobbs on **Raisins and Almonds**; *Montreal Star,* December 23, 1974, Joan Irwin on **Raisins and Almonds**; *Ici Radio-Canada,* vol. 8, no. 11 (1974), p. 5, on **La légende du vent**.

WOODS, GRAHAME

Director, cameraman and writer, Grahame Woods was born in London, England in 1934 and worked as a journalist before joining the CBC in 1956. Beginning as an assistant cameraman on a number of public affairs programs, Woods has since photographed numerous documentaries and dramas directed by himself and others. With Douglas Leiterman he worked on **Forty Million Shoes** and **The Chief**; with Allan King, **Dreams**; with Ron Kelly, **Caio Maria**, **Open Grave** and **The Gift**, with Terence Macartney-

Filgate, **Marshall McLuhan** and **Portrait of Karsh**; with Peter
Carter, **The Mercenaries** and **The Day They Killed the
Snowman**. Woods has also been director of photography for a
number of series, including "Wojeck", "Corwin" and "An-
thology". His scripts were included in the following productions:
Twelve and a Half Cents, **The Disposable Man**, **Kalinsky's
Justice** and **Vicky** (which won the 1973 ACTRA Script Award), all
directed by René Bonnière, **Rape**, directed by Don Haldane,
Strike and **The Mercenaries**, directed by Peter Carter. Woods
has written many of his own directed scripts, including **Winter's
Discontent** and **It's Winning That Counts**. Les Rose and Barry
Pearson wrote **Rodeo Rider** and playwright George Ryga wrote
The Ninth Summer. Woods is presently writing a stage play.

Filmography

The Miracle of Terezin (1966). Prod: G. Woods, CBC "Sunday
Night". 15 min. col.

Trudeau (1968). Prod: G. Woods, CBC "The Way It Is". 30 min.
b&w.

Aberfan (1968). Prod: G. Woods, CBC "Public Affairs". 30 min.
b&w.

Ginette Ravel (1969). Prod: G. Woods, CBC. 60 min. col.

Winter's Discontent (1971). Prod: G. Woods, CBC "Theatre
Canada". 30 min. col.

Thanks for the Ride (1971). Prod: G. Woods, CBC "Theatre
Canada". 30 min. col.

Rodeo Rider (1971). Prod: Ron Weyman, CBC "Anthology". 60
min. col.

Stop for a Moment . . . and Feel the Pain (1972). Prod: G.
Woods, CBC "Tuesday Night". 60 min. b&w.

The Ninth Summer (1972). Prod: CBC "To See Ourselves". 30
min. col.

Our Miss Hammond (1973). Prod: Ron Weyman, CBC "Anthology". 60 min. col.

It's Winning That Counts (1973). Prod: G. Woods, CBC "Tuesday Night". 60 min. col.

Till Divorce Do Us Part (1975). Prod: G. Woods, CBC "Date-
line". 60 min. col.

Bibliography

Canadian Cinematography, March-April 1964, pp. 11-14, "Film
Features Hand-held Camera", Grahame Woods on the making of
Open Grave.

WRIGHT, JOHN

Born in Pioneer Mine, B.C. in 1937, John Wright studied theatre and English at U.B.C. and received his B.A. in 1963. For two years he organized and directed a summer stock theatre, "Palace Grande Theatre", in Dawson City, returning to his theatre studies at Stanford Unviersity in 1964. He worked as an actor and stage manager in a Seattle theatre, returning to Vancouver in 1967 as artistic director of Stage II of the Playhouse Theatre Company. Wright subsequently taught drama at the University of Saskatchewan and the University of Calgary. Highwood Films Ltd. was co-founded with Robert Lockwood in 1972; this company produced Wright's first feature, **The Visitor**, with camera by Doug McKay and editing by Homer Powell; John Wright wrote the screenplay.

Filmography

Drumheller (1971). Prod: Highwood Films, CFCN. 27 min. col.
Drug Crisis (1972). Prod: University of Calgary, Communications
  Media. 20 min. b&w.
The Visitor (1974). Prod: Margaret Dallin, Highwood Films Ltd.
  93 min. col. Dist: Faroun.
"The Beachcomers" series (1975): **Boss Log**, **Cargo of Gold**,
  The Colonel's Day, **Win or Lose All**. Prod: CBC. 30 min.
  each. col.

Bibliography

Cinema Canada, no. 14, pp. 28-29, an interview with Wright by George Mendeluk; *Vancouver Province*, August 25, 1967, "The New Man at the Playhouse", James Barber; *Vancouver-Sun*, February 26, 1974, "Wright Hoping to Take Off — With a Canadian Movie", Les Wedman; *Film Culture*, N.Y., nos. 58-60 (1974), pp. 268-292, "Filmexpo and the New English Canadian Cinema", Seymour Stern discusses **The Visitor** (pp. 281-283); *Cinema Canada*, no. 16, p. 70, review of **The Visitor** by Mark Miller.

YAKIR, LEONARD

Born in Germany in 1947, Leonard Yakir emigrated to Canada a year later and grew up in Winnipeg. A student at the University of Manitoba and the University of Winnipeg, he received his B.A. in English and philosophy before attending Ryerson in Toronto as a student of photographic arts. Yakir's work in still photography has culminated in three exhibitions — at Ryerson in 1973, in Winnipeg in 1974 and a group show, "Canadian Photographers", at the Ontario Art Gallery. While a student at Ryerson, Yakir was assistant director on Murray Markowitz' **More than One** and later, in Winnipeg, cameraman and editor on Shin Sugino's **Shinshu**. Yakir's feature, **The Mourning Suit**, co-authored with Joe Wiesenfeld, was the official Canadian entry at the Locarno International Film Festival in 1975.

Filmography

My Home 1970 (1970). Prod: Independent. 3 min. b&w.
Main Street Soldier (1972). Prod: Paul Leindburd, Circle Films. 36 min. col. Dist: Canadian Filmmakers' Distribution Centre.
The Mourning Suit (1975). Prod: L. Yakir, March Films Ltd. 85 min. col. Dist: Cinepix.

Bibliography

Cinema Canada, no. 21, pp. 38-40, "Talking with Leonard Yakir", Natalie Edwards, also p. 48, review of **The Mourning Suit** by Stephen Chesley.

Film Groups

ASSOCIATION COOPERATIVE DE PRODUCTIONS AUDIO-VISUELLES (ACPAV)

Founded in Montreal in 1971, ACPAV is a co-operative production company funded, in part, by the CFDC, which makes sponsored films, shorts and features. This organization has all of the necessary filmmaking equipment, including editing facilities; ACPAV often collaborates on the production of shorts by furnishing technical assistance.

With a membership of about 60, ACPAV is directed by a five-person board headed by executive producer Marc Daigle. Daigle was born in St. Hyacinthe in 1947 and studied at the University of Montreal before making his first film in 1970, **Colombine**, a short for Radio-Canada. His feature **C'est ben beau l'amour** (1971), was produced by Jean-Pierre Lefebvre of the National Film Board in the cadre "Premières oeuvres". Since 1971, when Daigle became executive producer at ACPAV, he has produced a number of films, including **Le loup blanc** (Brigitte Sauriol, 1972, 30 min.) and **Y'a toujours un maudit bout**, a 45-minute work film sponsored by metal and chemical workers, miners, the audio-visual department of the Université de Québec at Trois-Rivières and the Shawinigan CEGEP.

ACPAV has produced two films by Jean-Guy Noël — a short, **Elle était un fois: une autre fois** (1971), and a feature, **Tu brûles... tu brûles** (1972). Born in Montreal in 1945, Noël studied philosophy at the University of Louvain before enrolling at INSAS in Brussels where he prepared "La 5e saison", an audio-visual presentation of Quebec poems for an international festival of young poets, held in Brussels in 1968. That same year Noël organized a two-week showing of Quebec cinema in Belgium and worked in theatrical design at the Théâtre africain de Louvain. Noël directed three short films at INSAS before his 1970 short, **Zeuzere de Zegouzie**. Jean-Guy Noël is presently preparing his second feature with ACPAV, **Ti-Cul Tougas**, and has directed sequences of Jacques Leduc's **Chronique de la vie quotidienne**.

Michel Bouchard, who served an apprenticeship on Almond's **Act of the Heart** and Carle's **La mort d'un bûcheron**, wrote and directed his first feature, **Noël et Juliette**, with ACPAV in 1973 with producer René Gueissaz. Other features produced by ACPAV include Mireille Dansereau's **La vie rêvée** (The Dream Life), Brigitte Sauriol's **L'absence**, Alain Chartrand's **Isis au 8** (Isis at 8) (1971) and **La piastre**, produced by Daigle and Bernard Lalonde with songs by Claude Gautier; Pierre Harel's **Bulldozer**, and Jean Chabot's **Une nuit en Amérique** are products of this co-operative. ACPAV has also co-produced a number of films: Bruno

Carrière's **La mort dans l'oeuf** (1973) is a 65-minute film co-produced with Cinetrie; **Jos Carbone**, directed by Hughes Tremblay, was produced by Bernard Lalonde, ACPAV and Soger Inc.; and André Forcier is presently preparing his feature, **La cène**, at ACPAV in conjunction with Les Films André Forcier. As well as features, ACPAV has produced a number of shorts: **7 dernières minutes dans la vie d'Archibald** by Jean Cousineau; **Au sujet d'un camp d'été**; **Pareil partout** by Maurice Rochette; **Y faut crier plus fort** by Bruno Carrière; **Une aventure** by Roger Cantin; **Les étoiles et autres corps** by Paul Tana; and **En garouine avec Philippe Gagnon** by Louis Hébert. Although the distribution of some features is handled by distribution companies, ACPAV distributes many of its own films.

Bibliography

Québec-presse, August 1, 1971, "Une trentaine de jeunes cinéastes fondent une coopérative de production", Carol Faucher; *Cinéma Canada*, no. 6 (February-March, 1973), pp. 22-23, "Association coopérative de productions audio-visuelles", Kirwan Cox; *Films du Québec 2: Tu brûles...tu brûles* (CQDC, 1973), includes an interview with Jean-Guy Noël and a discussion of the feature (available from the CQDC); *Relations*, no. 392 (April 1974), p. 125, a review of **Bulldozer** by Yves Lever; references to Marc Daigle in *Cinéma d'ici*.

LES ATELIERS DU CINEMA QUEBECOIS INC.

Founded in 1971, Les Ateliers du cinéma québécois is dedicated to the production of feature films; the organization is directed by Jean Dansereau, François Brault and Yves Gélinas. Director, editor, producer Jean Dansereau was born in Montreal in 1930; he began his career as a journalist with *La Patrie* and Canadian Press before joining the National Film Board in 1957 as an assistant director. In this role he worked on Fernand Dansereau's **La canne à pêche** and Louis Portugais' **Les 90 jours**, and went on to co-direct **Jeu de l'hiver** with Bernard Gosselin, **Congrès** with Fernand Dansereau, and **La guerre des pianos** with Jean-Claude Labrecque, and to direct **L'escale des oies sauvages**, **Parallèles et grand soleil** and **La bourse et la vie**. Jean Dansereau left the Board in 1964 to found, with Gilles Groulx, Denys Arcand and Bernard Gosselin, Les Cinéastes associés, which he directed until its demise in 1971: in these years he co-directed, with François Brault, **A soir on fait peur au monde**, a feature musical documentary on Robert Charlebois, and directed **Est-ce qu'on a le droit de faire un soleil?** for the Pavillon de l'homme at Terre des hommes and **Comment vit le Québécois** for the Quebec Pavilion at Osaka. Since the founding of Les Ateliers, Jean Dansereau has produced a number of features, including Bernard Gosselin's **Le Martien de Noël**, Pascal Gélinas' **Montréal blues**, André Forcier's **Bar salon** and François Brault's **M'en revenant par les épinettes.**

Director-cameraman François Brault was born in Montreal in 1941. His work as cameraman includes his co-directed **A soir on fait peur au monde**, **Comment vit le Québécois** and Kroitor's **Exercise Running Jump II**: he has directed films in Radio-Canada series "Prelude", "Action santé" and the "Telescope" segment, **The Mark of a Champion**. In the OFQ series, "Les ecrivains québécois", Brault directed **Marcel Dubé**. He has recently completed his second feature, **M'en revenant par les épinettes**.

Actor-musician Pascal Gélinas studied at the National Theatre School before beginning his work in film as a researcher and scriptwriter for the Radio-Canada series dedicated to cinema, "Images en tête". With Arthur Lamothe, Gélinas assisted on **Ce soir-là, Gilles Vigneault**, **Au-delà des murs** and "Actualités québécoises". He later worked with Fernard Dansereau, and directed, with Pierre Hamel, the political documentary, **Taire des hommes**; since then Gélinas has made **Une bonne journée pour les pionniers**, **En montage** and **La fête** for the OFQ, and **Montréal blues** with Les Ateliers, which stars the theatre group, Le grand cirque ordinaire, with a collective script improvised by them.

Bibliography

Montreal Gazette, August 2, 1969, "A Long Lens Look at Dansereau", Dane Lanken; *Films du Québec 2: Montréal Blues* (CQDC, 1972), synopsis, critique and interview with Pascal Gélinas.

THE ATLANTIC FILMMAKERS' CO-OPERATIVE

The Atlantic Filmmakers' Co-operative was formed in 1973 and now has a membership of 25, which is co-ordinated by Chuck Lapp with technical advisor Grant Crabtree. Women Co-op members worked on a series of one-minute films for women on filmmaking under executive producer Kathleen Shannon of the National Film Board. **The Tavern** (Edith Ray), **I'm Ready, Dear** (Gert Mabey), **Assembly Line** (Jay MacLean), **Women in Motion** (Shelagh McNab) and **Friends** (Sharon Mann) were some of lthe films produced in the series. Shelagh McNab also directed **Phenomenon**, a film about Peggy's Cove; Ramona MacDonald is working on an improvised drama, **Regan's Cove**, on **Black and**

White, and on **Dialogue**, with Randy Gaynor. John Brett's **Voices from the Landscape**, Chuck Lapp's **Nightwalk** and **Paradise**, Bill MacGillivray's **Lil and Mr. Bill**, Mike Williams' **Port Morien**, Harold Pearse's **Joe Sleep** and Lionel Simmons' **Masterpiece** are all recent productions. There are also a number of scripts in progress, including one on Acadian lifestyles by Monique Léger and Normand LeBlanc, a drama by Neal Livingston, and **Phaedra**, a film on skydivers, by Paul Mitcheltree. To borrow films contact the Co-op.

Bibliography

Cinema Canada, no. 17, pp. 26-29 Lon Dubrinsky and Liz Mullen interview three members of the Co-op.

ATLANTIC REGIONAL PRODUCTION CENTRE—NATIONAL FILM BOARD

This regional production unit was established in Halifax in 1973 under executive producer Rex Tasker. One of its first accomplishments was to assist in the creation of the Atlantic Filmmakers' Co-operative for professional and amateur filmmakers. It has also encouraged video activities through workshops held at many universities in the region. "Atlanticanada," a 2½ hour CBC special, was the result of the unit's work in combining the talents of many east coast filmmakers.

Rex Tasker has long advocated the story potential of all parts of Canada—not just of Montreal and Toronto—and is a longtime supporter of regional film production. As an editor, writer, director and producer, he has been involved in over 100 films since joining the National Film Board in 1960. Tasker's editing credits include **Fields of Sacrifice**, **Quebec as Seen by Cartier Bresson**, **Helicopter Canada** and **The Land**. (made for the Canadian Pavilion at Expo '70). Tasker co-directed (with Wolf Koenig) **Steeltown**, and directed **Loops to Learn By**, **The Oshawa Kid**, **Encounter at Kwacha House—Halifax**, **Celebration**, and more recently, **Don Breaks Out** and **The Queen, The Chief and the President** for "Atlanticanada". His work within the Challenge for Change projects has produced three films on urban transportation —**Where do We Go From Here?**, **A Bus for Us** and **Regina Telebus**. Before joining the Atlantic NFB in 1972, Tasker was involved in various cable television projects, particularly in Thunder Bay. **Simple histoire d'amour**, a dramatic videotape directed by Fernand Dansereau, was co-produced by Tasker.

Shelagh Mackenzie graduated from the University of Toronto in drama, and worked for the CBC for six years as researcher and story editor before joining the NFB in 1967 as Joe Koenig's assistant on educational films. As well as directing a film on an educational project, **Unstructured for a Summer**, she edited Tasker's **Loops to Learn By**, Barry Perles' **A Quiet Wave**, Robin Spry's **Action** and **Reaction** and the English version of **L'Acadie, L'Acadie**. As a teacher, Mackenzie was involved with the Thunder Bay Community Television Project in 1969-70, working with half-inch video. Mackenzie brought her experience as a researcher and editor to the Halifax unit in 1973.

Ted Haley, who joined the NFB in 1951, worked as a soundman on **Labyrinth**, **Tiger Child**, **Norman Jewison, Filmmaker**, **Blake, The Sea**, and on Kathleen Shannon's series, "Working Mothers". He has taught sound in colleges and on location with the Fogo Island project of Challenge for Change. Haley moved to Halifax in 1973, and has worked on many of the new unit's productions.

Kent Nason, a native of New Brunswick, worked for Crawley Films as a cameraman for **A Hospital Is** and **National Role**, and joined the Film Board in 1973 to shoot **Don Breaks Out**, **What's Up Doc**, and Bill Gough's **The Brothers Byrne** in the "Atlanticanada" series. Nason also brings teaching experience to his work in the Maritimes. He shot Cheryl Wright's **Cancer in Women** and directed **Tracker** for the Department of National Defence.

Cheryl Wright began **Cancer in Women** as a slide-tape show at the Halifax Infirmary; under the aegis of the Atlantic production unit this personal project became a film which was distributed through "Reel Life", a co-operative project brought to many communities in the Maritimes by van. She made **What's Up Doc** in 1974 for "Atlanticanada".

Kent Martin started filmmaking while at Carleton University, where he graduated in English in 1972. **Moses Coady** and **Milton Acorn, the People's Poet**, both directed by Martin, are moving portraits of Maritime folk heroes. He has worked as cameraman on a number of the Atlantic unit's productions, and has a feature, **Rustico**, in progress.

Michael Jones, born in St. John's, Newfoundland in 1944, joined the NFB in 1974 after freelancing as a photographer in Toronto and earning his Masters' degree at the Ontario Institute of Studies in Education. Jones taught English and film, and made films with his students, including **The Bullies**, which he directed and edited. He was assistant cameraman on **The Rowdyman**, and worked on **Tattoo** at Memorial University for the Department of National Defence. Jones is currently working at Memorial on a co-production with the NFB entitled **Barkin' the Spineless Servant** or **It's Hard to Get Good Help These Days.**

Diane Beaudry-Cowling was born in Montreal in 1946, and worked for the CBC as a researcher and editor before moving to Halifax in 1971. She directed **The Electric Ben**, a film about musician Ben McPeek, and edited **The Margaree People** for the "Atlanticanada" series. Beaudry-Cowling made **Maud Lewis: A World Without Shadows** in 1976.

Michael McKennirey was born in Ottawa in 1935, and in 1956 he joined the NFB as a lab technician, working eventually as sound editor, picture editor, director and producer. He edited **Best Damn Fiddler from Calabogie to Kaladar** and **Don't Let the Angels Fall**, and co-produced **People of the Seal** and **The Conquered Dream** in the "Netsilik" series. He wrote and edited as well as directed **Atonement**, and directed **I Don't Have to Work That Big** in the "West" series, **The Long View**, and **Eastern Graphics**; the latter was made with the Atlantic unit after McKennirey joined in 1974.

Barry Cowling came to Nova Scotia from England in his youth, and worked for advertising agencies as a scriptwriter before joining the film unit in Halifax in 1974. He wrote and directed **Changes by Degrees** for "Atlanticanada" and scripted Nason's **Tracker**.

Other young filmmakers who are part of the film unit include Bill McGillivray, whose **7:30 A.M.** was a prize-winning student film and who animated **Big Bus #5**; Stefan Wodoslawsky, who made **Desolation Row** and worked as a cameraman on "Atlanticanada"; Brian Pollard, whose collection of tapes, old photos and ballads of P.E.I. formed the basis of **The Islanders**; and John N. Smith, who made **Halifax Ukelales** for "Atlanticanada" as well as **We Sing More Than We Cry** and, with Douglas Kiefer, **Ready When You Are.**

Other results of the NFB's regional production in Halifax include: **Medoonak the Storemaker** by Les Krizsan, with the Mermaid Puppet Theatre; **Scoggie** by Cynthia Scott; **Gulf Stream** by Bruce MacKay; **Blind Mechanic** by Mike Mahoney and Ted Haley; **Citizen Sailor** by Whit Trecartin and Sam Grana; and **Gardening** by John Pederson. Two notable video productions are **Chapell's Diary**, from a screenplay by Ken Stetson on the diary of P.E.I.'s first settlers, and **Sister Theckla's Choice**, a colour video by Mike Boyle.

Bibliography

American Cinematographer, July 1970, "Film at Expo '70", special edition with a long article on **The Land** with an interview with co-director, editor Rex Tasker; *Montreal*, *Gazette*, April 13, 1973, "The Atlantic Just Super", Ian MacDonald; *The 4th Estate* (Halifax), July 19, 1973, p. 19 "NFB Here Only Two Months—But Involved in Seven Productions"; *The Chronicle-Herald* (Halifax), November 13, 1973, p. 18, "National Film Board Shoots **People of the Margaree**", Betsy Chambers; *The Mail-Star* (Halifax), November 13, 1973, "Personalities of Margaree Valley in NFB Film", Betsy Chambers; *L'Evangeline* (Moncton), September 26, 1973, p. 7, "Co-production Télé-Publik/ONF: **Une Histoire d'amour** dans le nord-est"; *Cinema Canada*, April-May, 1974, "Atlantic Provinces"; *Pot pourri*, March 1975, pp. 7-9, an article on Tasker's work with "Atlanticanada"; *Ottawa Citizen*, April 10, 1975, "Maritime Soul Caught", Frank Penn; *Calgary Herald*, March 24, 1975, "Atlanticanada Series a Change for 'Fun'", Bill Musselwhite; a *Film and Video Newsletter* published four times a year by The Atlantic regional NFB is available in English or French from the NFB at 1572 Barrington Street, Halifax, Nova Scotia.

CHERRY FILM PRODUCTIONS LTD.

Cherry Film Productions Ltd. was founded in 1961 by Evelyn Spice Cherry and her husband, Lawrence Cherry; the company, dedicated to filming local subjects, and located in Regina, Saskatchewan, consists of Evelyn Spice Cherry, Bill Cherry, and Gary Seib, cameraman. Ms. Cherry was born in Yorkton, Saskatchewan and attended the University of Manitoba before studying journalism in the United States. For a short time during the Depression she worked as a reporter, before travelling to England where she became a member of the British Documentary Group under John Grierson's direction; working as an editor and producer, Ms. Cherry learned her craft with Basil Wright, Arthur Elton and Stuart Legg. This unit was later taken under the wing of the GPO, and in 1941 many of its members, including Evelyn and Lawrence Cherry, joined Grierson in setting up the National Film Board. The NFB consisted of 12 units in the early forties and the Cherrys headed up the Agriculture Unit. In 1958 the Cherrys returned to their home province where Lawrence Cherry set up a provincial film unit for the Saskatchewan government and Evelyn Cherry freelanced as writer and editor. Cherry Film Productions Ltd. has completed a number of series; "The Nature Series", consisting of **The Squaw Rapids** (1964), **Harnessing the South Saskatchewan** (1966) and **Mastering the South Saskatchewan** (1967), were commissioned by (and are available from) the Saskatchewan Department of Education. "The Geology Series", consisting of **Dust Bowl Dividend** (which used archival footage), **Cypress Hills**, **Edge of Shield**, **Dunelands**, **Sanctuary—the Qu'Appelle Valley**, **On the Prairie** and and **Nature's Story—in Saskatchewan** are available from Cherry Film Productions Ltd. Other films include **Alcohol in My Land** (1972), made in the Inuit language with an English version available and a music score by Larry Crosley, **In the Workshop** (1975) about environmental diseases for the Department of Labour, **Community Revitalization: Old Towns New Life** (1975) and two films in a continuing series on "Prairie Artists", **I.H. Kerr** and **E. Lindner**.

Bibliography

Pot pourri, Summer 1975, the entire issue is devoted to the women at the early National Film Board, criticism and interviews.

CRAWLEY FILMS LTD.

F.R. "Budge" and Judith Crawley began their film careers with **Ile d'Orléans** in 1940, shot while they were honeymooning. **Ile d'Orléans** won the best amateur film award in an international festival held in New York and attracted the attention of John Grierson, first National Film Board commissioner. From 1940 to 1945 the Crawleys and a staff of six were commissioned by the NFB to make training films for the army. After the war the business community's interest in film allowed this small company to expand its location and staff, and in 1956 it was a company of 80 working in all aspects of filmmaking. It produced 71 films, a number of slide shows and over 100 television commercials. Much of the company's most impressive work has been done in the area of sponsored films, which have received numerous awards. **The Loon's Necklace** (1948) and **Newfoundland Scene** (1950) were produced for Imperial Oil Ltd.; **Zéro de conduite** (1950), **Power of Pennies** (1951), **Packaged Power** (1952), **The Power Within**, **Immediate Action**, **Les bouts d'chou** (1953), **Episode in Valleydale** (1954), **It's in the Cards** (1955), **Legend of the Raven**, **Canadian Wheat**, **Generator 4** (1958), **Money Minters** (1959), **It's People That Count** (1960), **Waters of the Whiteshell** (1961), **Abitibi**, **Campus on the Move** (1962), **Partners for Progress**, **The Annanacks** (1963), **Brampton Builds a Car** (1964), **The Entertainers**, **The Perpetual Harvest**, **Global Village** (1967), **Carstairs**, **Tell the People** (1968), **A Hospital Is** (1970), and **Child Behaviour Equals You** (1972) were all award winners.

A generation of filmmakers learned their skills with Crawley Films, including Grant Crabtree and Peter Cock, who in 1948 directed **Fortress For Freedom** for the Progressive-Conservative Party, Ed Reid, René Bonnière, Christopher Chapman, Peter Carter, Rob Iveson and Vincent Vaitiekunas, who directed **Motion** for the CN Pavilion at Expo' 67, **Multiplicity**, and **The Sun Don't Shine on the Same Dawg's Back All the Time**, which won the 1970 CFA award for the best sports and recreation film. Original music scores by William McCauley (**Newfoundland Scene**, **Beaver Dam**) and Larry Crosley (**Saskatchewan Jubilee**, **Journey to Power**) have helped to make Crawley films classics of sponsored work.

With the coming of television in Canada, Crawley Films collaborated with the CBC and Radio-Canada to make two important series, "RCMP" and "Au pays de Neuve France"; the director of the latter series, René Bonnière, directed Crawley's first feature film, **Amanita Pestilens**. The second feature, **The Luck of Ginger Coffey** (from the novel by Brian Moore), was co-produced with U.S. producers Roth-Kershner. Peter Carter's **The Rowdyman**, Bonnière's **Hamlet** and Crawley's **The Man Who Skied Down Everest** (which won the 1976 Academy Award for feature-length documentary) form an impressive number of feature productions. **Janis**, directed by Howard Alk and Seaton Findlay, won the award as best feature film—non-fiction at the 1975 Canadian Film Awards.

Bibliography

Ottawa Citizen, January 17, 1970, "Crawley Name is Synonymous With Film", Marie Riley; *The Canadian Film Digest*, March 1973, p. 13, "Budge Crawley: We've Got to Look for World Markets"; *La Presse*, June 7, 1975, "Janis Joplin sous son vrai jour", L.P.; *Maclean's*, May 17, 1976, p. 61, "The Man Who Skied Down the Balance Sheet", Marni Jackson; *Take One*, vol. 4, no. 6, pp. 20-22, "Putting **Janis** Together: The Inside Story", Doug Fetherling; *Cinema Canada*, no. 18, pp. 26-27, "**Janis** by Alk", George Köller and Tony Lofaro, and pp. 61-63, reviews of **Janis**; *Cinema Canada*, no. 22, p. 46, review of **The Man Who Skied Down Everest** by David McCaughna.

FILMWEST ASSOCIATES

Filmwest Associates was founded in Edmonton in 1971 on the original organization of Film Frontiers with Ken Pappes, Bill Thorsell, Tom Radford, Bob Reece and Peter Boothroyd. Although the personnel of Filmwest has changed (Lorna Rasmussen and Anne Wheeler have founded Prairie People Productions, and Mark Dolgoy, Reevan Dolgoy and Tom Radford have begun to freelance), the company is dedicated to making films in and about the west and providing opportunities for cooperative filmmaking. Each member handles a variety of production functions, and in this cooperative way Filmwest has produced more than fifty documentaries and dramatized documentaries, winning in 1973 the Golden Sheaf Award at the Yorkton International Film Festival, and in 1974 Best Film at the Alberta Film Festival for **Ernest Brown: Pioneer Photographer**: an original music score was performed and written by Bruce Cockburn. Other members of Filmwest are Dale Phillips, Harvey Spak, Peter Amerongen, Allan Stein, Freida Koplowicz and Samuel Koplowicz.

Filmography

Death of a Delta (1970). Prod: Film Frontiers for Alberta Department of Education. 27 min. col.
Lament for Woody (1970). Prod: Film Frontiers. 7 min. col.
Shelter (1971). Prod: CBC. 22 min. b&w.
Winter (1971). Prod: Filmwest for CBC. 26 min. col.
Urban Crisis (1971). Prod: Filmwest for CBC. 29 min. col.

To Be Young, Gifted and Western Canadian (1971). Prod: Filmwest for CBC. 29 min. col.

Hay River: The Way North (1971). Prod: Filmwest for Alberta Department of Education. 29 min. col.

To Live Good (1972). Prod: CBC. 25 min. col.

Country Doctor (1972). Prod: Roger Scott Kennedy, CBC "Take 30". 28 min. col.

Gung Fu: Fighting Back (1972). Prod: CBC. 25 min. col.

Mountain People (1972). Prod: CBC. 29 min. col.

Promises, Promises (1972) Prod: Len Chatwin, NFB. 28 min. col.

Ernest Brown: Pioneer Photographer (1972). Prod: Filmwest for Northwestern Utilities. 54 min. col.

Jimmy Simpson: Mountain Man (1972). Prod: Filmwest and Jon Whyte for Alberta Department of Education. 24 min. col.

Common Cause (1972). Prod: Filmwest for The United Way. 7 min. col.

Cardinal and **Art Recycling** (1973). Prod: Roger Scott Kennedy, CBC "Arts 73". Each 9 min. col.

One Woman (1973). Prod: Filmwest. 25 min. col.

Three Minutes to Live (1973). Prod: Filmwest for Alberta Workers' Compensation Board. 33 min. col.

Paul Kane: To the Wild Woods (1973). Prod: Filmwest for Alberta Department of Education. 22 min. col.

Trade-Off (1974). Prod: Filmwest for Syncrude. 25 min. col. Censured.

Following the Plough (Chant du tracteur) (1974). Prod: Filmwest for NFB for Agriculture Canada. 29 min. col.

Aerospace Medicine (1974). Prod: Filmwest for Canadian Aerospace Medical Association. 29 min. col.

The Solid Lands (1974). Prod: Filmwest for Alberta Department of Education. 29 min. col.

Prairie Women (1976) Prod: Filmwest for NFB. 29 min. col.

The Ukrainian Settlers (1976). Prod: Filmwest for Alberta Department of Education. 21 min. col. Video.

Work in progress: **Fort McMurray** for Alberta Department of Education.

Filmwest's distribution is handled by New Cinema, 35 Britain Street, Toronto, Ontario, M5A 1R7. Print sales are handled by Marvin Melnyk Associates, 464 McNicoll Avenue, Willowdale, Ontario, M2H 2E1.

Bibliography

Artscanada, no. 142-143 (April 1970), p. 48, "Filmmakers in Edmonton: An Interim Report", Norman Yates; *Interlock*, no. 2 and

3 (April-May 1975), pp. 21-30, "Pulling Focus", an interview with Lorna Rasmussen and Anne Wheeler by Barbara Halpern Martineau; *Cinema Canada*, no. 14, pp. 34-37, interview with Filmwest by T. Marner.

INSIGHT PRODUCTIONS

Insight Productions was formed in 1970 by Pen Densham and John Watson, members of a community of free-lancers which includes Bob Grieve. Both Watson and Densham were born in England; Densham began his career as a photographer, coming to Canada with his father who was shooting for the NFB. He and Watson met while they were both working for the educational film production company, Moreland-Latchford; their first film, **Playground**, set their future course—optimistic films often using the talents of children. **Life Times Nine**, which was nominated for an Academy Award, is a compilation of nine commercials for life prepared by children. Many of their films have been award winners: **Thoroughbred** was chosen best documentary in 1972 by the Canadian Film Editor's Guild and **White Days—Red Nites** won the same organization's award for best industrial and promotional film for 1973. With a number of other small independent film companies (Nelvana, Sunrise, Rosebud, Intercom, Gary Nicholl and Cinematics), Insight has formed a protective lobby — the Independent Producers' Group.

Filmography

Playground (1971). Prod: Insight. 10 min. b&w.
Lickity Split (1971). Prod: Insight. 3 min. col.
Sunburst (1972) Prod: Insight. 6 min. col.
Thoroughbred (1972). Prod: Insight. 22 min. col.
A Photographer's Britain (1973). Prod: Insight. 5 min. col.
Beaverman (1973). Prod: Insight. 7 min. col.
Life Times Nine (1973). Prod: Insight. 14 min. col.
Streetworker (1973). Prod: Insight. 16 min. b&w.
White Days—Red Nites (1973). Prod: Insight for Massey-Ferguson. 15 min. col.
Dull Day Demolition (1974). Prod: Insight. 25 min. col.
The Bricklin Story (1975). Prod: Insight CBC. 25 min. col.
Reflections on Violence (1975). Prod: Insight for the Ontario Government. 25 min. col.
Work in progress: two documentaries, **Morning Line** and **Toller Cranston**.

Insight films are distributed by Viking Films, 525 Dennison Avenue, Markham, Ontario.

Bibliography

Daily Racing Form (Toronto) October 8, 1972, "**Thoroughbred**, a Fine Film", Wally Wood; *Toronto Star*, March 15, "Two Young Filmmakers Bask in Applause", Clyde Gilmour reviews **Sunburst**; *Canadian Photography*, December 1973, "Money is By-product to Youthful Partnership of Insight Productions", Dean Walker; *Globe and Mail*, February 21, 1974, "Film by 9 Toronto Youngsters Nominated for Academy Award", Betty Less; *Motion*, March 1974, "The Insight Story", Claudia Wittgens; *American Cinematographer*, May 1974, "**Life times nine**", Pen Densham; *Cinema Canada*, no. 13, pp. 30-31, "Insight: The Philosophy of Success", Gunter Ott; *Motion*, May 1974, "Comments from Filmmakers: Pen Densham", Claudia Wittgens; *Rushes*, November 1974, "An Unworking Man's Guide to the Film Business", Pen Densham and John Watson; *The Canadian Film Editor*, December 1974, interview with John Watson.

INTERNATIONAL CINEMEDIA CENTER LTD.

Cinemedia was founded in 1969 as a production company specializing in films and related media for education. Producers Joe Koenig and John Kemeny have been joined by Donald Duprey as producer. Also on staff are editor Ian Ferguson, who graduated from the Communications Department of Loyola College and trained as editor at Crawley Films; Martin Rosenbaum, AV producer; David Verrall, who established the AV department and is production manager, Jane Churchill, researcher and slide and filmstrip editor; and Wendy Greenspoon, production manager. Over 70 films have been made and hundreds of film loops and filmstrips. Recently the company has been involved in the production of feature films, most notably **The Apprenticeship of Duddy Kravitz** and **White Line Fever.**

Joseph Koening was born in Dresden, Germany in 1930 and came to Canada in his youth. He attended Ryerson in Toronto, studying graphic arts and journalism, and worked for a Montreal magazine publisher. Koenig joined the National Film Board in 1955 as a writer and researcher in the film strip unit; he later directed and produced many educational films. Among his directing credits at the NFB are **The Tiny Terrors**, **The Origins of Weather**, **Jet Pilot**, **Change in the Western Mountains**, **The Changing Wheat Belt** and **The Ever Changing Lowlands**. He produced Martin Defalco's **Bird of Passage**, Eva Szasz's **Cosmic Zoom**, Josef Reeve's **Imperial Sunset**, Co Hoedeman's **Continental Drift** and **Matrioska**, Les Drew's **The Underground Movie** (co-produced with Drew and Bob Verrall), Gilles Gascon's **If at First**,

and Shelagh Mackenzie's **Unstructured for a Summer**. With
Bané Jovanovic, Koenig co-produced two films directed by
Jovanovic—**DNA** and **Question of Immunity**. **The Rise and Fall
of the Great Lakes** by Bill Mason, **Christopher's Movie Matinée**
by Mort Ransen and **Flowers on a One Way Street** by Robin Spry
were all produced by Koenig while he was at the National Film
Board. His production credits at Cinemedia include the series
"Inventions and Technology that shaped America", "Holt Reading
Filmstrips", "Holt Transformational Grammar Filmstrips",
"Students and Teachers", and "National Museums of Man"; his
films include **The Living City, Classroom Television: Instrument
for Educational Change**, as well as numerous segments for the
Children's Television Workshop in the U.S.

John Kemeny was born in Hungary, and worked in film there for
eight years before joining the National Film Board in 1957. As a
producer with the NFB he was involved in George Kaczender's
You're No Good, **The Game** and **Don't Let the Angels Fall**,
Donald Brittain's **Memorandum**, **Ladies and Gentlemen, Mr.
Leonard Cohen** (co-directed with Don Owen) and **Bethune**. With
Tom Daly he co-produced **Untouched and Pure** by Mort Ransen,
and with Barrie Howells co-produced **PowWow at Duck Lake**
(Bonnie Klein), **Encounter at Kwacha House-Halifax** (Bonnie
Klein and Rex Tasker), **Encounter with Saul Alinsky** (Bonnie
Klein) and **Halifax Neighborhood Center Project** (Rex Tasker).
Tanya Ballantyne's **The Things I Cannot Change** was also produced by Kemeny. Since co-founding Cinemedia, Kemeny has produced or co-produced a number of feature films, including **Sept
fois par jour**,   **Un enfant comme les autres**, **The Apprenticeship of Duddy Kravitz** and **White Line Fever**. He is presently
producing **The Shadow of the Hawk.**

Bibliography

Cinema Canada, no. 21, pp. 41-43, "Producing down South",
Connie Tadros on Kemeny, **White Line Fever**, and Cinemedia.

MEMORIAL UNIVERSITY EXTENSION SERVICE FILM UNIT

The Memorial University Extension Film Unit grew out of the joint
Memorial University-National Film Board Fogo Island Project; this
innovative use of film, which encourages a community to gain
control of its future, was directed by Colin Low who, as a result of
this experience, set up the Challenge for Change/Société nouvelle
program at the National Film Board. The Extension Service Film
Unit was built on a two-man unit that existed before 1967; Jeff
Evans and cameraman Nels Squires were joined by director-pro-

ducer Paul MacLeod, soundman Randy Coffin, and Joe Harvey. Their film work is an extension of the work done by the Community Development Officers (under the direction of Tony Williamson), who live in various Newfoundland and Labrador communities and attempt to respond to the needs of each community. They have produced a series of teaching films for fishermen called "Decks Awash" (**It's All Made Up of Moneywise**, **King of Fish**, **Not Many as Didn't Have a Finger In It**, **Fish Marketing in Montreal**) and "Port au Choix" produced by Harvey Best (**Port au Choix 3**, **I Take It As It Comes**, **The Past, the Present, and the Future**, **The Move**).

Paul MacLeod was born in Stratford, Ontario in 1941 and studied history at Mount Allison University and Canadian Studies at the University of Rochester. In 1966 he joined the NFB Halifax office as a distributor, and moved to the Extension Service at Memorial where he became involved in production, notably in the editing of the "Port au Choix" series. Since then MacLeod has directed the unit as well as many films in the "Decks Awash" series, the "Port au Choix" series and individual films—**If Just One of Us Does Something**, a fisheries co-op film course for CIDA, and **Reid Land Ownership**, produced by Don Snowden in 1973. He also directed **Tattoo** in 1974 and was assistant cameraman on NFB productions **A Memo from Fogo** and **A Little Fellow from Gambo**.

Nels Squires first worked as a newspaper photographer before becoming a television cameraman and editor for CJON in St. John's. In 1966 he freelanced for CJON, CBC and Memorial University as well as working in his own stills studio. Later that year he joined the Film Unit on a full-time basis. Along with other members of the Unit, Squires spent seven weeks training at the NFB and shot **Fish Marketing in Montreal** for "Decks Awash", as well as many others in the series. He has also shot **The Sea**, directed by Bané Jovanvic, **Reid Land Ownership**, **Sir Wilfred Grenfell**, **Tattoo**, **Sir William Coaker** and local segments of **A Little Fellow from Gambo**, directed by Julian Biggs.

Randy Coffin, a former teacher and a native of Fogo Island, began his film career as a researcher for the Fogo Island Project, which included acting as interpreter for the editing of the films. This was followed by two months of screening the Fogo films for participant approval as well as screenings for government officials. Coffin doubled as distribution officer and assistant cameraman in recording reaction to the series. As soundman Coffin has worked on the "Decks Awash", "Port au Choix" and "Labrador Coast" series. He is also responsible for sound on **A Little Fellow from Gambo**, **If Just One of Us Does Something** (with Wayne Sturge), **When I Go, That's It** and **A Memo from Fogo**.

Joe Harvey was born in Wabana, Bell Island, Newfoundland, joining the Film Unit in 1968 after working for the NFB as a driver in Montreal during Expo. Harvey has been assistant cameraman in the "Port au Choix" series and cameraman and editor on many "Decks Awash". His film work in Labrador led to the editing of **Introduction to Labrador** and his running for a seat in Labrador South which he held for two terms. Since then Harvey has directed a number of films for the Unit including **King of Fish**, **Marine Lab** and **Wabana**, a history of his home town told in old photographs and recent film.

See also COMMUNITY FILM AND VIDEO.

NELVANA LIMITED

Patrick Loubert, Michael Hirsh and Clive Anthony Smith founded Nelvana in 1972 to produce live-action features, documentary shorts, animated logos and children's programs. The three work as a creative team: for example, they organized "The Canadian Whites", the National Gallery of Canada comic book show, with Smith handling the design, catalogue and poster; **A Christmas Two-Step**, an animation/live-action special for CBC French and English Divisions, used animation by Smith, executive production by Loubert and was produced by Hirsh. The logo for "Sprockets", the CBC series showcasing independent Canadian films, was also produced by Nelvana.

Patrick Loubert directed **125 Rooms of Comfort** (Prod: Nelvana and Don Haig, Film Arts Ltd. 80 min. col.) in 1974 from a screenplay he wrote with assistance from Bill Fruet, which features a former rock star who returns to his home town to manage the family hotel. Loubert has directed **The Great Canadian Comic Books** (Nelvana for CBC "Telescope", 24 min. col.), **Madja** (for CBC "Gallery", 15 min.), **Homefront** (for the National Gallery, 7 min.), **Picture of Love** (for CBC, 7 min.), and six 15-minute dramatic shorts for CBC's Children's Department. *The Great Canadian Comic Books* (Toronto: Peter Martin Associates, 1971) was written with Hirsh; Loubert has also written a number of short scripts for CBC radio and CBC's Children's Department.

Michael Hirsh directed **The Happy Chalk Dog** and **Mr. Pencil Draws the Line** (for CBC, 13 Min.), **Lyle Leffer: Last of the Medicine Men** (24 min.), **Smile a Day** (13 min.), **Birds of Music** (13 min.), **Robert Markle: A Celebration of Woman** (15 min.) and **Voulez-vous coucher avec God?** (69 min.), an experimental film made with Jack Christie. He co-directed **The Great Canadian Comic Books**, co-authored *The Great Canadian Comic Books*, and directed and hosted numerous shows for CBC Radio, including "Bringing Back the Future". Hirsh has lectured in film at

Johns Hopkins University, York University, the University of
Baltimore, Conestoga College and Sheridan College. He worked
on animated films for "Sesame Street" at Cineplast in 1969.

Clive Anthony Smith is a graduate of the Ealing School of Art in
London, and has exhibited his work at the A.I.A. Gallery and the
I.C.A. Gallery in London, England. From 1962 to 1966 he worked
as a musician and a boutique designer. In 1967 he began working
in animation for Group II Animation, London, and for Al Guest,
and made a number of animated films for the CBC and OECA, and
logos for several CBC shows. He has done the animation for
Nelvana's children's films produced for CBC, including **Zounds of
Music**, **Battle of the Alphabets**, and **The Adventrues of Mr.
Pencil**, as well as the title sequence of **125 Rooms of Comfort**.

Bibliography

Motion, September-October 1974, pp. 13-14, "**125 Rooms**",
David McCaughna; *Variety*, November 20, 1974, review of **125
Rooms of Comfort**; *Cinema Canada*, no 17, pp. 48-50, "Notes
For an Article I Could Not Write", Á. Ibrányi-Kiss; *Cinema
Canada*, no. 18, pp. 32-34, "Nelvana Presents", an interview with
Loubert, Hirsh and Smith by Mark Miller, pp. 58-59, film review of
125 Rooms of Comfort by Robert Fothergill.

NEWFOUNDLAND INDEPENDENT FILMMAKERS' COOP

The Newfoundland Independent Filmmakers' Coop was founded in
St. John's in 1975. Born in 1949 in St. John's, Bill Doyle received
his B.Ed. from Memorial University and continued doing work
there in communications. Doyle's photographic work includes
"Women at Work", a series of photos distributed in high schools
which encouraged young women to work in various professions.
Bill Doyle's film career has been in Super 8, starting with his 1971
Head and Shoulders, a 15-minute critique of the school system.
He went on to direct **It Happened Last Night** (1973, 3 min.),
Flute Loose and Fancy Free (1973, 5 min.), **No Memoriam**
(1973, 20 min.), a film about the lack of town planning, **Dr. P.J.
McNicholos: Candidate for Mayor** (1974, 12 min.) and **Pure
Silver**, a satirical look at Newfoundland's 25th anniversary
celebrations. Doyle does his own editing and sound.

John Doyle works in video as well as Super 8. He attended the
University of Windsor and Ryerson in Toronto, and made his first
short film, **Regatta**, in 1970. His other films include **A Small
Deposit** (1970, 3 min.), **Saint John Youth Test** (1971, 11 min.)
shown on the local CBC, **The Graduate Film Workshop** (1972), a

film about the sexual revolution, **Too Hard to Touch** (1972, 6 min.), made while Doyle was still a student at Ryerson, and a drama starring Doyle in the role of St. John visiting St. John's— **The Visit of St. John the Baptist**; this comedy was shot on video by Kathy Cooper in 1973. Mike Jones, who has done camera work and has directed for a number of National Film Board productions, is presently working on **Codco**, a film-portrait of the Newfoundland satirical group.

NOVA SCOTIA COMMUNICATION AND INFORMATION CENTRE

This unusual provincial government department is a film unit under the aegis of the premier of Nova Scotia, and is available to all government departments. It has a long history of independent and creative documentary work. Its activities began in 1945 under Margaret Perry, who operated a one-woman unit for over 12 years, and made more than 50 films before her retirement in 1970. Since then Ned Norwood has headed the unit; Martin Alford, Charles Dean and Rod MacEachern are among the film-makers currently working out of the Nova Scotia Communication and Information Centre.

Born in Upper Mills, New Brunswick, Margaret Perry had two compelling interests — photography and nature—which led her into filmmaking in the early 1940s. Her experimental film work came to the attention of John Grierson, who invited her to the newly-founded National Film Board in 1942. She stayed for over two years, becoming familiar with scripting, directing, editing and photographing. In 1945 she joined the staff of the Nova Scotia Travel Bureau, Department of Trade and Industry, to make pub-licity films. Having been granted the freedom to make films that were more documentary than promotionals, she produced over 50 films for various departments of the Nova Scotia government. Until 1959 she ran a one woman film unit, whose films reflect her knowledge and love of the different regions of the province, as well as her skill as an editor. Perry has said that her personal favourite is **Glooscap Country**, made in 1961 with music by Larry Crosley; this story of Glooscap, the god of the Micmac Indians, was filmed "without benefit of people, using the elements of nature, animals and land areas frequented by Glooscap in a fanci-ful way." Other films she has directed inlude: **Artists** (1970), **Nova Scotia Sage** (1960), **Woodland Wealth** (1963), **New Nova Scotia** (1962), **Orison** (1968), **Royal Province** (1967), and **The Cape Islander** (1961).

Ned Norwood learned photography from his father, a profes-sional photographer, and joined what is now the Nova Scotia

Communication and Information Service in 1955 as a darkroom technician. He later worked as a photographer in the Stills Division, and in 1959 he was transferred to Margaret Perry's film unit as a cameraman-director. Since 1970 he has headed this unusual department. Norwood has photographed Margaret Perry's **Glooscap Country**, **Artists**, and **Nova Scotia Saga** (with Perry), among others; he directed and photographed **Discover Nova Scotia** (1972), **A Summer for All Ages** (1972) for the Department of Social Service, **Ologies and Isms** (1970), **Bluenose Shore** (1969), **Trees in the News** (1961) and **Free From Care** (1964).

Martin Alford was born in England in 1924 and emigrated to Canada in 1937. He joined Crawley Films in 1953 as a production assistant; there he received his film training, working later as a freelance editor, writer and co-director. Alford worked on CBC's "Inquiry", produced by Patrick Watson, and for the "20/20" series; after a stint with Canawest-Master's Film Productions in Calgary, he joined the Communications and Information Centre in 1968. He wrote and edited **Sable Island**, **A Summer for All Ages**, **Discover Nova Scotia**, and **Ologies and Isms**. As a director he worked on **Encounter Week** and **Bluenose Ghosts**, a dramatized folklore documentary based on stories collected by Helen Creighton in her book of the same title.

Charles Dean was born in Kentville, Nova Scotia, and after graduating from Ryerson Polytechnical Institute in film production he freelanced in 1973 for the Ontario Ministry of the Environment as editor, soundman and cameraman. With co-director and co-producer Hans Eijsenck, Dean made **Environment Ontario**, **Waste Control**, and a number of commercials, and edited videotape for the National Film Board. His film, **Don't You Ever Say Goodbye**, co-directed with Steve Shaw and Ian Leech, won first prize in the documentary category in the Montreal Student Film Festival in 1973. Dean joined the Communication and Information Service film unit in 1974.

Experience in distribution work in the National Film Board's Halifax office from 1969 to 1971 led Rod MacEachern into a community-oriented video program in his home city. Backed by a coalition of churches and with help from a LIP grant, he worked with four others to make a number of tapes attempting to use video as a viable educational tool. The series included tapes on learning disabilities, mental retardation, poverty (with Teled) and, in conjunction with the NFB's Challenge for Change unit, on welfare rights. MacEachern joined the Nova Scotia film unit in 1972, working as cameraman for **Evangeline Tract** and as assistant director for **Bluenose Ghosts**.

The film unit has made use of a number of other directors and cameramen, notably Les Kriszan (**Discover Nova Scotia** and **Sable Island**) and Charles Doucet, an underwater photographer. A member of the Bedford Oceanographic Institute Photographic Unit, Doucet has shot **Dive Nova Scotia** and **The Wreckhunters**.

PACIFIC FILM CO-OP

The Pacific Film Co-op in Vancouver has a membership of 25 film-makers, including a number who have made feature films. Peter Bryant studied at Simon Fraser University before beginning his career as a cameraman. In 1968 Bryant completed **Andy**, while studying at the National Film Board. His shorts include **Noohalk** (1970), a documentary on West Coast Indians, which won first prize at the Student Film Festival, **One Man Went to Mow** (1970), **Felix**, with camera by Tony Westman, **The Roof** (1971), **Deal** (1972), **Morning Line** and **Rocco Brothers** (1973), a fantasy-drama about re-created youth. **The Supreme Kid** is Bryant's first feature; completed in 1975 this drama was written by Bryant and shot by Tony Westman. It is available, as most of Bryant's films are, from the Canadian Filmmakers' Distribution Centre. Bryant, who received a scholarship from the American Film Institute to study at the Centre for Advanced Film Studies, is a contributor to *Cinema Canada*.

Byron Black was born in the United States and worked in film there before coming to Canada in 1971. He directed **At Home in Infinity, Master of Images** (1971), an 82-minute feature, and in 1974 a second feature, **The Holy Assassin**, both produced by Infinity Studio in Vancouver.

Al Ruzutis has set up Visual Alchemy, a production company experimenting in film opticals, videographs and holographs to produce innovative short works: **1967-1969** (1969, 4 min.), **Aaeon** (1968-1970, 26 min.), **Vortex** (1970, 12 min.), **Software** (1972, 3 min.), **Le Voyage** (1973, 7 min.), **The Beast** (1971-1973, 5 min.), **98.3 KHz: (Bridge at Electrical Storm)** (1966-1973, 13 min.), **Holographics/1973** (1974, 5 min.), **Inauguration** (1974, 15 min.), **Melie's Catalogue** (1974, 10 min.), **The Moon at Evernight...** (1974, 7 min.), **Aurora** (1972-1974, 6 min.). Phil Warren assisted Ruzutis with sound on **Aaeon** and Tony Westman did camera work on **The Beast** and **Holographics/1973**.

David Lee studied English, history and theatre at UBC; his film career grew out of playwrighting and the production of short 8mm dramas. In 1969 he was a one-man crew for **The Kind of September**, a 7-minute film produced by Stan Fox, CBC. Under his direction and co-produced with Don Wilson, **The Life and Times of Chester-Angus Ramsgood** was an inspired feature comedy; Wilson also produced the half-hour **The House That Jack Built** (1972). In 1974 under Barrie Howells, NFB, Lee directed **Summer Centre**, a short which dealt with youth activities, and worked as an assistant on two features, **Slipstream** and **Another Smith for Paradise**, before tackling his second feature, **Let Me Sing**, in 1975. Once again Don Wilson is producing with Ron Orieus on camera and sound by Zale Dalen.

Kirk Tougas, director of the Pacific Cinémathèque pacifique, has directed a number of short films, including **Far From Quebec**

(1971, 8 min.), **The Politics of Perception** (1973, 33 min.), which was selected for Canada Trajectoires '73 (Paris), **Letter from Vancouver** (1973, 33 min.) and **Feminist Portrait** (1973, 51 min.), co-directed with Joan Campana. Tougas shot Tom Braidwood's first film, **The Student Film**, produced by the UBC Film Society. Braidwood has gone on to direct experimental films in **Backbone** (1972, 10 min.), **Willow** (1973, 12 min.), **Wind from the West** (1973, 10 min.) and **Inside the Reflection** (1973, 56 min.). Bryan R. Small is another member of the Co-op who has directed a few short films: **Lullaby, Made in Canada,. . .August** and **Dancers**. He has assisted on **Another Smith for Paradise** and co-directed **Baby Ducks** with Peter Bryant. Bix Milanich directed **The Funeral Ship**, with camera by Westman; Dennis Wheeler directed **Potlatch**, produced by Tom Shandel for the Omista Society of Kwakiutl People; and Bill Roxborough directed **Imaged Dream**. A number of animators are also members of the Co-op: Mal Hoskin directed **Sunset, 35/16, AAAArgh** and **Bread and Water**, among others; Doug White and Ken Wallace animated a chicken carcass in **Thanksgiving**.

While many on the films made by Co-op members are available from the Canadian Filmmakers' Distribution Centre in Toronto, others may be rented from the Pacific Cinémathèque pacifique as part of its Film Study Collection.

Bibliography

Vancouver Sun, July 15, 1970, "No One Understood But the Viewers were Thinking" (on films by Al Ruzutis); *Artscanada*, October-November 1970, "Al Razutis' Film **Aeon**", Andreas Schroeder; *Vancouver Province*, March 5, 1971, "Underground Funnies", Michael Wash on Mal Hoskin; *The B.C. Photographer*, Winter 1971, pp. 11-14, "Peter Bryant"; *Artscanada*, October 1973, "Hybrid. . .a Collaborative Video Piece" (on Gary Lee-Nova and Al Razutis in an issue dedicated to video art); *Cinema Canada*, no. 12, p. 24, a discussion of **The Funeral Ship** by director Milanich; *Cinema Canada*, no. 12, p. 49, review of Wheeler's **Potlatch** by Peter Bryant; *Cinema Canada*, no. 16, p. 30, "Production Notes on a Low Budget Movie", Peter Bryant on **The Supreme Kid**; *Cinema Canada*, no. 19, pp. 50-53, an interview with Bryon Black; *Take One*, vol. 2, no. 7, pp. 17-18, "Making a Film in Bella Coola", Peter Bryant; *Take One*, vol. 2, no. 12, p. 20, review of **The Life and Times of Chester-Angus Ramsgood**.

TORONTO FILMMAKERS' CO-OP

The Toronto Filmmakers' Co-op was founded in 1971; while it offers a series of services, it is largely a production cooperative with over 100 active members. Although most of the films produced at the Co-op or by its members are shorts and experimental films, feature films are also being produced. Keith Lock's first feature, **Everything Everywhere Again Alive**, was produced by Lock in 1975, following a series of short films, many co-directed with Jim Anderson; they joined forces on **Base Tranquility**, an animated film which won top awards at the 1970 Canadian International Amateur Film Festival. **Touched** (1970), **Arnold** (1970), and **Work Bike and Eat** (1972) were all co-productions. Jim Anderson's animated short, **Screams of a Butterfly** (1969), has won many awards, including Best Animation Prize at the 1969 Canadian Student Film Festival; Anderson has made live-action films as well, including **Big Wave**, **Yonge St.** (1972), **Ontario Land** (1972), **Royal Ontario Museum** (1972), **Birth**, ▰▰▰▰ (1974) and **Canada** (1975). Dennis Zahoruk, a third graduate of York University, made his feature, **The Shakespeare Murders**, in 1973. Zahoruk made a number of Super 8 films before his short, **Jason Borwick**, which won second prize for its scenario at the 1972 Famous Players Student Film Festival; another of his short dramas, **The Last Freak in the World** (1974), is set in a circus. Two short dramas were made by Co-op members in 1975: **Scales** by Bill Boyle (Co-op director), and **The Understudy**, written by Keith Leckie and Paul Shapiro and directed by Shapiro. The Theatre Passe Muraille's production of "The Farm Show" forms the basis of poet Michael Ondaatje's **The Clinton Special: A Film about The Farm Show**, made in 1974; another portrait, of poet b.p. nichol, is seen in **Sons of Captain Poetry** (1970). Kim Ondaatje made **Black Creek** (1972) about the restoration of that area, **Factories** (1973), an impressionistic study, and **Quilts** (1974), a collage. In 1968 Clay Borris made his first film, **Parliament Street** (distributed by the Ontario Department of Education and Youth). His second short, **Paper Boy**, which starred his family, was completed under Tom Daly at the National Film Board. For CBC "Of All People" Borris made **One Hand Clapping**, and most recently he completed **Rose's House** (1976), an hour-long dramatized documentary with camera by John Phillips and music by Willie Dunn. Borris is presently resident filmmaker at Browndale, a children's home. Rick Hancox, originally from Prince Edward Island, made his first film, **Cab 16**, in 1969; it won Best Documentary Award at the first Canadian Student Film Festival. Hancox has since won numerous awards for his short inventive films: **Tall Dark Stranger** (1970), **Next To Me**, **I A Dog** (1971), **Rooftops**, **House Movie** (1972), **Wild Sync** (1973), **Landfall No. 1**, **Arrival & Departure of a Train**, and **East Side Blues** (1974). Hancox teaches his craft at Sheridan College. President and creative director of the advertising agency Ogilvy and Mather Ltd., John Straiton is an accomplished animator; his **Portrait of Lydia** won awards for best animated film and best amateur film at the 1965 Cannes Film Festival; Straiton's **The**

Banshees (1966), **Steam Ballet, Animals in Motion** (1968), a reworking of 19th-century Edward Muybridge's photographic studies, **Eurynome** (1970), featuring animated clay figures, and **Horseplay** (1972) are all available from the Canadian Filmmakers' Distribution Centre. While there are many other talented Co-op filmmakers and many other notable films, the following works deserve special mention: Lothar Spree's **Sarah's War**; Marie Waisberg's **The Journals of Susanna Moodie** and **Antheos (God Inside)**, with Michele Moses; and Patrick Lee's **Jugband Music**.

Most films made by Co-op members are distributed by the Canadian Filmmakers' Distribution Centre in Toronto.

Bibliography

Cinema Canada, no. 10/11, pp. 38-39, a review of **Sarah's War** and on interview with Lothar Spree by Á. Ibrányi-Kiss; *Cinema Canada*, no. 12, pp. 32-35, a review of **The Shakespeare Murders** by Laurinda Hartt.

VANCOUVER REGIONAL PRODUCTION CENTRE — NFB

Peter Jones, executive producer of the Vancouver Film Unit of the National Film Board, first joined the sound department in 1945, after service with the Navy; three years later he joined the music department as music and sound editor. With the series "Eye Witness", Jones began to write scripts, edit and direct those 10-minute theatrical screen magazine shorts in Nick Balla's unit. Eventually he became producer of the series which, when it was terminated in 1957, had over 100 segments. With the move of the NFB to Montreal in 1957, Jones became executive producer of Unit D, and produced sponsored films; with Larry Gosnell, Tom Farley, Wally Hewitson, and Stanley Clish, Unit D produced a new kind of sponsored film using dramatic scripts and actors. The "Canada at War" series, **Fields of Sacrifice, Ducks of Course, A Day in the Night of Jonathan Mole, The Enduring Wilderness** (Ernest Reid), **Coronet at Night** (Stanley Jackson) all flowed from Unit D. The first feature made at the NFB was produced by Peter Jones — **The Drylanders** started out as a documentary on prairie settlement. In 1966 Jones set up the Vancouver Unit, producing **Helicopter Canada, Jablonski**, Daryl Duke's **David and Bert**, and Reljic's **Soccer.**

Shelah Reljic, a native of Burnaby, B.C., began her career in theatre at the Seattle Repertory Theatre in 1950 and The Everyman Theatre in Vancouver. In 1952 she joined Lew Parry Films as an assistant to film editor Homer Powell; she stayed with the company cutting industrial films until she joined CBUT in 1958 as a film and sound editor, and worked on the sound editing of **A Bit of Bark**, **Spanish Village** and **Dark Gods**. Ms. Reljic has freelanced since 1961, working for CBC, independent filmmakers and Vancouver NFB; she edited Larry Kent's **Sweet Substitute**, George Robertson's **The Journey**, Sandy Wilson's **He's Not the Walking Kind**, Grant Munro's **Tour en l'air**, Tom Radford's **Every Saturday Night**, John Taylor's **Baby, This is for You**, and her own **Soccer**, the latter three for the "Pacificanada" series. As well she was assistant editor, with Homer Powell, on Shandel's **Another Smith for Paradise**. In 1966 Reljic started the 16mm workshop at Simon Fraser University; in 1969 she was resident i ' film at SFU, and her students included Sandy Wilson, Tony Westman, Peter Bryant and Bryan Small.

A native of Vancouver, cameraman Doug McKay began his film career there at Trans Canada Films working with Wally Hamilton and Arla Saare. In 1951 he joined the National Film Board as a student cameraman and assisted John Spotton, and later photographed the television series "On the Spot" and worked with Colin Low in animation. In 1958 he moved to CBC in Ottawa as a freelancer, and later freelanced for the corporation in Vancouver; from 1961 to 1964 McKay was cameraman with the CBC's Vancouver Film Unit working with Allan King, Arla Saare, Philip Keatley and Stan Fox, among others. Some of his camera credits in this period include episodes of "The Littlest Hobo", **Diary of a Curator** and **Japanese Gymnasts**. McKay has worked with many young west coast directors; he shot Sylva Spring's **Madeleine Is . . .**, Larry Kent's **When Tomorrow Dies**, Sandy Wilson's **Bridal Shower** and **He's Not the Walking Kind**, and Tom Shandel's **They Call Them Killers**. As well as working with the NFB film unit, McKay freelances; as a freelancer he shot Don Eccleston's **The Incredible Forest** and Boon Collin's **Sally Field-good & Co.** McKay has taught in the Film Department of the Vancouver School of Art.

Another cameraman working with the NFB unit, who was also a former member of the CBC Vancouver Film Unit, is Jack Long. Long was born in Calgary, Alberta, and studied music and still photography before joining a National Film Board crew shooting in Vancouver. As well as working as cameraman-director on NFB's early television series, "Eye Witness", Long shot (for the CBC unit) **Skid Row**, **Pemberton Valley** and **A Bit of Bark**, among others. More recently Long directed a number of films in the CBC series "Five Years in the Life of" and **Emily Carr**, **David and Bert** and **I Heard the Owl Call My Name**, the latter two directed by Daryl Duke, for the NFB. Long shared camera with Tony Westman on Tom Radford's **The Man Who Chose the Bush**.

Ray Hall was born in Norfolk Island in 1932 and first joined the CBC, Vancouver, in 1956 as a scenic carpenter, learning his craft as an editor with Stan Fox and Arla Saare. He edited George Robertson's **To the Volcano** and Philip Keatley's **How to Break a Quarterhorse** in the "Caribou Country" series. After a year with the U.N. as director of a film unit in Syria, Hall spent a year freelancing as a film editor for the BBC and returned to Canada in 1973. Hall's editing credits include **Diary of a Whale Hunter** (1965), "Camera West" series, **A Slow Hello** in "Pacificanada" series, **Torch to Tokyo**, directed by Doug Gillingham, and his own **Norfolk Island**, directed for the CBC in 1962. Ray Hall is one of the partners with Tom Shandel, Werner Aellen and Bill Nemtin of Image Flow Centre Ltd., which produced **Wolfpen Principle**, edited by Hall.

Sandy Wilson was born in Penticton, B.C. in 1947, studied English at Simon Fraser University and followed the film workshop offered by Stan Fox and Shelah Reljic. Her first film, **Garbage**, was independently made and shown on CBC's "Take Thirty"; **Penticton Profile**, which followed is distributed by NFB's Challenge for Change. Her ethnographic study, **Bridal Shower**, is a wonderfully amusing film shot by Doug McKay; it can be borrowed from the Pacific cinémathèque. **He's Not the Walking Kind**, a short documentary, stars her brother and was made for the NFB as was **Pen-Hi Grad** in the "Pacificanada" series. In 1973 Ms. Wilson made **Prairie Passing Through** with still photography by Ken Klassen and animation by John Taylor.

John Taylor attended the Vancouver School of Art and attended National Film Board's summer student animation program in 1966; he returned to Vancouver and started an animation club at the art school with Ken Klassen, Mal Hoskin, Howard and Jean Pedlar, and Ernie Schmidt, among others. As well as producing B.C. centennial clips for the NFB, he joined the Vancouver unit in 1972 to produce Hugh Foulds' **Citizen Harold** and **The Bear's Christmas** (with Don Worobey, Peter Jones and Bob Verrall) and Al Sens' **The Twitch**. Since then the animation production has been turned over to Don Worobey, and Taylor has produced Sandy Wilson's **Prairie Passing Through** (as well as animating for it), **A Slow Hello** and **Every Saturday Night**, directed by Radford; Taylor directed **Baby, This Is for You** for the "Pacificanada" series, with camera by Tony Westman.

Joanna Moss, currently working on feature scripts for the Vancouver production unit, came to Vancouver in 1971 from Kenya, where she was born in 1948. She began her film work in Vancouver, doing community video, making **The Meeting** with the East Indian community for CBC's video "Access" program, and working in video with older people. With producer Barrie Howells, Moss made **The 7th Step to Freedom** and **Bye Bye Blues**.

Bibliography

Montreal Star, January 23, 1975, "NFB's Pacificanada Not Very

Revealing'', Joan Irwin; *St. John's Evening Telegram*, January 25, 1975, "A Noble Effort", Wick Collins; *Penticton Herald*, February 10, 1975, "Fun Course Led to Career", Barbara Persson on Sandy Wilson; *The Western Producer*, February 13, 1975, "Pacificanada: New NFB Series", Dorothy Hall on **A Slow Hello**.

WEST WIND FILM GROUP

Founded in 1973, West Wind Film Group consists of four filmmakers, all former students of Jean Oser, professor of film at the University of Saskatchewan. Christine Welsh studied English at the U. of S.; as a former teacher she has been interested in the school system and in the use of modern dance in teaching. Robert Troff studied psychology and film and while a student made **Chrysalis** (with Norman Sawchyn), which won the best amateur film award at the 1971 Yorkton Film Festival. As well as acting as assistant cameraman on a number of educational films in Alberta, Troff, along with Ms. Welsh, was involved in 1972 with the Gopher Film Project, a basic film workshop for high school students. Norman Sawchyn studied social sciences and film, and became Jean Oser's assistant. In 1972 he was commissioned by the NFB to record the living history of Icelandic Day held in Gimli, Manitoba, Canada's largest Icelandic community. This ethnographic work is held by the Museum of Man. In 1974 Sawchyn was hired by the Department of Culture and Youth to record on video work being done in multi-cultural communities. With the fourth member of the group, Brock Stevens, they have made the following films: **Schizophrenia: A Changing World** (1973), produced by the Schizophrenia Foundation; **Poltoon: A Heritage of Dance**; **Dance About**; and **Crossing**. In addition they have directed promotion films for the Saskatchewan Department of Tourism and scripted Manpower training films.

Many of their independent films are distributed by the Canadian Filmmakers' Distribution Centre.

Bibliography

Leader-Post, Regina, April 16, 1974, "Filmmakers Determined to Stay Here".

WINNIPEG FILM GROUP

Formed in 1974, the Winnipeg Film Group has 30 members; the Group is co-ordinated by Len Klady. One of their members,

Leonard Yakir, made the feature **The Mourning Suit** (see individual filmmakers). Cameraman-director Richard Stringer graduated from Ryerson in 1967, and worked as a cameraman for small companies and television in Winnipeg, Toronto and Ottawa. With director David Springbett, Stringer shot **Powerline** for the Atomic Energy Commission, **Next Time Around** for the Manitoba Liberal Party and **Anniversary City** for Canadian Breweries. He also shot Vic Cowie's drama, **And No Birds Sing**, which won the 1968 award for best film over 30 minutes at the Vancouver Film Festival; the theatrical short, **The Match**, and the features **Out of Touch**, **The Proud Rider** and the Ukranian feature, **Marichka**, were photographed by Stringer. As a director he has made a number of promotion films and documentaries, including **Farmer's Factory Day** for Co-op Implements, **Paraplegic Pan-Am Games** with Pasquefilm Ltd. and his independent **Recess 10:15 — 10:30**; with editing by Robert Lower and camera by Stringer, it was nominated best documentary, 1972 Canadian Film Awards. Ian Elkin graduated in fine arts from the University of Manitoba beginning his film work in photography, slides and 8mm films; as well as acting as cameraman on a number of local productions, Elkin has directed in 1973, **Profits and the Puck: A Hockey Primer** which has been shown on CBC, Alberta. David Cherniack graduated in science from the University of Manitoba in 1967 and spent four years in study and production at F.A.M.U., the Czechoslovakian film school. Since returning to Canada he has directed a short film for the NDP in Manitoba and recently edited **A Better Choice**, directed by Vesna Cherniack for the Manitoba Department of Industry and Commerce. The film group also has a large membership of animators: Nancy Edell, Rich Condie, Brad Caslor and Leon Johnson have been animating segments for "Sesame Street", Nancy Edell directed **Black Pudding** and **Charlie Co.** and was joined by Joanne Jackson in co-directing **The Children's House**. A number of these animators, joined by Willi Ahrens, Al Pakarnyk and Betsy Thorsteinson animated sequences in "The Joys of Urban Living" and recently, Neil McInnes animated **Boardinghouse**. In 1975 the National Film Board set up a regional production office in Winnipeg and the co-op members are preparing various scripts for production; Rich Condie is working on a "funny money" story; Bob Lower is preparing work on the Winnipeg General Strike; and Vesna Cherniak is investigating the Winnipeg Contemporary Dancers. Sarah Yates and Len Klady have developed a script, **Mistaken Identities**.

Many of these films are available from the Canadian Filmmakers' Distribution Centre.

Bibliography

Cinema Canada, no. 25 (February 1976), ''of **Black Pudding** and Pink Ladies'', interview with Nancy Edell by Brian Clancey.

Community Film and Video

Canada is unique in the extent of its use of film and video as a tool of social change. The roots are, of course, in the Grierson philosophy and in the early activities of the National Film Board, which was a whirlwind of social and political action in the production and distribution of film. The intensity of that action was dampened by the Cold War and heavy bureaucracy, but we have seen a kind of revival with the development of compact film equipment and sophisticated video hardware. The revival was prompted by events in Newfoundland — in the community of Fogo Island fighting for its life — and that community, in demanding help from the NFB, gave rise to the Challenge for Change/Société nouvelle units which have, in turn, spawned film and video action groups across the country. What follows is a short description of some of these active projects and a bibliography for further research.

Extension Service, Memorial University of Newfoundland, 21 King's Bridge Road, St. John's, Newfoundland.

Unlike most university extension departments, Memorial's (under the direction of Donald Snowden) is actively involved in the educational, economic and social needs of the community. Community Development Officers, on staff with the Extension Service and living in various areas of Newfoundland and Labrador, work in helping the communities to define and to act on their needs. Their tools include media hardware — projectors, tape recorders, video and cameras. It was out of this innovative movement that the Extension Service began negotiations in 1967 with the National Film Board and, in particular, with Colin Low on a three-year collaboration in pioneering an approach to film in community development; the project—the Newfoundland Project or the Fogo Island Project—was designed "to investigate the reactions of a community when its people and its problems were filmed in depth and the results played back to them for discussion and criticism". Communication among the isolated villages on the island was initiated, and a dialogue was started between the islands and the government. As well as the continued existence of Fogo Island, the result of this project has been to train a number of people in film for the well-established Extension Service Film Unit which continues to use the "Fogo Process". (See FILM GROUPS: MEMORIAL UNIVERSITY EXTENSION SERVICE FILM UNIT.) The following filmography and bibliography will give some idea of the breadth and importance of this community organization.

For further reference see:

Cinema as Catalyst, a report (written by Sandra Gwyn) on the seminar on film, video-tape and social change, organized by the

Extension Service of Memorial University (March 13-24, 1972), available from the University; *Decks Awash*, a bi-monthly community newspaper working in conjunction with "Decks Awash" television series, published by the Extension Service, Memorial University of Newfoundland (21 King's Bridge Road, St. John's, Nfld.); *Film and Video-Tape Catalogue*, Extension Media, Memorial University of Newfoundland; *Fogo Island Film and Community Development Project* (published by NFB, 1968), a description of the experiment in Newfoundland which led to the Challenge for Change program; *Fogo Process in Communication*, available from Extension Service, Memorial University.

The Newfoundland Project films are available from any NFB Distribution Office. They include **Introduction to Fogo Island**, some basic facts on the project as well as nine other films. Also available from NFB are **A Memo from Fogo**, **The Specialists at Memorial Discuss the Fogo Films**, **When I Go...That's It** and **Billy Crane Moves Away**.

Video Theatre, 1571 Argyle Street, Halifax, Nova Scotia B3J 2B2 (902-426-5935).

The Video Theatre has a varied program of production, distribution and exhibition. A number of individuals and groups have been experimenting with dramatic productions as well as being closely involved with community groups in documenting issues. These tapes and tapes from other video production centres are in the Video Tape Library, catalogued and accessible. The Video Theatre also sponsors weekly workshop sessions for video workers.

For further reference see:

Film & Video: Atlantic Regional Newsletter/Communiqué régional de l'atlantique. Available from National Film Board, 1572 Barrington Street, Halifax, Nova Scotia B3J 1Z6 (902-426-6157).

Télé-publik, Bathurst College, Bathurst, New Brunswick E2A 2T7.

From its inception in 1972, Télé-publik was designed as a medium to furnish information exchange from and to northeast New Brunswick by broadcasting through station CHAU. It was approved by Société nouvelle and funded by SAR (Société d'amenagement régional) as a non-profit organization, and has continued to broadcast through funding by federal and provincial grants, the SAR and Bathurst College.

Télé-publik, with a permanent staff of five, shoots material in one-inch and half-inch video. Although they did produce a feature dramatic film on video, **Simple histoire d'amour**, they primarily produce documentaries on particular localities, industries and problems as well as news programs. Télé-publik works with local committees in their programing.

For further reference see:

L'Evangeline, September 26, 1973, p. 7, "Co-production Télé-publik—ONF: *Une histoire d'amour* dans le Nord-Est".

Centre Vidéo Educatif, F u st College, Bathurst, New Brunswick E2A 2T7 (506-546-9805).

The Centre vidéo éducatif works with groups in northeast New Brunswick, using video as a basis for communication and discussion. Its aim is the demystification of television and film techniques and to this end works with students to produce half-hour programs.

Vidéographe, 1604 St-Denis Street, Montreal, Quebec H2X 3K3 (514-842-9786).

Vidéographe began operation in 1971 as a pilot project of Challenge for Change/Société nouvelle. After a brief subsidization by the Canada Council, Vidéographe began operating in 1973 as an independent, non-profit company with the Quebec government as its chief subsidizer. Vidéographe is a centre for half-inch video production and distribution, available to individuals and groups whose ideas are approved by a production committee. Completed videotapes may be distributed through an established video network which operates at three levels: a theatre on the premises with four monitors and seats for 100 people at evening showings, individual monitors with video cassettes and a video exchange system. Vidéographe will transfer any tape in their library onto clean vidéotapes supplied by customers; catalogues are available. Vidéographe also assists in preparing promotional material, posters and information sheets for productions made with them.

For further reference see:

Image et son, no. 267 (January 1973) pp. 2-9, "Experience au Québec: Le Vidéographe — Le Bloc", Guy Gauthier; *Cinema Canada*, no. 4, pp. 16-18, "Vidéographe", Kirwan Cox; *Médium-média*, Vidéosphère issue, Michel Faubert and Jean-Yves Bégin on Vidéographe; and "Le film et les média communautaires comme instrument d'intervention sociale", special issue.

Parallel Institute, 2365 Grand Trunk, Montreal, Quebec H3K 1M8 (514-933-2262) and P.O. Box 6, Station D, Montreal, Quebec.

Parallel Institute for Community and Regional Development was formed in 1970 as a non-profit community development project to teach the practical skills of political community organizing in Point St. Charles. To this end they have produced a series of video teaching tapes which are available through the Challenge for Change program of the NFB. Videotape titles include **Why Build an Organization**, **Bad Publicity and More Publicity**, **Getting Better Publicity**, **Making Your Own Publicity**, **I Never Did It with a Banker Before**, **Research**, **Point Equal Rights Movement (PERM) vs. Samuel E. Cohen Slumlord**, **Chairing a Meeting** and **Common Group Problems**.

Challenge for Change/Société nouvelle

The Challenge for Change and the Société nouvelle units at the National Film Board both publish periodicals with recent community film and video information at the Montreal office and in regional centres. *Challenge for Change Film Catalogue* is a separate catalogue listing films produced by this special unit (available from any local NFB office). See also FILM PUBLICATIONS: PERIODICALS.

For further reference see:

Challenge for Change Newsletter, vol. 1, no. 3 (Winter 1968-1969), "**Saint-Jerome**: the Experience of a Filmmaker as Social Animator", Fernand Dansereau; *Artscanada*, April 1970, "Challenge for Change", Patrick Watson, a warm evaluation of the work at the National Film Board beginning with the Fogo Island Project; *Challenge for Change Newsletter*, no. 5 (Autumn 1970), "Cinema as a Form of Protest", Robert Daudelin; *Challenge for Change Newsletter*, no. 7 (Winter 1971-1972), "Fiction Film as Social Animator", an interview with Léonard Forest on the making of **La noce n'est pas finie**, a community-evolved feature; *Challenge for Change Newsletter*, no. 8 (Spring 1972), "Memo to Michelle about Decentralizing the Means of Production", John Grierson; *Take One*, vol. 4, no. 1, pp. 22-25, "What Challenge? What Change?", Marie Kurchak.

Monitor North, 324 John Street, Thunder Bay, Ontario P7B 1X1 (807-344-9156).

Monitor North is a broad-based community group working with half-inch video and providing action groups with free assistance and equipment. The agency grew out of a Challenge for Change program in Thunder Bay which provided the basic hardware. Projects include working with ethnic groups in preserving their history, instructional programs on medical problems, and training

people to operate video hardware. Providing cable television programing is not a high priority for Monitor North, but many of the
projects are produced in a format suitable for broadcast.

Alberta Native Communications Society, 11427 Jasper Ave.,
Edmonton, Alberta.

This unique organization produces radio shows in conjunction with
the Department of Education for school broadcasts, a weekly
video news magazine program for cable television, and films for
training people in isolated communities. In cooperation with Grant
MacEwan Community College, the Society has designed a training
program in native communications. The training films made by this
group of 35 native people are handled by the Department of Indian
and Northern Affairs.

Metro Media, 3255 Heather Street, Vancouver, B.C. V5Z 3K4
(604-876-8610).

Metro Media is an association of groups and individuals with slide
and sound equipment and a library of video tapes available to the
public.

Video Inn, 261 East Powell Street, Vancouver B.C. V6A 1G3 (604-
688-4336)

Video Inn is a distributor of community video tapes.

Other Organizations of interest:

Access, Canadian Broadcasting Corporation. Access is CBC-TV's
community programing branch which operates through local CBC
stations. Community groups with views of interest to television
audiences can present their ideas on half-inch video; CBC provides the facilities and technical and production assistance. Contact your local CBC station for further information.

**Canadian Cable Television Association/Association cana-
dienne de télévision par câble (CCTA)**, 85 Albert Street, Suite
405, Ottawa, Ontario.
The CCTA is an association of 200 licenced cable operators in
Canada.

Canadian Radio and Television Corporation (CRTC), 100 Met-
calf Street, Ottawa, Ontario K1A 0N2.
The CRTC controls cablevision in Canada. It has a number of
reports and policy statements which are useful, and a booklet, *A
Resource for the Active Community.*

Bibliography

Access to Information (Cat. no. 41-1/6B). Available from Publishing Centre, Supply and Services Canada, Ottawa.

Artscanada, October 1973. This issue is devoted to examining video as an art form.

Bashford, Ron, "Community Use of Cable TV". A talk to the Canadian Educational Communications Conference, 1971. Available on tape for $3.50 from the Edmonton Audio Visual Association, c/o Educational Media Division, Department of Extension, University of Alberta, Edmonton, Alberta.

Cinéma-Québec, vol. 2, no. 3, pp. 32-36, "L'audio-visuel au Québec à un carrefour", by Jacques Parent, NFB.

A Directory of Federal Funding Sources Available to Citizens' Organizations. This pamphlet is available by writing to the Secretary of State, 66 Slater Street, Ottawa, Ontario K1A 0M5.

Egly, Max, and others, *Conséquences de l'emploi des technologies "vidéo" pour l'éducation et la culture* (UNESCO). Includes an international bibliography on the relation of education and technology.

Film & Video, Autum 1974, pp. 22-71. "A Special Report on Cable Television in the Maritimes".

On a raison de se révolter (1973). Prod: CAU Montmorency, Prisma Films. 80 min. b&w. Made by a community of filmmakers, the film outlines the tools of definition and reorganization for the working class.

Radical Software, no. 4. Issue dedicated to Canadian facilities and experience. Available from Raindance Corporation, 8 East 12th Street, New York, N.Y. 10003.

A Resource for the Active Community. Explanations, suggestions and examples for community programers. Booklet available upon request from the CRTC.

Singer, Benjamin D., ed., *Communications in Canadian Society* (Toronto: Copp Clark, 1972).

Telecommunications and Participation (Cat. no. Co 41-1/6A). Available from Publishing Centre, Supply and Services Canada, Ottawa.

Telecommunications and the Arts (Cat. no. 41-1/6C). Available from Publishing Centre, Supply and Services Canada, Ottawa.

Vie des arts, vol. 20, no. 80 (Autumn 1975), pp. 62-63, "La vidéographie dans un contexte d'art", by Eric Cameron.

The Wired City (Cat. no. 41-1/6D). Available from Publishing Centre, Supply and Services Canada, Ottawa.

The Department of Communications of Canada publishes a number of booklets. To obtain a publications list, write to Communications Canada, Information Services, 100 Metcalfe Street, Ottawa K1A 0C8, or phone (613) 995-8185.

See also FILMMAKERS, in particular, the biblioigraphies of Colin Low, Michel Regnier, Fernand Dansereau and Léonard Forest. MAKING FILMS: COÖPERATIVE DISTRIBUTION; COÖPERATIVE PRODUCTION.

Native Peoples and Film

The Alberta Native Communications Society (11427 Jasper Avenue, Edmonton), founded in 1966, is a non-profit organization funded by the federal and the Alberta governments. With an elected board of six treaty Indians and six Métis, it produces a weekly newspaper, *The Native People*, radio shows for public and commercial broadcasting, a weekly newsmagazine for television, and training films which are distributed by the Department of Indian and Northern Affairs.

Filmography

Films on Indians

The Longhouse People (La grande maison) (1951). Prod: Tom Daly, NFB. 23 min. col. Dist: NFB. A number of religious ceremonies related to the Longhouse are enacted.

Circle of the Sun (Le soleil perdu) (1961). Dir: Colin Low. Prod: Tom Daly, NFB. 29 min. col. Dist: NFB. A gathering of the Blood Indians of Alberta for the Sun Dance as seen thrugh the eyes of a young member of the tribe who is caught in a changing world.

Age of the Buffalo (La légende du bison) (1964). Dir: Austin Campbell. Prod: A. Campbell, Nick Balla, NFB. 14 min. col. Dist: NFB. Animated nineteenth-century paintings of the buffalo hunts.

High Steel (Charpentier du ciel) (1965). Dir: Don Owen. Prod: Julian Biggs, NFB. 14 min. col. Dist: NFB. A picture of the work and traditions of the Mohawk Indians of Caughnawaga, famous for their skill in erecting the steel frames of skyscrapers.

The Indian Speaks (L'indien parle) (1967). Dir: Marcel Carrière. Prod: NFB for the Department of Citizenship and Immigration. 40 min. col. Dist: NFB. Indians living in cities talk about their concern for preserving their culture.

Cesar's Bark Canoe (César et son canot d'écorce) (1971). Dir: Bernard Gosselin. Prod: Paul Larose, NFB. 58 min. col. Dist: NFB. Cesar Newashish, a Cree from the Manowan Reserve, builds a canoe solely from materials that the forest provides.

Christmas at Moose Factory (1971). Dir: Alanis Obomsawin. Prod: Robert Verrall, Wolf Koenig, NFB. 13 min. col. Dist: NFB. A collage of children's drawing from Moose Factory with artists explaining their work.

Cold Journey (1972). Dir: Martin Defalco. Prod: George Pearson, NFB. 75 min. col. Available from NFB. Starring Buckley

Petawabano and Johnny Yesno, with songs composed by Willie Dunn, **Cold Journey** is a drama revolving around the decision to assimilate Indian children into the white man's educational system.

Who Were the Ones? (1972). Dir: Michael Mitchell. Prod: Denis Gillson, NFB. 7 min. col. Dist: NFB. An Indian's view of North American history after the arrival of European colonists. John Fadden did the art work which was animated to a song composed by Willie Dunn and sung by Bob Charlie.

The Other Side of the Ledger: An Indian View of the Hudson's Bay Company (1972). Dir: Martin Defalco, Willie Dunn. Prod: George Pearson, NFB. 42 min. col. Dist: NFB. On the 300th anniversary of the Hudson's Bay Company, Indians discuss their experiences on the company's reserve. Narrated by George Manuel of the National Indian Brotherhood.

The Colors of Pride (Fierté sur toiles) (1973). Dir: Henning Jacobsen. Prod: Henning Jacobsen Productions Ltd. 28 min. col. Dist: NFB. Four Indian painters — Norval Morrisseau, Alex Janvier, Allen Sapp and Daphne Odjig — are featured.

Kainai (1973). Dir: Raoul Fox. Prod: Colin Low, NFB. 27 min. col. Dist: NFB. A report on the Indians of the Blood Indian Reserve in Alberta who have moved into industrialized society.

Québec sauvage (1973). Dir: Pierre Marchand, Leo Henrichon (1973). 90 min. col. Silent with a magnetic unsynchronized sound track.

Starblanket (1973). Dir: Donald Brittain. Prod: D. Brittain, NFB. 27 min. col. Dist: NFB. A portrait of Noel Starblanket, young Indian chief of the Starblanket Reserve and vice-president of Saskatchewan Indians.

La chasse au Montagnais (1974). Dir: Arthur Lamothe, AVQ Dist: Ateliers audio-visuels du Québec.

Cree Hunters of Mistassini (Chasseurs cris de Mistassini) (1974). Dir: Tony Ianuzielo, Boyce Richardson. Prod: Colin Low, Len Chatwin, NFB, Challenge for Change. 58 min. col. Dist: NFB. Three hunting families of James Bay and Ungava Bay areas set up their winter camp. An intimate portrait of the Cree, their family relationships and their relationship with the land.

Job's Garden—The Land of the Great River People (Chissibi —la mort d'un fleuve) (1974). Dir: Jean-Pierre Fournier, Boyce Richardson. Prod: Fournier/Richardson Associates with Association for Quebec Indians and the Inuit Association of Quebec. 60 min. col. Dist: Canadian Filmmakers' Distribution Centre. A response from Job Bearskin and other Cree Indian trappers of the Fort George area of northern Quebec to the government's plan to flood 6,000 square miles around James Bay, displacing 4,500 Cree and 1,500 Inuit.

Like the Trees (1974). Dir: Kathleen Shannon. Prod: K. Shannon, NFB, "Working Mothers" series. 15 min. col. A Métis

woman from northern Alberta discusses her move from the city.
Mistashipu(La grande rivière)(1974). Dir: Arthur Lamothe. Prod:
AVQ 79 min. col. Dist: Faroun Films. An historical-critical study
of the Montagnais Indians who occupy a third of the province of
Quebec.
Our Land is Our Life (1974). Dir: Tony Ianuzielo, Boyce Richard-
son. Prod: Colin Low, Len Chatwin, NFB. Challenge for
Change. 58 min. col. Available from NFB. The Cree people of
the Mistassini area in northern Quebec meet to discuss the
Quebec government's offer for their land to build the James Bay
power project.
Pakuashipu (1974). Dir: Arthur Lamothe. Prod: AVQ 54 min. col.
Dist: Faroun Films. The Indians of the Pakuashipu River return
to the old way of life.
Ungava, terre lointain (1974).Dir: Pierre Marchand, Leo
Henrichon. 70 min. col. Dist: Société ciné-exploration Inc. (Box
1300, Trois-Rivières, Quebec). Two films on the Cree people.
Netsi Nana Shepen (On dirait que c'était notre terre) (1975). Dir:
Arthur Lamothe. prod: AVQ. Three parts, totalling 4 hours. col.
Dist: Faroun Films. A history of Sept-Iles from an Indian point
of view.
Potlatch: A Strict Law Bids Us Dance. Dir: Dennis Wheeler. 53
min. Dist: Pacific Cinémathèque Pacifique and the Canadian
Filmmakers' Distribution Centre. A documentary on Potlatch, a
ceremonial giving-away of surplus wealth, and the trials of 1922
(in B.C.) that arose as a result of the white government's
negative reaction to the Potlatch ceremony.

See also the National Film Board's Challenge for Change films
about and often by Indians:
God Help the Man Who Would Part with His Land (1971). 47
min. b&w.
Indian Dialogue (1967). 28 min. b&w.
PowWow at Duck Lake (1967). 15 min. b&w.
These Are My People (1969). 13 min. b&w. First film by an In-
dian film crew, directed by Mike Mitchell.
You are on Indian Land (1969). 37 min. b&w.
Encounter with Saul Alinsky Part II: Rama Indian Reserve
(1967). 32 min. b&w.

Multi-Media Kits

Indians of Canada. A multi-media resource kit containing
filmstrips, slides, photos, charts and printed material.
Manouan. Slides, filmstrips, photos, legends, maps, toys, records
and instructions on how to make puzzles, skis and snowshoes.
Produced by Alanis Obomsawin, NFB and the Department of
Indian Affairs and Northern Development.
Mount Currie. Filmstrips and raw stock, and instructions for mak-
ing filmstrips, books, colouring books, records and toys. Pro-

duced by A. Obomsawin, NFB and the Department of Indian Affairs and Northern Development.

All multi-media kits are available for sale only from Visual Education Centre in Toronto, SECAS in Montreal, and Harry Smith & Sons in Vancouver.

Films on Inuit

How to Build an Igloo (Comment construire votre iglou (1950). Dir: Douglas Wilkinson. Prod: NFB. 10 min. col. Dist: NFB. A step-by-step instruction film.

Angotee: Story of an Eskimo Boy (1953). Dir: Douglas Wilkinson. Prod: Michael Spencer, NFB. 31 min. col. Dist: NFB. The birth and maturation of a Inuit male filmed in the eastern Arctic.

The Living Stone (Pierres vives) (1958). Dir: John Feeney. Prod: Tom Daly, NFB. 31 min. col. Dist: NFB. An Inuit legend is the inspiration for a carver working in stone.

"Netsilik Eskimos" series (1963-1965). Prod: NFB and the Education Development Center, Inc. (Massachusetts). This series of nine films, in 21 half-hour parts, reconstructs the traditional Eskimo life as it was led before the arrival of the Europeans: **At the Caribou Crossing Place**; **At the Autumn River Camp**; **At the Winter Sea Ice Camp**; **Jigging for Lake Trout**; **At the Spring Sea Ice Camp**; **Group Hunting on the Spring Ice**; **Stalking Seal on the Spring Ice**; **Building a Kayak** and **Fishing at the Stone Weir** (1967). col. Dist: NFB. The "Netsilik Eskimos" series footage has been edited into other films: a series for children — "The Stories of Tuktu" ("Les récits de Tuktu") — consisting of 13 15-minute films (in colour) recording the adventures of an Eskimo boy; **Yesterday—Today—The Netsilik Eskimos** (Esquimaux) which combines more recent footage of the Netsilik in discussing their changing lifestyle; **Eskimo Summer** and **Eskimo Winter** (1971), two parts of the series, "People of the Seal", co-produced by the NFB and the BBC. (each 52 min. col.); **The Netsilik Eskimo Today** (1972) uses both old and new footage (18 min. col.); **The Eskimo: Fight for Life** (1970) also combines old and new footage (51 min. col.). All this material is available for rental or purchase from NFB.

The Annanacks (Les Annanacks) (1964). Prod: Crawley Films for NFB. 29 min. col. Dist: NFB. The Annanacks form working cooperatives in their northern Quebec community.

Eskimo Artist—Kenojuak (Kenojouak—artiste esquimau) (1964). Dir: John Feeney. Prod: Tom Daly, NFB. 20 min. col. Dist: NFB. A woman printmaker shows the process of transferring her drawings to stone and making prints.

Alcohol in My Land (1972). Dir: Evelyn Cherry, Cherry Films.
Filmed in Inuit with English titles. Dist: Cherry Films, Regina.
Pictures Out of My Life (1973). Dir: Zina Heczko. Prod: Wolf
Koenig, NFB. 13 min. col. Dist: NFB. The drawings and
recollections of Pitseolak, the Eskimo artist from Cape Dorset.
Sananguagat: Inuit Masterworks (1974). Dir: Derek May. Prod:
Tom Daly, Colin Low, NFB. 25 min. col. Dist: NFB. A
cinematic exhibition of Inuit carvings.
Animation from Cape Dorset and **Natsik Hunting**. Prod: NFB.
Dist: NFB. These two films are the results of animation
workshops held in Cape Dorset and Frobisher Bay.

Bibliography

Cinéma-Québec, vol. 2, no. 6/7 (March-April 1973), pp. 38-44, a
discussion by Gilles Marsolais on **Job's Garden—The Land of
the Great River People**; *Pot pourri*, June 1974, pp. 18-19, review
of **Cree Hunters of the Mistassini** by Dan Driscoll; *Pot pourri*,
Spring 1976, the whole issue is dedicated to "Media in the Arctic"; *Saturday Night*, June 1976, pp. 72, 74, "Movies", Marshall
Delaney on **Potlatch: A Strict Law Bids Us Dance**; *La Question
Amérindienne*, CQDC, 1976, a catalogue and critical evaluation of
recent films about the loss suffered by the Indians of northeastern
Quebec; The Association for Native Development in the Perform-
ing and Visual Arts publishes a newsletter on their activies,
available by writing *ANDPVA Newsletter* (30 Bloor Street W.,
Toronto, Ontario M4W 1A2); See also bibliographies of Arthur
Lamothe, Martin Defalco and Colin Low.

Political and Third World Films

All films are political in that each one expresses an attitude towards a social-political system and the people living within it. Some films either tacitly accept the status quo or wildly celebrate it, others consciously criticize it. This section deals with this latter group of films.

In Montreal in June 1974 Rencontres internationales pour un nouveau cinéma brought together 100 filmmakers and theoreticians from around the world to discuss and see a new and alternative cinema. André Pâquet, who had organized the retrospective of Canadian cinema at the Cinémathèque canadienne in 1966, was once again innovatively involved in the structure, scope and quality of Rencontre.

Filmography

Countdown Canada (1970). Dir: Robert Fothergill. Prod: York University Television Centre. 60 min. b&w. Dist: Canadian Filmmakers' Distribution Centre. Network coverage of one day in 1980 when Canada joins the United States.

Le mépris n'aura qu'un temps (Hell No Longer) (1970). Dir: Arthur Lamothe. Prod: SGC for Le Conseil des syndicats nationaux. 95 min. b&w. Dist: DEC Films. A document of the lives of Quebec construction workers.

Breathing Together: Revolution of the Electric Family (Vivre ensemble: la famille electrique) (1971). Dir: Morley Markson. Prod: Morley Markson and Associates Ltd. 84 min. b&w. Dist: New Cinema. A document and portrait of media heroes of the '60s in the U.S.

Down On The Farm (1972). Prod: Unconscious Collective. 25 min. b&w. Dist: DEC Films. Four days in the life of a National Farmers' Union organizer in Saskatchewan.

Action: The October Crisis of 1970 (Les évenements d'octobre 1970) and **Reaction: A Portrait of a Society in Crisis** (1973). Dir: Robin Spry. Prod: Tom Daly, Normand Cloutier and R. Spry, NFB. 87 min. 58 min. col. Dist: NFB. With the use of television footage, **Action** gives an analytic background and foreground to the October Crisis. **Reaction**, filmed solely during the Crisis, focuses on the reactions of different communities in Quebec.

Bleecker Street (1973). 25 min. b&w. and **The Tenants Act** (1973). 6 min. b&w. Two films on neighbourhood organizing. Dist: DEC Films.

On a raison de se revolter (1973). Prod: Comité d'information politique/Champ libre. Four one-hour documentaries. b&w. Dist: CIP. A political essay designed for workers and the trade union movement.

The Desert is Dying (1974). Dir: Deborah Peaker. Prod: Northern Film Production. 17 min. col. Dist: Viking Films Ltd. A documentary about a nomadic tribe in central Africa being strangled by drought.

Forget It Jack (1974). Prod: Local 220, Service Employees International Union. 23 min. b&w. Dist: DEC Films. A film made to generate support for the right to strike.

Buenos Dias, Companeras: Women in Cuba (Buenos Dias, Companeras: Les femmes de Cuba) (1975). Dir: Aviva Slesin. Prod: Vivienne Leebosh, Octopus Inc. 58 min. col. Dist: Viking Films Ltd., New Cinema.

Holy Ganges (1975). Dir: Carl Schiffman. prod: C. Schiffman, CBC. 28 min. col. Dist: Viking Films Ltd.

Il n'y a pas d'oubli (1975). A film trilogy made up of **J'explique certaines choses**, directed by Rodrigo Gonzalez; **Lentement**, directed by Marilu Mallet; and **Jours de fer**, directed by Jorge Fajardo. 99 min. col. Dist: NFB. A film by three exiled Chileans, **Il n'y a pas d'oubli** tells of the survival of Chilean refugees in Quebec.

Indira Ghandi: The State of India (1975). Dir: Paul Saltzman. Prod: Sunrise Films. 28 min. col. Dist: Viking Films Ltd. An interview with Ms. Ghandi shot in 1975.

I Remember Too (1975). Dir: Leuten Rojas. 14 min. col. Dist: DEC Films. Three Chilean children, now in Canada, draw and tell their story of the military Junta.

See also the work of Michel Brault (**Les ordres**), Denys Arcand (**Réjeanne Padovani**, **On est au coton**, **Gina**), Jean-Claude Lord (**Bingo**), Fernand Dansereau (**Faut aller parmi l'monde pour le savoir**), and Guy L. Côté (**Tranquillement, pas vite**, **Les deux côtes de la médaille**). Information and bibliographies for the films can be found in the section on individual filmmakers.

Organizations which Distribute Political and Third World Films

Canadian Filmmakers' Distribution Centre, 406 Jarvis Street, Toronto, Ontario M4Y 2G6, Tel: (416) 921-4121.

Comité d'information politique (CIP)/Champ Libre, P.O. Box 399, Outremont, Quebec, or 252 Mount Royal Street E., Montreal, Quebec. Formed in 1967, CIP, in line with its aims to produce films and video and to distribute these and other politically conscious films, arranges film festivals, discussions and publishes, erratically, *Champ libre*, a journal of political criticism largely related to film.

Coopérative cinéastes indépendants, 2026 Ontario Street East, Montreal, Quebec. H2K 1V3, Tel: (514) 523-2816.

Development Education Centre (DEC), 121A Avenue Road, Toronto, Ontario M5R 2G3, Tel: (416) 964-6560. DEC is a non-profit, independent group of people committed to critical education on Canada and the Third World, and engaged in research and in the provision of research tools: it offers a research library, the sale of a variety of publications, the rental and production of films, slide- tape montages and filmstrips. DEC also arranges film and discussion forums. Catalogue available on request.

International Development Education Resource Centre (IDERA), 2524 Cypress Street, Vancouver, B.C., Tel: (604) 738-8815. A resource and research group specializing in international affairs. Limited to distribution within British Columbia, IDERA has a collection of films and slide and tape shows. Catalogue available on request.

National Film Board. Contact your local distribution office. Films are available free of charge.

New Cinema Enterprises Corp. Ltd., 35 Britain St., Toronto, Ontario M5A 157 .

Toronto Committee for the Liberation of Southern Africa (TCLSAC), 121 Avenue Road, Toronto, Ontario M5R 2G3, Tel: (416) 967-5562. Speaker's Bureau, films and slide-tape shows available.

Viking Films Ltd., 525 Denison Street, Markham, Ontario L3R 1B8.

Bibliography

Travelling (Lausanne), no. 34 (November-December 1972), pp. 2-6, "Pour un definition du cinéma alternatif", André Pâquet; *Cinéma-Québec*, vol. 3, no. 8 (October 1974), "Dans un film rien n'est innocent", Jean-Patrick Lebel; *Cinéma-Québec*, vol. 2, no. 1, pp. 18-22, "Disséquer l'homme politique québécois", Jean-Pierre Tadros interviews Denys Arcand; *Cinéma-Québec*, vol. 4, no. 5, pp. 10-15, "Une histoire à suivre: octobre 70 dans le cinéma québécois", Yves Lever discusses **Faut aller parmi l'monde pour le savoir, Tranquillement, pas vite, Les smattes, Bingo, Les ordres, Action, Reaction, L'île jaune**; *Le cinéma québécois et les événements d'octobre*, CQDC, 1976, a catalogue and critical dossier of such films as **Bingo, Les orders, Action, Réaction, l'île jaune**; *Champ libre*, a journal (published erratically) of political criticism dealing largely with film, available from *Champ libre*, P.O. Box 399, Station Outremont, Quebec; Five cahiers resulting from the Rencontres internationales pour un nouveau cinéma have been published: *Cahier 1: Projets et resolutions, Cahier 2: Repertoire des groupes, Cahier 3: Conférences/textes/bibliographie, Cahier 4: Dossier de presse,* and the fifth cahier which will appear in 1976, available from the Comité d'action cinématographique, 360 McGill Street, Montreal, Quebec H2Y 2E9 (articles are in French, English and Spanish).

Women in Film

During the early years of the National Film Board women were very much in evidence; Evelyn Spice-Cherry with husband Lawrence Cherry headed up the Agriculture Unit, and Gudrun Bjerring Parker was in charge of the Education Unit. Margaret Perry was there too in those early days, leaving later to set up the Nova Scotia provincial film unit.

In the intervening years Canadian film women were seldom directors, although the award-winning Beryl Fox first came to prominence on the CBC series, "This Hour Has Seven Days". The women in film were and continue to be production assistants, editors and sometimes producers: Maxine Samuel produced the series "Forest Rangers"; Marguerite Duparc edits and produces feature films; Arla Saare, Judith Crawley, Louise Ranger, Monique Champagne are all solid and important film people.

In 1971 Tanya Ballantyne directed **The Things I Cannot Change**, a documentary for the NFB's Challenge for Change, and Sylvia Spring directed **Madeleine Is. . .**, the first fiction feature by a woman in Canada. This was followed in 1972 by **La vie rêvée**, a feminist feature by Mireille Dansereau. Since then women have been much more in evidence as directors, encouraged by two series coming out of the NFB, "En tant que femmes" and "Working Mothers", and the development of Unit D under Kathleen Shannon. In the private sector as well women such as Kim Ondaatje, Bonnie Kreps, Marie Waisberg, Daria Stermac, Lorna Rasmussen, Zale Dalen, Anne Wheeler and Deepa Saltzman have been making good films often with the help of such female technicians as Carol Betts and Aerlyn Weissman. And one is also encouraged by Joyce Wieland and Judy Steed's production of the feature, **The Far Shore**.

Women & Film: International Festival 1896-1973, an impressive pioneering multi-media event, was a comprehensive international retrospective of films by women, videotape showings and a photographic exhibition of Canadian entries. While the main festival was held in Toronto, touring festivals, co-organized by the cities on the tour circuit, visited communities from coast to coast. The immediate results of the festival were an historical awareness of the woman-artist and a sympathy for all women in their struggle to communicate and to educate. While the circuit as a formal entity no longer exists, there are a number of operations across the country which use film and video, linked together loosely as *Women & Film Etc.*

The following groups are directly involved in encouraging and supporting women in film:

Cine Videobec
562 St. Jean Street
Quebec, Quebec
(418) 524-1815

A feminist and community video centre.

Country Reels
143 Walnut Street
Winnipeg, Manitoba
(204) 786-4581

A loosely-knit group of women producing and distributing video and sound tapes. Contact Pam Atmikov and Sarah Berger.

Floralie
c/o Videographe
1604 St. Denis Street
Montreal, Quebec
(514) 842-9786

A collaborative project assisted by the Secretary of State to produce nine video tapes on special groups of women — Native women married to white men, women in prison, women in factories, etc. Contact Simone Trudeau.

Hummer House
252 Robert Street
Toronto, Ontario
(416) 925-8501

A video production and performance group. Contact Deanne Taylor, Janet Burke, Bobbe Besold or Marien Lewis for up-to-date information on women in film.

Isis
2214 West 5th Avenue
Vancouver, B.C.
(604) 736-1303

A production and distribution cooperative of films, video tapes and slide and sound tapes. Contact Mo Simpson, Liz Walker, Leigh Deering or Marian Penner.

Magpie Media
10805-124th Street, Suite 2
Edmonton, Alberta
(403) 452-4125

Michèle Spak and Donaleen Saul produce film and slide tapes and are available as production assistants.

Prairie People Products
9442-100A Street
Edmonton, Alberta
(403) 424-5891

A film production group which has also produced children's radio
scripts and photographs. Contact Anne Wheeler, Lorna
Rasmussen or Linda Rasmussen.

Reel Feelings
4973 Angus Street
Vancouver, B.C.
(604) 731-9496 or 263-6603

A feminist media collective producing film, video and slide and
sound tapes.

Reel Life
1671 Argyle Street
Halifax, Nova Scotia
(902) 423-7627

A cooperative involved in tapes, slides and films. They are also
distributors and have published the *Maritime Women's Access
Handbook.*

Women's Resource Centre
P.O. Box 2037
Charlottetown, P.E.I.
(902) 892-7564

A group producing slides, tapes, film and video. Contact Gail
MacEachern.

Bibliography

Globe and Mail, March 27, 1971, "Making a Movie Despite the
CFDC", Betty Lee on Sylvia Spring shooting **Madeleine Is...**;
Globe and Mail, April 24, 1971, "Refuting the Youth Movie Fantasy", Martin Knelman on **Madeleine Is...**; *Châtelaine,* January
1973, p. 19, "Naissance d'un cinéma féministe au Québec",
discussion by Mireille Dansereau and Anne-Claire Poirier; *Image
et son* (France), no. 267 (January 1973) pp. 10-17, "La femme
dans le cinéma québécois", interview with Michele Lalonde, Jean-
Claude Labrecque, Pierre Perrault and Bernard Gosselin; *Médium-
média,* vol. 2 (January 1973), issue dedicated to the NFB series,
"En tant que femmes"; *Miss Chatelaine,* Winter 1973, pp. 68-
71ff., "Women as Filmmakers: Hey, It's Happening", Myrna

Kostash; *This Magazine,* vol. 8, no. 1, (March 1974), p. 25, "The
Canadian Film Industry: The Land is Dead. The Women are Hang-
ing on to Corpses. Nobody Gets Paid Back", letter from Judy
Steed; *Montreal Star,* May 15, 1974, "Lens Focused Clearly on
her Career", Patricia Lowe interviews camerawoman Nesya
Shapiro; *Pot pourri,* June 1974, pp. 2-12, "Women Making Film:
Three Interviews", interviews with Kathleen Shannon, Barbara
Greene and Dina Lieberman; *Branching Out,* November-
December 1974, an interview with Anne Wheeler and Lorna
Rasmussen on their film, **Great Grand Mothers**; *Access,* no. 14
(Spring 1975), "Working with Film: Experiences with a Group of
Films about Working Mothers", (*Access* is available on request
from NFB); *Communique,* May 1975, a special issue: "Women in
the Arts in Canada" with an article by Barbara Halpern Martineau,
pp. 32-35, "Women in Film: Many Women Filmmakers, Few
Films" (available from The Canadian Conference of the Arts, 3
Church St., Suite 47, Toronto, Ontario M5E 1M2, Tel: 364-6351);
Pulse, June 1975, pp. 14-15, "Women in Film", Lynne McIlveen
interviews Pat Thompson; *Pot pourri,* Summer 1975, "The Grier-
son Years: They Wouldn't Have Been Worth a Damn Without the
Women", a special issue with interviews and conversations with
the Grierson women: Evelyn Spice-Cherry, Daphne Lilly Anstey,
Margaret Ellis, Edith Spencer Osberg, Marion Leigh Leventhal,
Jane Marsh Beveridge, Margaret Carter, Beth Bertram, Marjorie
McKay, Helen Watson Gordon, Janet Scellen-Bull, Grace Brown,
Margaret-Ann Bjornson (Lady Elton) and Laura Boulton —
fascinating look at the early NFB; *Books in Canada,* October
1975, pp. 5-6, "Arts and the Women", Catherine L. Orr, reviews
of **Lucy Maud Montgomery: The Road to Green Gables**
(directed by Macartney-Filgate) and **Emily Carr** (written, directed
and produced by Nancy Ryley); *Cinema Canada,* no. 12, pp.
12-13, "On Location: Israel—Soundperson Aerlyn Weissman"
(interview); *Cinema Canada,* no. 13, p. 61, "Two Visions", an
interview with Daria Stermac on her film, **Playground in Six
Acts;** *Cinema Canada,* no. 16, pp. 42-44, "Carol on Camera",
article on camerawoman Carol Betts; *Cinema Canada,* no. 17,
p. 80, review of **At 99 — A Portrait of Louise Tandy Murch** by
Á. Ibrányi-Kiss; *Interlock,* a newsmagazine and newsletter
establishing a communication link among film women in Canada.
Edited by Donna Dudinsky, it is available from *Interlock,* National
Film Board, P43—P.O. Box 6100, Station A, Montreal, Quebec
H3C 3H5; *Take One,* vol. 3, no. 2, a special "Women in Film"
issue with a Joyce Wieland interview, a filmography of Canadian
women directors, and a symposium which includes Sylvia Spring,
Tanya Ballantyne MacKay and Judy Steed; *Motion,* vol. 4, no. 5,
pp. 14-19, "Women in Documentary: the Early Years".

Catalogues

Canadian Women Filmmakers: An Interim Filmography, compiled by Alison Reid (Canadian Filmography Series, no. 108, 1972). Available for $1.00 from the Canadian Film Institute.

Films by Women, August 1975,. A catalogue of films available from the Canadian Filmmakers' Distribution Centre, 406 Jarvis Street,Toronto, Ontario M4Y 2G6, (416) 921-4121.

Film Women International. An organization which grew out of the 1975 UNESCO Symposium held in Italy and attended by women filmmakers from 17 countries. Canadian filmmaker, Anne-Claire Poirier, was elected as a member of the executive committee. Temporary headquarters: c/o Swedish Film Institute, Stockholm, Sweden.

4 Days in May, a Report: Films, Workshops, Share and exchange Ideas, edited by Olga Deisko. A catalogue of films screened and workshops held May 6-9, 1975. Available from Challenge for Change/Media Research, National Film Board in Montreal.

Maritime Women's Access Handbook. Lists films, books, individuals and groups concerned with women in the Maritimes. Available for $1.00 from *Reel Life,* 1671 Argyle Street, Halifax, Nova Scotia, (902) 423-7627.

Toronto Access Resource Catalogue of Women's Films in Toronto. This catalogue contains articles on women and films and lists about 900 titles available in Toronto. Contact Barb Cochrane, 444A Spadina Avenue, Toronto, Ontario, (416) 929-5846.

Women: A Filmography. A catalogue of over 200 films by and about women available from the Toronto Public Library system. Copies available from Toronto Central Library, 214 College Street, Toronto.

Women and Film/La femme et le film: 1896-1973, International Festival. An annotated catalogue of films shown at the festival held in Toronto in 1973 and in partial showings across the country. Available for reference in film study centres and available for 50c from Hummer House.

The Women's Kit. A multi-media kit (including filmstrips, slides and photographs) gathered by women on the historical and present state of women in Canada. Available for $57.50 from Publications Sales, The Ontario Institute for Studies in Education, 252 Bloor Street West, Toronto, Ontario, M5S 1V6.

Films on the status of women

Women on the March (1958), Parts 1 & 2. Each 29 min. b&w. Part 1 deals with the suffragette movement, using archival footage. Part 2 is concerned with gaining the vote and the UN Status of Women Committee. Available free from NFB.

Les femmes parmi nous (1961), Parts 1 & 2. Each 30 min. b&w. The struggles for emancipation. Available from NFB.

After the Vote (1969). Dir: Bonnie Kreps. 22 min. b&w. Dist: Canadian Filmmakers' Distribution Centre. A feminist documentary.

La Québécoise (1972). 27 min. col. A study of Quebec women today, produced as part of the "Adieu Alouette' series. Available free from NFB.

The Status of Women: Strategy for Change (1972). Dir: Jo MacFadden. Prod: Moira Armour, Judith Lawrence. 30 min. col. A film of the First National Status of Women Conference, with discussions of women in politics, native women's rights and education. Dist: Canadian Filmmakers' Distribution Centre.

"En tant que femmes" series (1973): **A qui apparient ce cage?** (Dir: Susan Gibbard); **Les filles du Roy** (Dir: Anne-Claire Poirier); **J'me marie, j'me marie pas** (Dir: Mireille Dansereau); **Souris, tu m'inquietes** (Dir: Aimée Danis). Prod: Anne-Claire Poirier. Each 56 min. col. Available from NFB. The series deals with women in Quebec society.

Buenos Dias, Companeras: Women in Cuba (Buenos Dias, Companeras: les femmes de Cuba) (1975). Dir: Aviva Slesin. Prod: Vivienne Leebosh. Associate Prod: Lise Segal. Researcher and translator: Selma Bryant Fournier. 58 min. col. Available from Viking Films and New Cinema.

A Token Gesture (1976). Dir: Micheline Lanctot, NFB for the Secretary of State. Available free from NFB.

The Visible Woman. 30 min. b&w and col. Covers 100 years in the history of women in Canada. Available free from the Federation of Women Teachers Association of Ontario (1260 Bay St., 3rd floor, Toronto, Ontario M5R 2B8, 964-1232 or (800) 261-7205).

Women Want. . . . Prod: IWY Secretariat. 25 min. col. Available free from NFB.

"Working Mothers" series. Eight films of varying lengths, from 7 to 16 min. Designed for discussion. Available free from NFB.

Making Films

Cooperative Distribution

There are a number of cooperative film collections in Canada.
Some handle only distribution while others are distributing arms of
production cooperatives. The collections include features, shorts,
experimental and animated films which may be purchased or
rented at reasonable rates (rental fees are usually $1.00 per
minute). The cooperatives offer independent filmmakers a distribution outlet and a better share of the gross rentals than other, more
commercial, distributors.

   There are two main distribution cooperatives which deal mainly
with independently-made Canadian films but also handle films from
Europe and the United States. Catalogues are available on request:

   Canadian Filmmakers' Distribution Centre
   Tess Taconis, director
   406 Jarvis Street
   Toronto, Ontario M4Y 2G6
   (416) 921-4121

Coopérative cinéastes indépendants/Independent Filmmakers'
Cooperative
Dimitri Eipides and Claude Chamberland, directors
2026 Ontario Street, E.
Montreal, Quebec H2K 1V3
(514) 523-2816

The following production cooperatives also distribute their films:

Association coopérative de productions audio-visuelles (ACPAV)
96 Sherbrooke Street W.
Montreal, Quebec H2X 1X3
(514) 849-1381

Atlantic Filmmakers' Co-operative
1671 Argyle Street
Halifax, Nova Scotia
(902) 423-8833

One film study centre has a distribution system for independent
West Coast filmmakers:

Pacific Cinémathèque Pacifique
1155 West Georgia Street
Vancouver, B.C. V6E 3H2

See also FILMMAKERS; COMMUNITY FILM AND VIDEO; NATIVE
    PEOPLES AND FILM; POLITICAL AND THIRD WORLD
    FILMS; WOMEN IN FILM

André Brassard (*left*) was one of the participants in **Backyard Theatre**, made in the "Adieu alouette" series.

Michel Brault (behind camera) with Claude Gautier during the shooting of **Les ordres**.

Mireille Dansereau with Liliane Lemaître-Auger who plays Isabelle in Dansereau's **La vie rêvée.**

A scene from Martin Duckworth's **Temiscaming, Quebec,** a film about the attempt by workers to control their own production.

Director Roger Frappier during the shooting of **Infonie inachevée.**

John Grierson (*left*) with Ralph Foster in a scene from Roger Blais' **Grierson.**

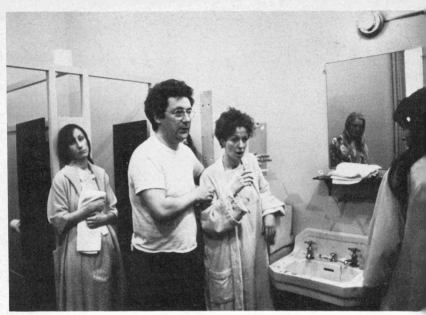

Claude Jutra directs Jane Eastwood in the CBC's 1977 production, **Ada**.
Photo courtesy CBC. Photographer: Barry Philp.

Allan King and crew filming **Who Has Seen the Wind**. *Left to right*: Ian Mc-Dougall, Allan King, Richard Leiterman, Christian Wangler, Henri Fiks.

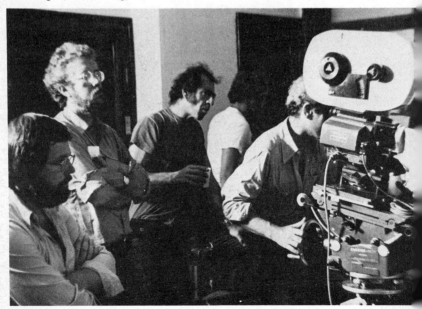

Director Jacques Leduc with Esther Auger (*left*) and Luce Guilbeault during the shooting of **Tendresse ordinaire.**

...ll Mason works with ...e of the "vicious" ...tors appearing in his ...y of the Wild, a ...m about the histori-...ly maligned wolves.

Dancers David and Anna Marie Holmes and director Grant Munro (*upper right*) with Norman McLaren during the shooting of **Tour en l'air.**

Jacques Godin who plays Paul Laliberté, director Marcel Carrière and cinematographer Thomas Vamos during the shooting of the NFB production, **OK . . . Laliberté.**

...ector and actor Frank Vitale (*left*) with Allan (Bozo) Moyle, Stephen ...ck and Peter Brawley in **Montreal Main.**

...irector Joyce Wieland (*right*) ...ith Céline Lomez who plays ...ulalie in **The Far Shore.**
...hoto: John Cressey

A scene from Peter Foldes' **La faim (Hunger)**. The film won the Palme d
at the 1974 Cannes Film Festival.

From **Animation of Cape Dorset**, an NFB film resulting from the Arctic
Workshop in animation.

Cooperative Production

There are cooperative production centres in every area of Canada. As opposed to film companies, cooperatives have open membership with a reasonable fee. Their services vary but all offer access to equipment and technical advice.

Association coopérative de productions audio-visuelles (ACPAV)
96 Sherbrooke Street W.
Montreal, Quebec H2X 1X3
(514) 849-1381

Established in 1971, ACPAV has approximately 60 members making sponsored film, shorts and features. ACPAV has all necessary equipment including editing facilities. The organization also collaborates on independent productions by furnishing technical assistance. Contact ACPAV for their catalogue of available films.

Atlantic Filmmakers' Co-operative
1671 Argyle Street
Halifax, Nova Scotia
(902) 423-8833

Formed in 1973, the Atlantic Filmmakers' Co-operative has a membership of approximately 25. It provides equipment and space to facilitate film production by its members, serving as a production agency and distributor. The Co-op has a close liaison with the Atlantic Regional Production Centre of the National Film Board.

Newfoundland Independent Filmmakers' Co-op
Box 9116
St. John's, Newfoundland

Founded in 1975, the Co-op has close ties with the Atlantic Filmmakers' Co-operative in Halifax and the Extension Services Department of Memorial University in St. John's.

Pacific Film Co-op
Box 46507
Vancouver, B.C. V6R 4G7

With a membership of 25, the Pacific Film Co-op distributes its films through the Canadian Filmmakers' Distribution Centre in Toronto and the Pacific Cinémathèque as part of their Film Study Collection.

Toronto Filmmakers' Co-op
67 Portland Street
Toronto, Ontario
(416) 366-3005

The Toronto Filmmakers' Co-op was founded in 1971 and has an active membership of approximately 100. Fully equipped, the Co-op offers practical filmmaking courses, lab discounts, screenings and a newsletter, *Rushes*. Their productions are distributed by the Canadian Filmmakers' Distribution Centre.

Winnipeg Film Group
24-221 McDermot Avenue
Winnipeg, Manitoba

Formed in 1974, the Winnipeg Film Group has a membership of approximately 30. Their films are distributed by the Canadian Filmmakers' Distribution Centre.

See also FILMMAKERS: FILM GROUPS; COMMUNITY FILM AND VIDEO; NATIVE PEOPLE AND FILM; POLITICAL AND THIRD WORLD FILMS; WOMEN IN FILM

Film Festivals and Competitions

Those international festivals which fall under official international regulations allow only one film from each country to be submitted. In Canada, the Film Festivals Bureau in the Department of the Secretary of State handles the details of preselection. Involved are two representatives from the art field, four representatives from film producers associations, two film critics, one representative from the Department of External Affairs and two knowledgeable people appointed by the Government Film Commissioner. These regulations are laid down by the International Federation of Film Producers Associations. For further information contact the Film Festivals Bureau/Bureau des festivals du film, Suite 1822, 66 Slater Street, Ottawa, Ontario K1A 0M5.

The Canadian Film Awards is an annual competition open to all Canadian films in various categories with presentations made during the first week of October. Public screenings are held of all selected films and the winning films shown following the awards in cities across the country. For further information and application forms, write:

Canadian Film Awards
916 Davie Street
Vancouver, B.C.
(604) 688-7757

Canadian Film Awards
175 Bloor Street E.
Toronto, Ontario M4W 1E1
(416) 924-3701

The Prix de la critique québécoise is given annually in November or December by the Association québécoise des critiques de cinéma (AQCC), Box 512, Station N, Montreal, Quebec H2X 1L0. (514) 738-0800.

The Canadian Student Film Festival is held each year at Concordia University in Montreal in September and is open to all Canadian student filmmakers. Further information and entry forms may be obtained by writing Canadian Student Film Festival, Conservatory of Cinematographic Art, H-109, 1455 de Maisonneuve Blvd. W., Montreal, Quebec H3G 1M8.

The best available source of information is the *Calendar of International Film & Television Events* published jointly by the International Film & Television Council and UNESCO each year. This calendar, which provides dates, addresses and purpose and specialities of festivals, can be obtained for $2.00. Write:

Calendar of International Film & Television Events
Via Santa Susanna 17
00187 Rome, Italy

Festival Diary is published monthly in newsletter form. Each issue provides a comprehensive listing of international film festivals for the coming twelve months. Subscription at £4 per year is available from:

Short Film Service Ltd.
122 Wardour Street
London W1, England

Further Sources of Film Festival Information:
Information Officer
Canadian Film Institute
1762 Carling Street
Ottawa, Ontario K2A 2H7
(613) 729-6193

Conseil québécois pour la diffusion du cinéma
3466 St-Denis Street
Montreal, Quebec H2X 3L3
(514) 879-4349

La Cinémathèque québécoise
360 McGill Street
Montreal, Quebec H2Y 2E9
(514)866-4688

Federation of Canadian Amateur Cinematographers/Fédération des cinéastes amateurs canadien (FCAC)
7485 Fabre Street
Montreal, Quebec

Society of Canadian Cine Amateurs
Box 984
St. Catharines, Ontario

Festival canadien international du film amateur (FCIFA)/Canadian International Amateur Film Festival (CIAFF)
c/o Armand Bélanger
39 rue du Crochet
Laval-des-Rapides, Québec
       or
c/o Mrs. Betty Peterson
4653 Dundas Street W.
Islington, Ontario

Almost all film periodicals and especially *New Canadian Film/Nouveau cinéma canadien*, published by La Cinémathèque québecoise, regularly carry detailed information on festivals and competitions.

Money Sources

The Canadian Film Development Corporation/Société de développement de l'industrie cinématographique canadienne is a bank set up to assist feature film production. The executive director is Michael Spencer, president is Gratien Gélinas. Addresses:

800 Place Victoria, Suite 2220
Montreal, Quebec H4Z 1A8
(514) 283-6363

111 Avenue Road, Suite 602
Toronto, Ontario M5A 3J8
(416) 966-6436

Most films demanded by federal government departments are channelled through the NFB, but only 50% are actually made by that organization; the remaining half are tendered by independent film producers. If you are interested in making sponsored films, contact:

Liaison Board
National Film Board
150 Kent Street
Ottawa, Ontario K1A 0M9.

A brochure is available from the Canada Council explaining the various programs of assistance to film and video workers. The grants cover production and post-production costs, script writing, apprenticeship, research and advanced studies, travel grants and short term grants. Write:

Canada Council
Box 1047
Ottawa Ontario K1P 5V8

If you are an Ontario citizen, the Film and Literature Section of the Ontario Arts Council has grants for production and pre-production. Contact:

Film and Literature Section
Ontario Arts Council
151 Bloor Street W.
Toronto, Ontario M5S 1T6

Bibliography

The Business of Film, by Stephen Chesley, is "an outline of the business aspects of Canadian feature and short film making from pre-production through marketing". Published in 1975 by the Cinema Canada Magazine Foundation, it is available from the

Canadian Filmmakers' Distribution Centre, 406 Jarvis Street, Toronto, Ontario M4Y 2G6.

Cinema Canada, no. 6 (February-March 1973) has three articles of interest: pp. 28-31, "How to make a profit doing what we really should be doing anyway", a brief presented to the Ontario Film Study Group by Kirwan Cox and Sandra Gathercole, representing the opinion of the Toronto Filmmakers' Coop and the Canadian Filmmakers' Distribution Centre; pp. 34-35 and 43, "The Film Industry in Ontario", a brief submitted to the Ontario Ministry of Industry and Tourism by John F. Bassett on behalf of the Exploration Team on Film Industry, January 1973; and pp. 38-42, "Canadian Film Industry Panel", held in 1973 with George Destounis, president of Famous Players, Canada; Bill Fruet and Allan King, filmmakers; John Hofsess and Gerald Pratley, critics; Michael Spencer, director of CFDC; and Sandra Gathercole, Canadian Council of Filmmakers.

See also MAKING FILMS: FILM FESTIVALS AND COMPETITIONS

Professional Organizations

Alberta Motion Picture Industries Association
347 Birks Building
Edmonton, Alberta T5J 1A1
(403) 424-4692

American Federation of Musicians (Canada)
101 Thorncliffe Park Drive
Toronto, Ontario M4H 1M1
(416) 425-1831

Association canadienne des distributeurs indépendants de films
d'expression française, (ACDIF)
245 Victoria Avenue, 7th floor
Montreal, Quebec H3Z 2M6
(514) 934-0869

Association des producteurs de films du Québec (APFO)
Box 686, Station Outremont
Montreal, Quebec H2V 4N6
(514) 277-6667

Association des propriétaires de cinémas du Québec Inc.
3720 Van Horne Avenue, Suite 405
Montreal, Quebec H3S 1R8
(514) 738-2715

Association des réalisateurs de film du Québec (ARFQ)
3466 St-Denis Street
Montreal, Quebec H2X 3L3
(514) 844-2457/844-6265

Association internationale du film d'animation (ASIFA-Canada)
49 rue du Moulin
Laval des Rapides, Québec H3C 3H5

Association of Canadian Television and Radio Artists (ACTRA)
105 Carlton Street
Toronto, Ontario M5B 1M2
(416) 363-6335

Association québécoise des critiques de cinéma (AQCC)
Box 512, Station N
Montreal, Quebec H2X 1L0
(514) 738-0800

Canadian Association of Motion Picture Producers
38 Isabella Street
Toronto, Ontario M4Y 1N1
(416) 964-6661

Canadian Film and Television Association
55 York Street, Suite 512
Toronto, Ontario M5J 1S2
(416) 363-8374

Association canadienne de cinéma-télévision
1103 St. Matthew Street
Montreal, Quebec H3H 2H3

Canadian Film Editors' Guild (CFE)
Box 46, Terminal A,
Toronto, Ontario M5W 1A2
(416) 924-8847

Canadian Society of Cinematographers (CSC)
22 Front Street W.
Toronto, Ontario M5J 1C4
(416) 363-4321

Composers, Authors and Publishers Association of Canada
1240 Bay Street,
Toronto, Ontario M5R 2C2

1245 Sherbrooke Street W.
Montreal, Quebec H3G 1G2

1 Alexander Street
Vancouver, B.C. V6A 1B2

Conseil québécois pour la diffusion du cinéma (CQDC)
3466 St-Denis Street, Suite 5-6
Montreal, Quebec H2X 3L3
(514) 842-5079

Council of Canadian Filmmakers (CCFM)
Box 1003, Station A
Toronto, Ontario M5W 1G5
(416) 869-0716

Directors Guild of Canada
22 Front Street W., Suite 815
Toronto, Ontario M5J 1C4
(416) 364-0122

Fédération québécoise des membres de l'industrie
cinématographique
3720 Van Horne Avenue, Suite 4-5
Montreal, Quebec H3S 1R8
(514) 738-2715

International Alliance of Theatrical Stage Employees
1590 Mount Royal E., Suite 303
Montreal, Quebec H2J 1Z2
(514) 527-1725

167 Church Street
Toronto, Ontario
(416) 364-8323

1356 Seymour Street
Vancouver, B.C.
(604) 688-4718

Manitoba Audio-Visual Industry Association (MAVIA)
Box 154
Winnipeg, Manitoba R3C 2G9

Motion Picture Theatres Association of Canada
167 Church Street
Toronto, Ontario

1590 Mont Royal E.
Montreal, Quebec H2J 1Z2

National Association of Broadcast Employees and Technicians
(NABET)
1010 St. Catherine Street, W., Suite 735
Montreal, Quebec H3B 3R3
(514) 878-3141

1019 Freshwater Drive
Richmond, B.C.
(604) 274-9941

105 Carlton Street, Suite 32,
Toronto, Ontario M5B 1M2
(416) 364-5185

Société des auteurs et compositeurs
1001 St-Denis Street
Montreal, Quebec H2X 3J1
(514) 288-3512

Society of Film Makers,
7451 Trans Canada Highway
Ville St. Laurent, Quebec
(514) 333-0722

Syndicat général du cinéma et de la télévision (SGCT)
1285 Hodge Street, Suite 205
Montreal, Quebec H4N 2B6
(514) 744-4989

Syndicat national du cinéma (SNC)
3466 St-Denis Street, Suite 8
Montreal, Quebec H2X 3L3
(514) 844-2457/844-6265

Union des artistes
1290 St-Denis Street
Montreal, Quebec H2X 3J7
(514) 878-3681

For further information on the activities of these professional organizations, consult the following publications:

Canadian Professional Film Directory
Filmcraft Publications
Phil Auguste, editor
116 Earlton Road
Agincourt, Ontario M1T 2R6
(416) 291-2834

Le cinéma au Québec: bilan d'une industrie
Les editions cinéma/Québec
Box 309, Station Outremont
Montreal, Quebec H2V 4N3
(514) 272-1058

Canadian Film Digest Year Book
c/o Film Publications of Canada Ltd.
175 Bloor Street E.
Toronto, Ontario M4W 1E1

Cinema Canada Bottin/Directory
Film Festival Bureau
Department of the Secretary of State
66 Slater Street, Suite 1822
Ottawa, Ontario K1A 0M5
(613) 996-3460

Film Canadiana Yearbook
Canadian Film Institute (CFI)
75 Albert Street, Suite 1105
Ottawa, Ontario K1P 5E7
(613) 238-7865

Technical Information, Services and Assistance

Sources of information on where to procure technical equipment and services:

> *Canadian Film Digest Year Book*
> Dan Krendal, editor
> c/o Film Publications of Canada Ltd.
> 175 Bloor Street E.
> Toronto, Ontario M4W 1E1

> *TV-Film Filebook*
> Arthur C. Benson, editor
> 2533 Gerrard Street E.
> Scarborough, Ontario

> *Le cinéma au Québec: bilan d'une industrie*
> Jean-Pierre Tadros, Connie Tadros, editors
> Editions cinéma/Québec
> Box 309, Station Outremont
> Montreal, Quebec H2V 4N3

The **Technical and Production Services** of the National Film Board publish an erratic quarterly report as material becomes available on technical developments. Available on request from:

> Director of Technical and Production Services
> National Film Board
> Box 6100
> Montreal, Quebec H3C 3H5

This same branch also makes technical information and service available to the private sector *only* if no commercial service of this kind is otherwise available in Canada.

The **Association of Motion Picture Producers and Laboratories of Canada** provides a booklet with a list of equipment and technical services available from member companies as well as a membership list. Contact:

> AMPPLC
> 55 York Street, Suite 512
> Toronto, Ontario M5J 1S2
> (416) 363-8374

> or

> Association des producteurs de films du Québec (APFQ)
> Box 686, Station Outremont
> Montreal, Quebec H2V 4N4
> (514) 277-6667

Les Laboratoires de film Québec has published a dictionary of cinematographic terms in which commonly used words and terms are listed in French and English. To obtain a free copy write:

Les Laboratoires de film Quebec
1085 Saint Alexandre
Montreal, Quebec H2Z 1P4
(514) 861-5483

Stockshot Libraries

Stockshot libraries consist of filmed materials divorced from their original use, gathered together in a film production library and broken down for possible inclusion in later complete productions. Stock may be extracted from newsreels, from the footage of completed films or from unused footage. UNESCO and the Royal Film Archives of Belgium have compiled the *World Directory of Stockshot and Film Production/ Un Répertoire mondial de cinémathèques de production,* ed, John Chittock (Paris: Pergamon Press). The directory covers 310 libraries in 59 countries, among them Canada. It should be noted, however, that while only seven companies in Canada are listed in this directory, virtually every film production organization (as well as the tv networks) is willing to supply stock material. The restrictions on the use of such material vary as do the prices; however, many companies that use film for public ralations provide stock free if it will not used for commercial purposes.

Special Effects

Two papers are available from *Pot pourri: Production Techniques Used in* Universe, Sidney Goldsmith (1968), 18pp., and *Special Effects,* an illustrated 16-page paper by Wally Gentleman. The July 1972 issue of *Pot pourri* is dedicated to the subject of special effects with articles by Wally Gentleman, Colin Low, Sidney Goldsmith and Pierre L'Amare.

Cameraless Animation/Cinéma d'animation sans caméra, by Norman McLaren, is available from the Information Division, NFB (reprinted from *Fundamental Education,* vol. 1, no. 4, 1939).

Most filmmakers' professional organizations offer technical training within their ranks to upgrade their own membership. If, however, you don't have the qualifications for membership, your local film cooperative offers technical workshops.

Association des cinéastes amateurs du Québec, 1415 Jarry Street E., Montreal, Quebec offers information and distribution services to amateur filmmakers.

Lexique du cinéma d'animation/ Amateur Movie Making Lexicon, Ray J. Pollet (Ottawa: Editions Ici Radio-Canada, 1971). Available from Leméac Inc.

Amateur filmmakers may find assistance by joining the **Canadian**

Society of Cine Amateurs/Société canadienne des ciné amateurs. Formed to foster and stimulate amateur filmmaking in Canada, the organization is open to amateur movie clubs, film production groups and individuals. Write:

Miss Dorothy Walter
2619 Lakeshore Blvd. W.
Toronto, Ontario
        or
Mr. Armand Bélanger
39 Crochet Street
Laval-des-Rapides, Quebec

Ciné guide Super18, André Lafrance (Ottawa: Les Editions de L'homme, 1974). Available from Agence de distribution populaire Inc., 955 Amherst Street, Montreal, Quebec H2L 3K4, (514) 523-1182.

See also MAKING FILMS: COOPERATIVE PRODUCTION;
            PRFESSIONAL ORGANIZATIONS
            FILM STUDY: MEDIA AND FILM COURSES
            FILM PUBLICATIONS: TRADE JOURNALS

ACTING

The Association of Canadian Television and Radio Artists (ACTRA) publishes a membership list of ACTRA members in Canada. This organization also publishes a 400-page book, *Face to Face with Talent,* which is an alphabetical listing, with photographs, of ACTRA members. Both are available to directors and producers on request from:

ACTRA
105 Carlton Street
Toronto, Ontario M5B 1M2
(416) 363-6335
        or
ACTRA
1434 St. Catharine Street, W., Suite 418
Montreal, Quebec
(514) 866-8149

In Quebec:
Union des Artistes
1290 St-Denis Street, 6th floor
Montreal, Quebec
(514) 288-6682

See also FILM STUDY: MEDIA AND FILM COURSES.

MUSIC

Two organizations which concern themselves with copyright and royalties regarding Canadian composers and wordsmiths are:

BMI Canada Ltd.
41 Valleybrooke Drive
Don Mills, Ontario
(416) 445-8700
    and
CAPAC (Composers, Authors and Publishers
Association of Canada)
1240 Bay Street
Toronto, Ontario
(416) 924-4427

Both these organizations publish a trade magazine which follows composers in Canadian cinema:

The Canadian Composer/Le compositeur canadien
40 St. Clair Street W.
Toronto, Ontario
(416) 925-5138

The Music Scene/La scène musicale
41 Valleybrooke Drive
Don Mills, Ontario M3B 2S6
(416) 445-8700

See also FILM STUDY: FILM STUDY CENTRES

WRITING

The script is a key element in any film despite the myth of the "unscripted" documentary in *"cinéma-vérité"*. Producers and backers (including the CFDC) demand a script before proceeding and many of our most impressive films testify to the skills of their writers.

The Canadian Film Development Corporation is the central clearinghouse for feature film scripts and this organization will put writers in touch with directors. Contact them at:

800 Place Victoria, Suite 2220
Montreal, Quebec H4Z 1A8

Another clearinghouse, although largely a source of new Canadian plays, is the Playwrights' Co-op. A number of writers who work in the film medium have had their stage plays reproduced by the Co-op. Write or telephone the Co-op for a catalogue:

8 York Street, 6th floor
Toronto, Ontario M5J 1R2
(416) 363-1581

The Toronto Filmmakers' Co-op conducts courses in all aspects of filmmaking including that of scriptwriting. Their address:

67 Portland Avenue
Toronto, Ontario

A few articles and books on scriptwriting are available as follows:

Write Me A Film?: A Symposium of Canadian Filmmakers, edited by Hugo McPherson, contains a number of articles: "Uneasy Riders" by William Weintraub, scriptwriter and director with the National Film Board; "The Fabled Movie Contract" by Ian MacNeill, director-producer, also with the National Film Board; "The Non-Literary Film" by Guy Glover, producer at the National Film Board; and "Le temps: la poésie du cinéma", by Jacques Godbout. This collection of articles can be found in *Canadian Literature,* no. 46 (Autumn 1970).

A number of articles on scriptwriting can be found in the special issue on film, "Cinéma si", in *Liberté,* vol. 8, no. 2-3 (March-June 1966).

"Hello, 'Caroline', Goodbye", by George Robertson can be found in *How to Make or Not to Make a Canadian Film.* "A Trap: The Script", by Jacques Godbout, is in the same book.

Pot pourri, Summer 1976. The issue is dedicated to "Writing for the Screen" and consists of interviews with Donald Brittain, Ken Dancyger, David Helwig, Ian MacNeill, William Weintraub and William Whitehead.

Script Writing for Short Films/Le scénario du film de court métrage was written by James A. Beveridge who teaches in the film department at York University, Toronto, It is available in the UNESCO series, *Reports and Papers on Mass Communication* (no. 57, UNESCO, 1969), for $1.25 from Publishing Centre, Supply and Services Canada, Ottawa.

Le métier de script, Monique Champagne (Montreal: Editions Leméac, 1973). Ms. Champagne discusses the experience involved in being a script assistant; the publication includes a glossary and a list of production functions.

Canadian Writer's Guide, prepared by the Canadian Authors' Association (Toronto: Fitzhenry & Whiteside Limited, 1973). Contains chapters on copyright, radio, television and theatre writing.

L'adaptation d'un roman au cinéma, by H. Queffelec, was published in the Collection cinéma et culture by the Centre diocesain du cinéma de Montréal in 1959. Available at film study libraries.

Particular film scripts available are indicated in the bibliographies of particular filmmakers. The National Film Board often makes available scripts from its productions; contact your local NFB office or the production office in Montreal. Many film study centres have copies of unpublished film scripts available for reference: see USING FILMS for addresses and accessibility of material.

Using Films

Films for Children

The international organization for children's cinema, **International Centre of Films for Children and Young People,** has its headquarters at 241 rue Royale, Brussels, 3, Belgium. Unfortunately, there is no longer a Canadian branch of this organization so information and reports released by them must be obtained directly.

Faroun Films in Montreal is a commercial organization which produces and distributes its own films as well as children's films from all over the world. For their catalogue, contact:

Faroun Films/Les Films Faroun
136A St. Paul Street E.
Montreal, Quebec H2Y 1G6
(514) 866—8831

Astral Television Films Ltd. distributes a number of films gathered together by the British Children's Film Foundation. For a catalogue contact:

Astral Television Films Ltd.
224 Davenport Road
Toronto, Ontario M5R 1J7
(416) 924-2155

The **National Film Board** has a 13-part series, "The Stories of Tuktu/Les récits de Tuktu", about the adventures of an Eskimo boy. See the NFB catalogue for other films for children.

See also FILMMAKERS, in particular the filmographies of Bernard Gosselin and Richard Lavoie who specialize in films for children; *Montreal Star*, April 10, 1976, "Why can't we have a children's cinema of our own?", Joan Irving.

Finding and Using Educational Material

A number of books, theses and pamphlets are available to the film educator. The following list is not meant to be exhaustive but rather to act as a guide to the types of material being published.

Beauchamp, René, *Photo / ciné / télé: trois agents de communication.* Montreal: Centre de psychologie et de pédagogie, 1970.

Beaudet Gérard, and Proteau, Donald. *Introduction au cinéma.* Montreal: Centre de psychologie et de pédagogie, 1966.

Bonneville, Léo, and Pelletier, Rosaire. *Cinema.* "Cahiers de bibliographie collèges Series" no. 4. Quebec: Ministère de l'éducation, Gouvernement du Québec, 1974.

Canada Cinematography in Research. Ottawa: National Science Film Library, Canadian Film Institute, 1971.

Charlesworth, Roberta. "The Quiet Revolution — Film in Education" in *Artscanada,* April 1970, pp. 21-23.

La contribution du film à l'enseignement du premier degré. Paris: UNESCO, 1963.

Cruikshank, Lyle Reid. *An Examination of the Current Approaches to and Effects of Screen Education in Selected Schools of the Toronto Area.* Thesis submitted to the College of Communication Arts, Michigan State University, 1969. Available for reference in the NFB library, Montreal.

————. *Media Study—Screen Education: A Comparison of British, American and Canadian Approaches.* Report submitted to Michigan State University, College of Education, 1970. Available for reference in the NFB library, Montreal.

Demers, Pierre. *Filmographie à l'usage des professeurs: philosophie, français, cinéma.* Presses collegiales de Jonquière, 1973. Distributed by Fides.

Educational Television Across Canada: The Development and State of ETV, 1968. Toronto: Metropolitan Educational Television Association of Toronto, 1969.

Egly, Max and others. *Conséquences de l'emploi des technologies "vidéo" pour l'éducation et la culture.* Paris: UNESCO. Contains an international bibliography on the relation of education and technology.

Gailitis, M.M. *The Costs of Information Retrieval Television: A Case Study in the Cost-effectiveness of Educational Media.* Occasional paper no. 12. Toronto: OISE, 1972.

Gillet, Margaret. *Educational Technology: Toward Demystification*. Critical Issues in Canadian Education Series. Toronto: Prentice-Hall, 1973.

Goombridge, Brian, ed. *Adult Education and Television: A Comparative Study in Three Countries — Canada, Czechoslovakia and Japan*. London: National Institute of Adult Education (England and Wales) and UNESCO, 1966.

Hall, E.M. and Dennis, L.A. *Living and Learning*. Report of the Provincial Committee on Aims and Objectives of Education in the Schools of Ontario. Toronto: Ontario Department of Education, 1968.

Hughes, A.E., ed. *Tribal Drums*. Toronto: McGraw-Hill, 1970. A collection of contemporary song lyrics and poetry with film and record references.

Irving, John A. *Mass Media in Canada*. Toronto: Ryerson Press, 1962.

Katz, John Stuart, ed. *Perspectives on the Study of Film*. Boston: Little, Brown, 1971. This collection contains "In Defense of Film History", by Peter Harcourt, pp. 258-59.

Katz, Oliver, Aird. *A Curriculum in Film*. Curriculum Series no. 13. Toronto: OISE, 1972. On the integration of the study of film with the study of literature.

Kidd, J.R., ed. *Learning and Society*. Toronto: Canadian Association of Adult Education, 1963.

Miller, Lewis, ed. *Educational Television: An Abstract of the Proceedings of the Educational Conference in Newfoundland and Labrador*. Ottawa: Queen's Printer, 1966. Available from Ministry of Supply and Services, Ottawa.

McLaughlin, G. Harry. *Educational Television on Demand: An Evaluation of the Ottawa IRTV Experiment*. Occasional paper no. 11. Toronto: OISE, 1972.

McLuhan, Marshall. *Understanding Media: The Extensions of Man*. Toronto: McGraw-Hill, 1964.

Möller, Hans. *Media for Discovery*. Toronto: Maclean-Hunter, 1970.

Nuttall, James, ed. *Screen Education in Canadian Schools*. Toronto: Canadian Education Association, Ontario Department of Education, 1969.

Phillips, Charles, E. *To Begin Making Movies*. Toronto: Information Division, Canadian Education Association.

Repath, Austin, ed. *Getting Out of the Box*. Toronto: Longman, 1972.

————. *Mass Media and You.* Toronto: Longman, 1966.

Rutledge, Donald and others, eds. *Experiments with Film in the Art Classroom.* Toronto: OISE, 1970.

Screen Education in Ontario. Toronto: Queen's Printer, 1970.

Slade, Mark. *Language of Change: Moving Images of Man.* Toronto: Holt, Rinehart and Winston, 1970.

The Uses of Film in the Teaching of English. Report of the English Study Committee Office of Field Development, Curriculum Series no. 8. Toronto: OISE, 1971. A thorough study of references to elementary, secondary and college teaching with a full bibliography and film sources.

Waniewicz, Ignacy. *La radio-télévision au service de l'éducation des adultes: les leçons de l'expérience mondiale.* Paris: UNESCO. Includes an international bibliography.

On Classification of Non-Book Material

Lamy-Rousseau, Françoise. *Inventoriez et classez facilement vos documents audio-visuels/Easy Method for Inventory-taking and Classification of Audio-visual Material.* Lamy-Rousseau, 1972, rev. 1975. Available from Mme F. Rousseau, 187 Brais Street, Longueuil, Quebec J4H 1T7.

————. *Traitement automatisé des documents multi-média avec les systèmes ISBD unifié, Lamy-Rousseau et PRECIS — propositions SILP.* Quebec, 1974. Available from Ministère de l'éducation du Québec.

————. *Uniformisation des règles de catalogage des documents visuels et sonores: description d'une expérience.* Montreal, 1973. Available from Ministère de l'éducation du Québec.

Riddle, Jean; Lewis, Shirley; and MacDonald, Janet. *Non-book Materials: The Organization of Integrated Collections.* Ottawa: Canadian Library Association, 1970.

Periodicals and Catalogues

School Progress: A national monthly periodical listing distributors of educational media, film programs, and hardware as well as articles on educational media. Subscriptions are available for $10.00 per year from:
    Maclean-Hunter Ltd.
    481 University Avenue
    Toronto, Ontario M5W 1A7

Canadian University and College. A bi-monthly journal for administrators and educators at the university and college level. Each issue carries a section on audio-visual equipment and availability, software and printed material. The magazine is available at $10.00 per year from:

> Maclean-Hunter Ltd.
> 481 University Avenue
> Toronto, Ontario M5W 1A7

Access. An educational quarterly published by the Alberta Educational Communications Authority (AECA) which concerns itself with all levels of educational broadcasting and television, available from:

> AECA
> Central Services, Room 400
> Barnett House, 11010 - 142 Street
> Edmonton, Alberta   T5N 2R1

CBC Educational Films. The catalogue is available from:

> CBC
> Box 500, Terminal A
> Toronto, Ontario M5W 1E6

Selections: Federal Government and International Publications for Educators. This catalogue is available from Publishing Centre, Supply and Services Canada, Ottawa.

Sources of Non-Book Material

Multi-media products and visual education material (other than 16mm films) produced by the National Film Board are distributed by three private companies. Such materials filmstrips, 8mm concept films, multi-media kits, overhead projectuals, slides and film loops can be obtained from the following organizations:

> in Ontario:
> Visual Education Centre
> 95 Berkeley Street
> Toronto, Ontario

> east of Ontario:
> SECAS
> 400 Notre Dame E.
> Montreal, Quebec

> west of Ontario:
> Harry Smith & Sons
> 1150 Homer Street
> Vancouver, B.C.

Loops to Learn By. A film on the use of film loops directed by Rex Tasker, NFB. 25 min. col.

Audio cassettes of talks given at the 1971 Canadian Educational

Communications Conference are available at $3.50 each from the Edmonton Audio-Visual Association, c/o Educational Media Division, Department of Extension, The University of Alberta, Edmonton, Alta. The following are some of the talks catalogued:

Canadian Science Films in Higher Education (no. 19), Dr. Lucien Kops;

Colloque: matériel de média en langue française (no. 7), P.A. Lamoureux;

Libraries and the Wired City (no. 16), Thomas Ferguson;

Research Films: Science (no. 18), Stephen Rothwell;

Selection and Evaluation of Educational Films (no. 6) Anne Davidson;

Should University Professors Produce Their Own Science Films Without Technical Assistance? (no. 20), A. Leitner.

The CBC offers publications and audio tapes of many of their radio programs. A number of them would be of interest to educators. For catalogues of publications and audio tapes, contact:

CBC Learning Systems
Box 500, Terminal A
Toronto, Ontario M5W 1E6

The Video-Tape Programme Service of the Ontario Educational Communications Authority provides video copies of some 3,000 programs to educational institutions in Ontario only. Catalogue available from VIPS Order Desk, OECA, 2180 Yonge Steet, Toronto, Ontario M4S 2C1.

Organizations

Association for Media and Technology in Education in Canada (AMTEC) 797 Don Mills Road, Suite 701,
Don Mills, Ontario M3C 1V1
(416) 429-6073

AMTEC is a coordinating body for individuals and organizations involved in educational media. It holds within it the Educational Media Association of Canada (EMAC) which concerns itself in the public school area and the Educational Television and Radio Association of Canada (ETRAC) involved in the college and university area.

Canadian Science Film Association (CSFA)
Ontario Science Centre
770 Don Mills Road
Don Mills, Ontario M3C 1T3

CSFA is concerned with the use of films in research science and in the field of education. They publish the *CSFA Newsletter*.

General Service of Teaching Media
Department of Education
Government of Quebec
255 Crémazie Blvd. E.
Montreal, Quebec
(514) 873-3241

Ministère de l'éducation
Service général des moyens d'enseignement
Centre de documentation
600 Fullum Street
Montreal, Quebec H2K 4L1

Ministère de l'éducation du Québec
Service général des moyens d'enseignement
Cité parlementaire, edifice G
Québec, Québec G1A 1H2

The Naltional Science Film Library (NSFL)
Canadian Film Institute
75 Albert Street
Ottawa, Ontario K1P 5E7
(613) 729-6193

The National Science Film Library is a special collection within the
CFI of films on the sciences and social sciences, holding over
4,000 titles. The NSFL offers three services in addition to their
film resources: information and research; film evaluations and
film programing.

Office du film du Québec (OFQ)
360 McGill Street
Montreal, Quebec
(514) 873-2234

or

1601 Hamel Blvd.
Quebec, Quebec
(418) 643-5168

A provincial government agency producing films for provincial
departments including the Department of Education.

Ontario Educational Communications Authority (OECA)
Canada Square
2180 Yonge Street
Toronto, Ontario M4S 2C1
(416) 484-2600

OECA is a provincial Crown corporation concerning itself with
educational broadcasting in Ontario.

Ontario Film Association
Box 521
Barrie, Ontario

OFA is an organization of film producers, distributors, educators and film librarians who meet each year at the Grierson Seminar to exchange ideas and information.

Free Films

Many organizations and companies offer to lend films without charge, as a means of education and/or publicity. These films are generally deposited in a central clearing house and the borrower is usually expected to pay transportation costs either one or both ways. **Crawley Films** — the country's largest producer of sponsored films — has gathered together titles and sources of free 16mm films; their *Free Film Directory* lists almost 500 sources, giving access to over 16,000 free films. The directory can be obtained without charge by writing to Crawley Films Limited at either of the following addresses:

> 19 Fairmont Avenue
> Ottawa, Ontario

> Box 580, Station F
> Toronto, Ontario M4Y 2L8

Don't overlook the **National Film Board libraries** and **public library collections.** Public libraries are also good places to borrow a 16mm projector and, indeed, learn how to run one efficiently. Another source of good free films are the foreign embassies and trade offices as well as tourist bureaus. Furthermore, every province produces trade and tourist films usually under the aegis of the Department of Trade or Industry; in Quebec, it is under the Department of Cultural Affairs. Write to your provincial government seat for their source of free films.

See also FILM PUBLICATIONS: CATALOGUES

Special Film Collections

A large number of specialized film collections exists in Canada; where these collections have been discussed in some detail under other headings, they will be referred to in this section without further discussion.

Film on the Arts

The Canadian Centre for Films on Art is the outcome of the 1963 UNESCO Seminar, *"Films on Art"*, which was held in Ottawa. The Centre operates under the joint sponsorship of the National Gallery and the National Film Board of Canada in cooperation with the Canadian Film Institute which acts as distributor. The Centre has a number of collections under its aegis:

Films on Art/Films sur l'art. This collection is made up of those films gathered by the National Gallery of Canada and supplemented by other films on art from the CFI's collection, embassies, galleries and universities, totaling over 2,000 films in English and French. Films are borrowed through the Canadian Film Institute at their usual rates.

> Film Library, CFI
> 303 Richmond Road
> Ottawa, Ontario K1Z 6X3
> (613) 729-6193

For catalogues, advice on programing and program notes, contact:

> Canadian Centre for Films on Art
> 150 Kent Street
> Ottawa, Ontario K1A 0M9

As an extension of the *Films on Art* collection, films on art have been deposited in each province. Arrangements for borrowing these films should be made with the provincial organization concerned:

> Educational Media Division
> University of Alberta
> Edmonton, Alberta

> Film Library
> University of Manitoba
> Winnipeg, Manitoba

> Audio-Visual Centre
> Memorial University
> St. John's, Newfoundland

London Public Library
305 Queens Ave.
London, Ontario

Le Centre artistique
Université de Sherbrooke
Sherbrooke, Quebec

Extension Department
University of British Columbia
Vancouver, B.C.

Owen's Art Gallery
Mount Allison University
Sackville, New Brunswick

Audio-Visual Education
Department of Education
Box 578
Halifax, Nova Scotia

Confederation Art Gallery
Charlottetown, P.E.I.

Film Library
University of Saskatchewan
Saskatoon, Sask.

Films on the Performing Arts/Films sur les arts d'interpréta-tion. In conjunction with the National Arts Centre, a catalogue is available of over 300 titles of films on the performing arts. They can be booked through the Canadian Film Institute. Catalogues and information are available from the Canadian Centre for Films on Art.

Films on the Dance/Films sur la danse. A collection of over 60 titles of films on the dance have been put together in conjunction with the National Arts Centre. They can be booked through the Canadian Film Institute at their going rates. Further information and catalogues are available from the Canadian Centre for Films on Art.

The National Gallery of Canada in Ottawa has gathered together a collection of films which they use within their education program. This film study collection is available at the Gallery in Ottawa for individual viewing on request. Ask for the Canadian Filmmakers Series.

Science Films Collections

Two collections of science films exist in Canada. The National Film Board collection is wholly Canadian and films may be borrowed through your local library. Catalogues are also available at the nearest NFB office.

The second collection is at the Canadian Film Institute with The National Science Film Library/La Cinémathèque nationale scienti-fique. This collection has over 3,500 films from all over the world catalogued under the following headings: *The Earth Sciences and Related Subjects, Films on Engineering and Technology, Films on the Physical Sciences, Films on Anthropology and Ethnology.* These catalogues, available for a small fee, give descriptions of films listed (with their nominal rental rates).

> The National Science Film Library/La Cinémathèque nationale scientifique
> Canadian Film Institute Film Library
> 303 Richmond Road
> Ottawa, Ontario K1Z 6X3
> (613) 729-6193

The Travel Film Library is a branch of the Canadian Government Travel Bureau which aims to promote tourism in Canada. Admini-stered by the National Film Board in cooperation with the depart-ments of tourism in each of the provinces, the Travel Film Library distributes provincially-made films through 500 outlets around the world.

See also FILMMAKERS: NATIVE PEOPLE AND FILM; POLITICAL AND THIRD WORLD FILMS; WOMEN IN FILM; COMMUNITY FILM AND VIDEO
USING FILMS: FILMS FOR CHILDREN; FINDING AND USING EDUCATIONAL MATERIAL
MAKING FILMS: COOPERATIVE DISTRIBUTION.

Film Study

Media and Film Courses

CANADA

The Canadian Film Institute annually compiles *A Guide to Film and Television Courses in Canada* which lists those courses offered by universities and community colleges (CEGEPS in Quebec) across Canada. Organized by province, the guide offers a description of each course, degrees and certificates awarded, and addresses for further information.

> *A Guide to Film and Television Courses in Canada/Un guide des cours de cinéma et de télévision offerts au Canada*
> Canadian Film Institute
> 75 Albert Street, Suite 1105
> Ottawa, Ontario K1P 5E7

Film Studies Association of Canada was formed in 1976 with a five-person executive committee to promote exchanges between teachers of film in colleges and universities across Canada. For further information, contact the organization through the Department of Communications, McGill University, Montreal, Quebec.

The **Media Division** of the National Film Board conducts screen study seminars in conjunction with educational institutions across the country. For further information write to the Summer Institute of Film and Media Study, National Film Board, Box 6100, Montreal, Quebec H3C 3H5.

The **Drama Development Programme** within the National Film Board is attempting to develop skills in dramatic writing, directing and acting. Regional workshops at the NFB regional production centres have been and will be held. For further information, contact your local NFB production office or The Drama Development Programme, NFB, Box 6100, Montreal, Quebec H3C 3H5. See *Pot pourri*, Winter 1976, for a discussion of the program.

The **National Theatre School of Canada** (5030 St-Denis Street, Montreal, Que. 842-7954) offers the country's toughest and best acting course (three years). Only 32 students are accepted each year into the acting course (16 English, 16 French) following nation-wide auditions.

Offered as a service by BMI Canada Ltd., the **Film Music Workshop** is open to professional lyricists and composers to stimulate and encourage new creative talent in the film music field. Started in December 1970, the workshops are led by various composers working in film. For further information, contact:

> BMI Canada Ltd.
> 41 Valleybrooke Drive
> Don Mills, Ontario M3B 2S6
> (416) 445-8700

UNITED STATES

The American Film Institute has compiled a *Guide to College Film Courses*. More than 400 universities are listed. The pamphlet is available for $2.50 from the American Library Association, 50 East Huron Street, Chicago, Illinois 60611, or from the American Film Institute, 1815 H Street N.W., Washington, D.C. 20006.

ABROAD

The *International Film Guide,* edited by Peter Cowie on a yearly basis, gives up-to-date information on the prominent film schools in Europe. A.S. Barnes & Co. is the American publisher.

Les institutions cinématographiques, no. 68 in series "Etudes et documents d'information", published by the CITC (Conseil international du cinéma et de la télévision) of UNESCO, 1973. French edition ISBN 92-3-2010763; English edition ISBN 92-3-101073-X. Available from Publishing Centre, Supply and Services Canada, Ottawa.

See also MAKING FILMS: COOPERATIVE PRODUCTION; PROFESSIONAL ORGANIZATIONS; TECHNICAL INFORMATION, SERVICES AND ASSISTANCE.

Film and Photography Archives

As opposed to film collections, film archives are depositories of public records and historic documents which are held in the public trust. While the National Film Board and the Canadian Broadcasting Corporation maintain archival material produced within and outside those organizations, it is, in fact, selected material reflecting their, rather than the public's needs and views.

A true public archive has the responsibility of preserving, without preselection, films and other related material from its own national heritage and that of other heritages as well if such material is made available. Because such work is part of the national interest, it is carried out without prejudice of copyright laws. Furthermore, the archivist has the responsibility of organizing and researching this material in order to promote effectively the preservation and study of the film heritage.

This work is accomplished by an archive in a number of ways:

1) by membership in FIAF (Féderation internationale des archives du film/International Federation of Film Archives). This organization lays down international standards for archival operations, facilitates cooperation between member organizations and oversees the publication of archival documentation;

2) by publishing and encouraging the publication of film study material which will detail and elucidate the archival material which they and sister archives hold;

3) by providing access to the archives through exhibition, lectures and the discussion of the material held in their trust.

Film material from public and private production is preserved in a number of archives across the country:

National Film Archives, Public Archives Canada/Les Archives nationales du film, Archives publiques Canada

(mailing address)
395 Wellington Street
Ottawa, Ontario K1A 0N4

56 O'Connor Street
Ottawa, Ontario K1P 5Z6
(613) 992-1383, 922-0635 and 996-6009

The National Film Archives was established in 1972 to hold the film, sound tapes and video tapes of the Public Archives Canada as well as the archival collection of the former Canadian Film Archives of the Canadian Film Institute. The present holdings include 20,000 films, 4,000 books on film, 800 periodical titles, 200,000 stills as well as vertical files on film subjects and filmmakers. Their large title index is international in scope made possible through cooperative arrangement with FIAF; the Archives is, at the time of publication, a provisional member of FIAF. All these important holdings are open to researchers.

La Cinémathèque québécoise

360 McGill Street
Montreal, Quebec H2Y 2E9
(514) 866-4688

This archive (which became a full member of FIAF in 1966) specializes in preserving Canadian and animated films. Unlike the National Film Archives, La Cinémathèque québécoise exhibits its archival collection and films of other FIAF members in frequent public showings. Its stills library holds over 80,000 pieces, many archival in nature. It also preserves taped interviews and cinematographic apparatus in the museum, also on McGill Street. La Cinémathèque québécoise works closely with the Département de documentation cinématographique, also at 360 McGill Street, which holds printed material, much of it archival in nature. Many of the publications of La Cinémathèque are archival expositions; in particular, *How to Make or Not to Make a Canadian Film, Hommage à Maurice Jaubert* and *Une Exposition Georges Meliès.*

There are a number of other archives across Canada (at least one exists in each of the ten provinces); while their holdings in this area of interest are generally limited to archival photographs, some few have archival films as well:

Alberta

Provincial Museum and
   Archives of Alberta
12845 — 102 Avenue
Edmonton, Alberta

British Columbia

Vancouver Public Library
Historical Photo Section
750 Burrard Street
Vancouver, B.C.

Visual Records
Provincial Archives
Victoria, B.C.

Manitoba

Provincial Archives
Provincial Library
Winnipeg, Manitoba

New Brunswick

Provincial Archivist
Bonar Law — Bennett Building
University of New Brunswick
Fredericton, New Brunswick

Newfoundland

Provincial Archivist
Colonial Building
Military Road
St. John's, Newfoundland

Nova Scotia

Public Archives of Nova Scotia
Dalhousie Campus
Coburg Road
Halifax, Nova Scotia

Ontario

Department of Public Records
   and Archives
Queen's Park
Toronto, Ontario

Prince Edward Island

Provincial Archives
Box 1000
Charlottetown, P.E.I.

Quebec

Provincial Archives
Department of Cultural Affairs
Quebec, Quebec

Saskatchewan

Archives Division
Legislative Library
Regina, Sask.

Provincial Archivist
Saskatchewan Archives Board
Regina Campus Library
University of Saskatchewan
Regina, Sask.

Western Development Museum
1839 11th Street W.
Saskatoon, Sask.

Three other specialized collections exist:

Photographic Services
Canadian Pacific Railways
Windsor Station
Montreal, Quebec

Over 300,000 archival photographs taken since the building of the CPR. Open to the public weekdays from 8:30-1:00 and 2:15-5:00. Photographs can be reproduced for a fee on request.

Curator of Photography
Notman Photo Archives
690 Sherbrooke Street W.
Montreal, Quebec
(514) 392-4781

Including the Notman collection dating from 1856 to 1934, which traces the building of the CPR railway. Also the McCord Collection dating from 1847. Over 500,000 photos accessible weekdays by appointment.

Glenbow Archives,
Glenbow-Alberta Institute
902-11th Avenue S.W.
Calgary, Alberta

As well as a few archival films and stills from early films made in western Canada, this archives has a large collection of photographs of early Eskimo settlements, the building of the CPR, ranching and immigration to the west. They hold the collection of the Lomen Brothers, circa 1900-1945, dealing with western and southwestern Alaska.

See also FILM STUDY: FILM STUDY CENTRES

Film Societies

The Canadian Federation of Film Societies/La Fédération canadienne des ciné-clubs (CFFS/FCCC) is a federated group coordinating the efforts of all those interested in the appreciation of the film as art. Among their services are the following: guidelines for starting a film society; film information for the preparation of program notes; a quarterly newsletter; access to the CFFS Film Library; a membership directory and the *Index* of feature length films available in Canada with over 9,000 films cross-referenced. The annual May general meeting provides an opportunity to see new films available to film societies. For membership contact:

> Canadian Federation of Film Societies (CFFS)
> 6718 Legare Drive S.W.
> Calgary, Alberta T3E 6H2
> (403) 246-8117

Index of 16mm and 35mm Feature Length Films Available in Canada listing more than 9,000 films including the director, leading players, country, running time, year released, available print versions and distributors. The *Index* is available for $25.00.

> CFFS Index Committee
> Box 484, Terminal A
> Toronto, Ontario

Another handbook of interest to film societies is *Le ciné-club: méthodologie et portée sociale,* by Léo Bonneville (Montreal: Fides, 1968.)

Film Study Centres

Some film study centres listed in this section have been set up solely for that purposes, but more often they are part of a larger organization such as archives, a public library, university program, film distribution or production organization, or an arm of a film publication. Students of film will be generously assisted by the dedicated staff in these centres.

See also FILM STUDY: FILM AND PHOTOGRAPHY ARCHIVES
        USING FILMS: FINDING AND USING EDUCATIONAL
        MATERIAL; SPECIAL FILM COLLECTIONS
        FILM PUBLICATION: PERIODICALS
        BIBLIOGRAPHY

CANADIAN FILM INSTITUTE/INSTITUT CANADIEN DU FILM

> 75 Albert Street
> Ottawa, Ontario K1P 5E7
> (613) 238-7865

The Canadian Film Institute is no longer an archive (having turned over all its archival material to the Public Archives of Canada) but has intensified its various functions as a centre for film study:

National Film Library, Canadian Film Institute, 303 Richmond Road, Ottawa, Ontario K1Z 6X3, (613) 729-6193. The National Film Library is the distribution arm of the Institute with a complete collection of over 7,000 films. The Film Study Collection of classic films and compilations is available along with the reference guide, *800 Films for Film Study*. A second, most important collection is the National Science Film Library (NSFL) with films on science and social sciences (see USING FILMS: SPECIAL FILM COLLECTIONS). Numerous small collections exist and catalogues are available for films on sports, labour and management, humanities, law, etc. The complete *Title Index* is available for $25.00. Film borrowers must become Institutional Members.

Exhibitions Section, Canadian Film Institute, 75 Albert Street, Suite 1105, Ottawa, Ontario K1P 5E7, (613) 238-7866. The Exhibitions Section has a number of responsibilities. The National Film Theatre programs films from three to seven nights a week at the National Library and Public Archives Building, 395 Wellington Street, in Ottawa. Programs consist of thematic studies, retrospectives of particular filmmakers, national cinema programs and, on Tuesday evenings, the Canadian series regularly in collaboration with the National Film Archives. Program notes are generally available. Memberships are available at the door for $3.00 and entrance is $1.50 a showing. The Regional Film Theatre branch works in programing cooperation with a number of film theatres across the country. The ones that now exist are as follows:

National Film Theatre/Edmonton, c/o Edmonton Public Library, 10630 77 Avenue, Edmonton, Alberta, (403) 439-0209.

National Film Theatre/Winnipeg, c/o Winnipeg Art Gallery, 300 Memorial Blvd., Winnipeg, Manitoba R3C 1V1, (204) 786-6641.

National Film Theatre/Kingston, c/o Department of Film Studies, Queen's University, Kingston, Ontario K7L 3N6, (613) 547-5573.

National Film Theatre/Cornwall, c/o St. Lawrence College, Windmill Point, Cornwall, Ontario K6H 4Z1, (613) 933-6080.

National Film Theatre/Halifax, c/o Dalhousie Art Centre, Dalhousie University, Halifax, Nova Scotia, (902) 424-2067.

In addition, the National Film Theatre cooperates with the Ontario Film Theatre in Toronto and the Pacific Cinémathèque Pacifique in Vancouver which are discussed in detail below. The Exhibitions Section also organizes an annual August "Ottawa Festival", an international film festival sanctioned by the International Federation of Film Producers' Associations.

Publications, Canadian Film Institute, 75 Alberta Street, Suite 611, Ottawa, Ontario K1P 5E7; (613) 238-7865. The Publications Branch of CFI has four main areas of work:

Film Canadiana. An annual listing of films produced in Canada in the preceding year, production index, information and addresses of institutions, organizations and companies, bibliographies, festivals and awards and statistics;

Reference material, such as *800 Films for Film Study,* and *A Guide to Film and Television Courses in Canada;*

International Series;

Canadian Filmography Series, on filmmakers such as Gilles Carle, Don Shebib, Paul Almond, etc.

Particular CFI publications are listed in the Introduction of this book, in bibliographies of particular filmmakers, or in the Bibliography.

Information Division, Canadian Film Institute, 303 Richmond Road, Ottawa, Ontario K1Z 6X3, (613) 729-6193. A service provided to National Film Library users on the materials available for their particular needs.

Print Sales Division, Canadian Film Institute, 303 Richmond Road, Ottawa, Ontario K1Z 6X3, (613) 729-7193. Contact them for their available prints.

LA CINEMATHEQUE QUEBECOISE

360 McGill Street
Montreal, Quebec H2Y 2E9
(514) 866-4688

The Cinémathèque is first of all a film archive which aims to preserve both Canadian and foreign films. It is also a centre for documentation on Canadian cinema with vertical files carrying information on films, filmmakers, distribution and festivals; and it is the repository for about 90,000 stills, posters, tapes and archival materials. The Cinémathèque specializes in information on animation and possesses a large number of drawings and other materials. Its museum, recently opened to the public (Monday to Friday, 9:30 a.m. to 5:30 p.m.), is the first of its kind in Canada. This museum offers a large display of antique and modern cinematographic apparatus, an exhibition of film posters, and drawings relating to animated cinema.

Much of the topical material on new films across the country, festivals around the world and other activity is published in the quarterly, *New Canadian Film/Nouveau cinéma canadien* which is available from the Cinémathèque. They also publish an annual *Film Index/Annual de la production cinématographique* which includes all feature films made in Canada and short films made in Quebec. A number of studies of national and international cinema are also available. Contact them for a publication and price list.

From Tuesdays to Fridays, La Cinémathèque québécoise has twice-nightly film showings in the basement of La Bibliothèque nationale du Québec, 1700 St-Denis Street, Montreal, Quebec. National and international cinema, classics and recent productions offer a complete film education. Entrance fee is minimal; monthly programs may be obtained at the Cinémathèque, the theatre or by mail (include a stamped, 4 x 9 envelope with each request).

LE CONSEIL QUEBECOIS POUR LA DIFFUSION DU CINEMA (CQDC)

3466 St-Denis Street
Montreal, Quebec
(514) 842-5079

Le Conseil was formed by a number of professional and commercial organizations as a method of making Quebec cinema known at home and abroad, as a method of dovetailing their common interest and efforts, and as a means of organizing festivals and study sessions on Quebec film. The CQDC has attempted to bring films and often the filmmakers to the public in and outside of Montreal; to this end they have organized "Soirées rencontre", workshop meetings with young film students, and "La Quinzaine nationale du cinéma", a film blitz. Their publications include the important series "Cinéastes du Québec", critiques of important new films, the *Répertoire des long métrages produits au Québec 1960-1970* and *Bottin cinéma*, a catalogue of Quebec film people.

CONSERVATOIRE 'ART CINEMATOGRAPHIQUE/ CONSERVATORY OF CINEMATOGRAPHIC ART

Concordia University
1455 de Maisonneuve Blvd.
Montreal, Quebec H3G 1M8
(514) 879-4349

The Conservatory is a unique organization showing rich and varied programs of recent and archival films international in scope. Programs can be picked up at the Hall Building Auditorium; the entrance fee is 75c per showing. As part of Concordia University's extension program, the Conservatory has organized a series of film courses. As an extension of their critical interest in film, they also hold each September the Canadian Student Film Festival with an international jury.

DEPARTEMENT DE DOCUMENTATION CINEMATOGRAPHIQUE

La Bibliothèque nationale
360 McGill Street
Montreal, Quebec H2Y 2E9
(514) 874-5398

The basis of this library is the rich collection of Guy-L. Côté, founder of La Cinémathèque canadienne (now La Cinémathèque québécoise). The library consists of 1,500 periodical titles, many historical in nature, as well as current titles. The 8,000 books on the cinema cover critical and technical works, biographies and scenarios. Card indexes offer information on filmmakers, films, distributors and critical reviews. Press cuttings, pamphlets and other printed material are available in a vertical file system. Although the library is international in scope, special emphasis is placed on the documentation of Canadian cinema. Other services include microfilm, some photo slides, reproduction of documentation, telex and a reading room. The most important film library in Canada, it has published the *Catalogue des acquisitions de documents cinématographiques 1974* compiled by the head librarian, Pierre Allard; this catalogue is available to any Canadian library or university.

NATIONAL FILM ARCHIVES

56 O'Connor Street
Ottawa, Ontario K1P 5Z6
(613) 992-1383, 992-0635, 996-6009

Primarily an archive (see FILM STUDY: FILM AND PHOTOG-
RAPHY ARCHIVES), it is also a film study centre of current and
archival film information. The library of printed material is accessible to all students of film; it holds over 4,000 books, 800 recent
and defunct periodical titles (many on microfilm), clipping files on
films and filmmakers, and a title index of Canadian and international films and filmmakers. This library also holds 200,000 stills
related to film and a collection of film posters.

NATIONAL FILM BOARD HALIFAX REFERENCE LIBRARY

1572 Barrington Street
Halifax, Nova Scotia B3J 1Z6
(902) 426-6157

This library is open to individuals for reference and books may be
borrowed on their film library card. Resources include over 80
periodicals, film catalogues and publicity files. In addition to these
resources, the library has telex and telephone access to the NFB
Montreal library, the CFI and the National Film Archives in
Ottawa.

NATIONAL FILM BOARD INFORMATION DIVISION

Box 6100
Montreal, Quebec H3C 3H5
(514) 333-3452

The Information Division of the NFB handles all requests for in-
formation on filmmakers, NFB films and related information. *A
Brief History: The National Film Board of Canada,* by James
Lysyshyn, and *History of the National Film Board of Canada,* by
Marjorie McKay, are available on request as is a special edition of
News Clips/Revue de presse, a collection of articles on the opera-
tions, achievements and aims of The National Film Board of
Canada. A monthly edition of *News Clips/Revue de presse* is avail-
able for reference in any local or regional office of the National
Film Board.

National Film Board films are available in public showings in
every office across the country or may be borrowed from them or
from the local public library. Catalogues, English and French, are
available without charge from any NFB office. Not all films are
listed in each catalogue so it is wise to obtain both; many films
listed only in the French catalogue would offer no barrier to an
English-speaking student of cinema.

NATIONAL FILM BOARD LIBRARY

3155 Côte de Liesse Road
Saint-Laurent, Quebec
(514) 333-3141

The library at the National Film Board's main office is basically an internal resource library to serve the staff of filmmakers, the regional offices and offices abroad. Permission can be obtained, however, for use of the library by graduate students of communications.

While much of the material within the library does not deal with film or related topics, it does offer 20,000 volumes and 100 current periodicals. Press clippings, pamphlets and catalogues offer information on all audio-visual media and, in particular, information on the National Film Board itself. Many periodicals are now on microfilm and photocopy service is available as well as a reading room.

The library also makes available current specialized bibliographies on many aspects of national and international film and other media.

ONTARIO FILM INSTITUTE/CINEMATHEQUE DE L'ONTARIO

770 Don Mills Road
Don Mills, Ontario M3C 1T3
(416) 429-4100

The Ontario Film Institute was founded in 1969 by its present director, Gerald Pratley. Its areas of interest are twofold:

Ontario Film Theatre, Ontario Science Centre, 770 Don Mills Road, Don Mills, Ontario, programs between three and five films a week by Canadian and international filmmakers who are relatively unknown on the commercial circuit. Theatre memberships are available at the door. In addition, there are two film theatres which are programed by local committees with booking and documentation assistance from the Ontario Film Theatre: Ontario Film Theatre—Windsor, Supercinema, Windsor, Ontario (519) 966-1656; and Ontario Film Theatre—Brockville, Civic Auditorium, Brockville, Ontario (613) 345-1855. As part of their program, the Ontario Film Theatre organizes the annual Stratford International Film Festival each September in Stratford, Ontario.

Ontario Film Archive, Ontario Science Centre, 770 Don Mills Road, Don Mills, Ontario, is a major source of printed material on film; the resources include 5,000 book titles, film periodicals, original screenplays, biographical files on actors, directors and producers, and subject files on numerous areas. The archive also holds a collection of posters and photographs and a special collection of the original scores of over 3,000 films.

L'OFFICE DES COMMUNICATIONS SOCIALES

4635 de Lorimier
Montreal, Quebec H2H 2B4
(514) 526-9165

The communication library of L'Office des communications sociales is not strictly a film study library but deals with all media and, in particular, the relationship between religion and mass media. Open to the general public, the library offers a book collection and periodical collection international in scope. The vertical file system offers critical reviews and documentation on over 25,000 films, personalities and directors.

L'Office des communications sociales publishes the film periodical *Séquences,* edited by Léo Bonneville and available quarterly, and *Recueil des films,* an annual listing with synopses of films distributed in Quebec, noting their artistic and moral value.

PACIFIC CINEMATHEQUE PACIFIQUE

1616 West 3rd Avenue
Vancouver, B.C. V6J 1K2
(604) 732-5322, 732-6119

The Pacific Cinémathèque Pacifique has a three-pronged program. Canadian and international as well as archival films are presented at the NFB Mini-Theatre, 1155 West Georgia Street, Vancouver, B.C. (604) 682-5621. In association with CFI and the Cinémathèque québécoise, the Cinémathèque offers programs four evenings a week as well as tours of special extension programs throughout the province. Film study is another aspect of the Cinémathèque which includes a small library of books and periodicals, film catalogues, and files on films and filmmakers with special emphasis on those on the West Coast. An important part of this arm is the Film Study Collection, groups of programs of archival films dating from 1900 to 1940 and collections of West Coast filmmakers such as Tom Braidwood, David Rimmer, Sandy Wilson and Al Razutis. Distribution and sales concentrate on those films produced in British Columbia by independent filmmakers. A catalogue is available on request.

Of Further Interest:

Film Music Study

La Cinémathèque québécoise has a large amount of information available on Canadian composers who have written scores for films other than those produced by the National Film Board. In 1965, La Cinémathèque published a pamphlet, *Musique et cinéma,* on the occasion of their homage to two composers, Eldon Rathburn and Maurice Blackburn; this contains filmographies and articles on a number of composers who have worked within the National Film Board.

The **Music Department of the National Film Board** keeps detailed records and original recordings of their film music. Contact the archivist, Music Department, National Film Board, Box 6100, Montreal, Quebec H3C 3H5.

The **Ontario Film Institute** has a large number of recordings available for students of film music. Arrangements can be made for access by contacting the secretary, Ontario Film Institute, c/o Ontario Science Centre, 770 Don Mills Road, Don Mills, Ontario.

Cine Books are unique film bookshops selling books, magazines, pictures, records and posters. Their catalogue is available for $3.50 and they offer mail and telephone service.

692A Yonge Street
Toronto, Ontario M4Y 2A6
(416) 964-6474

570 Granville Street
Vancouver, B.C. V6C 1W6
(604) 681-0329

A number of public libraries are building up impressive film study collections. The **Vancouver Public Library** for example, has a good book collection on films and a vertical file on local filmmakers in particular. The **London Public Library** in London, Ontario and the **Metropolitan Toronto Central Library** are also good sources of film study information.

See also MAKING FILMS: TECHNICAL INFORMATION, SERVICES
          AND ASSISTANCE — MUSIC

Film Publications

CATALOGUES

Annual de la production cinématographique/Film Index. A detailed cross-referenced yearly index of all feature films in Canada and short films in Quebec. Published in collaboration with the Bibliothèque nationale, the *Film Index* is available from La Cinémathèque québécoise.

The Association for Films in Adult Education Catalogue. The Association shows and rents its collection of over 300 films to promote adult education within the province of British Columbia. Available from the Association for Films in Adult Education, 703-318 Homer Street Rm. 703, Vancouver, B.C.

Behavioural Sciences Filmography. An annotated list of some 600 films available in Ontario and Quebec. The catalogue is available from CIEAI, Hospital Sainte-Justine, 3100 Ellendale Street, Montreal, Quebec H3S 1W3.

British Broadcasting Corporation Catalogue. A 16mm film catalogue giving details of BBC television programs available for purchase or rental. Write: BBC Film Sales, 135 Maitland Street, Toronto, Ontario.

Canadian Filmmakers' Distribution Centre Catalogue. A catalogue of films by independent filmmakers in Canada, U.S. and Europe. Write: Canadian Filmmakers' Distribution Centre, 406 Jarvis Street, Toronto, Ontario M4Y 2G6. (416) 921-4121.

Catalogue of 16mm Educational Motion Pictures. Lists a large collection of films available in western Canada from the University of Alberta. Catalogues are available for $3.00 from the Educational Media Division, Department of Extension, University of Alberta, Edmonton, Alberta.

Catalogue des productions OFQ. Under the Ministry of Cultural Affairs, the Office du film du Québec produces educational films available free of charge. Catalogue available from OFQ, 360 McGill Street, Montreal, Quebec.

Catalogues of Special Libraries. A number of foreign embassies, the Royal Architectural Institute of Canada, the Canadian Centre for Films on Art, Films on the Performing Arts, The Department of National Health and Welfare, and UNESCO have deposited their films with CFI. Catalogues of these special collections are available for 25c from the Canadian Film Institute.

Challenge for Change Film Catalogue. A separate catalogue listing the films produced by this special unit. Available from any NFB office.

Coopérative cinéastes independants/Independent Filmmakers' Cooperative Catalogue. Lists over 600 films, features and shorts — experimental, poetic and political — from Canada, United States and Europe. Available from the Coopérative cinéastes indépendants/Independent Filmmakers' Cooperative, 2026 Ontario Street East, Montreal, Quebec.

CTV Film Distribution Service Catalogue. A small numbr of television-made films are available for sale or rental. Write: Educational Film Distributor, CTV Television Network Ltd., 42 Charles Street East, Toronto, Ontario M4Y 1T4. (416) 924-5454, ext. 335.

Film Canadiana: The Canadian Film Institute Yearbook of Canadian Cinema. An alphabetical listing of Canadian film productions for the preceding year. Information includes director, producer, time, colour and a short description plus an index number for each title.

Film Study Collection Catalogues. A number of catalogues for students of film covering the historical face of filmmaking. Available for a small fee from the Canadian Film Institute.

Free Films Directory. A sourcebook of over 16,000 free 16mm films available in Canada. For a copy of the Directory write: Crawley Films Limited, 19 Fairmont Ave., Ottawa, Ontario K1Y 3B5.

In Canada Travel Film Programme/Programme de films touristiques au Canada. Catalogues and films available from any NFB office.

Index of 16mm and 35mm Feature Length Films Available in Canada. A listing of more than 9,000 films, published by the Canadian Federation of Film Societies. Available from CFFS Index Committee, Box 484, Terminal A, Toronto, Ontario.

National Film Board French Language Films in Ontario. An information bulletin available from National Film Board, 1 Lombard Street, Toronto, Ontario. (416) 369-4093.

National Film Board of Canada: Film Catalogue/Office national du film du Canada: Catalogue des films. Available on request from the NFB, Box 6100, Montreal, Quebec and from any local NFB office.

National Film Board 16mm Films Relating to Native Culture. A specialized bulletin available from the National Film Board, 1 Lombard Street, Toronto, Ontario. (416) 369-4093.

National Industrial Relations Film Library Catalogue/Répertoire de la cinématheque nationale des relations industrielles. Catalogue and films are available free from the National Industrial Relations Film Library, Public Relations Branch, Canada Department of Labour, 340 Laurier Avenue West, Ottawa, Ontario K1A OJ2.

National Science Film Library Catalogues. A collection of ten catalogues of films dealing with all aspects of science. All films listed and the catalogues are available from the Canadian Film Institute.

Nursing Media Index. Edited and compiled by Marilynne Sequin and John S. Bradley, published by the Nursing Educational Media Association. A reference tool for those interested in the health sciences — administration, behavioral sciences and family life. Resumés for over 1200 16mm films and sources, many free. Available for $12.00 from 26 Edgar Avenue, Toronto, Ontario.

Pacific cinémathèque pacifique catalogue. A list of films made on the west coast and distributed cooperatively. Write: Pacific Cinémathèque, 1616 West 3rd Avenue, Vancouver, B.C. V6J 1K2.

Recueil des films. An annual listing of films distributed in Quebec, with artistic and moral criticism. Available for $3.00 per year, $34.00 for collected works (1956-1970) from Office des communications sociales, 4635 de Lorimier, Montreal, Quebec.

Répertoire des longs metrages produits au Québec. Organized by year with complete information on credits and availability, plus a resumé for each film. Available for $1.50 from the Conseil québécois pour la diffusion du cinéma, 3466 St-Denis Street, Montreal, Quebec.

16mm Film Directory, Film Federation of Eastern Ontario. A catalogue of film blocks which move around eastern Ontario, largely through public libraries. Catalogue available from the Ottawa Film Council, Box 359, Ottawa, Ontario.

Special Subject Catalogue. Covers subjects of available films — education, fire prevention, human rights, labour and management, literature, political science, old age, sports. Available from the Canadian Film Institute.

Vancouver Film Council Catalogue. Lists over 600 films, many of screen study value, available within the province of British Columbia only. Write: Vancouver Film Council, 1701 West Broadway, Vancouver, B.C. (604) 733-3414.

See also FILMMAKERS: COMMUNITY FILM AND VIDEO;
             NATIVE PEOPLES AND FILM; POLITICAL AND THIRD
             WORLD FILMS; WOMEN IN FILM
             FILM STUDY
             USING FILMS
             MAKING FILMS: COOPERATIVE DISTRIBUTION

DIRECTORIES AND ANNUAL REPORTS

Directories

Bottin des membres. Available from Syndicat national du cinéma (SNC), 3466 St-Denis Street, Montreal, Quebec H2X 3L3.

Canadian Film Digest Year Book. A handbook for the industry, with lists of production and distribution companies, equipment, taxes, studios, statistics. Available from 175 Bloor Street East, Toronto, Ontario M4W 1E1.

Canadian Government Photo Centre Price List/Tarifs du Centre de photographie du gouvernement canadien. A catalogue giving information on ordering, colour and black and white services, finishing and special services, commercial and special consultation services. Catalogue available from Canadian Government Photo Centre, Tunney's Pasture, Ottawa, Ontario K1A 0M9.

Canadian Professional Film Directory. Lists the membership of the Canadian Film Editors Guild, Canadian Society of Cinematographers, Directors Guild of Canada, Talent Agents Association of Canada, Toronto Commercial Producers Association, Canadian Association of Motion Picture Producers, and the Canadian Film and Television Association. Available from Filmcraft Publications, 116 Earlton Road, Agincourt, Ontario M1T 2R6, (416) 291-2834.

Canadian Women Filmmakers: An Interim Filmography. Compiled by Alison Reid in the Canadian Filmography Series no. 108. Available from the Canadian Film Institute.

Cahier des films visés par catégories de spectateurs/Catalogue of Films Approved by Spectator Category. An annual listing of films categorized by the Quebec Cinema Supervisory Board and the rules governing that board. Available at no charge from the Bureau de surveillance du cinéma, 360 McGill Street, Montreal, Quebec, (514) 873-2371.

Cine Books. A catalogue of film books, posters, magazines from Canada's only film bookshop. Available for $1.00 from Cine Books, 692A Yonge Street, Toronto, Ontario.

Le cinéma au Québec: bilan d'une industrie. An annotated directory of organizations, production and distribution houses in Quebec. Write: Cinéma-Québec, Box 309, Station Outremont, Montreal, Quebec H2V 4N3.

Cinema Canada Bottin/Directory. Lists organizations, associations and companies. Published each year by the Film Festival Bureau, Department of the Secretary of State, Ottawa, Ontario.

Creative Canada: A Biographical Dictionary of Twentieth-Century Creative and Performing Artists. 2 vols. Edited by Helen MacGretor Rodney. Toronto: University of Toronto Press, 1972.

Film & Video, January 1976. "A Directory of Film & Video Production People in the Atlantic Region".

Film Canadiana: A Yearbook of Canadian Cinema/L'annuaire du cinéma canadien. An annual directory of films, organizations. Available from the Canadian Film Institute.

A Guide to Film and Television Courses in Canada. An annual guide to courses offered in colleges. Available from the Canadian Film Institute.

The Guidebook to Movie Theatres. Lists all theatres in Quebec with addresses. Available from the Cinema Supervisory Board of Quebec/Bureau de surveillance du cinéma.

TV-Film Filebook. A twice-yearly handbook for the television and cinema industries listing services available and a myriad of information. Available at $3.00 a copy from TV-Film Filebook, 2533 Gerrard Street East, Scarborough, Ontario.

UNESCO Publications — Communication. Annual catalogue of books and other publications on communications. Available from UNESCO or through Publishing Centre, Supply and Services Canada.

Annual Reports

The Canada Council: Annual Report. Available at no charge from Canada Council, 151 Sparks Street, Ottawa, Ontario K1P 5V8.

Canadian Film Development Corporation: Annual Report/Société de développement de l'industrie cinématographique canadienne: rapport annuel. Available at no charge from CFDC.

The Cinema Supervisory Board of Quebec Annual Report. Contains information on film classification, film distribution and revenues. Available from the Board/Bureau de surveillance du cinéma.

La Cinémathèque: Rapport annuel. Back copies from 1966 available at no charge from La Cinémathèque québécoise, 360 McGill Street, Montreal, Quebec.

Conseil québécois pour la diffusion du cinéma: rapport annuel. from CQDC, 3466 St-Denis Street, Montreal, Quebec.

Motion Picture Production/Production cinématographique. An annual statistical study of theatrical, non-theatrical and television films and video tape production in Canada. Catalogue no. 63-206. Available from Publishing Centre, Supply and Services Canada.

Motion Picture Theatres and Film Distributors/Cinémas et distributeurs de films. An annual statistical study of indoor and outdoor theatres and of film distributors operating in Canada.

Catalogue no. 63-207. Available from Publishing Centre, Supply and Services Canada.

National Film Board of Canada: Annual Report/Office National du film du Canada: rapport annuel: Available on request from the National Film Board, Box 6100, Montreal, Quebec.

PERIODICALS

Access: Challenge for Change/Société nouvelle, edited by Elizabeth Prinn. An exchange of information newsletter appearing 3-4 times a year in connection with the Challenge for Change Unit at the NFB. Available from: National Film Board, Box 6100, Montreal, Quebec H3C 3H5.

Champ libre. A critical collection on Quebec and international cinema. Edited by a number of film critics, including Dominique Noguez and Yvan Patry. Available for $3.50 an issue from: Box 399, Outremont Station, Montreal, Quebec.

Cinécrits, edited by Paul Warren. A critical magazine written by students of Laval University. Available from: Prof. Paul Warren, editor, Pavillon de Koninck, Faculté des lettres, Université Laval, St.-Foy, Quebec.

Cinema Canada, published 10 times a year, is dedicated to developing a critical awareness of Canadian cinema. Film news, organization and technical information can also be found in each issue. Editor and publisher: Jean-Pierre and Connie Tadros. Subscriptions are $8.00 a year, available from Montreal address: Box 398, Outremont Station, Montreal, Quebec, H2V 4N3, (514) 272-5354. Toronto address: 406 Jarvis Street, Toronto, Ontario M4Y 2G6, (416) 924-8045.

Cinéma-Québec is a critical film magazine published 10 times a year in French with a special emphasis on Quebec cinema. Edited by Jean-Pierre Tadros, *Cinéma-Québec* is available for $8.00 per year from: Box 309, Outremont Station, Montreal, Quebec H2V 4N1.

Culture Vivante is a quarterly published in French by Quebec's Ministry of Cultural Affairs. Covering all aspects of Quebec's cultural life, it invariably has articles on film. Subscriptions are available at $2.00 per year ($1.00 for students) from: Ministère des affaires culturelles, Hôtel du gouvernement, Québec, Québec.

*Film & Video: Atlantic Regional Newsletter/*Communiqué régional de l'atlantique. An information newsletter prepared by the Atlantic regional production office of the NFB; it covers the whole Atlantic area. Available by writing: National Film Board, 1572 Barrington Street, Halifax, N.S. B3J 1Z6, (902) 426-6157.

Interlock is an information newsletter for those involved in films by and about women. Edited by Donna Dudinsky, it is available by writing: National Film Board, P. 43, Box 6100, Station A., Montreal, Quebec H3C 3H5.

Médium-Média is the information magazine of Société nouvelle, the French counterpart of the Challenge for Change program administered by the National Film Board in conjunction with federal government departments. The magazine covers the history of the program, its operations and aims, cable and video television. Available from: Société nouvelle, National Film Board, Box 6100, Montreal, Quebec H3C 3H5.

Motion is a bi-monthly publication featuring short interviews and portraits with emphasis on Canadian production. Subscriptions at $4.00 a year are available from: Box 5558, Station A, Toronto, Ontario M5W 1N7, (416) 964-3510.

New Canadian Film/Nouveau cinéma canadien, published about four times a year in English and French by the Cinémathèque québécoise, keeps track of film production across the country. The editor encourages filmmakers and producers to send news of their activities. *New Canadian Film* also publishes information on festivals, and on Canadian films which have been released. *New Canadian Film* is available from: La Cinémathèque québécoise, 360 McGill Street, Montreal, Quebec H2Y 2E9.

Ontario Film Association *Newsletter* offers news on its own activities and film news from across Canada. A monthly, it is available from: Ontario Film Association, Box 521, Barrie, Ontario L4M 4T7.

Performing Arts in Canada covers all aspects of Canadian cultural activity and often touches on cinema. Published quarterly, it is available for $3.00 per year from: 52 Avenue Road, Toronto, Ontario M5R 2G3.

Pot pourri is published monthly by the National Film Board's Ontario regional office. Edited by Patricia Thorvaldson, *Pot pourri* includes film criticism, happenings around Ontario and interviews with filmmakers inside as well as outside the Board. Available by contacting: National Film Board, 1 Lombard Street, Toronto, Ontario M5C 1J6.

Pulse, "The Practical Film and TV Newsletter", is an eclectic publicaton with views and information from United States and Canada. Editor and publisher is Rick Harris and subscriptions are $5.00 a year from: Box 5268, Terminal A, Toronto Ontario M5W 1N5.

Rushes is an erratic monthly published for the Toronto Filmmakers' Co-op, offering technical information, local and national film news, festival information and articles on filmmakers. Available from Toronto Filmmakers' Co-op, 67 Portland Street, Toronto, Ontario.

Screen. An information exchange depot published by the Media Division of the National Film Board. *Screen* carries and invites articles, reviews and comments. Published irregularly, *Screen* is available at no charge from: National Film Board, Box 5100, Station A, Montreal, Quebec H3C 3H5.

Séquences is a quarterly critical periodical published in French by the Office des commnications sociales. Edited by Léo Bonneville, *Séquences* covers international cinema with a particular emphasis on the Canadian scene. Subscriptions are $3.50 per year ($3.00 for students) from: 4635 de Lorimier Street, Montreal, Quebec 2H2 2B4.

Take One is a critical film periodical with international coverage. Edited by Peter Lebensold, *Take One* is published bi-monthly; a two year subscription is available for $5.00 From Box 1778, Station B, Montreal, Quebec H3B 3L3.

Vie des arts covers all aspects of Quebec cultural life and carries, irregularly, articles on film. Subscriptions are available at $9.00 per year from: 360 McGill Street, Suite 409, Montreal, Quebec H2Y 2E9.

Also of interest:

Catalogue des acquisitions de documents cinématographiques 1974 includes a list of new books, current periodicals, names and addresses of film book publishers and names and addresses of current film magazines. The catalogue is available free to any library or university in Canada. It has been compiled by the chief librarian, Mr. Pierre Allard. Available from: Bibliothèque nationale du Québec, Département de documentation cinématographique, 360 McGill Street, Montreal, Quebec H2Y 2E9.

The *International Film Guide* lists about 60 film periodicals and trade magazines around the world. Examples of articles, evaluations, prices, and addresses are given in most cases. Published yearly by The Tantivy Press, the *International Film Guide* is available in most bookstores.

The International Index to Film Periodicals indexes 80 film periodicals including *Take One, Cinema Canada* and *Cinéma Québec* under the headings, "General Subjects", "Films" and "Biography". Available from Collier-Macmillan Canada.

TRADE JOURNALS

Actrascope, the house organ of ACTRA. Available from: 105 Carlton Street, Toronto, Ontario M5B 1M2, (416) 363-6336.

The Canadian Composer/Le Compositeur canadien is a bilingual publication appearing 10 times a year and published by the Composers, Authors and Publishers Association of Canada (CAPAC). For a subscription write: 40 St. Clair Street West, Toronto, Ontario.

Canadian Film Digest Year Book includes lists of exhibitors and personnel; a limited listing of both 16mm and 35mm distributors; production and distribution associations; equipment sales and service; updated industry statistics; censorship boards and rates; listing of recipients of Academy and Canadian Film Awards; provincial amusement taxes and theatre licence fees; studios and producers; laboratories; a listing of television film studios, their distributors and record companies. Edited by Dan Krendel, the *Year Book* is available from: 175 Bloor Street East, Toronto, Ontario M4W 1E1, (416) 924-3701.

The Canadian Film Editor is the organ of the Canadian Film Editors Guild. Issues include technical information and profiles. For a subscription write: Box 46, Terminal A, Toronto, Ontario M5W 1A2.

Le cinéma au Québec: bilan d'une Industrie is a heavily annotated list of public organizations and groups, production and distribution houses, laboratories and associations. The emphasis is on Quebec in the private sector list. This annual publication is available from: Editions cinéma/Québec, Box 309, Station Outremont, Montreal, Quebec H2V 4N3.

The Music Scene/La scène musicale are two companion publications of Broadcast Music Inc. Canada Limited (B.M.I.), published six times per year, and edited by Nancy Gyokeres. Covering news and information for and about their membership, it carries a regular column on film music. *The Music Scene* is available to organizations and individuals interested in the performance of Canadian music. Write: 41 Valleybrooke Drive, Don Mills, Ontario M3B 2S6.

TV-Film Filebook is published yearly or twice-yearly for the television and film industry. It is packed with all kinds of well-researched information: films for television and educational film distributors; a listing of syndicated television programs and their distributors; studios and production laboratories; government film departments; sound recording studios; editing services; special effects; music services; talent; post-production services;

technical services; film equipment rentals; motion picture equipment; listing of equipment and technical services available from member companies of the Association of Motion Picture Producers and Laboratories of Canada; marketing research organizations; associations and guilds; unions; television networks; television stations; British television groups; educational film groups and advertising agencies. The editor of the publication is Arthur C. Benson. Write: 2533 Gerrard Street East, Scarborough, Ontario.

PUBLISHERS' ADDRESSES

L'Agence de distribution
   populaire Inc.
955 Amherst Street
Montreal, Quebec H2L 3K4

Artscanada
3 Church Street
Toronto, Ontario M5E 1M2

Branching Out
Box 4098
Edmonton, Alberta T6E 4S8

CBC Learning Systems
Box 500, Station A
Toronto, Ontario M5W 1E6

Canadian Film Institute
75 Albert Street, Suite 1105
Ottawa, Ontario K1P 5E7

Collier Macmillan Canada Ltd.
1125B Leslie Street
Don Mills, Ontario M3C 2T5

Communications Canada
300 Slater Street
Ottawa, Ontario K1A 0C8

Conseil québécois pour
   la diffusion du cinéma (CQDC)
3466 St-Denis Street
Montreal, Quebec H2X 2X4

Les Editions de l'aurore
1651 St-Denis Street
Montreal, Quebec H2X 3K5

Les Editions du jour
5705 Sherbrooke Street E.
Monteal, Quebec H1N 1A7

Editions Hurtubise — HMH Ltée.
380 Craig Street W.
Montreal, Quebec H2Y 1J9

Editions Lémeac Inc.
5111 Durocher Street
Montreal, Quebec H2V 3X7

Fides
245 Dorchester Blvd.
Montreal, Quebec H2X 1N9

Lidec Inc.
1083 Van Horne Street
Montreal, Quebec H2V 1J6

McClelland & Stewart Ltd.
25 Hollinger Road
Toronto, Ontario M4B 3G2

McGraw-Hill Ryerson Ltd.
330 Progress Avenue
Scarborough, Ontario M1P 2Z5

Ministère des affaires culturelles
Hôtel du gouvernement
Québec, Québec

Ontario Institute for Studies
   in Education (OISE)
Publications Sales
252 Bloor Street W.
Toronto, Ontario M5S 1V6

Peter Martin Associates Ltd.
280 Bloor Street W.
Toronto, Ontario M5S 1W1

Les Presses de l'Université
   de Montréal
Box 6128
Montreal, Quebec

Les Presses de l'Université
   du Québec
Box 250, Station N
Montreal, Quebec

Publishing Centre
Supply and Services Canada
270 Alberta Street
Ottawa, Ontario K1A 0S9

Tundra Books of Montreal
1374 Sherbrooke Street W., Suite 17
Montreal, Quebec H3G 1J6

Bibliography

HISTORY

Backhouse, Charles. *Canadian Government Motion Picture Bureau, 1917-1941.* Canadian Filmography Series, no. 9. Ottawa: Canadian Film Institute, 1974.

Bouchard, René. *Filmographie d'Albert Tessier.* Collection documents filmiques du Québec. Les Editions du Boréal Express, 1973. Priest, photographer and filmmaker Albert Tessier documented life in rural Quebec from 1925 to 1953 and is the precursor of "cinéma direct" and a cinema of social intervention. Available from Fides.

Canadian Feature Films 1913-1969. Part 1: 1913-1940, Part 2: 1941-1969. Canadian Filmography Series nos. 106 and 107. These documents are detailed filmographies giving production credits, synopses, notes on production and extracts from reviews for in-digenous and non-indigenous films shot in Canada. Each part is available for $3.00 from the Canadian Film Insitute.

Cinema Canada, no. 15 (August — September, 1974). A special issue on the occasion of the 35th anniversary of the National Film Board.

Côté, Guy L., ed. *Hommage à M.L. Ernest Ouiment.* Montreal: La Cinémathèque canadienne, 1966. Though out of print, this pamphlet on Canada's pioneer filmmaker and cinema-operator is available in film study libraries.

Daudelin, Robert, *Vingt ans de cinéma au Canada français.* Quebec: Ministère des affaires culturelles, 1967. Daudelin is the former director-general of Le Conseil québécois pour la diffusion de cinéma and is now director of La Cinémathèque québécoise. Beginning with an excellent historical background, the discussion centres around the important directors and technicians in Quebec cinema. Published as part of the "Collection art, vie et sciences au Canada français", it is available at no charge from the Ministère des affaires culturelles, Quebec.

Handling, Piers, ed. *Canadian Feature Films 1913—1969. Part 3: 1964-1969. Canadian* Filmography Series, no. 10. Ottawa: Canadian Film Institute, 1975. A detailed annotated look at more than 100 features.

Homage to the Vancouver CBC Film Unit. Montreal: La Cinémathèque canadienne, 1964. Now out of print, the pamphlet is available in film study centres.

Lafrance, André, and Marsolais, Gilles, eds. *Cinéma d'ici.* Montreal: Editions Leméac, 1973. A historical look at Quebec cinema through interviews first heard on Radio-Canada in the series "Cinema d'ici".

Marsolais, Gilles. *Le cinéma canadien.* Montreal: Editions du jour, 1968. This gives an excellent historical background up to the present, concentrating on the interaction of developments. Productions are listed chronologically in a separate section. Available from Editions du jour.

Martin, André. *Origine et âge d'or du dessin animé américain de 1906 à 1941.* Montreal: La Cinémathèque canadienne, 1967. A chart published on the occasion of the World Retrospective of Animation Cinema. Available for $10.00 from La Cinémathèque québécoise.

McKay, Marjorie. *History of the National Film Board of Canada.* Ottawa: National Film Board, undated. A 147-page history of the NFB from its inception to 1964, written by a former staff member. Available on request from any NFB office.

Morris, Peter, ed. *The National Film Board of Canada: The War Years.* Canadian Filmography Series, no. 103. Ottawa: Canadian Film Institute, 1965. This 32-page book reviews the formative years under John Grierson, giving a complete filmography and articles written by contemporaries. Available from the Canadian Film Institute.

Paquet, André, ed. *Comment faire ou ne pas faire un film canadien/How to Make or Not to Make a Canadian Film.* This was published by La Cinémathèque canadienne on the occasion of a retrospective of Canadian cinema presented in 1967. It contains a chronological history of Canadian cinema, a list of 100 essential films and a number of articles by filmmakers. Priced at $1.00, it is available in English or French from La Cinémathèque québécoise.

Watt, Harry. *Don't Look at the Camera.* England: Elek Books Limited, 1974. Memories of Grierson and the G.P.O.

See also Notes accompanying AN INTRODUCTION TO CANADIAN FILM.

CRITIQUES

Artscanada, no. 142-143 (April 1970). The entire issue is dedicated to "The Moving Image — Current Trends in Canadian Film". Two articles deal with animators: "Six Filmmakers in Search of an Alternative", by Terry Ryan, discusses the work of Arthur Lipsett, Ryan Larkin and Pierre Hébert; "Nine Film Animators Speak", by Guy Glover, contains words and pictures by Laurent Coderre, Ryan Larkin, Sidney Goldsmith, Bernard Longpré and Norman McLaren. Thorough and still relevant, the issue has been reprinted and is available for $5.00 from *Artscanada.*

Berton, Pierre. *Hollywood's Canada: The Americanization of Our National Image.* Toronto: McClelland & Stewart, 1975.

Bérubé, Renald, and Patry, Yvan, eds. *Le cinéma québécois: tendance et prolongements.* Montreal: Editions Sainte-Maire, 1968. A collection of critical articles on Quebec filmmakers and their films plus discussions of film education and the problems of mass media. Available from Editions Sainte-Marie.

Boissonnault, Robert. *Les cinéastes québécois: un aperçu.* Master's thesis presented to the Département de sociologie, Université de Montréal, 1971. An analysis of the structure of filmmaking in Quebec, related to Radio-Canada, the CBC, the NFB, large theatre chains and cinemas. Available for reference at the Bibliothèque nationale, Montreal.

Briefs and Reports submitted to various government organizations by the Council of Canadian Filmmakers. (Box 1003, Station A, Toronto).

Champ libre 1 (July 1971). "Cinéma/Ideologie/Politique". Hurtubise HMH.

Champ libre 2 (November-December 1971). "La critique en question". Hurtubise HMH.

Cox, Kirwan and Morris, Peter. *History of Canadian Film 1895-1941*. Toronto: Gage Publishing. Publication date 1977.

Crean, S.M. *Who's Afraid of Canadian Culture?* Toronto: General Publishing, 1976. Crean writes a series of articles on aspects of Canadian culture, their history of growth and the political struggle to survive. Chapter 3, "Nightmares in Dreamland" (pp. 65-114), discusses film.

Criteria, vol. 2, no. 1 (February, 1976). Issue on "The Politics of Film in Canada". Available from *Criteria*, 1145 West Georgia Street, Vancouver, B.C. V6E 3H2.

Daudelin, Robert. *Rapport sur la situation du cinéma au Québec.* Montreal, 1970. Photocopies available et Bibliothèque nationale, Montreal.

Dossiers de cinéma: 1. A 12-section critique of 12 short films by Canadian filmmakers. As well as an analysis of the film, the sections give background of the filmmaker, a filmography, bibliography and an approach to the film suggested in a series of questions. Among the films discussed are **60 Cycles** by Jean-Claude Labrecque, **High Steel** and **Runner** by Don Owen, **Percé on the Rocks** by Gilles Carle and **Corral** by Colin Low. Available from Editions Fides.

Drabinsky, Garth. *Motion Pictures and the Arts in Canada: The Business and the Law*. Toronto: McGraw-Hill Ryerson, 1976.

Evans, Gary. *The War For Men's Minds*. Toronto: Peter Martin Associates. Publication date 1978. A history of government- sponsored film propaganda in Canada and Britain.

Exposition mondiale du cinéma d'animation. Montreal: La Cinémathèque canadienne, 1967. Catalogue published on the occasion of the World Retrospective of Animation Cinema. Available from La Cinémathèque québécoise.

Feuilletoscopes/Flip-Books. Montreal: La Cinémathèque canadienne, 1967. Published on the occasion of the World Retrospective of Animation Cinema, it includes:

1. *Man and His World*
2. *Metamor-Flip*
3. *Le Dompteur*
4. *First Cigarette*
5. *Baccanal*
6. *Gaminerie*
7. *Infidelité*
8. *Le Papillon*
9. *Flix*
10. *The Room*

11. *Nudnik*
12. *Felix*

Available from La Cinémathèque québécoise.

Feldman, Seth, and Nelson, Joyce, eds. *Canadian Film Reader.* Toronto: Peter Martin Associates, 1977.

Fulford, Robert. *Marshall Delaney at the Movies.* Toronto: Peter Martin Associates, 1974. A collection of reviews on Canadian and foreign cinema.

Hofsess, John. *Inner Views: Ten Canadian Film-makers.* Toronto: McGraw-Hill Ryerson, 1975.

Lever, Yves. *Cinéma et société québécoise.* Montreal: Editions du jour. A sociological appreciation of international cinema in a Quebec context; Lever's articles have been gathered from the Catholic periodical, *Relations.* Available from Editions du jour.

Liberté, nos. 44-45 (March-June 1966). A special issue on Canadian cinema entitled "Cinema si," containing reports submitted to government bodies, reflections and opinions. Available from Agence de distribution populaire, 11300 La Gauchetière Street E., Montreal, Quebec H1B 2G5.

MacDonald, Dick, ed. *The Media Game.* Montreal: Content Publications, 1972. This collection discusses the documentary, problems of content, research and public access.

Marcorelles, Louis. *Elements pour un nouveau cinéma.* Paris: UNESCO, 1970. A study of "cinema direct" in Europe, Canada and the U.S.

Marsolais, Gilles. *L'aventure du cinéma direct.* Collection Cinéma/Club. Paris: Editions Seghers, 1974. A discussion of work from around the world with emphasis on Canada.

Noguez, Dominique. *Essais sur le cinéma québécois.* Montreal: Editions du jour, 1970. A collection of essays on the relationship of Quebec cinema to the educational, social, cultural and political life of the province. Available from Editions du jour.

Pay TV. A project of the Council of Canadian Filmmakers which ran as a special insert in the August 1976 issue of *Cinema Canada.* Available free from the CCFM, Box 1003, Station A, Toronto.

Pot pourri. The April 1972 issue is dedicated to National Film Board animators with articles on or by Robert Verrall, René Jodoin, Wolf Koenig, Mike Mills, Co Hoedeman, Don Arioli, Evelyn Lambert, George Geertsen and Yvon Mallette. Available from *Pot pourri,* Ontario Regional Office, NFB, 1 Lombard St., Toronto, Ontario.

Pot pourri, November 1974. The whole issue is devoted to a discussion of film criticism.

Predal, René. *Jeune cinéma canadien.* Lyon: Premier plan, 1967. A background to Canadian cinema that largely concentrates on the individual filmmakers and critiques of their work. Published by the review *Premier plan* it is now available from *Premier plan,* B.P. 3, Lyon-Prefecture, 69 — Lyon, France.

Québec 75 cinéma. Published by La Cinémathèque québécoise on the occasion of a three-part exhibition of art, cinema and video. Available from La Cinémathèque québécoise, the booklet contains articles on the state of Quebec cinema and detailed information and short critiques on recent features and shorts made in Quebec.

Sociologue et sociétés, vol. 8, no. 1 (April 1976). Published by Les Presses de l'Université de Montréal. A special issue dedicated to "Pour une sociologie du cinéma".

Tadros, Jean-Pierre. "A Conversation with Hugh Falkner". *Cinema Canada,* no. 28 (May 1976), pp. 30-34. The Secretary of State talks about the evolution of a film policy.

Walser, Lise, and Hamelin, Lucien, eds. *Cinéma québécois, petit guide.* Published by the Conseil québécois pour la diffusion du cinéma. First of a series, this guide has been published to permit a first contact with the cinema of Quebec. Contains a selection of short and feature films, an index and a bio-filmography of the most important cinéastes with addresses and a bibliography. Available at the CQDC.

See also AN INTRODUCTION TO CANADIAN FILM
          FILMMAKERS: FILM PEOPLE (Bibliographies)
          USING FILMS: FINDING AND USING EDUCATIONAL
          MATERIAL

Index

Included are film titles, series titles and people referred to in the Filmmakers section. Page numbers in boldface type indicate an individual entry.